PETERSO

#1 IN COLLEGE PREP

GMAT

SUCCESS

READING, JANET SCHAEFFER • MATHEMATICS, MARK WEINFELD
WRITING, NILA GANDHI-SCHWATLO • SENTENCE CORRECTIONS,
BRUCE KIRLE • CRITICAL REASONING, SUSAN J. BEHRENS

Peterson's

Princeton, New Jersey

About Peterson's

Peterson's is the country's largest educational information/communications company, providing the academic, consumer, and professional communities with books, software, and online services in support of lifelong education access and career choice. Well-known references include Peterson's annual guides to private schools, summer programs, colleges and universities, graduate and professional programs, financial aid, international study, adult learning, and career guidance. Peterson's Web site at petersons.com is the only comprehensive—and most heavily traveled—education resource on the Internet. The site carries all of Peterson's fully searchable major databases and includes financial aid sources, test-prep help, job postings, direct inquiry and application features, and specially created Virtual Campuses for every accredited academic institution and summer program in the U.S. and Canada that offers in-depth narratives, announcements, and multimedia features.

The passages listed below were reprinted with permission, as follows:

Pages 8–9 excerpted from "A People's History of the American Revolution: A New Age Now Begins," Vol. I, by Page Smith. Reprinted by permission of the author's estate.

Pages 12–13, excerpted from "Never Cry Wolf," by Farley Mowat. Used by permission of McClelland & Stewart, Inc., Toronto, *The Canadian Publishers.*

Pages 88–90, excerpted from "In The Rainforest," by Catherine Caufield. Copyright © 1984 by Catherine Caufield. Reprinted by permission of Alfred A Knopf, Inc.

Pages 229–230, excerpted from "Nomads of the World." Reprinted by permission of The National Geographic Society, Washington, D.C.

Visit Peterson's Education Center on the Internet (World Wide Web) at
www.petersons.com

Library of Congress Cataloging-in-Publication Data
GMAT success / Janet Schaeffer . . . [et al.].
   p.   cm.
   ISBN 0-7689-0233-9
   1. Graduate Management Admission Test. 2. Management— Examinations, questions, etc. I. Schaeffer, Janet.
HF1118.G634 1996
650′.076—dc20   96-21076
                                                CIP

Printed in the United States of America

10 9 8 7 6 5 4 3 2

CONTENTS

Red Alert: The GMAT CAT and Study Plans 1

Diagnostic Test 8

Quick-Score Answers to the Diagnostic Test 34

Explanatory Answers to the Diagnostic Test 35

Unit 1: Sentence Correction Strategies and Review 51

Unit 2: Basic Grammar Strategies and Review 70

Unit 3: Reading Comprehension Strategies and Review 87

Unit 4: Critical Reasoning Strategies and Review 108

Unit 5: Analytical Writing Assessment Strategies and Review................ 121

Unit 6: Mathematical Problem Solving and Review 130

Unit 7: Data Sufficiency Strategies and Review 187

Practice Test 1... 204

Quick-Score Answers to Practice Test 1.................................. 232

Explanatory Answers to Practice Test 1 233

Practice Test 2.. 249

Quick-Score Answers to Practice Test 2................................. 273

Explanatory Answers to Practice Test 2 274

Financing Your Graduate and Professional Education 286

What Is the GMAT?

The Graduate Management Admission Test (GMAT) measures verbal, quantitative, and analytical writing skills. The GMAT is used by graduate schools of business to assess the qualifications of applicants to graduate management programs. The GMAT is only one of several factors that will determine your admission to business school. Admission committees also may consider information such as undergraduate grade point average, work or internship experience, an application essay describing your career goals, and references.

The GMAT is designed to predict how well you will perform in the first year of a graduate management program. The GMAT tests neither specific knowledge of business nor achievement in a particular subject. The verbal, quantitative, and analytical writing skills that appear on the GMAT are those that you have already encountered or developed in your academic career.

Until recently, the GMAT was available throughout the world as a paper-and-pencil test. Since October 1997, however, the GMAT is available in North America and many other parts of the world *only* as a computer-adaptive test. Research has shown that scores from the paper-based test are comparable to those from the computer-based test. If you need more information

about registering for the GMAT, visit **http://www.gmat.org** on the World Wide Web or contact:

GMAT
Educational Testing Service
PO Box 6103
Princeton, NJ 08541-6103
Telephone: 609-771-7330
Fax: 609-883-4349
E-mail: gmat@ets.org

What Is a Computer-Adaptive Test (CAT)?

A computer-adaptive test is—as the title says—adaptive. That means that each time you answer a question, the computer adjusts to your responses when determining which question to present next. For example, the first question will be of moderate difficulty. If you answer it correctly, the next question will be more difficult. If you answer it incorrectly, the next question will be easier. The computer will continue presenting questions based on your responses, with the goal of determining your ability level.

It is very important to understand that questions at the beginning of a section affect your score more than those at the end. That's because the early questions are used to determine your general ability level. Once the computer determines your general ability level, it presents questions to identify your specific ability level. As you progress farther into a section, it will be difficult to raise your score very much, even if you answer most items correctly. That's because the later questions affect your score less, as they are used to pinpoint your exact score once the computer has identified your general ability level. Therefore, take as much time as you can afford to answer the early questions correctly. Your score on each section is based on the number of questions you answer correctly, as well as the difficulty level of those questions.

You need only minimal computer skills to take the computer-based GMAT. You will have plenty of time at the test center to work through a tutorial that allows you to practice such activities as answering questions, using the mouse, using the word processor (which you will need for your essay responses), and accessing the help function.

WHAT KINDS OF QUESTIONS WILL BE ON THE GMAT CAT?

The GMAT consists of essay responses to two analytical writing questions, a verbal section, and a quantitative section, as shown in the table below. You will key in the answers to the two essay questions first, then proceed to the remaining sections. Note that questions are not grouped by type within the quantitative and verbal sections. You must be mentally prepared to switch back and forth among the different types of questions.

You will be allowed to take a 5-minute break after completing the analytical writing section and a 5-minute break between the quantitative and verbal sections. Your testing appointment, including the tutorial, will take about 4 hours.

SCORING

One advantage of the CAT is that you can see your scores for the multiple-choice sections immediately after the test. Prior to seeing your scores, however, you have the option of canceling the results if you have reason to believe you did not perform as well as you could have. Official score reports are mailed about two weeks later and include scores for the analytical writing assessment. You will receive four separate scores:

1. *Total Score.* This score is a composite of your verbal and quantitative scores only. Analytical writing scores are not included in the total score. The range for total scores is 200 to 800.

2. *Verbal Score.* This score range is 0 to 60.

3. *Quantitative Score.* This score range is 0 to 60.

4. *Analytical Writing Assessment Score.* This score range is 0 to 6. This score is the average of four ratings of your responses to the two essay topics.

Section	Number of Questions	Time (minutes)
Analytical Writing		
Analysis of an Issue	1 Writing Topic	30
Analysis of an Argument	1 Writing Topic	30
Quantitative	37	75
Data Sufficiency		
Problem Solving		
Verbal	41	75
Sentence Correction		
Reading Comprehension		
Critical Reading		

You will receive a percentile rank for each of the four GMAT scores. This percentile will indicate the percentage of examinees who scored below you.

TEST-TAKING TIPS FOR THE
GMAT CAT

The purpose of *GMAT Success* is to help you prepare for the GMAT. You will increase your chances of scoring high on the GMAT by being completely familiar with the content and format you will encounter on test day. The strategies and review sections of this book, as well as the practice tests, provide lots of opportunity to review relevant content. Keep in mind the following test-taking tips, most of which are unique to the CAT format.

Understand the directions for each question type. Learn the directions for each type of question. The directions in this book are very similar to those on the actual test. Understanding the directions for each question type will save you valuable time on the day of the test.

Take your time with questions at the beginning of each section. Remember that questions at the beginning of a section affect your score more than questions at the end. Be especially careful in choosing answers to questions in the first half of both the quantitative and verbal sections. Once the computer determines your general ability level with these initial questions, you will be unable to dramatically improve your score, even if you answer most of the questions toward the end correctly.

Be completely sure of each answer before proceeding. With a CAT, you must answer each question as it is presented. You cannot skip a difficult question and return to it later as you can with a paper-and-pencil

test. Nor can you review responses to questions that you have already answered. Therefore, you must be confident about your answer before you confirm it and proceed to the next question. If you are completely stumped by a question, eliminate as many answer choices as you can, select the best answer from the remaining choices, and move on.

Pace yourself. To finish both the verbal and quantitative sections, you will need to establish a pace that allows you to spend an average of just under 2 minutes per item. You will need to work both quickly and accurately to complete each section within the 75-minute time constraint. You will still receive a score, even if you do not complete all of the questions in a section.

Be mentally prepared to receive a mix of different question types within each section. On the paper-and-pencil GMAT, questions are typically grouped by type. For example, in the math section, data sufficiency questions appear together as a group, followed by problem-solving questions. On the GMAT CAT, however, the computer may select one of several question formats, depending on whether you answered the previous question right or wrong. Therefore, you must be mentally ready to switch back and forth between questions that have very different formats, both in the quantitative section and in the verbal section, to maintain focus during the test.

Use the scratch paper provided at the test center. You will not be allowed to bring any paper or other materials into the test center, and since there is no test booklet, you will have no opportunity to underline, circle, or otherwise make notes on actual questions or problems. The test center does, however, provide as much scratch paper as you need to make notes during the test. You may want to develop a simple system for recording which answer choices you have eliminated or a way of noting key information in a reading passage. Use scratch paper to solve math problems, draw diagrams, and record any other information that helps you work accurately and quickly.

How to Use This Book

Review the study plans that follow and select the one that best serves your needs. Then take the Diagnostic Test that begins on page 8. Depending on how much time you have before your test date, you can work through each section separately or take the entire test at one sitting. All of the tests and exercises in this book include answer explanations to help you understand the reasoning and problem solving behind the answers. The strategies and review sections of this book, as well as the practice tests, provide lots of opportunity. The more familiar you are with the content of the test, the better your chances for scoring high on the GMAT.

The Study Plans

It is entirely likely that as you are preparing to take the GMAT, you are also studying for your regular college courses. As a result, your time may be limited. This section will help you prepare your own study schedule. We offer you three separate study plans. The first is the **9-Week Plan**, which involves concentrated studying, twice a week. The second, the more leisurely plan, is the **18-Week Plan**. This is essentially the former study plan, but gives you more time in which to review your work, and you can study only once a week, if you wish. Finally, we offer you the **Panic Plan**, for those of you who only have a few weeks to prepare

for the test. Of course, the more time you have to study, the easier it will be to review all of the material in this book. It will also help you feel more relaxed when you take the exam.

These plans are not set in stone. Feel free to modify them to suit your needs and your own study habits. Also, take into account your strengths and weaknesses, which can be determined from the introductory diagnostic test in this book. Focus more of your study efforts on those areas that need greater attention.

The 9-Week Plan—2 Lessons Per Week

Week 1

Lesson 1: Diagnostic Test. Take the Problem Solving (Mathematics) and Sentence Completion sections of the diagnostic GMAT.

Lesson 2: Diagnostic Test. Take the Data Interpretation and Reading Comprehension of the diagnostic GMAT.

Week 2

Lesson 1: Diagnostic Test. Take the Critical Reasoning section of the diagnostic GMAT. Also, check all of the answers for the entire test.

Amend this entire plan to take into account those areas in which you need to concentrate your studying.

Lesson 2: Problem Solving. Begin with the overview of this section, including the Introduction, and read through all of the sections from Arithmetic through Fractions. Complete the sample problems and check your answers.

Week 3

Lesson 1: Sentence Correction. Read the chapter on Sentence Corrections, and answer the review questions. Check your answers. Refer to the Grammar section to help clarify any of the points that were unclear in the Sentence Correction problems.

Lesson 2: Problem Solving. Read through the sections from Decimals through Powers, Exponents and Roots. Complete the sample problems and check your answers.

Week 4

Lesson 1: Reading Comprehension. Read and study the techniques for answering Reading Comprehension questions. Complete the sample questions and check your answers.

Lesson 2: Problem Solving. Read through the Algebra section of the review section. Complete the sample problems and check your answers.

Week 5

Lesson 1: Critical Reasoning. Review this chapter, particularly the strategies and explanations of the different types of questions you will encounter on the GMAT. This is a section where an understanding of the directions is extremely important. Read them carefully and try to memorize them, in order to save time on the actual test.

Lesson 2: Problem Solving. Complete this chapter by reading the Plane Geometry portion. Complete the sample problems and check your answers.

Week 6

Lesson 1: Critical Reasoning. Answer the questions that follow the review section. Complete the sample problems and check your answers.

Lesson 2: Data Sufficiency Review. Read and study the Strategies portion of this chapter. Answer the solved problems and check your answers. Like the directions for the Critical Reasoning section, these directions are also complicated and important to memorize. Take the time to learn them by heart.

Week 7

Lesson 1: Analytical Writing Assessment. There are two types of essays you will be required to write: The first is analyzing an issue stated in the topic, and the second, critiquing an argument presented in the topic. Read through the explanations and strategies and then try to *outline* some of the practice essays presented at the end of the chapter. You won't have time to write complete essays, but outlining will help you formulate the process of developing an effective essay.

Lesson 2: Data Sufficiency Problems. Answer the supplementary questions that appear at the end of the review section. Check your answers carefully. If your mistakes were predominately mathematical, go back to the appropriate sections in the Problem Solving Mathematics review chapter. If your errors were more in the nature of not understanding *how* to answer the questions, reread the overview section that precedes the practice questions, and again, memorize the directions.

Week 8

Lesson 1: Practice Test #1. Under test-taking conditions, take the entire test in one sitting. Don't worry about time on this test. Instead, focus on answering the question, and following directions.

Lesson 2: Practice Test #1. Check your answers and explanations and review any questions that gave you trouble.

Week 9

Lesson 1: Practice Test #2. Under test-taking conditions, take the entire test in one sitting. On this exam, try to time yourself.

Lesson 2: Practice Test #2. Check your answers and explanations and review any questions that gave you trouble.

THE 18-WEEK PLAN—1 LESSON PER WEEK

If you are fortunate enough to have the time, the **18-Week Plan** will give you much more time to study at your leisure. This plan is ideal because you are not under any pressure, and you can take more time to read through the review sections and practice as many problems as possible. You will also have more time to go back and repeat a section of the test that might have given you trouble. Because the primary focus of this book is to provide you with as much practice as possible, you will have more time to spend on this study plan.

In this plan, each lesson should be done in one week. You can surely be more relaxed about the studying, although if you wish, in order not to lose continuity or your train of thought, there is no reason you can't combine lessons where necessary. For example, the Problem Solving portion is spread out over several weeks in the **9-Week Plan.** The reason for this is to give you a breather, in order to permit the material to be retained, while spending time on other topics at the same time. In this plan, you can study all of the mathematics in one week. That week becomes "Problem Solving Week." It's why we recommend altering the plan to suit your needs.

THE PANIC PLAN

Not everyone is lucky enough to have a full eighteen weeks to study for this test, nor even nine weeks. Thus, the **Panic Plan.** Although this is not the best way to study for this, or any test, here are some pointers.

1. Read through the official test booklet or this *GMAT Success* book and *memorize* the directions. We've stated this several times in this chapter and in other chapters. If you don't have to read the directions when you take the actual exam, you will have saved yourself valuable time.

2. Read "Introduction to the GMAT," which can be found in this Red Alert section. This will help you prepare for the different types of questions that you will encounter. The introduction makes an important point about how much time you will have for each question, depending upon which test you are taking. Learn to pace yourself.

3. Take the Diagnostic GMAT test, as well as the two Practice GMAT tests. You'll learn a lot by checking your answers. You will also become familiar, very quickly, with the different types of questions that will be on the actual exam.

4. Focus whatever time you have left on those areas of the test that gave you the most difficulty when you took the full-length tests in this book. If you have the time, read the review sections, and answer the questions in those chapters.

5. Practice filling in the blanks when you take the practice tests. Nothing will hurt you more than skipping a question to come back to later on, and then filling in the wrong blanks on your answer sheet. If you are not going to answer some questions (and remember that it often pays to skip some problems), make sure you establish your own system for leaving those answer ovals blank.

Diagnostic Test

Directions: Each passage in this group is followed by questions based on its content. After reading a passage, choose the best answer to each question and fill in the corresponding space on the answer sheet. Answer all questions following a passage on the basis of what is *stated* or *implied* in that passage.

READING 1

Diversity in unity is one of the major themes in American history; certainly it is the essence of the idea of a federal union. The diversity is simple enough to state and to understand. It lay in the variousness of the original settlements—from feudal Maryland to democratic Rhode Island—and in the extraordinary variety of immigrants—from members of the English gentry to convicted felons. The unity is more difficult to explain, although two key factors were a common allegiance to the British Crown and, if we except small settlements scattered here and there where Germans or Swiss or Dutch clung to their native tongues, a common English language. Among the other common denominators was the fact that the charter of each colony guaranteed its inhabitants "all the rights, privileges and immunities of Englishmen" and that the colonists were, if anything, more aware of these rights and more determined to protect them than their cousins across the Atlantic.

If England in the seventeenth century had flamed with a zeal for "rights" that had produced the classic immunities of the famous English Bill of Rights, the dedication to those principles had cooled considerably by the middle of the next century. Those Englishmen who determined, in large part, the mood and temper of the country were too prosperous, too complacent, and too arrogant to be concerned about the miserable conditions in which the mass of the poorer people lived. They continued, however, to congratulate themselves on the glories of the British constitution and its superiority to any other form of government in the world. This is not to say, of course, that the constitution was without substantial virtues, or that the middle ranks of Englishmen as well as the aristocracy did not enjoy broader rights than those enjoyed by the citizens of other European countries. But a self-congratulatory spirit can be dangerous for a country as for an individual, for it blinds those possessed of it to a proper sense of their own shortcomings and of the mutability of all earthly enterprises.

The colonists, on the other hand, interpreted "the rights of Englishmen" much more practically and directly. They still lived in the "glorious" spirit of the Revolution of 1689. They did not have to view those splendid rights through intervening layers of exceptions and exemptions. Where the Englishman, challenged on some glaring inequity quite at odds with the sacred principles of English justice, would doubtless have replied haughtily, "But my dear fellow, that is the way we have always done it," considering that quite a sufficient answer, the English colonist, confronted with a similar discrepancy between principle and fact, would have been at some pains to effect a reconciliation. Even in the case of slavery, many Southern slaveholders were profoundly troubled by the moral implications of the institution.

The colonists were continuously reminded of their rights by what they considered abuses of them—abuses that led to constant minor friction between the colonial legislative assemblies and the agencies of the Crown in England—the Board of Trade and Plantations and the Privy Council—and, in the colonies, between the Americans and the royal governors (where the colony was a royal one), and the customs officials. Parliament and the ministry thus became increasingly bored with the continual clamor of the colonists over their precious "rights as Englishmen." "Ask a colonist for some money to help protect his borders against the French and Indians," said one exasperated official, "and he will deliver you a lengthy lecture on his rights."

1. The passage overall is a discussion of:
    (A) common grievances among the colonists.
    (B) factors that tended to unify the colonists.
    (C) the colonists' view of freedom.
    (D) diversification in colonial America.
    (E) abuses of rights by the British.

2. Which of the following best presents the author's opinion of eighteenth-century Englishmen?

    (A) The British view of freedom was determined and controlled by a comfortable elitist group far removed from the status and needs of the common man.
    (B) The British felt that Englishmen everywhere had gained sufficient rights, largely because of their zeal in the eighteenth-century.
    (C) The British believed that all Englishmen still lived in the glorious spirit of the Revolution of 1689.
    (D) The British continued to lead the civilized world in acquisition of rights because of their unfaltering attention given to this issue.
    (E) The British were firmly committed to the concept of equality under the law.

3. According to the passage, disagreements between the British and the colonies in interpretation of rights:

    (A) affected every colony.
    (B) were intermittent in nature.
    (C) annoyed the British.
    (D) resulted only from decisions made in England.
    (E) were of serious proportion.

4. Which of the following was neither stated nor implied in the passage as a contribution to the unity of the colonies?

    (A) Language.
    (B) Allegiance to the Crown.
    (C) The terms of each colony's charter.
    (D) Interpretation of "rights".
    (E) Common danger.

5. The passage suggests that Englishmen below the middle-class level:

(A) were more sympathetic to the colonists than were the upper classes in England.

(B) were more conscious of their rights than the higher classes were.

(C) had rights that were equivalent to or less than the rights of citizens in other European countries.

(D) were a minority in England.

(E) were blinded to their shortcomings.

6. The purpose of the second and third paragraphs is:

(A) to give evidence in support of a previously stated generalization.

(B) to compare and contrast.

(C) to define a key term.

(D) to establish a cause-effect relationship.

(E) to refute a premise.

7. Which of the following situations, assuming that all occurred during the eighteenth century, does NOT present a conflict with this author's views or opinions?

(A) An upper-class eighteenth-century Englishman advocates for the lower class.

(B) Citizens of a European country enjoy greater rights than upper-class Englishmen.

(C) A colonist did not live in the spirit of the Revolution of 1689.

(D) The British meet to consider how to increase the rights of Englishmen everywhere.

(E) American slaveholders are troubled by the moral implications of slavery.

READING 2

The treacherous island of Antikythera, the site of a vast trove of classical works of art recovered from the sea at the beginning of the current century, lies at the gate of the Aegean. By 1900, when Captain Dimitrios Kondos and his crew of sponge divers came upon the Antikythera shipwreck, Aegean sponge divers had learned to use the helmet diving gear with reasonable safety, putting in about 1 million hours on the bottom per year.

As it became necessary, the bravest and most adventurous began to specialize in deep diving at depths of well over 200 feet in crews of twenty divers all using the same helmet and pump—a system that remained largely unchanged until the industry waned after the invention of plastics. Kondos and his men, who wore watch fobs of black coral that grows at great depths off Africa where few men have been even today, were unaware that the salvage task the Greek government eventually employed them to undertake at a depth of 180 feet was the deepest ever attempted at that time.

Kondos and his crew were to salvage what was left of a magnificent Roman argosy that had been freighted with plundered Greek bronze and marble sculpture. After more than 2,000 years it appeared as a concreted mound protruding from the sandy bottom that lay at the foot of the steep cliff of Pinakakia. Ordinary citizens, as well as government officials, took great interest in this, the first major archaeological sea discovery made in Greece by Greeks. Supervision of the project was entrusted to an accountant in the archaeology department, an appointment that set a disastrous pattern characteristic of archaeology of the day.

Kondos worked his six divers at the extreme edge of safe diving, two or three times a day in 5-minute shifts, taking the time from when the diver hit the bottom. A diver's reasoning ability deteriorates under pressure, possibly because of a buildup of excess carbon dioxide; divers begin to be affected soon after 100 feet. The effect of narcosis upon the Antikythera divers was exacerbated by their diving helmets. When the divers reported that the wreck itself was covered by great, immovable stones, difficult operations were carried out to maneuver them down the slope of the sea bed and into the abyss. One "great boulder" brought to the surface was a huge statue of Hercules with club and lion skin; all had been statues, so improbably big, so corroded and over-grown, that the divers had failed to recognize them. By the summer of 1901, when all visible objects had been removed from the site, work was suspended. Materials taken from the site were stored in the National Museum in Athens, where piecemeal study of them in ensuing years fueled controversy over the date, later established as first century B.C., and provenance of the ship.

A calcified lump of corroded bronze contained fragments that looked like clockwork. Study of this evidence in 1958 and later in 1971 using new techniques of X-ray investigation determined that it dated from the first century B.C. and was a calendric sun and moon computing device. The Antikythera "computer" with its complicated mechanism, the earliest extant example of the use of sophisticated gears and differentials, is thus a relic of major historical importance that challenges the widely held view that the Greeks were scientifically backward.

8. The best title for this passage is:

   (A) Kondos and His Sponge Divers.
   (B) Dangers of the Deep.
   (C) Treasures of the Sea.
   (D) Early Underwater Archaeology.
   (E) The Antikythera Shipwreck.

9. The passage indicates that:

   (A) sponge diving declined as the plastics industry grew.
   (B) the plastics industry made it unnecessary for several divers to share a helmet.
   (C) the diving helmet industry grew as the plastics industry developed.
   (D) as the use of plastic became widespread, divers were no longer needed.
   (E) the plastic industry propelled the diving industry to new heights.

10. It can be inferred that it became necessary for the divers to specialize in deeper dives because:

   (A) improved plastic equipment allowed them to do so.
   (B) deeper dives were necessary to salvage treasure.
   (C) most sponges had been harvested from shallower levels.
   (D) black coral was in great demand by rich tourists.
   (E) the government required it.

11. It can be inferred that the Antikythera computer was:

   (A) Greek in origin.
   (B) a Roman navigational instrument.
   (C) not among items on board the Antikythera when it sank.
   (D) of great interest to the salvors of the Antikythera.
   (E) stored in a location other than the National Museum in Athens.

12. Which of the following statements can NOT be supported by the passage?

(A) Kondos and his crew had worked off the coast of Africa.

(B) Kondos's men specialized in deep dives.

(C) Using the helmet diving gear involved risks.

(D) The Romans had stolen the cargo of the ship from the Greeks.

(E) The use of the diving helmet enabled a sponge diver to work for prolonged periods before surfacing.

13. The most probable reason that the Antikythera computer remained a mystery for so long is:

(A) it was extant, therefore not available for consideration.

(B) there was inadequate technology to study it sufficiently.

(C) it was removed from the ship surreptitiously by the divers.

(D) no one expected it to have gears and differentials.

(E) it was assumed to be of little value.

14. It can be inferred that the use of diving helmets:

(A) was remarkably safe.

(B) enabled divers to stay underwater for long periods of time.

(C) obstructed a diver's view of the site.

(D) was unnecessary for most divers.

(E) increased the carbon dioxide levels of the divers.

READING 3

As I entered manhood and found that my avocation must now become my vocation, the walls began to close in. The happy days of the universal scholar were at an end, and I was forced to recognize the unpalatable necessity of specializing if I was to succeed as a professional biologist. Nevertheless, as I began my academic training at the university, I found it difficult to choose the narrow path.

For a time I debated whether or not to follow the lead of a friend of mine who was specializing in scatology—the study of the excretory droppings of animals—and who later became a high-ranking scatologist with the United States Biological Survey. But although I found the subject mildly interesting, it failed to rouse my enthusiasm; besides, the field was overcrowded.

My personal predilections lay toward the studies of living animals in their own habitats. Being a literal fellow, I took the word *biology* at face value and was sorely puzzled by the paradox that many of my contemporaries tended to restrict themselves to the aseptic atmosphere of laboratories where they used dead—often very dead—animal material as their subject matter. The new biologists were concentrating on statistical and analytical research, whereby the raw material of life became no more than fodder for the nourishment of calculating machines.

My inability to adjust to the new trends had an adverse effect upon my professional expectations. While my fellow students were already establishing themselves in various esoteric specialties, most of which they invented for themselves on the theory that if you are the *only* specialist in a given field you need fear no competition, I was still unable to deflect my interests from the general to the particular. As graduation approached I found that the majority of my contemporaries were assured of excellent research jobs, while I seemed to have nothing particular to offer in the biological marketplace. It was inevitable that I should end up working for the government.

The die was cast one winter's day when I received a summons from the Dominion Wildlife Service informing me that I had been hired at the munificent salary of $120 a month and that I *would* report to Ottawa at once. I obeyed this order with hardly more than a twitch of subdued rebelliousness, for if I had learned anything at the university, it was that the scientific hierarchy requires a high standard of obedience, if not subservience, from its acolytes. I presented myself to the chief mammalogist, whom I had known as a school chum, but who had now metamorphosed into a full-blown scientist so shrouded in professional dignity that it was all I could do to refrain from making him a profound obeisance. The next few days were orientation, during which I visited legions of Dantesque bureaucrats in their gloomy, Formalin-smelling dens where they spent interminable hours compiling dreary data or originating meaningless memos. During this period, which did nothing to rouse in me much devotion to my new employment, the only thing I actually learned was that, by comparison with the bureaucratic hierarchy in Ottawa, the scientific hierarchy was a brotherhood of anarchy.

15. The main point of the selection is that:

(A) the author's career preferences were unusual.

(B) the author was unable to narrow his interest in his field.

(C) most biologists were not interested in living things.

(D) working for the government required few skills.

(E) choosing a career is difficult.

16. The author's statement that "the raw material of life became no more than fodder for the . . . calculating machines" suggests that:

(A) animals had to be sacrificed in the interest of scientific advancement.

(B) statistical and analytical researchers were incorrect in their actions.

(C) sophisticated calculators enabled the scientific community to advance, learning much more about living animals.

(D) living things were regarded only as a source of data for analysis.

(E) the author was beginning to gain a sense of his future in biology.

17. This passage is best described as:

(A) a humorous narrative discussing the author's transition into his early career.

(B) a comparison of the author's feelings and beliefs about his field and the beliefs of established biologists.

(C) a vehicle to enable the author to present his views of the Canadian government.

(D) an allegory.

(E) a personal prose narrative without clear intention.

18. According to the author, which does NOT pertain to the established scientific community?

    (A) Interested primarily in research.
    (B) Impressed with its own self-importance.
    (C) Involved in narrow specialties.
    (D) Well established as a hierarchy.
    (E) More bureaucratic than the government.

19. When the author states that "by comparison with the hierarchy in Ottawa, the scientific hierarchy was a brotherhood of anarchy," his intention is:

    (A) to imply that the scientific hierarchy needed to be tightened up.
    (B) to inform the reader that the government hierarchy was more structured than the scientific hierarchy.
    (C) to suggest that the government hierarchy was excessive.
    (D) to imply that one cannot escape structure.
    (E) to point out that the scientific community should model itself after the government.

20. The author's statement that he "found it difficult to choose the narrow path" should be interpreted to mean that:

    (A) he could not find a job.
    (B) he could not find a suitable avocation.
    (C) he could not find a discipline of interest.
    (D) he could not determine a specialty.
    (E) he could not select a university.

21. A paradox pointed out by the author involves the difference between:

    (A) definition and restatement.
    (B) literal language and figurative language.
    (C) surface meaning and implied meaning.
    (D) living animals and dead animals.
    (E) theory and practice.

SECTION 2   TIME—25 MINUTES   16 QUESTIONS

Directions: In this section solve each problem, using any available space on the page for scratchwork. Then indicate the best of the answer choices given.

Numbers: All numbers used are real numbers.

Figures: Figures that accompany problems in the text are intended to provide information useful in solving the problems. They are drawn as accurately as possible EXCEPT when it is stated in a specific problem that its figure is not drawn to scale. All figures lie in a plane unless otherwise indicated.

1. A student's marks are 75, 92, 68, and 95. What must his next mark be in order for him to have an average of 85?

   (A) 100
   (B) 95
   (C) 85
   (D) 80
   (E) 90

2. Which of the following fractions is larger than $\frac{3}{5}$?

   (A) $\frac{1}{2}$

   (B) $\frac{39}{50}$

   (C) $\frac{7}{25}$

   (D) $\frac{3}{10}$

   (E) $\frac{59}{100}$

3. Find the perimeter of the adjoining figure if the area of each square is 25.

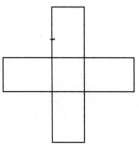

   (A) 36
   (B) 40
   (C) 48
   (D) 60
   (E) 80

Use the accompanying graph for questions 4 and 5.

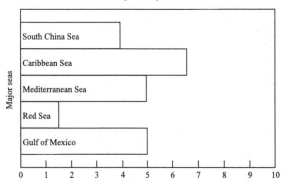

4. What is the approximate ratio of the depth of the South China Sea to the depth of the Red Sea?

   (A) 7:10
   (B) 3:1
   (C) 7:3
   (D) 7:5
   (E) 1:3

15

5. Approximately what is the depth of the Caribbean Sea?

(A) 6.5
(B) 65
(C) 650
(D) 6,500
(E) 65,000

6. When $\dfrac{x^2 - 9}{x}$ is divided by $\dfrac{x - 3}{5x}$ the quotient is:

(A) $\dfrac{(x - 3)^2(x + 3)}{5x^2}$

(B) $5x(x + 3)$

(C) $5(x + 3)$

(D) $5(x - 3)$

(E) $\dfrac{5x}{x - 3}$

7. A department store advertised a summer sale on fur coats, quoting the following prices:

 I. $1350 coats reduced to $1200
 II. $800 coats reduced to $650
 III. $2250 coats reduced to $2000
 IV. $1000 coats reduced to $900
 V. $3000 coats reduced to $2500

Which group of coats had the greatest rate of discount?

(A) I
(B) II
(C) III
(D) IV
(E) V

8. The sum of three consecutive integers is 33. Find the largest integer.

(A) −10
(B) 10
(C) −11
(D) 11
(E) 12

9. If $a + b = \dfrac{5}{6}$ and $\dfrac{1}{(a - b)} = \dfrac{3}{10}$, then $\dfrac{(a + b)}{(a - b)} =$

(A) $\dfrac{1}{4}$

(B) $\dfrac{9}{25}$

(C) $\dfrac{25}{9}$

(D) 4

(E) $\dfrac{25}{6}$

10. If a boy spent $60, which was $37\dfrac{1}{2}\%$ of the money he earned during the Christmas holidays, then the amount that he earned during the Christmas holidays was:

(A) $100
(B) $140
(C) $160
(D) $180
(E) $240

11. The perimeter of a square is R meters. The area of the square is:

(A) $4R$

(B) R^2

(C) $\dfrac{R^2}{4}$

(D) $\dfrac{R^2}{16}$

(E) $2R^2$

12. At a club meeting, five friends decide to buy a plaque for the club that will cost D dollars. One person later decides not to participate in the plan. What will be the increase in dollars to for each of the four remaining people?

(A) $\dfrac{D}{3}$

(B) $\dfrac{D}{20}$

(C) 2D

(D) $\dfrac{D-5}{2}$

(E) $\dfrac{D}{5}$

13. On a map, a line segment 3 inches long represents a distance of 15 miles. Using the same scale, how many miles long is a road that is $4\dfrac{3}{8}$ inches on a map?

(A) $21\dfrac{3}{4}$

(B) $12\dfrac{3}{8}$

(C) $21\dfrac{7}{8}$

(D) 33

(E) $62\dfrac{3}{8}$

14. If the width of a rectangle is increased by 10%, and the length is decreased by 20%, by what percent does the area decrease?

(A) 2%

(B) 12%

(C) 16%

(D) 20%

(E) 21%

15. The expression $\dfrac{1}{2}\sqrt{28}$ is equivalent to:

(A) $\sqrt{14}$

(B) $2\sqrt{7}$

(C) $\sqrt{7}$

(D) 7

(E) $4\sqrt{7}$

16. If x units are added to the length of the radius of a circle, what is the number of units by which the circumference of the circle is increased?

(A) x

(B) 2

(C) 2π

(D) $2\pi x$

(E) x^2

SECTION 3 | **TIME—25 MINUTES** | **20 QUESTIONS**

Directions: Each of the following data sufficiency problems consists of a question and two statements, labeled (1) and (2), in which certain data are given. You have to decide whether the data given in the statements are *sufficient* for answering the question. Using the data given in the statements *plus* your knowledge of mathematics and everyday facts (such as the number of days in July or the meaning of *counterclockwise*), you are to fill in the corresponding answer oval on your answer sheet.

A. If statement (1) ALONE is sufficient, but statement (2) alone is not sufficient to answer the question asked;

B. If statement (2) ALONE is sufficient, but statement (1) alone is not sufficient to answer the question asked;

C. If BOTH statements (1) and (2) TOGETHER are sufficient to answer the question asked, but NEITHER statement ALONE is sufficient;

D. If EACH statement ALONE is sufficient to answer the question asked;

E. If statements (1) and (2) TOGETHER are NOT sufficient to answer the question asked, and additional data specific to the problem are needed.

Numbers

All numbers used are real numbers.

Figures

A figure in a data sufficiency problem will conform to the information given in the question, but will not necessarily conform to the additional information given in statements (1) and (2).

Note

In questions that ask for the value of a quantity, the data given in the statements are sufficient only when it is possible to determine exactly one numerical value for the quantity.

Example

In $\triangle PQR$, what is the value of x?

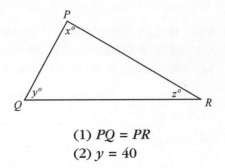

(1) $PQ = PR$
(2) $y = 40$

Explanation

According to statement (1), $PQ = PR$; therefore, $\triangle PQR$ is isosceles and $y = z$. Since $x + y + z = 180$, it follows that $x + 2y = 180$. Since statement (1) does not give a value for y, you cannot answer the question using statement (1) alone. According to statement (2), $y = 40$; therefore, $x + z = 140$. Since statement (2) does not give a value for z, you cannot answer the question using statement (2) alone. Using both statements together, since $x + 2y = 180$ and the value of y is given, you can find the value of x. Therefore, the answer is C.

1. A truck is carrying a load to city A, which is 180 miles away. It will return empty. How much will the gas cost?

   (1) The truck gets 15 miles a gallon when it is empty.
   (2) The truck gets 12 miles a gallon when it is loaded.

2. How much money did Brian earn last year?

   (1) The total of Brian's and Janet's salaries last year was $90,000.
   (2) Janet earned 20% more than Brian did last year.

3. Will farm income be up in 1996?

   (1) Farmers are planting 20% less land in grain in 1996 than 1995.
   (2) Exports of grain will increase in 1996.

4. Is A or C closer to B?

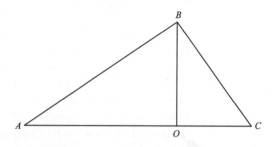

   (1) BO is perpendicular to AC.
   (2) AO is less than OC.

5. What are the coordinates of point B?

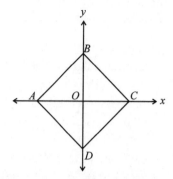

   (1) ABCD is a square
   (2) Perimeter of ABCD = 20.

6. Did MN Company have larger losses in 1992 or 1993?

   (1) The profits for 1994 and 1995 wiped out the combined losses for 1992 and 1993.
   (2) The profit for 1994 was more than one and a half times the loss for 1992.

7. What is the value of x?

   (1) y divided by 7 is equal to 8.
   (2) y is equal to 7 more than 3 times x.

8. ABCDEF is a regular hexagon inscribed in a circle with its center at O. What is the length of arc AB?

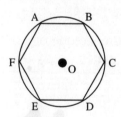

   (1) OA = 6 inches.
   (2) Triangle OAB is equilateral.

9. What is the average (arithmetic mean) annual salary of the members of the executive board?

   (1) The average (arithmetic mean) annual salary of the board members who attended the January meeting is $45,000.

   (2) The average (arithmetic mean) annual salary of the two members who missed the January meeting is $42,000.

10. Find $x + y$.

   (1) $\dfrac{x}{y} = 12$

   (2) $y = \dfrac{7}{8}$

11. If ACB is a straight angle, how large is angle ACD?

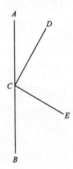

   (1) DC is perpendicular to CE.

   (2) Angle ECB is $1\dfrac{1}{2}$ times angle ACD.

12. Find the altitude of a triangle.

   (1) The area of the triangle = the area of the square.

   (2) The base of the triangle = the side of the square.

13. How far does John have to drive in the last 2 hours in order to average 55 miles an hour?

   (1) John has already completed four hours of driving.

   (2) Up to this point, his average speed is 50 mph.

14. Is $\dfrac{N}{35}$ an integer?

   (1) $\dfrac{N}{21}$ is an integer.

   (2) $\dfrac{N}{10}$ is an integer.

15. What is the value of $\dfrac{(x^2\,y^3\,z^7)^8}{(x^4\,y^2\,z^{14})^4}$

   (1) $x = 12$

   (2) $y = 5$

16. What is the area of triangle MNP?

   (1) $\angle$ MNP is a right angle.

   (2) NP = 7 and MN = 6.

17. How many different routes can be used to go from New York City to Washington, D.C., if a stop is made in Philadelphia?

   (1) There are four different routes from New York City to Philadelphia and three different routes from Philadelphia to Washington, D.C.

   (2) It is possible to travel the entire distance from New York City to Washington, D.C., on a turnpike.

18. A club has 100 members. It has an executive committee of twelve. From how many members may the finance committee be chosen?

    (1)   The appropriations committee is chosen from the executive committee.

    (2)   None of the six members of the finance committee may be members of the appropriations committee.

19. Angle *ACB* is inscribed in circle *O*. What is the formula to determine the length of the radius in terms of the length of *CB*?

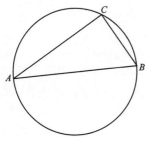

    (1)   *C* is a right angle.
    (2)   *AC* is twice the length of *CB*.

20. Each shift is responsible for completing half a job. If all workers work at the same rate, in how many hours will the job be completed?

    (1)   The first shift has eleven workers and completes its share of the work in 6 hours.

    (2)   The second shift has only five workers.

SECTION 4   TIME—25 MINUTES   16 QUESTIONS

> *Directions:* For each question in this section, select the best of the answer choices given.

1. A poll of all voters in the state shows that only 11 percent of all people who voted were younger than 29 years old. These results prove that young Americans are not as interested in voting as are older generations.

   Which of the following statements, if true, would most seriously weaken the author's conclusion?

   (A) The number of voters in the state under the age of 29 has increased for each of the past five years.
   (B) The average age of all voters in the state is 50 years old.
   (C) Of all people in the state who are old enough to vote, only 13 percent are younger than 29 years old.
   (D) Most of the voters in the state are Republicans, and the winning candidate is a Democrat.
   (E) The total number of voters this year was the lowest it has been in ten years.

2. Acme Company markets high-tech recording and videotaping materials for sale to parents of small children for the purpose of secretly recording the activities of their baby-sitters and nannies while they are away from home. In defending their products, an Acme representative argued, "More than 75 percent of the parents buying our surveillance equipment fire their baby-sitters or nannies within two weeks of their starting work. This proves that we have a nationwide problem with misconduct by all baby-sitters and nannies."

   Which of the following, if true, would most contradict the Acme representative's argument?

   (A) Secretly recording or videotaping people without their consent is unconstitutional.
   (B) The customers who use Acme Company's products are indicative of the nationwide population.
   (C) Of all the nannies who are fired in this country, more than 75 percent are illegal aliens.
   (D) Most of the people who use Acme Company's products suspected their baby-sitters of misconduct before using the equipment.
   (E) After six months of use, Acme Company's surveillance equipment tends to break down and become unreliable.

Questions 3 and 4 are based on the following:

Studies indicate that the job market for new graduates from U.S. law schools is as competitive as it has been in thirty years, and 40 percent of new law school graduates in 1998 are expected to remain unemployed for the first year. As a result, law schools, anticipating smaller enrollments in the near future, are decreasing the size of their teaching staffs.

3. Which of the following presents a pattern of thinking that is most closely analogous to the preceding situation?

   (A) A college football coach limits the size of his recruiting staff because his team lost most of its games this year.

   (B) The mayor of a small town increases the budget for road maintenance because car sales in the past two years have increased by 40 percent.

   (C) Meteorologists are predicting that next year will produce more hurricanes than any year in recent history, so hardware stores are stocking extra lumber supplies for boarding over windows.

   (D) A history teacher plans to assign extra homework every night this week because the students have to prepare for their final exams soon.

   (E) A bookstore manager returns 1000 copies of a book to its publisher because the book remained on the shelves for weeks without selling as predicted.

4. Which of the following statements, if true, would most strengthen the conclusion made by the law schools that enrollments will be decreasing?

   (A) The accuracy of methods for predicting graduate school enrollments has been a subject of study for many years.

   (B) Nationwide enrollments in medical schools have decreased by 25 percent over the past two years.

   (C) Predictions regarding future enrollments in professional graduate schools are based on factors including unemployment rates for those professions.

   (D) The last time that the unemployment rate among lawyers was as low as it is now, the nation had half as many lawyers as it does today.

   (E) Measuring unemployment levels in any profession historically has been an accurate method for predicting future graduate school enrollment.

5. When our savants characterize their golden age in any but scientific terms, they emit a quantity of down-at-the-heels platitudes that would gladden the heart of the pettiest politician.

If the word *savant* is used to mean "learned person" or "scholar," then one can reason that the term is used here in which of the following ways?

   (A) Pedantically
   (B) Metaphorically
   (C) Ironically
   (D) Symbolically
   (E) Literally

6. Let's take a few samples. "To render human nature nobler, more beautiful, and more harmonious." What on earth can this mean? What criteria, what content, do they propose? Not many, I fear, would be able to reply. "To assume the triumph of peace, liberty, and reason." "Fine words with no substance behind them." "To eliminate cultural lag." What culture? And would the culture they have in mind be able to subsist in this harsh social organization? "To conquer outer space." For what purpose? The conquest of space seems an end in itself, which dispenses with the need for reflection.

If the scientists claim that they seek "to eliminate cultural lag," then it is the author's view that:

(A) culture is thriving in the contemporary world.
(B) education is failing to promote culture.
(C) social classes must be eliminated in a cultured society.
(D) culture has first to be defined.
(E) ethnic groups have deserted their cultural values.

7. Real estate developer: "We expect that the formation of this new corporation to create a business park will make access easier for commuters to new businesses that we hope will locate in this area. As a result, tax revenues will increase and the quality of life in this area will improve."

Which of the following, if true, would most weaken the developer's conclusion?

(A) The town's crime rate has steadily increased for each of the past three years.

(B) The tax rate for new businesses in this area is higher than any other community in the state.
(C) High unemployment rates have never been a problem in this town.
(D) People who invest in the new corporation for town development will be motivated by their desire for a positive return on their investments and not by concern for the quality of life in this area.
(E) If new businesses open in this area, new money will be available to improve educational materials for local schools.

8. If the cost of building materials increases in any year over the cost of the previous year, then the cost of purchasing new homes increases for that year. New home sales always decrease when purchase costs increase. In 1995, the nationwide sales of new homes increased by 35 percent.

Which of the following can be concluded from the above information?

(A) The cost of building materials in 1995 must have increased by at least 35 percent.
(B) The sales of new homes in 1996 will increase by less than 35 percent.
(C) The cost of purchasing new homes in 1995 was less than it will be in 1996.
(D) Building materials are not as readily available this year as they were last year.
(E) The cost of building materials in 1994 must have been at least as high as in 1995.

9. In 1960, the weekly *L'Express* of Paris published a series of extracts from texts by American and Russian scientists concerning society in the year 2000. As long as such visions were purely a literary concern of science fiction writers and sensation journalists, it was possible to smile at them. Now, we have like works from Nobel Prize winners, members of the Academy of Science of Moscow, and other scientific notables. The visions of these men put science fiction in the shade.

Which of the following pieces of information reveal the comparison of the future in the view held by science fiction writers when compared to that held by scientists?

(A) They are completely different.
(B) The scientific conception is grounded to a greater degree on reality.
(C) The scientific conception is more solidly grounded in research.
(D) The scientific is more extravagant.
(E) The science fiction writers' conceptions are plausible.

10. The most remarkable predictions concern the transformation of educational methods and the problem of human reproduction. Knowledge will be accumulated in "electronic banks" and be transmitted directly to the human nervous systems by means of coded electronic messages. There will no longer be any need of reading or learning mountains of useless information; everything will be received and registered according to the needs of the moment. There will be no need of attention or effort. What is needed will pass directly from the machine to the brain without going through consciousness.

Which of the following most reasonably reproduces the scientific view of the future for knowledge to be accumulated?

Knowledge will be stored:

(A) in the minds of a specially trained intelligentsia.
(B) in centrally located "electronic banks."
(C) in mammoth libraries containing millions of books.
(D) in a communion of scientists and artists.
(E) on tapes in a large number of underground vaults.

11. The serious, although relatively minor, problems that were provoked by the industrial exploitation of coal and electricity 150 years ago still exist. In fact, there is one and only one means to their solution—a worldwide totalitarian dictatorship that will allow technology its full scope, and at the same time resolve its concomitant difficulties. It is not difficult to understand why the scientists and worshipers of technology prefer not to dwell on their solutions, but rather to leap numbly across the dull and uninteresting intermediary period of unanswered questions, and land squarely in the golden age of change and progress. We might indeed ask ourselves if we will succeed in getting through the transition period without universal cooperation. Is the price of progress perhaps too high a price to pay for this golden age?

The conclusion drawn in this selection implies that the problems created by industrial exploitation are

(A) national in nature.
(B) unsolvable realistically.
(C) exciting to handle.
(D) solvable by technology.
(E) solvable and inexpensive.

12. Officials reviewing conditions of a local police station are considering whether major structural renovations are required. "The chances are good that a police officer will be killed or injured by a prisoner because of cramped space and poor design of the holding cells," one official concluded.

The official's conclusion is based most upon which of the following assumptions?

(A) In crowded conditions, dangerous criminals will have more access to weapons and closer contact with police officers.
(B) All criminals who are brought to this particular holding cell are violently dangerous and present a serious threat to safety.
(C) Storage of and access to police files will be more efficient if the planned renovations are accomplished.
(D) Police officers will be able to perform their public duties more effectively if they are provided with new office spaces.
(E) Holding prisoners in small, cramped holding cells is unconstitutional because it constitutes cruel and inhuman punishment.

13. Banker: By transferring income to a retirement account at our bank, people can save money by delaying paying taxes.

Accountant: That plan won't actually save money, because the taxes will have to be paid sometime in the future when the money is withdrawn.

Which of the following best explains the conflict between the banker and the accountant?

(A) The banker is primarily concerned with recruiting new customers for the bank.
(B) The accountant misunderstands the application of the tax laws.
(C) The banker and the accountant disagree on the application of the term "save."
(D) Retirement accounts are nothing more than a tax shelter, which Congress intends to cut out of next year's tax amendments.
(E) The cost of living in the town where the banker and the accountant work is lower than in most other cities, so there is less need for saving money.

Questions 14, 15, and 16 come from the following selection.

By the year 2000, voyagers to the moon will be commonplace: so will be commonplace inhabited, artificial satellites. All food will be completely synthetic. The world's population will have increased fourfold but will have been stabilized. Sea water and ordinary rocks will yield all the necessary metals. Disease, as well as famine, will have been eliminated, and there will be universal hygienic inspection and control. The problems of energy production will have been completely resolved. Serious scientists, it must be repeated, are the source of these predictions, which hitherto were found only in Utopia.

14. Which of the following terms, if true, would most accurately describe the author's tone when discussing the "ideal" world of the future?

(A) Appreciative
(B) Captious
(C) Humorous
(D) Satirical
(E) Objective

15. The author of this passage concludes that the world of 2000 will:

(A) closely resemble that of today.
(B) feature a dependence on natural resources.
(C) require the elimination of scientific investigation.
(D) depend on scientific investigation.
(E) require continuing dreams of a Utopian society.

16. The conclusion concerning the world of the future as conceived by scientists is based LEAST upon which of the following assumptions?

(A) Travel in space will be commonplace.
(B) Instead of embattled nationalities there will be one world.
(C) Human beings will be free from disease.
(D) All food will be artificially produced.
(E) A unique and varied creativity will exist in the arts.

SECTION 5   TIME—25 MINUTES   22 QUESTIONS

Directions: In each of the following sentences, some part of the sentence or the entire sentence is underlined. Beneath each sentence you will find five ways of phrasing the underlined part. The first of these repeats the original; the other four are different. If you think the original is better than any of the alternatives, choose answer A; otherwise, choose one of the others. Select the best version and fill in the corresponding oval on your answer sheet.

This is a test of correctness and effectiveness of expression. In choosing answers, follow the requirements of standard written English; that is, pay attention to grammar, choice of words, and sentence construction. Choose the answer that expresses most effectively what is presented in the original sentence; this answer should be clear and exact, without awkwardness, ambiguity, or redundancy.

1. The gang went into their shack in order to exchange views on their problem.

   (A) exchange views on their problem.
   (B) vent their opinions.
   (C) rap about their problem.
   (D) interrelate about their problem.
   (E) air their problem.

2. The meter maid said he had transgressed the law as she saw it.

   (A) transgressed
   (B) evaded
   (C) broken
   (D) obstructed
   (E) averted

3. To perpetrate such a scheme, he felt, would be just plain mean.

   (A) just plain mean.
   (B) just plainly mean.
   (C) dreadfully unkind.
   (D) just plain awful.
   (E) just plain nasty.

4. The reward was divided between the four neighbors who had discovered the thief.

   (A) between the four neighbors who
   (B) to the four neighbors who
   (C) among the four neighbors who
   (D) between the four neighbors that
   (E) between the four neighbors which

5. Regardless of his position at this time, being that he once broke the law, he must be penalized.

   (A) being that
   (B) seeing that
   (C) since
   (D) being
   (E) as a result of

6. As far as I am concerned, it will be <u>alright</u> for them to take their leave.

   (A) alright
   (B) satisfactorily
   (C) all right
   (D) allright
   (E) well

7. Despite the doctor's warning, he continued to <u>itch</u> his wound.

   (A) itch
   (B) itch at
   (C) stitch
   (D) avoid
   (E) scratch

8. He drove carefully, but the accident <u>couldn't hardly be</u> avoided.

   (A) couldn't hardly be
   (B) could hardly be
   (C) couldn't hardly have been
   (D) couldn't have been
   (E) couldn't have hardly been

9. They decided to shift their headquarters, <u>irregardless</u> of the consequences.

   (A) irregardless
   (B) regarding
   (C) disregardless
   (D) regardless
   (E) irregarding

10. Responding to their appeal, she found them <u>already</u> to escape.

   (A) already
   (B) allready
   (C) All-ready
   (D) all-ready
   (E) all ready

11. He <u>was laying in his bed when I came</u> home from work.

   (A) was laying in his bed when I came
   (B) was laying in his bed as I came
   (C) was lying in his bed when I came
   (D) had been laying in his bed when I came
   (E) will be laying in his bed when I come

12. <u>Having less possessions, she was more able</u> to move unencumbered from place to place.

   (A) Having less possessions, she was more able
   (B) She had less possessions, so she was more able
   (C) Having fewer possessions, the ability
   (D) Having had less possessions, she was more able
   (E) Having fewer possessions, she was more able

13. <u>Listening to his singing the song</u> was obviously a hit.

   (A) Listening to his singing the song
   (B) While listening to his singing, the song,
   (C) While listening to his singing, the song
   (D) Listening to his singing, they could tell that the song
   (E) Listening to him, the song

14. They worried about her mental condition <u>having lost all her money</u>.

   (A) having lost all her money.
   (B) since she had lost all her money.
   (C) being she lost all her money.
   (D) losing all her money.
   (E) as she lost all her money.

15. We were frightened by the noises. We fled immediately.

  (A) We were frightened by the noises. We fled immediately.
  (B) Being that we were frightened by the noises, we fled immediately.
  (C) Because we were frightened by the noises, we fled immediately.
  (D) The noises frightened us, we fled immediately.
  (E) Being we were frightened by the noises, we fled immediately.

16. Challenged by the sentry, it was a shock to him.

  (A) Challenged by the sentry, it was a shock to him.
  (B) Being challenged by the sentry, it was a shock to him.
  (C) Being that he was challenged by the sentry, he was shocked.
  (D) Being challenged by the sentry shocked him.
  (E) Challenged by the sentry, it came as a shock to him.

17. Everyone except Dana and she automatically fail the exam.

  (A) except Dana and she automatically fail
  (B) accept Dana and her automatically fail
  (C) accept Dana and her automatically fail
  (D) except Dana and her automatically fail
  (E) except Dana and her automatically fails

18. Neither the boys or Robin want anything to do with the old man.

  (A) or Robin want
  (B) or Robin wants
  (C) nor Robin wants
  (D) nor Robin want
  (E) want or Robin wants

19. I'd behave differently if I were he.

  (A) if I were he.
  (B) if I was him.
  (C) if I was he.
  (D) if I were him.
  (E) if I were not him.

20. The producer was to be honored being that he made Shakespeare accessible to the masses.

  (A) being that he made Shakespeare
  (B) on account he made Shakespeare
  (C) when he made Shakespeare
  (D) although he made Shakespeare
  (E) since he made Shakespeare

21. His outlook on life, together with his disposition and his temper, make him a dangerous criminal.

  (A) together with his disposition and his temper, make
  (B) in addition to his disposition and his temper, make
  (C) along with his disposition and his temper, make
  (D) as well as his disposition and his temper, makes
  (E) as well as his disposition and his temper, make

22. The data is proof of the thesis.

  (A) is proof of the thesis.
  (B) are proof of the thesis.
  (C) prove the thesis.
  (D) proves the thesis.
  (E) is proof that the thesis is correct.

| SECTION 6 | TIME—25 MINUTES | 16 QUESTIONS |

1. If the length and the width of a rectangle are both tripled, the ratio of the area of the original rectangle to the area of the enlarged rectangle is:

   (A) 1:3
   (B) 1:6
   (C) 1:9
   (D) 1:8
   (E) 2:9

2. How many degrees are in the sum of the measures of the interior angles of a regular polygon with 10 sides?

   (A) 1200
   (B) 1600
   (C) 2440
   (D) 1800
   (E) 1440

3. If two fractions, each of which has a value between 0 and 1, are multiplied together, the product will be:

   (A) always greater than both of the original fractions.
   (B) always less than both of the original fractions.
   (C) sometimes greater and sometimes less than both of the original fractions.
   (D) the same.
   (E) never less than both of the original fractions.

4. An inheritance of $120,000 is divided among 3 people in a ratio of 3:4:5. How much was the largest share?

   (A) $30,000
   (B) $40,000
   (C) $45,000
   (D) $50,000
   (E) $55,000

5. A certain dress requires $2\frac{2}{3}$ yards of material. How many dresses of this type can a manufacturer make from 120 yards of material?

   (A) 60
   (B) 55
   (C) 65
   (D) 40
   (E) 45

6. The solution set of the inequality $3x - 4 > 8$ is:

   (A) $x > 4$
   (B) $x < 4$
   (C) $3x > 4$
   (D) $x = 4$
   (E) $x = -4$

7. If the fractions $\dfrac{x+y}{3}$ and $\dfrac{x-y}{4}$ are added, the result is:

(A) $\dfrac{7x+y}{12}$

(B) $\dfrac{2x}{7}$

(C) $\dfrac{7x-y}{12}$

(D) $\dfrac{5x+4y}{12}$

(E) $\dfrac{x^2-y^2}{7}$

8. If the price of an item triples, the increase is what percent of the new price?

(A) $16\dfrac{2}{3}\%$

(B) $33\dfrac{1}{3}\%$

(C) $66\dfrac{2}{3}\%$

(D) 200%

(E) 300%

9. Ms. A and Mr. B leave at the same time from points that are 300 miles apart and travel toward each other. If Ms. A travels at 60 miles per hour and Mr. B travels at 40 miles per hour, in how many hours will they meet?

(A) 3
(B) 4
(C) 5
(D) 6
(E) 2

10. If the yearly income from a $1000 investment is $30, the annual interest rate is:

(A) $33\dfrac{1}{3}\%$
(B) 30%
(C) 3%
(D) .3%
(E) 3.3%

11. The sum of two consecutive integers is 39. Find the value of the smaller integer.

(A) 11
(B) 12
(C) 18
(D) 19
(E) 20

12. A number of dimes and quarters are worth $2.55. If the number of dimes and quarters were interchanged, the resulting new amount would be $2.70. How many of each kind of coin were there before the interchange?

(A) 6 dimes, 9 quarters
(B) 9 dimes, 6 quarters
(C) 7 dimes, 7 quarters
(D) 8 dimes, 7 quarters
(E) 7 dimes, 8 quarters

13. A father can do a certain job in x hours. His son takes twice as long to do the job. Working together, they can do the job in 6 hours. How many hours does it take the father to do the job?

(A) 9
(B) 18
(C) 12
(D) 20
(E) 16

14. Six years ago in a state park, the deer outnumbered the foxes by 80. Since then, the number of deer has doubled and the number of foxes has increased by 20. If there are now a total of 240 deer and foxes in the park, how many foxes were there six years ago?

(A) 10
(B) 20
(C) 30
(D) 40
(E) 100

15. If $x < y$ and $y < z$, which statement about the integers x, y, and z must be true?

(A) $x < z$
(B) $x = z$
(C) $x > z$
(D) $y - x = z$
(E) $y > z$

16. If x is an integer, the solution set of $5 < x \leq 6$ is:

(A) 6
(B) 5
(C) 5, 6
(D) 0
(E) x

QUICK-SCORE ANSWERS

DIAGNOSTIC TEST ANSWERS

Section 1 Reading Comprehension	Section 2 Problem Solving	Section 3 Data Sufficiency	Section 4 Critical Reasoning	Section 5 Sentence Corrections	Section 6 Problem Solving
1. B	1. B	1. E	1. C	1. C	1. C
2. A	2. B	2. C	2. D	2. C	2. E
3. C	3. D	3. E	3. C	3. C	3. B
4. E	4. C	4. C	4. E	4. C	4. D
5. C	5. D	5. C	5. C	5. C	5. E
6. B	6. C	6. E	6. D	6. C	6. A
7. E	7. B	7. C	7. B	7. E	7. A
8. E	8. E	8. A	8. E	8. C	8. C
9. A	9. A	9. E	9. D	9. D	9. A
10. C	10. C	10. C	10. B	10. E	10. C
11. A	11. D	11. C	11. D	11. C	11. D
12. E	12. B	12. E	12. A	12. E	12. D
13. B	13. C	13. C	13. C	13. D	13. A
14. E	14. B	14. C	14. D	14. B	14. B
15. B	15. C	15. B	15. E	15. C	15. A
16. D	16. D	16. C	16. E	16. D	16. A
17. A		17. A		17. E	
18. E		18. E		18. C	
19. C		19. C		19. A	
20. D		20. C		20. E	
21. E				21. D	
				22. C	

16/21

11/16

12/16

16/16

81/111 73%

12/20

14/22

EXPLANATORY ANSWERS TO THE DIAGNOSTIC TEST

READING COMPREHENSION

1. The correct answer is B. The passage discusses factors that unified the colonists. These included allegiance to the crown, a common language, and common grievances. In mentioning grievances alone, choice A is too narrow. Choice C is, likewise, too narrow. Choice D is incorrect, for no diversification is discussed in the passage. Choice E is incorrect because the passage does not discuss specific abuses.

2. The correct answer is A. The author states that the Englishmen in control were "too prosperous, too complacent, and too arrogant" to be concerned about the conditions of the masses. Choice B can be eliminated because the first sentence of paragraph 2 mentions the zeal of the seventeenth century, not the eighteenth. Choice C incorrectly identifies the Englishmen, rather than the colonists, as those living the glorious spirit. Choice D should be eliminated because those who were too complacent and arrogant to be concerned cannot be described as giving unfaltering attention. Choice E has no basis in the passage.

3. The correct answer is C. The last sentence of the passage expresses the annoyance of the British. Choice A is beyond the scope of the passage. When the author refers to "the colonies," the reader cannot determine whether the author refers to colonies in general or to all colonies without exception. Because the passage states that the colonists were continuously reminded of their rights, the reader would not select choice B. Choice D should be eliminated because the passage refers to disagreements between the colonists and the royal governors, who lived in the colony they governed. The passage cites "constant minor friction," eliminating choice E.

4. The correct answer is E. No reference or implication in the passage suggests that common danger drew the colonies together as a unit. The first paragraph cites choices A, B, and C. Choice D is implied by the last three paragraphs, which discuss rights in England, in the colonies, and in conflict between England and the colonies.

5. The correct answer is C. The second paragraph states that middle ranks of Englishmen and aristocracy enjoyed broader rights. Lower ranks are excluded from the statement and, therefore, must have rights at a comparatively reduced level. No basis in the passage exists to enable a reader to learn the attitude of the lower classes in England (choice A) or their consciousness of their own rights (choice B). In order to select choice D, the reader would need to know relative numbers in each class, and these are not provided. Choice E is mentioned in the passage, but it refers to the self-congratulatory spirit of the dominant upper classes.

6. The correct answer is B. The second and third paragraphs compare the British concepts and attitudes with those of the colonists. This discussion refers to no generalization of the first paragraph; hence, choice A is not appropriate. Although the word *rights* is in quotes in the second line of the second paragraph, the second and third paragraphs do not define that term. Choices D and E cannot be justified.

7. The correct answer is E. The third paragraph states that a colonist would notice and attempt to reconcile a discrepancy between principle and fact. Since slavery presents such a discrepancy, choice E would support the author's statement. Choice A would conflict with the author's beliefs since the author has presented English political authorities as unconcerned about the masses of poorer people. Choice B conflicts with the author's point in paragraph 2 that middle ranks and aristocracy enjoyed broader rights. Choice C conflicts with the author's opening statement in the third paragraph. Choice D conflicts since the author feels the British dedication to rights had "cooled considerably."

8. The correct answer is E. "The Antikythera Shipwreck" is the best title, for it is what unifies and drives the author's commentary. Choice A is not correct since the passage also focuses on the cargo of the ship and the significance of it. Choices B, C, and D are too broad to be appropriate titles. Each choice does represent one aspect of the Antikythera recovery process, but the three choices (B, C, and D) all lack diction specific enough to link them with the Antikythera. In other words, the passage does NOT discuss dangers, treasures, or underwater archaeology IN GENERAL.

9. The correct answer is A. The first paragraph states that the shared-helmet and pump system remained unchanged until the (sponge-diving) industry waned, or declined, after the invention of plastics (which produced synthetic sponges, making it unnecessary for such a great supply of natural sponges). Other choices present misinterpretations of the sentence. Choice D might be tempting. It is true that divers were no longer needed to obtain natural sponges, but certainly they were needed for other purposes.

10. The correct answer is C. The first paragraph discusses sponge divers, who would make more dangerous dives only if their work (obtaining sponges) demanded it. Choice A is inappropriate since plastic was invented after the time period this article discusses. Choice B is not suggested since the discussion involves *sponge* divers. Their black coral gives evidence that Kondos's men were accustomed to deeper dives, but cannot be used as evidence to assume the presence of rich tourists. The government became a factor only after it hired the sponge divers; thus, the diving specialty of Kondos's men was unrelated to the government.

11. The correct answer is A. If this instrument challenges the view that the Greeks were scientifically backward, the instrument itself can be assumed to be Greek. If it were a Roman instrument (choice B), it would prove that the Romans were scientifically advanced. Nothing in the passage suggests that the instrument came from another wreck. Choice D can be eliminated since an item of great interest would not lie in a museum/warehouse for fifty to seventy years. Choice E is unwarranted since no evidence suggests that the instrument was anywhere other than the Athens museum.

12. The correct answer is E. Since multiple divers sharing one helmet worked in five-minute shifts, choice E is not supported by the passage. Kondos and his crew wore watch fobs of black coral from the coast of Africa, supporting their presence there (choice A). Choice B is supported by the depth of black coral (180 feet) and Kondos's agreement to work the Antikythera salvage job. Choice C is supported by the passage's reference to using the helmet gear with "reasonable safety." Choice D is supported since a Roman ship carrying plundered Greek items indeed relieved the Greeks of those items.

13. The correct answer is B. It was use of X-ray technology that solved the computer mystery. The reader can assume that advancing X-ray technology was instrumental in understanding the device. In choice A, *extant* means "currently existing." Choice C is contraindicated since, if divers had secretly removed the computer, no one would have studied it. Choice D is a true statement, but one that does not explain why study of the computer was not completed for years. While choice E may be true, one cannot make that assumption based on information from the passage.

14. The correct answer is E. Narcosis was exacerbated (made worse) by the helmets. If the helmets were remarkably safe (choice A), divers would not have attained "reasonable" safety in using them. Choice B is incorrect since the passage states that the divers worked in five-minute shifts. Choice C might be tempting since the divers failed to realize that the "boulders" they reported were actually huge statues, but this would be caused by their reduced

mental functions (as explained in the beginning of the paragraph) rather than by impaired vision. Choice D is beyond the data of this passage. These divers wore the helmets, and the reader can assume that, even with the risks, it was preferable to wear them.

15. The correct answer is B. The author describes some scientists with very narrowed interests (scatology) and others who prefer the theoretical. He, however, was unable to "deflect" his interests from the general to the particular. Choice A is incorrect since the author's problem is in finding a career preference. Choice C can be eliminated, even though the author states that many (not most) biologists prefer the laboratory. The author suggests, tongue in cheek, that choice D might be correct when he states that since he seemed to have nothing to offer, it was inevitable that he would work for the government. This, however, is not the main point. Choice E is extraordinarily general. This passage deals with one man's career, not careers in general.

16. The correct answer is D. Fodder is food for animals, just as animals are "food" for the machines that process data. Choice A cannot be supported because the author expresses no outrage or comment over killing animals and because he expresses no feeling of progress. Because the author sees the situation presented in the question stem as regrettable, but not necessarily wrong, choice B is not correct. Choice C is not discussed at all in the passage. The question stem tells the reader where the author's interests will definitely NOT lead him; choice E should be eliminated.

17. The correct answer is A. The author's clear intention is humor. He takes aim at the established scientific community as well as at the government. His own incipient career is his vehicle. Allegory (choice D) is a symbolic narrative used to teach a moral lesson.

18. The correct answer is E. As the final sentence of the passage indicates, the government is more bureaucratic, so much so that in comparison the scientific hierarchy looks like anarchy. Choice A finds support in the third paragraph when the author comments about scientists who prefer laboratories and statistical analytical research. Choice B is supported when the author (in the final paragraph) refers to his former friend as a "full-blown scientist" shrouded in professional dignity. Choice D is well supported. The author first mentions that the scientific hierarchy demanded a high standard of obedience. The hierarchy is mentioned again in the final sentence of the passage.

19. The correct answer is C. Although this question refers to a particular statement, the reader must be guided by the larger context of this statement, appreciation of the author's use of hyperbole (obvious exaggeration), and recognition of the author's agenda. If the scientific community, already portrayed as rigid, looks like anarchy in comparison to the government hierarchy, then the government hierarchy is excessive. Choice B would be the best second choice. The author does inform, but his intention is to ridicule.

20. The correct answer is D. The author points out in the first paragraph that his days as a universal (general) scholar had come to an end and that he had to select a specialty. Choice B is not correct since the author states that his avocation (interest) now had to become his vocation (work). Choice C is incorrect because the author had a discipline— biology. Nothing stated or implied in the passage supports choice E.

21. The correct answer is E. The author discusses at length the phenomenon of biologists (whose title would lead one to believe that they studied living things) preferring to study dead animals, very dead animals, or data generated. In theory, a biologist would study living things; in practice (according to the author), this was not the case. A paradox is an apparently contradictory statement or situation that, nevertheless, is true. There are no paradoxes involving definition and restatement (choice A), literal and figurative language (choice B), surface and implied meaning (choice C). Choice D might tempt one, but the contradiction lies not in the animals, but in the scientists.

PROBLEM SOLVING

1. (B) Let x be the fifth mark:

$$\frac{75 + 92 + 68 + 95 + x}{5} = 85$$

Cross-multiply and solve for x:

$$75 + 92 + 68 + 95 + x = 85(5)$$
$$330 + x = 425$$
$$x = 95$$

2. (B) Find the least-common denominator for all the fractions, which is 100. Convert each fraction to an equivalent fraction with a denominator of 100.

$$\frac{3}{5} \times \frac{20}{20} = \frac{60}{100}$$

(A) $\dfrac{1}{2} \times \dfrac{50}{50} = \dfrac{50}{100}$

(B) $\dfrac{39}{50} \times \dfrac{2}{2} = \dfrac{78}{100}$

(C) $\dfrac{7}{25} \times \dfrac{4}{4} = \dfrac{28}{100}$

(D) $\dfrac{3}{10} \times \dfrac{10}{10} = \dfrac{30}{100}$

(E) $\dfrac{59}{100} \times \dfrac{1}{1} = \dfrac{59}{100}$

Hence, $\dfrac{39}{50} > \dfrac{3}{5}$

3. (D) The area of a square = s^2

$$25 = s^2$$
$$5 = s$$

Each side is 5 units and there are 12 exterior sides. Hence, (5)(12) = 60.

4. (C) The depth of the South China Sea is $3\frac{1}{2}$; the depth of the Red Sea is $1\frac{1}{2}$.

$$\frac{3\frac{1}{2}}{1\frac{1}{2}} = \frac{\frac{7}{2}}{\frac{3}{2}} = \frac{7}{2} \times \frac{2}{3} = \frac{7}{3} \text{ or } 7:3$$

5. (D) Each unit stands for 1000 feet. The length of the bar for the Caribbean Sea is 6.5.

$$\begin{array}{r} 1{,}000 \\ \times\ \ 6.5 \\ \hline 6{,}500.0 \end{array}$$

6. (C) Invert the divisor so that the fractions can be multiplied:

$$\frac{x^2 - 9}{x} \cdot \frac{5x}{x - 3}$$

Factor: $x^2 - 9 = (x - 3)(x + 3)$

$$\frac{(x - 3)(x + 3)}{x} \cdot \frac{5x}{x - 3}$$

Cancel out any common factors:

$$\frac{(\cancel{x - 3})(x + 3)}{\cancel{x}} \cdot \frac{5\cancel{x}}{\cancel{x - 3}}$$

Multiply: $5(x + 3)$

7. (B) Find the ratio:

$$\frac{\text{amount of decrease}}{\text{original price}} = \frac{\text{percent}}{100}$$

(A) $\dfrac{150}{1350} = \dfrac{1}{9} = 11\%$

(B) $\dfrac{150}{800} = \dfrac{3}{16} = 19\%$

(C) $\dfrac{250}{2250} = \dfrac{1}{9} = 11\%$

(D) $\dfrac{100}{1000} = \dfrac{1}{10} = 10\%$

(E) $\dfrac{500}{3000} = \dfrac{1}{6} = 16\frac{2}{3}\%$

8. (E) Let x = first consecutive integer

$x + 1$ = second consecutive integer
$x + 2$ = third consecutive integer

$$x + x + 1 + x + 2 = 33$$
$$3x + 3 = 33$$
$$3x = 30$$
$$x = 10$$
$$x + 1 = 11$$
$$x + 2 = 12$$

9. (A) $\dfrac{(a+b)}{(a-b)} = \dfrac{a+b}{1} \cdot \dfrac{1}{a-b}$

$$= \frac{5}{6} \cdot \frac{3}{10} = \frac{15}{60} = \frac{1}{4}$$

10. (C) $37\frac{1}{2}\%$ of N = 60

First, find the fractional equivalent of $37\frac{1}{2}\%$.

$$37\frac{1}{2}\% = \frac{37\frac{1}{2}}{100} = \frac{\frac{75}{2}}{\frac{100}{1}} \quad \text{Change to an improper fraction.}$$

$$\frac{\frac{75}{2}}{\frac{100}{1}} = \frac{75}{2} \div \frac{100}{1} \quad \text{Rewrite.}$$

$$\frac{75}{2} \div \frac{100}{1} = \frac{\overset{3}{\cancel{75}}}{2} \times \frac{1}{\underset{4}{\cancel{100}}} = \frac{3}{8} \quad \begin{array}{l}\text{Invert}\\\text{divisor}\\\text{and}\\\text{multiply.}\end{array}$$

Thus, we have:

$\dfrac{3}{8} \times N = 60$. Then,

$N = 60 \div \dfrac{3}{8}$ divide both sides by $\dfrac{3}{8}$.

$N = \overset{20}{\cancel{60}} \times \dfrac{8}{\underset{1}{\cancel{3}}} = 160$ Multiply.

11. (D) The perimeter of a square is 4s.

$$R = 4s$$

$$\frac{R}{4} = s$$

The area of a square is s^2.

$$A = s^2$$

$$= \left(\frac{R}{4}\right)^2$$

$$= \frac{R^2}{16}$$

12. (B)

$$\frac{\text{Total amount}}{\text{Number of people}} = \frac{D}{4}$$

Subtract:

$$\frac{\text{Total amount}}{\text{Original number of people}} = \frac{D}{5}$$

Find equivalent fractions.

$$\frac{D}{4} = \frac{5D}{20}$$

$$-\frac{D}{5} = \frac{4D}{20}$$

$$\text{Difference} = \frac{D}{20}$$

13. (C) Let x = number of miles.

Set up proportion. $\dfrac{x}{15} = \dfrac{4\frac{3}{8}}{3}$

Crossmultiply: $3x = (15)\left(4\frac{3}{8}\right)$

$$3x = (15)\left(\frac{35}{8}\right)$$

Cancel out 3's, $\left(\dfrac{1}{3}\right)3x = (15)\left(\dfrac{35}{8}\right)\left(\dfrac{1}{3}\right)$

$$x = (5)\left(\frac{35}{8}\right)$$

$$x = 21\frac{7}{8} \text{ miles}$$

14. (B) Let the original length of the rectangle be L, and the original width be W. Then, the original area is LW. The new length is .8L, and the new width is 1.1W. Thus, the new area is:

A = (.8L)(1.1W) = .88LW

The area has been decreased by 12%.

15. (C) Find two factors of 28, one of which is a perfect square.

$$\frac{1}{2}\sqrt{28} = \frac{1}{2}\sqrt{4}\sqrt{7}$$

$$= \frac{1}{2}\sqrt{4}\sqrt{7} \quad \text{reduce perfect square}$$

$$\sqrt{4} = 2$$

$$= \frac{1}{2}(2)\sqrt{7}$$

$$= 1\sqrt{7} = \sqrt{7}$$

16. (D) Circumference of original circle:

$$c = 2\pi r$$

Circumference of new circle:

$$c = 2\pi(r + x)$$

$$= 2\pi r + 2\pi x$$

Difference between new circle and original circle:

$$2\pi r + 2\pi x - 2\pi r = 2\pi x$$

DATA SUFFICIENCY

1. (E) is the correct answer. Statements (1) and (2) tell us how much gas the truck will use, but since there is no information about the price per gallon for the gas, the question cannot be answered.

2. (C) is the correct answer. Neither (1) nor (2) contains any information about Brian's salary alone. However, if we let J = Janet's salary and B = Brian's salary, then from (2) we know J = 1.2B. Plugging this information into (1), we obtain B + 1.2B = 90,000. This equation can be solved for B.

3. (E) is the correct answer. Statements (1) and (2) indicate that there will be a smaller amount of grain available for domestic use in 1996. However, there is no information to determine that prices will increase. Although it is apparent that farmers will not decrease the size of their crops unless there is an anticipated increase in price, it does not say so here.

4. (C) is the correct answer. Both statements are necessary.

According to (1)
$$(AO)^2 + (BO)^2 = (AB)^2$$
$$(OC)^2 + (BO)^2 = (BC)^2$$

According to (2), AO is less than OC. Therefore, $(AB)^2$ would be less than $(BC)^2$.

5. (C) is the correct answer. Both statements are necessary. Because $ABCD$ is a square, $\triangle OBC$ is an isosceles triangle and $OC = OB$. According to (2), $BC = 5$ (perimeter is $20 \div 4 = 5$). Therefore, $OC^2 + OB^2 = BC^2$, or $2OC^2 = 25$. Solving the equation gives you the length of OC and OB, and the coordinates can be determined.

6. (E) is the correct answer. Neither (1) nor (2) gives you a relationship between the loss years, 1992 and 1993 individually, or a relationship that can relate a specific profit year to a specific loss. All (2) tells you is that the 1994 profit is one and a half times the 1992 loss, but the 1993 loss could be greater.

7. (C) is the correct answer. (1) tells us that $y = 56$. (2) tells us that $y = 7 + 3x$. Plugging $y = 56$ into this equation will enable you to find x.

8. (A) is the correct answer. Angle AOB equals 60°, since the inscribed hexagon is regular. The circumference of the circle is $2\pi r$, or 12π. Arc AB is $\frac{1}{6}$ of the circumference, or 2π.

9. (E) is the correct answer. We never are told how many people are on the executive board. Without this information, we cannot find the average.

10. (C) is the correct answer. Both statements are needed. It does not matter what x is or what y is. You are simply asked to find $x + y$. This can be done with the information supplied. It does not have to be worked out.

11. (C) is the correct answer. Both statements are needed. From (1), angle DCE is a right angle. Therefore, angles $ACD + ECB = 90°$. Statement (2) gives you another relationship between the angles, so that it is possible to find angle ACD.

12. (E) is the correct answer. No numbers are given in the problem, so it is not possible to answer it.

13. (C) is the correct answer. Both statements are necessary. The entire trip will take 6 hours, and John will have to cover 330 miles (6 hours × 55 miles) in order to average 55 miles per hour. He has driven four hours with an average speed of 50 miles an hour, so he has driven 200 miles and has another 130 miles to drive.

14. (C) is the correct answer. (1) tells us that N is divisible by 21, which means that N is divisible by 3 and 7. (2) tells us that N is divisible by 10, which means that N is divisible by 2 and 5. Taking (1) and (2) together, we see that N is divisible by both 5 and 7, which tells us it is divisible by 35.

15. (B) is the correct answer.

$$\frac{(x^2y^3z^7)^8}{(x^4y^2z^{14})^4} = \frac{x^{16}y^{24}z^{56}}{(x^{16}y^8z^{56})} = \frac{y^{24}}{y^8} = y^{16}$$

Thus, we only need to know the value of y to find the value of the expression.

16. (C) is the correct answer. (1) contains no numbers, so it is insufficient. (2) tells us the lengths of two of the sides, but nothing about the angle between them. Taking (1) and (2) together, however, tells us that we are given the two legs of a right angle. Using one leg as the base of the triangle, and one leg as the height, we can determine the area as $\frac{1}{2}$ bh.

17. (A) is the correct answer. (1) gives you all the information you need. There would be 4×3, or 12 ways of going from New York City to Washington, D.C., to allow a stopover in Philadelphia. (2) is irrelevant.

18. (E) is the correct answer. Neither (1) nor (2) tells you how the number of members on the appropriations committee are chosen or how large the committee is. Since these committee members are excluded from sitting on the finance committee, it is impossible to determine how many remaining members are eligible for the finance committee.

19. (C) is the correct answer. Since angle C is a right angle, according to (1), it is inscribed in a semicircle; therefore, AB is a diameter. There is not enough information to determine the length of the diameter and from that the length of the radius. (2) gives us a relationship between the sides of the right triangle. If $CB = x$, then $AC = 2x$.

$$(2x)^2 + x^2 = AB^2$$
$$AB = \sqrt{4x^2 + x^2}$$

The radius $= \dfrac{\sqrt{5x^2}}{2}$ or $\dfrac{\sqrt{5(CB)^2}}{2}$

20. (C) is the correct answer. Based on (1), 66 work hours (11 × 6) are needed to complete half of the job. Five workers (2) on the second shift would have to complete the same 66 work hours, or $\dfrac{66}{5}$, which = $13\dfrac{1}{5}$ hours. Both statements are needed.

CRITICAL REASONING

1. The correct answer is C. This author assumes that a low percentage of voters under 29 years old in comparison to the entire population of voters corresponds to a lack of interest among younger voters. Choice C contradicts this assumption by showing that the entire voting population of the state has a small percentage of voters younger than 29 years old, so the 11 percent who turn out to vote actually represent a large percentage of that group of voters. Choice A provides information that might be relevant to the argument, but it is insufficient to attack the conclusion by not including information about the actual number of young voters. Choices B and D provide information that is completely irrelevant to the argument. Choice E, like A, provides information that addresses only half the argument.

2. The correct answer is D. This argument depends on a generalization, assuming that the sample of Acme customers provides a representative sample of the nationwide population. Choice D attacks this assumption by showing that Acme users, who already suspect misconduct, could be overly suspicious people who would fire their baby-sitters for minor infractions. Choice A, regardless of whether it may or may not be true, is irrelevant to the argument about misconduct by baby-sitters. Choice B repeats the speaker's assumption and therefore strengthens, not weakens, the argument. Choice C suggests why some nannies might be fired, but it says nothing about the product. Choice E would be a good selection, because it attacks the product's reliability, except that the

argument focuses on the first two weeks after use of the product, and E focuses on some time after six months.

3. The correct answer is C. The argument can be simplified by considering that it begins with a prediction about the future, followed by someone's action based on that prediction. Choice C is the selection that follows this pattern, with the school officials taking action (decreasing the staff) based on a prediction about the future (low enrollment). Choices A and B have people taking action based on past events, not a future prediction. Choice D involves an action based on a future event, but the future event is not a "prediction" in the same sense of the prediction in the problem or choice C. Choice E involves no prediction at all.

4. The correct answer is E. The conclusion that schools will have low enrollments in the future depends on an assumption that unemployment rates act as an accurate predictor of the future. Choice E is the selection that repeats this assumption. Choice A is close, but it does not say whether the studies have shown the method of prediction to be accurate or inaccurate. Choice B addresses medical schools rather than law schools, and therefore is irrelevant. Choice C explains the method of making predictions, but it does not say whether the predictions are accurate. Choice D does not address the future and does not explain why the past is relevant.

5. The correct answer is C A *savant* is a "learned person" or a "scholar." The word is used not in a pedantic (narrow and self-serving) sense, nor as a metaphor (comparing two unlike things), nor as a symbol or icon, and certainly NOT in a literal sense. Therefore, the answer is C, because the learned observation must be one of intelligence and separating what is real from the unreal.

6. The correct answer is D. In order to determine the "cultural lag," one must first ascertain "What is culture?" Obviously, if culture were thriving, there would be no need to address a lag; and education could well be failing to promote culture, because the definition is unknown; social classes would be defined if they were unnecessary in culture; and the same is true of ethnic groups. Therefore, in order to eliminate the cultural lag, we must first know what is culture.

7. The correct answer is B. The argument assumes that businesses will want to locate in this town. Choice B provides evidence of a reason that may keep them away, despite the formation of the new corporation. Choices A and C provide information about the town, but that information does not directly address the question of whether businesses will locate in the town. Choice D is irrelevant because it addresses the motivations of the investors, but not the businesses themselves. Choice E discusses a positive result of the new corporation, but does not address the actual question of attracting businesses.

8. The correct answer is E. This is a direct application of an if-then syllogism. With the information that sales of new homes increased in 1995, one can conclude that the purchase costs did not increase since the previous year. In turn, if purchase costs did not increase, one can conclude that the cost of building materials did not increase from 1994 to 1995. Choice E is the answer that repeats this conclusion. The other four answers make statements that are not supported by the argument. Choice A directly contradicts the conclusion. Choices B and C discuss the future, but the argument provides no information about predicting the future. Choice D is irrelevant, because the argument only addresses the cost of materials, not the availability.

9. The correct answer is D. Certainly, we have known for some time, especially since *Star Trek*, that science fiction writers can go only so far, the limitations of man's mind; however, with the advent of so many strides forward, mankind has begun to realize that there is no boundary with science; therefore, the conception of the scientific would be more extravagant. Science fiction and scientific conception have much in common; therefore, the differences would not contribute, nor would the need to base all in reality. Also, much of science fiction is no more plausible than the farthest reaches of space.

10. The correct answer is B. The importance of accumulating information is having it available for succeeding generations; therefore, the mind of man, mammoth libraries, communes, and even underground vaults would be finite holding places and of no value.

11. The correct answer is D. The answer is correct because the author states that only technology can contribute to the solution. The problems are indicated to be "worldwide," which precludes choice A being correct. There is a solution, but it is unrealistic, making choice B incorrect. The handling of the problems is described as "dull and uninteresting," which makes choice C incorrect, and the last line asks whether the price is too high, making choice E incorrect.

12. The correct answer is A. The police official assumes that the cramped space will somehow contribute to attacks by prisoners. Choice A provides information that supports this assumption. Choice B goes too far beyond the scope of the argument, because it is not necessary to assume that "all" criminals are dangerous. Choices C, D, and E are irrelevant to the issue of attacks on police officers.

13. The correct answer is C. The banker focuses on the immediate effect of saving money by not paying taxes immediately, while the accountant considers the long-term application of the term "save." Because they both have different ideas of what it means to "save," the conflict arises. Choices A and B may or may not be true, but they do not address the conflict between the two speakers. Choices D and E draw on outside information that might address someone's motivation for saving but does not affect this particular argument.

14. The correct answer is D. The author is critical, but in a witty manner. There is no indication of appreciation, nor intent to deceive.

15. The correct answer is D. The case being made is that scientific development will be the means of reaching the future. While some of the choices may seem to be correct, the question asks to identify the author's conclusion.

16. The correct answer is E. When dealing with the scientific, there is no dependence upon the arts. Instead, travel in space, the one-world concept, freedom from disease, and artificial production of food would be definite parts of the scientific future.

SENTENCE CORRECTIONS

1. The correct answer is C. Since we are speaking about a "gang," the level of speech is probably lower than that indicated by the other choices. This is slang.

2. The correct answer is C. The other choices are too formal.

3. The correct answer is C. While this phrase—*dreadfully unkind*—sounds somewhat formal, it fits in with the use of the word *perpetrate*.

4. The correct answer is C. *Among* instead of *between* is used when more than two people or objects are involved.

5. The correct answer is C. There is no such expression as *being that*.

6. The correct answer is C. The correct spelling is *all right*.

7. The correct answer is E. *Scratch* is the correct verb. It means *to scrape or rub lightly* (as to relieve itching).

8. The correct answer is C. Avoid the double negative.

9. The correct answer is D. Remember that there is no such word as *irregardless*.

10. The correct answer is E. The meaning here is that *all (of them)* were *ready*.

11. The correct answer is C. *Laying* means the action of putting an object down.

12. The correct answer is E. *Fewer* is used when it is a question of a number of separate objects; *less* is used to indicate a relative portion or degree, as in *less water in the glass*. C is incorrect because the sentence has no subject.

13. The correct answer is D. The original contains a dangling participle. It sounds as though the *song* was doing the *listening*.

14. The correct answer is B. The original sentence makes it sound as though the *condition* had *lost all her money*.

15. The correct answer is C. Combining the two related sentences into one makes for a better expression. D is a run-on sentence.

16. The correct answer is D. The gerund phrase—*being challenged*—is the subject.

17. The correct answer is E. This question tests subject-verb agreement and pronoun case. *Everyone* is singular and must take a singular subject—thus, C and D are incorrect. B is incorrect because *accept* is misused. The correct word is *except*, which is a preposition rather than a verb. A is incorrect because *she* is the nominative case. *Her* is the correct pronoun since it is the object of the preposition *except*. Thus, E is correct.

18. The correct answer is C. With the construction "neither . . . nor," the number of the word or phrase closest to the verb determines the number of the verb. Since *Robin* is singular, the verb must be *wants*. A, B, and E are incorrect since *or* is used instead of *nor*.

19. The correct answer is A. Since *if I were he* is contrary to fact, the subjunctive mood is correct. Consequently, B and C are incorrect choices. *Were* takes a predicate rather than an object, so *him* is the wrong case, which eliminates D and E.

20. The correct answer is E. This question tests proper subordination of a dependent clause. The dependent clause should be introduced by a subordinate conjunction, which should narrow the choices to D, C, and E. *Although* changes the meaning of the clause (D). Since the relationship between the dependent and independent clauses is one of cause and effect, *since* is a better choice than *when*.

21. The correct answer is D. The subject is *outlook* and must take a singular verb. The only choice that qualifies is D. Only *and* can join two singular subjects and make them plural.

22. The correct answer is C. This is a relatively difficult question. *Data* is a plural noun, and must take a plural verb. The only two choices that qualify are B and C. C is a better choice since it is less wordy and avoids the nominalization *proof* and the unnecessary prepositional phrase.

PROBLEM SOLVING

1. (C) Let the original rectangle be expressed as:

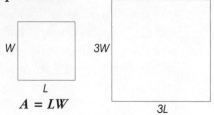

$$A = LW$$

$$A = (3L)(3W)$$
$$A = 9LW$$

$$\text{ratio} = \frac{\text{original rectangle}}{\text{enlarged rectangle}} = \frac{1LW}{9LW}$$
$$= \frac{1}{9} = 1:9$$

2. (E) The sum of the interior angles of a regular polygon:

$$= 180(N-2) \ (N = \text{number of sides})$$
$$= (180)(10-2)$$
$$= (180)(8)$$
$$= 1440$$

3. (B) The product of two fractions between 0 and 1 is always less than both of the original fractions.

Example: $\frac{1}{2}$ and $\frac{3}{4}$

$$\frac{1}{2} \times \frac{3}{4} = \frac{3}{8}$$

$$\frac{1}{2} = .50$$

$$\frac{3}{4} = .75$$

$$\frac{3}{8} = .37\frac{1}{2}$$

Hence, only B can be true.

4. (D) The largest share is $\frac{5}{12}$ of the total.

$$\frac{5}{\cancel{12}}_{1} (\cancel{120,000})^{10,000} = 50,000$$

5. (E) Divide 120 by $2\frac{2}{3} = \dfrac{120}{2\frac{2}{3}} = \dfrac{120}{\frac{8}{3}}$

$$= 120 \times \frac{3}{8} = 45 \text{ dresses.}$$

6. (A) Solve the inequality:

$$3x - 4 > 8$$
$$3x > 8 + 4$$
$$3x > 12$$
$$x > 4$$

7. (A) Combine $\dfrac{x+y}{3}$ and $\dfrac{x-y}{4}$ into a single fraction. The least-common denominator is 12. Change each fraction into an equivalent fraction.

$$\frac{x+y}{3} = \frac{4x+4y}{12}$$

$$\frac{x-y}{4} = \frac{3x-3y}{12}$$

Combine like terms in the numerator:

$$\frac{4x+4y+3x-3y}{12} = \frac{7x+y}{12}$$

8. (C) The easiest way to do the problem is to assume that the original price of the item was some nice number like $100. Then, the price increases to $300, which is an increase of $200.

Thus, $\dfrac{\text{increase}}{\text{new price}} = \dfrac{200}{300} = \dfrac{2}{3} = 66\dfrac{2}{3}\%$

9. (A) Let t = number of hours:

$$\text{rate} \cdot \text{time} = \text{distance}$$
$$\text{(mph)(hours)}$$
$$60(t) + 40t = 300$$
$$60t + 40t = 300$$
Divide by 100: $100t = 300$
$$t = 3 \text{ hours}$$

10. (C) Use the formula

income = (amount of money invested)(interest rate)

$$30 = (1,000)(x)$$

$$\frac{30}{1,000} = x$$

$$\frac{3}{100} = x$$

$$3\% = x$$

11. (D) Let

$$x = \text{first number}$$
$$x + 1 = \text{second consecutive number}$$
$$x + x + 1 = 39$$
$$2x + 1 = 39$$
$$2x = 38$$

Divide by 2: $x = 19$ smaller

$$x + 1 = 20 \text{ second number}$$

12. (D) Let d = number of dimes

Let q = number of quarters

total value in cents for dimes = $10d$
total value in cents for quarters = $25q$

$$10d + 25q = 255 \text{ (cents)}$$
$$10q + 25d = 270 \text{ (cents)}$$

Multiply (A) by 2: $2(10d + 25q = 255)$ $20d + 50q = 510$

Multiply (B) by 5: $5(10q + 25d = 270)$ $\underline{125d + 50q = 1350}$

Subtract (B) from (A): $-105d \qquad\quad = -840$

Divide by -105: $\dfrac{-105d}{-105} = \dfrac{-840}{-105}$

Substitute value in (A): $d \quad = \quad 8$

$$10(8) + 25q = 255$$
$$80 + 25q = 255$$
$$25q = 175$$
$$q = 7$$

Check in (B):

$$10(7) + 25(8) = 270$$
$$70 + 200 = 270$$
$$270 = 270$$

13. (A) Let

x = number of hours to complete the job (father)

$\dfrac{1}{x}$ = fraction of job completed in 1 hour (father)

Let

$2x$ = number of hours to complete the job (son)

$\dfrac{1}{2x}$ = fraction of job completed in 1 hour (son)

(fraction of job completed in 1 hour) · (number of hours worked) = part of job done

$\dfrac{1}{x}(6) + \dfrac{1}{2x}(6) = 1$ job (completed)

$$\dfrac{6}{x} + \dfrac{6}{2x} = 1$$

Multiply by $2x$: $2x\left(\dfrac{6}{x} + \dfrac{6}{2x} = 1\right)$

$$\dfrac{12x}{x} + \dfrac{12x}{2x} = 2x$$

Reduce: $12 + 6 = 2x$

$$18 = 2x$$
$$2x = 18$$

Divide by 2:

$x = 9$ (hours for father to complete the job alone)

$2x = 18$ (hours for son to complete the job alone)

14. (B) Let f = number of foxes six years ago

(A) $d = f + 80$ = number of deer six years ago

(B) $2d + f + 20 = 240$ (present time)

Substitute (A) for d in (B):
$$d = f + 80$$

$$2(f + 80) + f + 20 = 240$$
$$2f + 160 + f + 20 = 240$$
$$3f + 180 = 240$$
$$3f = 60$$

Divide by 3: $f = 20$ foxes six years ago

15. (A) If $x < y$ and $y < z$, then $x < z$. If one number is less than the second number and the second number is less than the third number, then the first number is less than the third number.

16. (A) $5 < x \le 6$ implies all integers bigger than 5 and less than or equal to 6.

Unit 1

The sentence corrections do not test spelling or capitalization. They do test grammar and rhetoric (usage, clarity, conciseness, and logic of expression). Although the exam will not test punctuation per se, occasionally issues of punctuation will arise in connection with a grammatical problem (run-on sentences, for example).

It is important to read the underlined portion of the sentences carefully. You will be given five choices to substitute for the underlined portion. The first choice—A—will be the same as the underlined part of the sentence. Choices B, C, D, and E will offer alternative answers. As always in a multiple-choice test, pick the best answer. Be aware that the underlined portions of the sentences can contain more than one error. Select the answer that corrects *all* the problems in the underlined part of the sentence (if there *are* any problems).

This review will start with common grammatical and rhetorical problems found on the test: dangling modifiers, subordination, faulty parallelism, arbitrary tense shifts, fragments, run-on sentences, noun-pronoun agreement, subject-verb agreement, illogical comparisons, wordiness, and idiomatic usage. Each of these problems will be illustrated by a sample question similar to those you will encounter on the exam. That section is followed by a basic grammar overview including the parts of speech, which you may or may not need to consult, depending on how successfully you deal with the sample questions. Use the overview as a reference if you don't understand the explanations of the correct answers for the sample questions.

Dangling Modifiers

To make sure his research was accurate, <u>all secondary sources were checked twice.</u>

(A) all secondary sources were checked twice.

(B) most of the secondary sources were checked thoroughly.

(C) Don checked all his sources, both primary and secondary.

(D) Don checked all his secondary sources twice.

(E) all secondary sources were checked twice by Don.

The correct answer is D. Choices A, B, and E contain no word that the infinitive phrase "to make sure" can effectively modify. The answer has to be either C or D, and choice C alters the meaning of the sentence.

Clauses and Subordinates

Clauses are groups of words that contain a subject and predicate (verb part of the sentence). There are two main kinds of clauses. One kind is the independent clause, which makes sense when it stands alone. Independent clauses are joined by coordinating conjunctions.

I know how to clean silver, but I never learned how to clean copper.

(The two independent clauses could stand alone as complete sentences.)

I know how to clean silver. I never learned how to clean copper.

The other kind of clause is a dependent or subordinate clause. Although this type of clause has a subject and a predicate, it cannot stand alone.

When I learn to clean copper, I will keep my pots sparkling.

"When I learn to clean copper," by itself, does not make sense. Dependent clauses are always used as a single part of speech in a sentence. They function as nouns or adjectives or adverbs. When they function as nouns, they are called noun clauses. When they function as adjectives, they are called adjective clauses. When they are adverbs, they are called adverbial clauses. Since a dependent or subordinate clause cannot stand alone, it must be joined with an independent clause to make a sentence. A subordinate conjunction does this job. A relative pronoun (*who, that, which, what, whose,* and *whom*) may act as the subordinate conjunction. For adjective and adverbial clauses, a relative adverb (*while, when*) may act as the subordinating conjunction.

I noticed that he was very pale.

"That he was very pale" is a noun clause—the object of the verb "noticed." That is the subordinating conjunction.

"Who was guilty" is not known.

"Who was guilty" is a noun clause—subject of the verb "is." "Who" is the subordinating conjunction.

She lost the belt, which was a present.

"Which was a present" is an adjective clause—describing belt.

"Which" is the subordinating conjunction.

She lost the belt when she dropped her bag.

"When she dropped the bag" is an adverbial clause answering the question "when" about the predicate. "When" is the subordinating conjunction.

Clauses should refer clearly and logically to the part of the sentence they modify.

We bought the dress at Bloomingdale's that was expensive.

(Misplaced adjective clause. Did the writer mean Bloomingdale's was expensive?)

Correct: We bought a dress that was expensive at Bloomingdale's

When finally discovered, not a sound was heard.

(Misplaced adverbial clause. Who or what is discovered?)

Correct: When finally discovered, the boys didn't make a sound.

Sample Questions (Illogical Subordination)

The author won the Pulitzer Prize <u>on account his book was timely and artistic.</u>

(A) on account his book was timely and artistic.

(B) being that his book was timely and artistic.

(C) his book was timely and artistic.

(D) when his book was timely and artistic.

(E) because his book was timely and artistic.

The correct answer is E. The underlined portion of the sentence is a subordinate clause—that is, a clause that cannot stand by itself as a complete thought, but must be joined to the rest of the sentence with a subordinate conjunction. The only possibilities are D and E. D is incorrect because "when" indicates time, not cause and effect. "Being that" is improper English usage. "On account" is incorrect; it should read "on account of," which would be much wordier than choice E.

Faulty Parallelism

Elements within a sentence of equal importance should have parallel structure or similar form.

> To sing, dancing, and to laugh make life happy. (Incorrect)

> To sing, to dance, and to laugh make life happy. (Correct)

> He wants health, wealth, and to be happy. (Incorrect)

> He wants health, wealth, and happiness. (Correct)

Sample Questions

Sue anticipates <u>hearing from her friends and to have</u> the opportunity to see them again at her home.

(A) hearing from her friends and to have

(B) hearing from her friends and having

(C) to hear from her friends and having

(D) not only to hear from her friends but also having

(E) not only hearing from her friends but to have

The correct answer is B. "Hearing" and "having" are both gerunds. The other choices use a gerund phrase with an infinitive phrase, which is not parallel. Two infinitives ("to hear" and "to have" would

be correct also, but they are not among the choices listed.)

Watch Arbitrary Tense Shifts

Make sure verb tenses indicate proper cause and effect. When two events take place simultaneously, their tenses should match.

> He complained while his father listens. (Incorrect)

> He complained while his father listened. (Correct)

When I saw Joanne at the class reunion, <u>I realized that I forgot how much I'd loved her.</u>

(A) I realized that I forgot how much I'd loved her.

(B) I realized that I had forgotten how much I'd loved her.

(C) I had realized that I forgot how much I'd loved her.

(D) I had realized that I had forgotten how much I loved her.

(E) I realized that I had forgot how much I loved her.

The correct answer is B. "Realized" and "saw" happened at the same time; they should be in the same tense. That eliminates C and D. "Forgot" and "I'd loved" describe a similar time. The past participle of "forget" is "forgotten," which eliminates E. Choice A is incorrect because "forgot" and "loved" do not show the proper relationship in time. Thus, B is correct.

Sentences

A sentence is a group of words that expresses a complete thought. An independent clause can stand by itself and may or may not be a complete sentence.

Beth and Terry rode the Ferris wheel; they enjoyed the ride. (Two independent clauses connected by a semicolon.)

Beth and Terry rode the Ferris wheel. They enjoyed the ride. (Two independent clauses—each is a sentence.)

1. A simple sentence has one independent clause. A dependent clause is never a sentence by itself. Here are some simple sentences:

   John and Fred played.

   John laughed and sang.

   John and Fred ate hot dogs and drank beer.

   The following is NOT an independent clause:

   Fred said. (Incorrect—"said" is a transitive verb. It needs a direct object.)

   Fred said hello. (Correct)

2. A compound sentence has at least two independent clauses.

   Darryl bought the meat, and Laverne bought the potatoes.

3. A complex sentence has one independent clause and at least one dependent clause.

   Because she left early, she missed the end.

   ("Because she left early" is the dependent clause. "She missed the end" is an independent clause.)

4. A compound-complex sentence has two independent clauses and one or more dependent clauses.

   You prefer math, and I prefer music, although I am the math major.

("You prefer math, and I prefer music" are the independent clauses. The dependent clause is "although I am a math major.")

Common Sentence Errors

Sentence Fragments

These are parts of sentences that are incorrectly written with capitals and punctuation of a sentence.

Around the corner.

Because she left early.

Going to the movies.

A terrible tragedy.

Remember that sentences must have at least a subject and a verb. A dependent clause cannot stand alone as a sentence (see Clauses and Subordinates).

Sample Question

The enrollment for Theater 101 is noticeably down this semester. All suggesting that the course is either too hard or that the instructor is incompetent.

(A) All suggesting that

(B) Which suggests that

(C) This statistic suggests that

(D) Suggesting that

(E) Suggesting the fact that

The correct answer is C. A finite verb is missing in all the other answers. The only choice that is an independent clause is choice C. A, B, D and E would all be dependent clauses.

Run-on Sentences

These are sentences that are linked incorrectly.

The rain was heavy, lightning was crackling he could not row the boat. (Incorrect)

Because the rain was heavy and lightning was crackling, he could not row the boat. (Correct)

The rain was heavy. Lightning was crackling. He could not row the boat. (Correct)

Sample Question

Many reasons have been suggested for the decline in literacy, the main reason is the way students are taught history.

(A) literacy, the main

(B) literacy, the

(C) literacy the main

(D) literacy. The main

(E) literacy The main

Choice D is correct. The clause preceding "the main reason" is an independent clause and cannot be connected to another independent clause with a comma, which eliminates choices A and B. Two independent clauses cannot be joined without punctuation or subordination, so C and E are also incorrect.

Noun-Pronoun Agreement

See the sections on pronouns and nouns. Some nouns are always singular, such as "everyone," "someone," "somebody," "each," "anyone," "anybody," "everybody," and "one." They must always take a singular pronoun.

A person may pass if they study. (Incorrect)

A person may pass if he studies. (Correct)

Sample Question

The libertarian maintains that everyone is an individual in their own right.

(A) in their own right.

(B) in their own way.

(C) and they are responsible for their actions.

(D) in what they do.

(E) in his own right.

The correct answer is E. "Everyone" is a singular noun, and the pronoun referring to it must agree. Only E has a singular pronoun.

Review the section on case under Pronouns. If a pronoun is the object of a preposition, it must be in the objective case.

Sample Question

Everyone failed the exam except Bob and her.

(A) except Bob and her.

(B) excepting Bob and her.

(C) outside of Bob and she.

(D) besides Bob and she.

(E) except Bob and she.

The correct answer is A. "Except" is a preposition and must take an object. "Her" is the objective case of "she," so only A and B are possibilities. The correct form of the preposition is "except." Thus, answer A is correct.

If a pronoun is the subject of a clause, it must be in the nominative case.

Sample Question

The guards were ordered to shoot <u>whomever tried to escape.</u>

(A) whomever tried to escape.

(B) whoever tried to escape.

(C) whomever escaped.

(D) whomever might escape.

(E) whoever might try to escape.

The correct answer is B. "Whoever" is the subject of the clause, so the answer must be in the nominative case. Only B and E are possible choices, and E changes verb tense without reason.

Watch Subject/Verb Agreement

Verbs must agree in number and person with their subjects. Singular verbs take singular subjects; plural verbs match plural subjects.

The boy walks the dog.

The boys walk the dog.

See the section on Verbs for more detailed information regarding subject-verb agreement. Be aware of collective nouns. Collective nouns are singular but denote a group. Examples are "association," "group," "society," "union," and "army." When the collective noun refers to a group as a whole, it takes a singular verb; when it refers to the individuals that comprise the group, it takes a plural verb.

The family is the most precious unit in American society.

("The family as a unit" is the subject; the verb is singular.)

After years of struggle, the family begins to go their separate ways.

(Each member is leaving separately.)

Sample Question

The group <u>insists that they have a right</u> to police the airwaves.

(A) insists that they have a right

(B) insist that they have a right

(C) insists that it has a right

(D) insist that is has a right

(E) insist that it has rights itself

The answer is C. "Group" here is used as a collective noun; it takes a singular verb, and any pronoun reference must be singular. Only C fits the criteria.

Comparisons

Beware of illogical comparisons. Only like things should be compared.

Sample Question

Your temper is <u>as bad as Bob.</u>

(A) as bad as Bob.

(B) worse than Bob.

(C) as bad as Bob when you get mad.

(D) as bad as Bob when he gets mad.

(E) as bad as Bob's.

The correct answer is E. The two items being compared are the "tempers" of the two individuals. Only E refers to Bob's temper. The other choices all refer to Bob.

Watch These DON'TS

DON'T use *being that*; use *since* or *because*.

DON'T use *could of, should of, would of*; use *could have, should have, would have*.

DON'T use the preposition *of* in the following; off *of* the table, inside *of* the house.

DON'T use *this here* or *that there*; use just *this* or *that*.

DON'T misuse *then* as a coordinating conjunction; use *than* instead.

He is better *than* he used to be. (Correct)

He is better *then* he used to be. (Incorrect)

Use of the Rhetorical

Good writing is clear and economical.

1. Avoid Ambiguous Pronoun References

   Tom killed Jerry. I feel sorry for him. (Who is "him"? Tom? Jerry?)

   Burt is a nice man. I don't know why they insulted him. (Who does "they" refer to?)

2. Avoid Clichés

   Betty is sharp as a tack.

   The math exam was easy as pie.

   It will be a cold day in August before I eat dinner with Louisa again.

3. Avoid Redundancy

   Harry is a man who loves to gamble. (Redundant—we know that Harry is a man.)

   Harry loves to gamble. (Correct)

   Claire is a strange one. (Redundant—"one" is not necessary)

   Claire is strange. (Correct)

   This July has been particularly hot in terms of weather. (Redundant—"in terms of weather" is not necessary.)

   This July has been particularly hot. (Correct)

4. Avoid Wordiness

   The phrases on the left are wordy. Use the word or phrase on the right.

Wordy	*Preferable*
the reason why is that	because
the question as to whether	whether
in a hasty manner	hastily
be aware of the fact that	know
due to the fact that	because
in light of the fact that	since
regardless of the fact that	although
for the purpose of	to

   Sample Question

   I am crying due to the fact that my wife left me.

   (A) due to the fact that my wife left me.

   (B) when my wife left me.

   (C) in light of the fact that my wife left me.

   (D) my wife left me.

   (E) because my wife left me.

   E is correct. This is a simple cause-effect statement. A and C are needlessly wordy. D is a run-on sentence; two independent clauses need to be connected by punctuation or subordination. B distorts the meaning—"when" does not denote cause and effect.

5. Avoid Vague Words or Phrases

   It is always preferable to use specific, concrete language rather than vague words and phrases.

   The reality of the situation necessitated action. (Vague)

   Bill shot the burglar before the burglar could shoot him. (Specific)

6. Be Articulate. Use the Appropriate Word or Phrase

The following are words or phrases that are commonly misused.

1. **Accept** — to receive or agree to (verb)
   I ACCEPT your offer.

   Except — preposition that means to leave out
   They all left EXCEPT Dave.

2. **Adapt** — to change (verb)
   We must ADAPT.

3. **Affect** — to influence (verb)
   Their attitudes may well AFFECT mine.

   Effect — result (noun)
   What is the EFFECT of their attitudes?

4. **Allusion** — a reference to something (noun)
   The teacher made an ALLUSION to Milton.

   Illusion — a false idea (noun)
   He had the ILLUSION that he was king.

5. **Among** — use with more than two items (preposition)
   They pushed AMONG the group of soldiers.

   Between — use with two items (preposition)
   They pushed BETWEEN both soldiers.

6. **Amount** — cannot be counted (noun)
   Sue has a large AMOUNT of pride.

   Number — can be counted (noun)
   Sue bought a NUMBER of apples.

7. **Apt** — capable (adjective)
   She is an APT student.

   Likely — probably (adjective)
   We are LIKELY to receive the prize.

8. **Beside** — at the side of (prepositional)
   He sat BESIDE me.

   Besides — in addition to (preposition)
   There were others there BESIDES Joe.

9. **Bring** — toward the speaker (verb)
   BRING that to me.

   Take — away from the speaker (verb)
   TAKE that to him.

10. **Can** — to be able to (verb)
    I CAN ride a bike.

    May — permission (verb)
    MAY I ride my bike?

11. **Famous** — well-known (adjective)
    He is a FAMOUS movie star.

    Infamous — well-known but not for anything good (adjective)
    He is the INFAMOUS criminal.

12. **Fewer** — can be counted (adjective)
    I have FEWER pennies than John.

    Less — cannot be counted (adjective)
    I have LESS pride than John.

13. **Imply** — the speaker or writer is making a hint or suggestion (verb)
    He IMPLIED in his book that dogs were inferior to cats.

    Infer — to draw a conclusion from the speaker or writer (verb)
    The audience INFERRED that he was a dog-hater.

14. **In** — something is already there (preposition)
    He is IN the kitchen.

    Into — something is going there (preposition)
    He is on his way INTO the kitchen.

15. **Irritate** — to annoy (verb)
    His whining IRRITATED me.

    Aggravate — to make worse (verb)
    The soap AGGRAVATED his rash.

16. Teach   to provide knowledge (verb)

           She TAUGHT him how to swim.

    Learn   to acquire knowledge (verb)

           He LEARNED how to swim from her.

17. Uninter-
    ested   bored (adjective)

           She is UNINTERESTED in everything.

    Disinter-
    ested   impartial (adjective)

           He wanted a DISINTERESTED jury at his trial.

Sample Question

Realizing how difficult it is to adopt to the new ways, I chose among two miserable alternatives.

(A) adopt to the new ways, I chose among

(B) adopt to the new ways, I chose between

(C) adapt to the new ways, I chose among

(D) adapt to the new ways, I chose between

(E) adopt to the new ways, I selected

This question tests word choice. The correct word here is "adapt" as in "change" rather than "adopt," which means incorporate. "Among" is used with more than two items; "between" is used with two items. Choice D represents the correct answer.

The following chapter presents a brief overview and reference section of basic grammar principles that you should also understand. Although these principles may not be directly tested on the exam, it is important to understand these basics in order to more fully understand the Sentence Correction section of the GMAT. In addition, there are numerous questions to provide additional practice. Answer the questions and carefully check your answers. This is the best way to prepare for the exam.

SENTENCE CORRECTION PRACTICE QUESTIONS

Directions: In each of the following sentences, some part of the sentence or the entire sentence is underlined. Beneath each sentence you will find five ways of phrasing the underlined part. The first of these repeats the original; the other four are different. If you think the original is better than any of the alternatives, choose answer A; otherwise, choose one of the others. Select the best version and blacken the corresponding space on your answer sheet.

This is a test of correctness and effectiveness of expression. In choosing answers, follow the requirements of standard written English; that is, pay attention to grammar, choice of words, and sentence construction. Choose the answer that expresses most effectively what is presented in the original sentence; this answer should be clear and exact, without awkwardness, ambiguity, or redundancy.

1. The train rolled into the station pulled by a diesel engine.

   (A) The train rolled into the station pulled by a diesel engine.
   (B) The train, pulled by a diesel engine, rolled into the station.
   (C) The train rolled into the station by a diesel engine.
   (D) Pulled by a diesel engine into the station rolled the train.
   (E) The train rolled into the station which was pulled by a diesel engine.

Analysis

   (B) The misplaced modifier is corrected by this form. Obviously the station was not pulled by an engine.

2. My mother was delighted to learn of me doing so well at the piano.

   (A) me doing so well
   (B) my doing so well
   (C) my well doing
   (D) my doing so good
   (E) myself doing so well

Analysis

   (B) The possessive pronoun used with the gerund.

3. She was moved to advice him about his program for the future.

   (A) advice
   (B) council
   (C) revise
   (D) admonish
   (E) advise

60

Analysis

> (E) This is the verb form meaning "to suggest." The noun is <u>advice</u>.

4. Many women feel that men have been domineering, tyrannical, and <u>they humiliate their wives</u>.

    (A) they humiliate their wives.
    (B) humiliating toward there wives.
    (C) humiliating toward their wives.
    (D) humility toward their wives.
    (E) humiliate their wives.

Analysis

> (C) To retain the parallelism—domineering, tyrannical, and humiliating.

5. It is discouraging to read about so much crime, <u>poverty, and degradation. And war too</u>.

    (A) poverty, and degradation. And war too.
    (B) And also warfare.
    (C) And war also.
    (D) poverty, degradation, and war.
    (E) and poverty and degradation and war.

Analysis

> (D) Parallel structure. In addition, *and war too* is not a sentence.

6. I told you that a baseball team <u>is comprised of</u> nine players.

    (A) is comprised of
    (B) comprises
    (C) was comprised of
    (D) consists
    (E) is consisted of

Analysis

> (B) <u>Comprises</u> means <u>is made up of</u>.

7. Their manner of speech is forthright, candid, and <u>right on</u>.

    (A) right on
    (B) with it
    (C) sharp
    (D) nitty-gritty
    (E) precise

Analysis

> (E) The original, A, and choices B through D all indicate slang expressions. These are unsuitable in this sentence.

8. <u>He awakened early in the morning, and then he showered, and then he left</u>.

    (A) He awakened early in the morning, and then he showered, and then he left.
    (B) He awakened early in the morning. And then he showered, and then he left.
    (C) He awakened early in the morning, Then he showered and left.
    (D) He awakened early in the morning after showering, and then he left.
    (E) He awakened early in the morning, showered, and left.

Analysis

    (E)   This correction avoids the awkward repetition of the original.

9. His shyness made it impossible for him to step forward <u>to except</u> the prize.

    (A)   to except
    (B)   to accept
    (C)   accepting
    (D)   expecting
    (E)   to expect

Analysis

    (B)   *Accept* means "to receive"; *except* means "to omit."

10. <u>Feeling it was shameful, their action was deplored by all</u>.

    (A)   Feeling it was shameful, their action was deplored by all.
    (B)   Their action was deplored shamefully by all.
    (C)   Their action, feeling it was shameful, they all deplored it.
    (D)   Feeling their action was shameful, all deplored it.
    (E)   Their action, feeling it was shameful, was deplored.

Analysis

    (D)   This corrects the dangling participle.

Sentence Correction Practice

1. There is a possibility <u>of him being barred</u> from practice.

    (A)   of him being barred
    (B)   of he being barred
    (C)   of his barring
    (D)   that his being barred
    (E)   of his being barred

2. When a poor woman came to them, <u>she was always given help</u>.

    (A)   she was always given help.
    (B)   she always helped.
    (C)   she always gave.
    (D)   they were always given help.
    (E)   they were always helped.

3. <u>In accordance to</u> the rules, smoking is prohibited.

    (A)   In accordance to
    (B)   According with
    (C)   In accordance with
    (D)   In accord to
    (E)   Accordingly

4. No one, <u>including Steve and me, have a greater right than he</u> to be president.

    (A)   including Steve and me, have a greater right than he
    (B)   including Steve and I, have a greater right than he
    (C)   including Steve and me, has a greater right than he
    (D)   including Steve and me, has a greater right than him
    (E)   including Steve and I, has a greater right than him

5. <u>However much we tried the motor</u> would not start.

    (A)   However much we tried the motor
    (B)   However much we tried; the motor
    (C)   However much we tried, The motor
    (D)   However much we tried, the motor
    (E)   However much we tried and the motor

6. Discretion involves the idea of choice, the exercise of will, and judging fairly.

   (A) the idea of choice, the exercise of will, and judging fairly.
   (B) the idea of choice, the exercise of will, and the practice of fair judgment.
   (C) the idea of choice; the exercise of will; and judging fairly.
   (D) choice ideas, willing exercise, and fair judgment.
   (E) the idea of choice, the exercise of will and judging fairly.

7. The climax of the play occurs when the villain admitted his crime.

   (A) occurs when the villain admitted
   (B) is when the villain admitted
   (C) occurred when the villain admits
   (D) occurs—when the villain admits •
   (E) occurs when the villain admits

8. The storm having stopped, the ship regained its balance.

   (A) The storm having stopped, the ship
   (B) Having stopped, the ship
   (C) The storm having stopped, it
   (D) The storm having stopped; the ship
   (E) It having stopped, it

9. David Edelson, the famous surgeon is also a practicing attorney.

   (A) David Edelson, the famous surgeon
   (B) David Edelson, the famous surgeon,
   (C) David Edelson the famous surgeon
   (D) David Edelson the famous surgeon,
   (E) David Edelson is the famous surgeon

10. Each of the students have passed the GMAT.

    (A) Each of the students have
    (B) Each of the students has
    (C) Each, of the students, has
    (D) Each, of the students, have
    (E) Each of the passing students have

11. Legal terminology is confusing, being unable to memorize the necessary definitions.

    (A) Legal terminology is confusing, being unable
    (B) Legal terminology confuses me, I am unable
    (C) Legal terminology is confusing because I am unable
    (D) Being that legal terminology is confusing, I am unable
    (E) Legal terminology is confusing and being unable

12. The student was bright however he failed the test.

    (A) bright however he
    (B) bright, however he
    (C) bright however; he
    (D) bright; however, he
    (E) bright. however, he

13. There was such a crowd that she could not find her parents.

    (A) There was such a crowd that she could not find her parents. •
    (B) There was such a crowd; that she could not find her parents.
    (C) There was such a crowd. That she could not find her parents.
    (D) There was such a crowd and that she could not find her parents.
    (E) There was such a crowd because she could not find her parents.

14. A serf's economic position <u>was comparable to a slave</u>.

    (A)   was comparable to a slave.
    (B)   was a slave.
    (C)   was comparable with a slave.
    (D)   was as comparable to a slave.
    (E)   was comparable to a slave's.

15. The boy felt <u>he should of come</u>.

    (A)   he should of come.
    (B)   , he should of come.
    (C)   , he should have come.
    (D)   he should have come.
    (E)   he should have came.

16. No sooner had the class begun <u>than Will started laughing</u>.

    (A)   than Will started laughing.
    (B)   when Will started laughing.
    (C)   and Will started laughing.
    (D)   then Will started laughing.
    (E)   but Will started laughing.

17. The term expresses a formula containing three elements, consisting <u>of amount charged "a percentage,"</u> the amount loaned, and the time.

    (A)   of amount charged "a percentage,"
    (B)   with amount charged (a percentage),
    (C)   of the amount charged (a percentage),
    (D)   of charging an amount of percentage,
    (E)   a percentage,

18. The court system <u>should resolve cases more rapidly and with greater economy</u>.

    (A)   should resolve cases more rapidly and with greater economy.
    (B)   should resolve cases more rapidly and more economically.
    (C)   should resolve rapid and economic cases.
    (D)   should resolve cases, more rapidly and with greater economy.
    (E)   should resolve cases with speed and economically.

19. <u>I had meant during the afternoon to call on him</u>.

    (A)   I had meant during the afternoon to call on him.
    (B)   I had meant, during the afternoon, to call on him.
    (C)   During the afternoon, I had meant to call on him.
    (D)   I had meant to call him.
    (E)   I had meant to call on him during the afternoon.

20. <u>All the raincoats are waterproof</u>.

    (A)   All the raincoats are waterproof.
    (B)   All the foregoing types of raincoats have the property of being waterproof.
    (C)   All these raincoats have waterproof properties.
    (D)   The properties of waterproof qualities are found in all these categories of raincoats.
    (E)   Water-repellent raincoats are waterproof.

21. They gave presents to the top graduating seniors, <u>Dave and I.</u>

    (A) , Dave and I.
    (B) , Dave and myself.
    (C) , me and Dave.
    (D) , Dave and me.
    (E) among which were Dave and me.

22. Although she has two <u>Ph.D.'s, her I's are illegible and her miss's look like mess's.</u>

    (A) Ph.D.'s, her I's are illegible and her miss's look like mess's.
    (B) Ph.D.'s, her I's are illegible and her miss s look like mess s.
    (C) Ph.D.es, her I'es are illegible and her misses look like messes.
    (D) Ph.D.s, her Is are illegible and her miss's look like mess's.
    (E) Ph.D.s, her Is are illegible and her miss s look like mess s.

23. She <u>had laid the book aside because she wanted to lie</u> in the sun.

    (A) had laid the book aside because she wanted to lie
    (B) had laid the book aside because she wanted to lay
    (C) had lain the book aside because she wanted to lie
    (D) had lain the book aside because she wanted to lay
    (E) had lied the book aside because she wanted to laid

24. <u>There were three guests, Mark, an actor, Emily, a dancer, and Dave, a musician.</u>

    (A) There were three guests, Mark, an actor, Emily, a dancer, and Dave, a musician.
    (B) There were three guests: Mark, an actor; Emily, a dancer; and Dave, a musician.
    (C) There were three guests: Mark an actor, Emily a dancer, and Dave a musician.
    (D) There were three other guests: Mark, an actor, Emily, a dancer, and Dave, a musician.
    (E) There were three guests: Mark; an actor, Emily; a dancer, and Dave; a musician.

25. I told them I had been there only <u>once or twice before.</u>

    (A) I told them I had been there only once or twice before.
    (B) I am there before once.
    (C) I was once or twice there I told them.
    (D) Once or twice I told them I was there.
    (E) I was there I told them once or twice before.

26. <u>The bridge towered above them in their car.</u>

    (A) The bridge towered above them in their car.
    (B) They could see the bridge towering above them in their car.
    (C) In their car the bridge towered above them.
    (D) From their car, they could see the bridge towering above them.
    (E) Towering above them in their car was the bridge.

27. <u>Being the girl of my dreams, I am sure she will marry me.</u>

(A) Being the girl of my dreams, I am sure she will marry me.
(B) She, being the girl of my dreams, will surely marry me.
(C) I am sure she will marry me, being the girl of my dreams.
(D) I am sure she will marry the girl of my dreams.
(E) I, being the girl of my dreams, am sure she will marry me.

28. It is many years <u>since I see</u> such good playing.

(A) since I see
(B) since I will have seen
(C) since I've seen
(D) since I'd seen
(E) since I will see

29. Before I left, <u>I have told</u> them to close the door.

(A) I have told
(B) I am telling
(C) I tell
(D) I told
(E) I had told

30. <u>From the very beginning, thinking as they did, are wrong.</u>

(A) From the very beginning, thinking as they did, are wrong.
(B) They are wrong, thinking as they did from the very beginning.
(C) From the very beginning, thinking as they did, is wrong.
(D) From the very beginning, thinking as they did, they were wrong.
(E) They, thinking from the very beginning as they did, are wrong.

31. <u>Founded in the nineteenth century, the City University.</u>

(A) Founded in the nineteenth century, the City University.
(B) The City University was founded in the nineteenth century.
(C) The City University, found in the nineteenth century.
(D) In the nineteenth century, founded the City University.
(E) The City University, founded in the nineteenth century.

32. <u>Rudyard Kipling, the famous British author, writing in the 1900s.</u>

(A) Rudyard Kipling, the famous author, writing in the 1900s.
(B) Rudyard Kipling, the famous British author, written in the 1900s.
(C) Writing in the 1900s, Rudyard Kipling, the famous British author.
(D) In the 1900s, the famous British author, Rudyard Kipling.
(E) Rudyard Kipling, the famous British author, wrote in the 1900s.

$\frac{26}{32}$ 81%

66

ANSWERS AND EXPLANATIONS TO THE SENTENCE CORRECTION PRACTICE QUESTIONS

1. **(E)** is correct. A pronoun preceding a gerund (an *ing* verb used as a noun) must be in the possessive case. C changes the meaning of the sentence. D introduces the relative pronoun *that* incorrectly because there is no subordinate clause that follows.

2. **(A)** is correct. The meaning is clear. The poor woman was given help. In the other choices the meaning of the sentence is changed.

3. **(C)** is correct. The correct idiomatic expression is *in accordance with*.

4. **(C)** is correct. This is the only choice that corrects the following errors: *no one* is a singular subject and must use the singular verb *has*. *Including* is a preposition and takes the objective form *me*. *He* must be used as the subject of the understood verb *has*.

5. **(D)** is correct. The subordinate clause, when preceding the main clause, must be separated by a comma. All the other choices use incorrect separations between the subordinate clause *however much we tried* and the main clause *the motor would not start*.

6. **(B)** is correct because it supplies parallel structure among the stated elements of discretion. In C the semicolon is used incorrectly. In D, the meaning of the sentence is changed. In E, although the punctuation is correct, the structure is not parallel. Note that it is correct either to use a comma before *and* in a series or to leave it out.

7. **(E)** is correct since both verbs (*occurs* and *admits*) should be in the present tense. B uses the verb *is*, which is idiomatically incorrect. D incorrectly uses the dash in the middle of the sentence.

8. **(A)** is correct. *Storm* and *ship* are correctly used as subjects. The meaning is clear. In B, the meaning is changed. In C, the pronoun *it* does not have a logical antecedent. The use of the semicolon is incorrect in D. In E, the use of *it* is unclear.

9. **(B)** is correct. An appositive is separated from the rest of the sentence by commas. In this sentence *the famous surgeon* is the appositive. C and D use only one comma. E has two predicates without any conjunction.

10. **(B)** is correct because *each* is singular and must take a singular verb. C and D use the commas incorrectly. E changes the meaning of the sentence.

11. (C) is correct because it replaces the dangling participle *being unable* with a subordinate clause. B is a run-on sentence. In D, *being that* is an incorrect beginning. E still contains the same dangling participle as the original sentence.

12. (D) is correct. This choice separates the two independent clauses by a semicolon and places a comma after the introductory word *however*. A and B are run-on sentences. C misplaces the semicolon. E has a period but does not use a capital to begin the new sentence.

13. (A) is correct. B uses the semicolon incorrectly. C forms two sentence fragments. In D, *and that* is incorrect. E changes the meaning of the sentence.

14. (E) is correct. The elliptical *economic position* makes it necessary to use *'s* after *slave*. The *economic position* is being compared. In B, the comparison is unclear. In C, *comparable with* is idiomatically incorrect. In D, the addition of *as*, which is a conjunction, is incorrect.

15. (D) The correct form is *should have*. *Of* can't be used as an auxiliary verb. In B and C, the comma is used incorrectly. In E, the incorrect past participle (came) is used.

16. (A) The only correct construction is *No sooner . . . than . . .*

17. (C) is correct. *A percentage* should be set off within parentheses. A uses an incorrect idiom, *consisting with*. In D, *charging an amount* could not be an element. E does not give a complete description.

18. (B) is correct because it balances two adjectives (*rapidly* and *economically*). In A, there is no parallel structure because an adjective, *more rapidly*, is used with a phrase, *with greater economy*. C changes the meaning of the sentence. D misuses the comma. E contains the same type of error as A.

19. (E) is correct because the phrase *during the afternoon* is placed so that the meaning of the sentence is clear. B uses commas incorrectly. C misplaces the phrases. D omits the phrase and changes the meaning of the sentence.

20. (A) is correct. It is a simple, concise, correct statement. Choices B, C, and D are all wordy, repetitive, awkward sentences. E changes the meaning of the sentence.

21. (D) is correct. The antecedent of *me* is *seniors*, which is the object of the preposition *to*. *Me* is correct because it is in the objective case. In B, the reflexive pronoun *myself* is incorrect. In C, the speaker incorrectly mentions himself before Dave. In E, *which* is incorrectly used to refer to people.

68

22. **(A)** is correct because it is the only choice that follows this rule: Use an apostrophe (') and *s* to form the plural of abbreviations followed by periods *(Ph.D.'s)*, of letter *(I's)*, and of words referred to as words *(miss's* and *mess's)*.

23. **(A)** is correct. *Laid* is the past participle of the transitive verb *to lay*. It takes an object. *To lie* is intransitive and does not take an object. All the other choices use incorrect verb forms.

24. **(B)** is correct. A semicolon is used to separate a series of items that contain commas. The series is introduced by a colon. The other colons do not use the marks of punctuation correctly.

25. **(A)** is correct. The sentence should be *past tense* and *past perfect* to indicate two actions in the past, one preceding the other.

26. **(D)** is correct. A misplaced modifier. Obviously the bridge was not in their car.

27. **(B)** is correct. The dangling participle is corrected by this answer.

28. **(C)** is correct. The present perfect tense is called for.

29. **(E)** is correct. The sequence of *past tense* and *past perfect* is correct.

30. **(D)** is correct. Two elements are involved here—keeping the tenses consistently *in the past* and eliminating the dangling participle.

31. **(B)** is correct. This is the only complete sentence.

32. **(E)** is correct. This is the only choice that is a complete sentence.

Unit 2

BASIC GRAMMAR STRATEGIES AND REVIEW

PARTS OF SPEECH

NOUN

A NOUN is the name of a person, place, or thing.

    actor, city, lamp

There are three kinds of nouns according to the type of person, place, or thing the noun names.

1. A *common* noun refers to a general type: *girl, park, army.*

2. A *proper* noun refers to a particular person, place, or thing, and always begins with a capital letter: *Mary, Central Park, U.S. Army.*

3. A *collective* noun signifies a number of individuals organized into one group: *team, crowd, Congress.*

Singular/Plural

Every noun has number. That means every noun is either singular or plural. The singular means only one; the plural means more than one. There are four ways to form the plurals of nouns:

1. by adding *s* to the singular (*horses, kites, rivers*)

2. by adding *es* to the singular (*buses, churches, dishes, boxes, buzzes*)

3. by changing the singular (*man* becomes *men, woman* becomes *women, child* becomes *children, baby* becomes *babies, alumnus* becomes *alumni*)

4. by leaving the singular as it is (*moose, deer,* and *sheep* are all plural as well as singular)

    Note: When forming the plural of letters and numbers, add 's: A's, 150's. Otherwise, *s* denotes possession.

Case

Nouns also have case, which indicates the function of the noun in the sentence. There are three cases—the nominative case, the objective case, and the possessive case.

1. Nominative case

    A noun is in the nominative case when it is the subject of a sentence: The *book* fell off the table. The *boys* and *girls* ran outside.

    The subject of a sentence is the person, place, or thing that the sentence is about. Thus, "The *book* fell off the table" is about the book.

    A noun is in the nominative case when it is a predicate noun. This is a noun used after a linking verb. In such cases, the predicate noun means the same as the subject.

        Einstein was a *scientist*. (Einstein = scientist)

        Judith was a brilliant *scholar* and gifted *teacher*. (Judith = scholar and teacher)

    A noun is in the nominative case when it is used in direct address. A noun in direct address shows that someone or something is being spoken to directly. This noun is set off by commas.

> *Claudel*, please answer the phone.
>
> Go home, *Fido*, before you get hit by a car.

A noun is in the nominative case when it is a nominative absolute. This is a noun with a participle (see Verbs) that stands as an independent idea but is part of a sentence.

> The *rain* having stopped, we went out to play.
>
> The *bike* having crashed, the race was stopped.

A noun is in the nominative case when it is a nominative in apposition. This is one of a pair of nouns. Both nouns are equal in meaning and are next to one another. The noun in apposition is set off from the rest of the sentence by commas.

> Steve, my *son*, is going to college.
>
> That man is Syd, the *musician*.

2. Objective case

A noun is in the objective case when it is the direct object of a verb. A direct object is the receiver of the action of a verb. A verb that has a direct object is called a transitive verb.

> The team elected *David*.
>
> The team won the *game*.

A noun is in the objective case when it is the indirect object of a verb. This is a noun that shows *to* whom or *for* whom the action is taking place. The words *to* and *for* may not actually appear in the sentence but they are understood. An indirect object must be with a direct object.

> Pedro threw *Mario* the ball. (Pedro threw the ball to Mario.)

Anya bought her *mother* a gift. (Anya bought a gift for her mother.)

A noun is in the objective case when it is an objective complement. An objective complement is a noun that explains the direct object. The word *complement* indicates that this noun *completes* the meaning of the direct object.

> The team elected Terry *captain*.

A noun is in the objective case when it is an objective by apposition. An objective by apposition is very much like a nominative in apposition. Again, we have a pair of nouns that are equal in meaning and are next to one another. The noun in apposition explains the other noun, but now the noun being explained is in the objective case. Therefore, the noun in apposition is called the objective by apposition. The objective by apposition is set off from the rest of the sentence by commas.

> The bully pushed Steve, the little *toddler*, into the sandbox.
>
> He gave the money to Sam, the *banker*.

A noun is in the objective case when it is an adverbial objective. This is a noun that denotes distance or time.

> The storm lasted an *hour*.
>
> The troops walked five *miles*.

A noun is in the objective case when it is an object of a preposition.

> The stick fell into the *well*. (*Into* is the preposition.)
>
> The picture fell on the *table*. (*On* is the preposition.)

See the section on prepositions.

3. Possessive case

A noun is in the possessive case when it shows ownership. The correct use of the possessive case is often tested on the exam. The following rules will help you answer such questions correctly.

(A) The possessive case of most nouns is formed by adding an apostrophe (') and s to the singular.

the *boy's* book

Emile's coat

(B) If the singular ends in *s,* add either just an apostrophe or an apostrophe plus a final *s.*

the *bus'* wheels; the *bus's* wheels

Charles' books; *Charles's* books

(C) The possessive case of plural nouns ending in *s* is formed by adding just an apostrophe.

the *dogs'* bones

Note: If the dog was singular, the possessive case would be *dog's.*

(D) If the plural noun does not end in *s,* then add an apostrophe and an *s.*

the *children's* toys

the *men's* boots

(E) The possessive case of compound nouns is formed by adding an apostrophe and an *s* to the last word if it is singular, or by adding an *s* and an apostrophe if the word is plural.

my *brother-in-law's* house

my *two brother's* house

(F) To show individual ownership, add an apostrophe and *s* to each owner.

Joe's and *Jim's* boats (Each owns his own boat.)

(G) To show joint ownership, add an apostrophe and *s* to the last name.

Joe and *Jim's* boat (They both own the same boat.)

PRONOUNS

A pronoun is used in place of a noun. The noun for which a pronoun is used is called the *antecedent*. The use of pronouns, particularly the relationship between a pronoun and its antecedent, is one of the most common items found on the test. Always make sure a pronoun has a clear antecedent.

John had a candy bar and a cookie. He ate *it* quickly. (Ambiguous) (What is the antecedent of *it*—candy bar or cookie?)

The boy rode his bike through the hedge, *which* was very large. (Ambiguous) (What was very large—the bike or the hedge?)

The captain was very popular. *They* all like him. (Ambiguous) (Who liked him? *They* has no antecedent.)

There are ten kinds of pronouns.

1. An expletive pronoun

The words *it* and *there* followed by the subject of the sentence are expletive pronouns.

There were only a few tickets left.

It was a long list of chores.

When using an expletive, the verb agrees with the subject.

There *remains* one *child* on the bus.

There *remain* many *children* on the bus.

2. An intensive pronoun

This is a pronoun, ending in *self* or *selves*, which follows its antecedent and emphasizes it.

> He *himself* will go.
>
> The package was delivered to the boys *themselves*.

3. A reflexive pronoun

This is a pronoun, ending in *self* or *selves*, which is usually the object of a verb or preposition, or the complement of a verb.

> I hate *myself*.
>
> They always laugh at *themselves*.

> *Myself, yourself, himself, herself*, and *itself* are all singular. *Ourselves, yourselves*, and *themselves* are all plural. There is NO such pronoun as *hisself* or *theirselves*. Do NOT use *myself* instead of *I* or *me*.

4. A demonstrative pronoun

This is used in place of a noun and points out the noun. Common demonstrative pronouns are *this, that, these*, and *those*.

> I want *those*.

5. An indefinite pronoun

This pronoun refers to any number of persons or objects. Following is a list of some singular and plural indefinite pronouns.

> SINGULAR
>
> *anybody, anyone, each, everybody, everyone, no one, nobody, none, somebody, someone*
>
> PLURAL
>
> *all, any, many, several, some*

If the singular form is used as a subject, the verb must also be singular.

> *Everyone* of them *sings*. (One person sings.)

If the singular form is used as an antecedent, its pronoun must be singular.

> Did *anybody* on any of the teams lose *his* sneakers? (One person lost *his* sneakers.)

6. An interrogative pronoun

This pronoun is used in asking a question. Such pronouns are *who, whose, whom, what*, and *which*. *Whose* shows possession. *Whom* is in the objective case. *Whom* is used ONLY when an object pronoun is needed.

7. A reciprocal pronoun

This pronoun is used when referring to mutual relations. The reciprocal pronouns are *each other* and *one another*.

> They love *one another*.
>
> They often visit *each other's* houses.

Note that the possessive is formed by an *'s* after the word *other*.

8. A possessive pronoun

This pronoun refers to a noun that owns something. The possessive pronouns are as follows:

> SINGULAR
>
> *mine (my), yours, his, hers, its*
>
> PLURAL
>
> *ours, yours, theirs*

Notice that possessive pronouns do not use an *'s*. *It's* means "it is"; *its* denotes possession.

9. A relative pronoun

Nominative case—*who, that, which*

Objective case—*whom, that, which*

Possessive case—*whose*

A relative pronoun used as the *subject* of a dependent clause is in the nominative case.

> I know *who* stole the car.

> Give the prize to *whoever* won it.

A relative pronoun used as the *object* of a dependent clause is in the objective case.

> He is the thief *whom* I know. (Object of verb *know*)

Note that the difficulty always comes between choosing *who* or *whom*. Remember that *who* is in the nominative case and is used for the appropriate situations discussed under Nominative Case in the section on nouns. *Whom* is in the objective case and is used for the appropriate situations discussed under Objective Case in the section on nouns.

> *Who* is coming? (*Who* is the subject.)

> *Whom* are you going with? (*Whom* is the object of the preposition *with*.)

The relative pronoun in the possessive case is *whose*. Notice there is no apostrophe in this word. The contraction *who's* means "who is."

> I know *whose* book it is. (Denotes possession)

> I know *who's* on first base. (*Who's* means "who is.")

10. Personal pronouns

NOMINATIVE CASE		
	Singular	Plural
First person	I	we
Second person	you	you
Third person	he, she, it	they

OBJECTIVE CASE		
First person	me	us
Second person	you	you
Third person	him, her, it	them

POSSESSIVE CASE		
First person	mine (my)	ours (our)
Second person	yours (your)	yours (your)
Third person	his, hers, its	theirs (their)
	(his, her, its)	

Personal pronouns denote what is called *person*. First-person pronouns show the person or thing that is speaking.

> *I* am going. (First person speaking)

Second-person pronouns show the person or thing being spoken to.

> *You* are my friend. (Second person spoken to)

Third-person pronouns show the person or thing being spoken about.

> Bea did not see *her*. (Third person spoken about)

IMPORTANT FOR THE EXAM

Pronouns must agree with their antecedents in person, number, and gender.

1. *Who* refers to persons only.

2. *Which* refers to animals or objects.

3. *That* refers to persons, animals, or objects.

> I don't know *who* the actor is. (Person)
>
> They missed their dog, *which* died. (Animal)
>
> I finished the book, *which* you recommended. (Object)
>
> They are the people *that* started the fight. (Person)
>
> That is the tiger *that* ran loose. (Animal)
>
> The light *that* failed was broken. (Object)

Note that the singular indefinite antecedents always take a singular pronoun.

> *Everyone* of the girls lost *her* hat.
>
> *None* of the boys lost *his*.
>
> *Someone* left *his* bike outside.

Note that collective singular nouns take singular pronouns; collective plural nouns take plural pronouns.

> The *choir* sang *its* part beautifully.
>
> The *choirs* sang *their* parts beautifully.

Note that two or more antecedents joined by *and* take a plural pronoun.

> Dave *and* Steve lost *their* way.

Note that two or more singular antecedents joined by *or* or *nor* take a singular pronoun.

> Tanya *or* Charita may use *her* ball.
>
> Neither Tanya *nor* Charita may use *her* ball.

If two antecedents are joined by *or* or *nor* and if one is plural and the other is singular, the pronoun agrees in number with the nearer antecedent.

> Neither the *ball* nor the *rackets* were in *their* place.

CASE

Remember that pronouns must also be in the correct case.

1. A pronoun must be in the nominative case when it is the subject of a sentence.

   > James and *I* went to the airport.
   >
   > *We* freshmen helped the seniors.
   >
   > Peter calls her more than *I* do.
   >
   > Peter calls her more than *I*. (Here, the verb *do* is understood, and *I* is the subject of the understood verb *do*.)

2. A pronoun is in the objective case when it is a direct object of the verb.

   > Leaving James and *me*, they ran away.
   >
   > John hit *them*.
   >
   > The freshmen helped *us* seniors.

   A pronoun is the in the objective case when it is the indirect object of a verb.

   > Give *us* the ball.

3. A pronoun is in the objective case when it is an object of a preposition.

   > to Ben and *me*
   >
   > with Sheila and *her*
   >
   > between you and *them*

4. A pronoun is in the possessive case when it shows ownership.

   > *Her* car broke down.
   >
   > *Theirs* did also.

A pronoun is in the possessive case when it appears before a gerund (see Verbs).

His going was a sad event.

For a more detailed analysis of the three cases, see the section on Cases of nouns.

ADJECTIVES

An adjective describes or modifies a noun or a pronoun. An adjective usually answers the question *which one*? Or *what kind*? Or *how many*? There are a number of types of adjectives you should know.

(1) Articles (*a, an, the*)

An article must agree in number with the noun or pronoun it modifies.

a boy

an apple

the girls

If the noun or pronoun begins with a consonant, use *a*. If the noun or pronoun begins with a vowel, use *an*.

a pear

an orange

2. Limiting adjectives point out definite nouns or tell how many there are.

Those books belong to John.

The *three* boys didn't see *any* birds.

3. Descriptive adjectives describe or give a quality of the noun or pronoun they modify.

the *large* chair

the *sad* song

4. Possessive, demonstrative, and indefinite adjectives look like the pronouns of the same name. However, the adjective does not stand alone. It describes a noun or pronoun.

This is *mine*. (Demonstrative and possessive pronouns)

This book is *my* father's. (Demonstrative and possessive adjectives)

5. Interrogative and relative adjectives look the same, but they function differently. Interrogative adjectives ask questions.

Which way should I go?

Whose book is this?

What time is John coming?

Relative adjectives join two clauses and modify some word in the dependent clause.

I don't know *whose* book it is.

IMPORTANT FOR THE EXAM

An adjective is used as a predicative adjective after a linking verb. If the modifier is describing the verb (a nonlinking verb), an adverb must be used.

The boy is *happy*. (Adjective)

Joe appeared *angry*. (Adjective)

The soup tasted *spicy*. (Adjective)

Joe looked *angrily* at the dog. (Adverb—*angrily* modifies *looked*)

POSITIVE, COMPARATIVE, AND SUPERLATIVE ADJECTIVES

1. The positive degree states the quality of an object.

2. The comparative degree compares two things. It is formed by using *less* or *more* or adding *er* to the positive.

3. The superlative degree compares three or more things. It is formed by using *least* or *most* or adding *est* to the positive.

Positive	Comparative	Superlative
easy	easier; more easy; less easy	easiest; most easy; least easy
pretty	prettier; more pretty; less pretty	prettiest; least pretty; most pretty

DO NOT USE TWO FORMS TOGETHER

She is the most prettiest. (Incorrect)

She is the prettiest. (Correct)

She is the most pretty. (Correct)

VERBS

A verb denotes either action or a state of being. There are four major types of verbs: transitive, intransitive, linking, and auxiliary.

1. Transitive verbs are action words that must take a direct object. The direct object, which receives the action of the verb, is in the objective case.

Joe *hit* the ball. (*Ball* is the direct object of *hit*.)

Joe *kissed* Helen. (*Helen* is the direct object of *kissed*.)

2. Intransitive verbs denote action but do not take a direct object.

The glass *broke*.

The boy *fell*.

IMPORTANT FOR THE EXAM

Set, *lay*, and *raise* are always transitive and take an object. *Sit*, *lie*, and *rise* are always intransitive and do NOT take a direct object.

Set the book down, *lay* the pencil down, and *raise* your hands. (*Book, pencil,* and *hands* are direct objects of *set, lay,* and *raise*.)

Sit in the chair.

She *lies* in bed all day.

The sun also *rises*.

The same verb can be transitive or intransitive, depending on the sentence.

The pitcher *threw* wildly. (Intransitive)

The pitcher *threw* the ball wildly. (Transitive)

3. Linking verbs have no action. They denote a state of being. Linking verbs mean "equal." Here are some examples: *is, are, was, were, be, been, am* (any form of the verb *to be*), *smell, taste, feel, look, seem, become, appear.*

Sometimes, these verbs are confusing because they can be linking verbs in one sentence and action verbs in another. You can tell if the verb is a linking verb if it means "equal" in the sentence.

He felt nervous. (*He* equals *nervous.*)

He felt nervously for the door bell. (*He* does not equal *door bell.*)

Linking verbs take a predicate nominative or predicate adjective. (See sections on Nouns, Pronouns, and Adjectives.)

It *is I.*

It *is she.*

4. Auxiliary verbs are sometimes called "helping" verbs. These verbs are used with an infinitive verb (*to* plus the verb) or a participle to form a verb phrase.

The common auxiliary verbs are:

all forms of *to be, to have, to do, to keep*

the verbs *can, may, must, ought to, shall, will, would, should*

He *has to go*. (Auxiliary *has* plus the infinitive *to go*)

He *was going*. (Auxiliary *was* plus the present participle *going*)

He *has gone*. (Auxiliary *has* plus the past participle *gone*)

There is no such form as *had ought*. Use *ought to have* or *should have*.

He *ought to have gone*.

He *should have gone*.

Every verb can change its form according to five categories. Each category adds meaning to the verb. The five categories are: *tense, mood, voice, number,* and *person.*

Tense: This indicates the *time*, or *when*, the verb occurs. There are six tenses. They are:

present   past   future
present perfect   past perfect   future perfect

Three principal parts of the verb—the present, the past, and the past participle—are used to form all the tenses.

The *present tense* shows that the action is taking place in the present.

The dog *sees* the car and *jumps* out of the way.

The present tense of a regular verb looks like this:

	Singular	Plural
First person	I jump	We jump
Second person	You jump	You jump
Third person	He, she, it jumps	They jump

Notice that an *s* is added to the third-person singular.

The *past tense* shows that the action took place in the past.

The dog *saw* the car and *jumped* out of the way.

The past tense of a regular verb looks like this:

	Singular	Plural
First person	I jumped	We jumped
Second person	You jumped	You jumped
Third person	He, she, it jumped	They jumped

Notice that *ed* is added to the verb. Sometimes just *d* is added, as in the verb *used*, for example. In regular verbs the past participle has the same form as the past tense, but it is used with an auxiliary verb.

The dog *had jumped*.

The *future tense* shows that the action is going to take place in the future. The future tense needs the auxiliary verbs *will* or *shall*.

The dog *will see* the car and *will jump* out of the way.

The future tense of a regular verb looks like this:

	Singular	Plural
First person	I shall jump	We shall jump
Second person	You will jump	You will jump
Third person	He, she, it will jump	They will jump

Notice that *shall* is used in the first person of the future tense.

To form the three *perfect tenses,* the verb *to have* and the past participle are used.

- The present tense of *to have* is used to form the *present perfect.*

- The dog *has seen* the car and *has jumped* out of the way.

The present perfect tense shows that the action has started in the past and is continuing or has just been implemented in the present.

- The past tense of *to have* is used to form the *past perfect.*

- The dog *had seen* the car and *had jumped* out of the way.

The past perfect tense shows that the action had been completed in the past.

- The future tense of *to have* is used to form the *future perfect.*

- The dog *will have seen* the car and *will have jumped* out of the way.

The future perfect tense shows that an action will have been completed before a definite time in the future.

Following is a table that shows the present, past, and future tenses of *to have.*

PRESENT TENSE

	Singular	Plural
First person	I have	We have
Second person	You have	You have
Third person	He, she, it has	They have

PAST TENSE

	Singular	Plural
First person	I had	We had
Second person	You had	You had
Third person	He, she, it had	They had

FUTURE TENSE

	Singular	Plural
First person	I shall have	We shall have
Second person	You will have	You shall have
Third person	He, she, it will have	They shall have

The perfect tenses all use the past participle. Therefore, you must know the past participle of all the verbs. As we said, the past participle usually is formed by adding *d* or *ed* to the verb. However, there are many irregular verbs. Following is a table of the principal forms of some irregular verbs.

PRESENT	PAST	PAST PARTICIPLE
arise	arose	arisen
awake	awoke, awaked	awoke, awaked, awakened
awaken	awakened	awakened
be	was	been
bear	bore	borne
beat	beat	beaten
become	became	become
begin	began	begun
bend	bent	bent
bet	bet	bet
bid (command)	bade, bid	bidden, bid

PRESENT	PAST	PAST PARTICIPLE	PRESENT	PAST	PAST PARTICIPLE
bind	bound	bound	rid	rid	rid
bite	bit	bitten	ride	rode	ridden
bleed	bled	bled	ring	rang	rung
blow	blew	blown	rise (go up)	rose	risen
break	broke	broken	run	ran	run
bring	brought	brought	saw (cut)	sawed	sawed
build	built	built	say	said	said
burn	burned, burnt	burned, burnt	see	saw	seen
burst	burst	burst	set	set	set
buy	bought	bought	shake	shook	shaken
catch	caught	caught	shine (light)	shone	shone
choose	chose	chosen	shine (to polish)	shined	shined
come	came	come	show	showed	shown
cost	cost	cost	shrink	shrank	shrunk, shrunken
dig	dug	dug			
dive	dived, dove	dived	sing	sang	sung
do	did	done	sit	sat	sat
draw	drew	drawn	slay	slew	slain
dream	dreamed, dreamt	dreamed, dreamt	speak	spoke	spoken
drink	drank	drunk	spend	spent	spent
drive	drove	driven	spit	spat, spit	spat, spit
eat	ate	eaten	spring	sprang	sprung
fall	fell	fallen	stand	stood	stood
fight	fought	fought	steal	stole	stolen
fit	fitted	fitted	swear	swore	sworn
fly	flew	flown	swim	swam	swum
forget	forgot	forgotten, forgot	swing	swung	swung
			take	took	taken
freeze	froze	frozen	teach	taught	taught
get	got	got, gotten	tear	tore	torn
give	gave	given	throw	threw	thrown
go	went	gone	wake	waked, woke	waked, woken
grow	grew	grown	wear	wore	worn
hang (kill)	hanged	hanged	weave	wove, weaved	woven, weaved
hang (suspended)	hung	hung	weep	wept	wept
			win	won	won
hide	hid	hidden	write	wrote	written
hold	held	held			
know	knew	known			
lay	laid	laid			
lead	led	led			
lend	lent	lent			
lie (recline)	lay	lain			
lie (untruth)	lied	lied			
light	lit	lit			
pay	paid	paid			
raise (take up)	raised	raised			
read	read	read			

Another aspect of tense that appears on the test is the *correct sequence* or *order of tenses*. Be sure if you change tense you know why you are doing so. Following are some rules to help you.

- When using the perfect tenses remember:

  - The present perfect tense goes with the present tense.

    present
    As Dave *steps* up to the mound, the

    present perfect
    pitcher *has thrown* the ball to first

    present perfect
    and I *have caught* it.

  - The past perfect tense goes with the past tense.

    past
    Before Dave *stepped* up to the

    past perfect
    mound, the pitcher *had thrown* the

    past perfect
    ball to first and I *had caught* it.

  - The future perfect goes with the future tense.

    future
    Before Dave *will step* up to the

    future perfect
    mound, the pitcher *will have thrown*

    future perfect
    the ball to first and I *shall have caught* it.

- The present participle (verb + *ing*) is used when its action occurs at the same time as the action of the main verb.

  John, *answering* the bell, *knocked* over the plant. (*Answering* and *knocked* occur at the same time.)

- The past participle is used when its action occurs before the main verb.

The elves, *dressed* in costumes, will *march* proudly to the shoemaker. (The elves dressed *before* they will march.)

MOOD

The mood or mode of a verb shows the manner of the action. There are three moods.

1. The *indicative mood* shows the sentence is factual. Most of what we say is in the indicative mode.

2. The *subjunctive mood* is used for conditions contrary to fact or for strong desires. The use of the subjunctive mood for the verb *to be* is a TEST ITEM.

Following is the conjugation (list of forms) of the verb *to be* in the subjunctive mood.

	PRESENT	
	Singular	Plural
First person	I be	We be
Second person	You be	You be
Third person	He, she, it be	They be

	PAST TENSE	
First person	I were	We were
Second person	You were	You were
Third person	He, she, it were	They were

If I *be* wrong, then punish me.

If he *were* king, he would pardon me.

Also, *shall* and *should* are used for the subjunctive mood.

If he *shall* fail, he will cry.

If you *should* win, don't forget us.

3. The *imperative mood* is used for commands.

Go at once!

If strong feelings are expressed, the command ends in an exclamation point. In commands, the subject "you" is not stated but is understood.

VOICE

There are two voices of verbs. The active voice shows that the subject is acting upon something or doing something *to* something else. The active voice has a direct object.

> subject   object
> The *car* hit the *boy*.

The passive voice shows that the subject is acted upon *by* something. Something was done *to* the subject. The direct object becomes the subject. The verb *to be* plus the past participle is used in the passive voice.

> subject
> The *boy* was hit by the car.

NUMBER

This, as before, means singular or plural. A verb must agree with its subject in number.

> The *list was* long. (Singular)
> The *lists were* long. (Plural)

Nouns appearing between subject and verb do not change subject-verb agreement.

> The *list* of chores *was* long. (Singular)
> The *lists* of chores *were* long. (Plural)

Subjects joined by *and* are singular if the subject is one person or unit.

> My *friend and colleague has* decided to leave. (Singular)

> *Five and five is* ten. (Singular)
> *Tea and milk is* my favorite drink. (Singular)

Singular subjects joined by *or, either-or,* and *neither-nor* take singular verbs.

> Either Alvin or Lynette *goes* to the movies.

If one subject is singular and one is plural, the verb agrees with the nearer subject.

> Either Alvin or the girls *go* to the movies.

The use of the expletive pronouns *there* and *it* do not change subject-verb agreement.

> There *is no one* here.
> There *are snakes in* the grass.
> Think: No one is there; snakes are in the grass.

A relative pronoun takes a verb that agrees in number with the pronoun's antecedent.

> It is the *electrician who suggests* new wiring. (Singular)
> It is the *electricians who suggest* new wiring. (Plural)

Singular indefinite pronouns take singular verbs.

> Everybody *buys* tickets.

It is hard to tell if some nouns are singular. Following is a list of tricky nouns that take singular verbs.

> Collective nouns—*army, class, committee, team*
> Singular nouns in plural form—*news, economics, mathematics, measles, mumps, news, politics*

Titles, although plural in form, refer to a single work—*The New York Times*, Henry James's *The Ambassadors*

The *army is* coming.

News travels fast.

Jaws is a good movie.

Don't (do not) is incorrect for third-person singular. *Doesn't (does not)* is correct.

He *doesn't* agree.

PERSON

Person, as before, refers to first person (speaking), second person (spoken to), third person (spoken about). A verb must agree with its subject in person.

I study. (First person)

He studies. (Third person)

Intervening nouns or pronouns do not change subject-verb agreement.

He as well as I *is* going. (Third person)

If there are two or more subjects joined by *or* or *nor*, the verb agrees with the nearer subject.

Either John or *we are* going. (First-person plural)

ADVERBS

An adverb describes or modifies a verb, an adjective, or another adverb. Adverbs usually answer the questions *why? where? when? how? to what degree?* Many adverbs end in *ly*. There are two types of adverbs similar in use to the same type of adjective.

• *Interrogative adverbs* ask questions.

  • *Where* are you going?

  • *When* will you be home?

• *Relative adverbs* join two clauses and modify some word in the dependent clause.

  • No liquor is sold *where* I live.

As with adjectives, there are three degrees of comparison for adjectives and a corresponding form for each.

1. The *positive degree* is often formed by adding *ly* to the adjective.

   She was *angry*. (Adjective)

   She screamed *angrily*. (Adverb)

2. The *comparative* is formed by using *more* or *less* or adding *er* to the positive.

3. The *superlative* is formed by using *most* or *least* or adding *est* to the positive.

Here are two typical adverbs:

POSITIVE DEGREE	COMPARA-TIVE DEGREE	SUPERLATIVE
easily	easier, more easily, less easily	easiest, most easily, least easily
happily	happier, more happily, less happily	happiest, most happily, least happily

CONJUNCTIONS

Conjunctions connect words, phrases, or clauses. Conjunctions can connect equal parts of speech.

> and
>
> but
>
> for
>
> or

Some conjunctions are used in pairs:

> either . . . or
>
> neither . . . nor
>
> not only . . . but also

Here are some phrases and clauses using conjunctions:

> John *or* Mary (Nouns are connected)
>
> On the wall *and* in the window (Phrases are connected)
>
> Mark had gone *but* I had not. (Clauses are connected)
>
> *Either* you go *or* I will. (Clauses are connected)

If the conjunction connects two long clauses, a comma is used in front of the coordinating conjunction:

> Julio had gone to the game in the afternoon, but Pedro had not.

Some conjunctions are transitional:

> therefore
>
> however
>
> moreover
>
> finally
>
> nevertheless

These conjunctions connect the meaning of two clauses or sentences.

IMPORTANT FOR THE EXAM

Do not use *comma splices*. Comma splices occur when one connects two independent clauses with a comma, rather than with a semicolon or with a comma followed by a coordinating conjunction. An independent clause is a clause that can stand alone as a sentence.

> His bike was broken; therefore, he could not ride. (Correct)
>
> His bike was broken. Therefore he could not ride. (Correct)
>
> His bike was broken, and, therefore, he could not ride. (Correct)
>
> His bike was broken, therefore, he could not ride. (Incorrect)
>
> He found his wallet, however he still left the auction. (Incorrect)

The last two sentences are comma splices and are incorrect. *Remember, two independent clauses cannot be connected by a comma.*

PREPOSITIONS

A preposition shows the relationship between a noun or pronoun and some other word in the sentence.

The following are all prepositions:

about	of
above	off
across	over
around	through
behind	to
beneath	under
during	up
for	upon
in	within
inside	without
into	

Sometimes groups of words are treated as single prepositions. Here are some examples:

according to

ahead of

in front of

in between

The preposition together with the noun or pronoun it introduces is called a prepositional phrase.

under the table

in front of the oil painting

behind the glass jar

along the waterfront

beside the canal

Very often on the test idiomatic expressions are given that depend upon prepositions to be correct. Following is a list of idioms showing the correct preposition to use:

abhorrence of: He showed an *abhorrence of* violence.

abound in (or *with*): The lake *abounded with* fish.

accompanied by (a person): He was *accompanied by* his friend.

accompanied with: He *accompanied* his visit *with* a house gift.

accused by, of: He was *accused by* a person *of* a crime.

adept in: He is *adept in* jogging.

agree to (an offer): I *agree to* the terms of the contract.

agree with (a person): I *agree with* my son.

agree upon (or *on*) (a plan): I *agree upon* that approach to the problem.

angry at (a situation): I was *angry at* the delay.

available for (a purpose): I am *available for* tutoring.

available to (a person): Those machines are *available to* the tenants.

burden with: I won't *burden* you *with* my problems.

centered on (or *in*): His efforts *centered on* winning.

compare to (shows similarity): An orange can be *compared to* a grapefruit.

compare with (shows difference): An orange can be *compared with* a desk.

conform to (or *with*): He does not *conform to* the rules.

differ with (an opinion): I *differ with* his judgment.

differ from (a thing): The boss's car *differs from* the worker's car.

different from: His book is *different from* mine. (Use *different than* with a clause.)

employed at (salary): He is *employed at* $25 a day.

employed in (work): He is *employed in* building houses.

envious of: She is *envious of* her sister.

fearful of: She is *fearful of* thunder.

free of: She will soon be *free of* her burden.

hatred of: He has a *hatred of* violence.

hint at: They *hinted at* a surprise.

identical with: Your dress is *identical with* mine.

independent of: I am *independent of* my parents.

in search of: He went *in search of* truth.

interest in: He was not *interested in* his friends.

jealous of: He was *jealous of* them.

negligent of: He was *negligent of* his responsibilities.

object to: I *object to* waiting so long.

privilege of: He had the *privilege of* being born a millionaire.

proficient in: You will be *proficient in* grammar.

wait for: We will *wait for* them.

wait on (service): The maid *waited on* them.

Like is used as a preposition. He wanted his dog to act *like* Lassie.

Now that you have reviewed the Principles of Grammar, answering the Sentence Correction Questions should be easier. In the practice section that follows, answer the questions as you would on the actual examination and then check your answers. If you still don't understand the answers, go back to this section and rereview the appropriate material.

Unit 3

As you work with GMAT practice materials and as you take the actual GMAT test, keep in mind three important principles:

1. RELAX!
2. MAINTAIN A BALANCE.
3. DO WHAT WORKS FOR *YOU*.

Relax! You have been reading and comprehending for many years in a variety of situations. It is only reasonable to assume that on GMAT day you will be able to perform.

Maintain a Balance. You cannot be leisurely about reading three 500-word passages and responding to 20 questions in 25 minutes. On the other hand, you will accomplish little by racing through the work just to "finish." Your job is to establish a "rate-to-results" ratio that seems best for you.

Do What Works for You. No one can dictate exactly what you, a unique individual, must do to achieve the best balance of efficiency and accuracy of results. Use the practice materials as a trial-and-error experiment to determine a pace and approaches that work for you. Don't try to force yourself to adopt reading approaches that cause you to think more about them (the approaches) than the real task (the test). Some approaches may simply be mismatches with your own reading styles and/or personality patterns. *There is not just one way to succeed; there are many ways.*

Read the questions carefully. No points are given for the "right answer" to a question no one asked you.

Be calm when reading the question. If you don't understand it, read it again. Read all answer choices before selecting one. Unless you are *positive* of your choice, return to the passage to double-check.

The following suggestions have been helpful to students in multiple-choice situations.

The 1-Minute Overview: Look Over Your Map

Let's say you are driving from New York to Los Angeles and need to arrive as soon as possible. You would not leave without taking a look at your map. Exactly what you focus your attention upon on the map would be determined by the nature of your journey and the time you had available to browse. Much of the information available on the map would be irrelevant in view of your purpose. You would not, for example, spend time contemplating the size of the population of Houston and comparing it to the size of the population of Phoenix if what you really wanted was a general idea of how to get to Los Angeles.

The purpose of your first glance at the map is to determine the magnitude and general direction of your travel. As you glance, you might happen to notice a few other details that do not distract you from your general purpose.

Overviewing Your Reading Task Is Like Your First Glance at the Map.

To overview your reading task you might:

1. read the first few sentences of the passage.

2. read the first and final sentences of each paragraph (and glance through it very quickly just to see what else you might notice).

3. read the final few sentences of the passage.

4. read the question stems themselves and take a fast glance through the choices.

   You should now be able to:

1. identify the topic of the passage, at least in general terms.

2. have a sense of what information the questions require you to focus on.

3. Evaluate your own level of comfort with this kind of material.

4. have some idea about the content of each paragraph.

Remember:

- Don't be compulsive. This first run through the passage is simply a way to pick up as much as you can about the general nature of the task as rapidly as you can. If you stop to worry about any particular aspect of the passage or questions, you are defeating your purpose. You are, after all, going to read the passage carefully later.

- Some paragraphs will have topic sentences that state the main idea. However, not every paragraph has a stated topic sentence, and some stated topic sentences don't appear first or last in the paragraph. Therefore, some of the information you encounter in your overview may not seem to add a great deal to your hypothesis about what the passage entails. Don't worry, just keep going.

- Your job is to run in and "steal" information and ideas as quickly as possible. You are "casing" the reading material. Run in, get what you can, and don't be alarmed by your inability to "remove the refrigerator" at this time.

- Your overview will usually *not* enable you to *answer* any questions. Your purpose is simply to determine a general sense of direction.

- This process should take about a minute.

   Now practice. Following is a practice passage. Do an overview of the passage and the questions.

Passage

For 600 years, while Western Europe groped through the Dark Ages, a magnificent culture flourished in the rain forests of Central America. The Maya were the only people in the Americas to develop an original system of writing. Their mathematics was many centuries ahead of the European system. The Mayan calendar was more accurate than the Gregorian calendar we use today. Mayan ceremonial buildings—their frescoes, sculptures, and bas-reliefs—are still admired for their grace and harmony. At its height, in the eighth century, the Mayan civilization supported 14 million people in the fragile and difficult rain forest environment. The key to it was the Mayas' sophisticated system of agriculture.

Since the time when the Lacandon Maya of Guatemala fled to the Chipas rain forest in southern Mexico after the Spanish conquest, they have been able to practice a simplified version of their ancient Mayan agriculture in peace, farming in the forest more effectively and efficiently than either modern experts or recent immigrants. In determining where to locate each plot, the Lacandon differentiate among seven types of soil, only three of which are considered appropriate for farming. Indigenous plant growth is also given careful consideration. Plots with mahogany and tropical cedar are avoided since the soils that support them are considered too wet for cultivation. In April the Lacandon clear a small plot (*milpas*) of 2 to 3 acres by setting it ablaze after clearing a firewall, generating ash that provides nutrients in which the crops can flourish.

With the forest cover gone and the danger of erosion ever-present, the Lacandon quickly plant fast-growing trees—such as banana, to provide shade—and root crops, like taro, to anchor the soil. A few weeks later they plant the staple crop, maize. Watching certain forest "indicator" plants, the Lacandon determine when to plant selected crops. Tobacco plants, for example, are planted when the wild tamarind trees flower in the forest. The entire plot, every inch, is covered with several layers of growth, representing perhaps eighty different types of vegetation. Trees shade the medium-height crops, and vines cover the ground that contains distinct subterranean layers. Each crop has unique soil, water, and light requirements as well as different responses to close associations with every other plant. To make optimum use of available nutrients and prevent the spread of plant-specific disease, each clump of one variety is separated by a minimum of 10 feet from another of the same variety.

Depending on the effectiveness of weed control, the same plot can be cultivated from three to seven years without appreciable drops in yield. Weed invasion is reduced by locating plots in the midst of mature forest, by burning debris after each harvest, and by weeding by hand, uprooting the plants. When a plot is no longer suitable for intensive cultivation, it is planted with rubber, cacao, citrus, and other trees and left fallow for five to twenty years. During this time the Lacandon harvest wild plants: useful species they have planted there for food, fiber, and construction material; and old crop plants. Although most animals require the mature forest at critical times during their life cycles, certain wild animals that the Lacandon rely upon for protein are more common in regenerating farm plots than in the pristine forest.

In the 1940s when the Lacandon lands were reclassified as national territory, eighty thousand peasant farmers migrated into the forest. The settlers learned that when they were unable to make a living by farming, the land could be cleared and sold to cattle ranchers for profit. By 1971 the Lacandon consolidation into three small reservations created circumstances that made it difficult for them to continue their traditional way of life. The Lacandon now number only about four hundred individuals, fewer than 20 percent of whom practice their traditional agriculture.

Since each settlement is quite a distance from the *milpas*, daily weeding is not possible. Additionally, increased use of machetes scatters weeds widely, entrenching them rather than reducing them. The Lacandon are encouraged to depend on manufactured goods, a development that entices them to abandon their centuries-old practices to become low-paid laborers for the ranchers and loggers who now occupy former Lacandon lands.

1. Select the best statement of the main idea for paragraph 1.

    (A) Because the Gregorian calendar was generated during the Dark Ages, the Mayan calendar was more accurate.

    (B) The Maya lived in the fragile rain forest environment, supporting 14 million people.

    (C) The Maya lived in the fragile rain forest environment as Europe experienced the Dark Ages.

    (D) The Mayan civilization, which supported 14 million people, left evidence that demonstrated their remarkable skill and knowledge in several disciplines.

    (E) Older civilizations may prove to be more advanced than civilizations that coexist with them or follow them.

2. Mahogany and cedar are mentioned in paragraph 2:

    (A) as evidence supporting the author's statement that the Lacandon methods are effective.

    (B) as a contrast to the reference to indigenous vegetation.

    (C) as an example of Lacandon use of indigenous vegetation as a guide to *milpas* location.

    (D) as an example of the phenomenal success of the Lacandon in preserving natural forest land.

    (E) as a transition statement.

3. It can be inferred that the Lacandon farmers:

    (A) moved into the Chipas rain forest in southern Mexico in order to improve their agriculture.

    (B) were able to correct for seasonal variations such as those in temperature or rainfall by using indicator plants.

    (C) were more advanced than modern farmers, who rely upon technology.

    (D) regenerate their *milpas* in order to attract animals to provide them with protein

    (E) have successfully resisted efforts to modernize their methods.

4. Paragraph 2 focuses on:

    (A) the differences between the Lacandon methods and those of the ancient Maya.

    (B) the use of native plants as indicators of when Lacandon plants should be planted.

    (C) the efficiency of Lacandon methods, which modern farmers have not been able to duplicate.

    (D) the Lacandon methods of selecting and clearing the *milpas*.

    (E) Spanish oppression of Guatemalan natives.

5. This passage suggests that the most significant factor affecting the productivity of the *milpas* is:

(A) the frequency, method, and effectiveness of weed control.

(B) whether the indicator plants follow their usual cycles.

(C) the number of years the *milpas* must lie fallow.

(D) the proper layering and organization of crops within the *milpas*.

(E) the degree to which those who work the *milpas* have assimilated the ancient Mayan knowledge.

6. Select the choice that contains all items that can be inferred from the passage:

I. The presence or absence of certain indigenous plants would indicate optimum moisture for a Lacandon plot.

II. The *milpas* remains useful to the Lacandon beyond its three- to seven-year maximum productivity cycle.

III. The Mexican government erred in placing the Lacandon on reservations.

IV. A Lacandon farmer might not be able to explain why certain crops should be separated from each other in the *milpas*.

V. Peasant farmers owned the land they settled when Lacandon territory was reclassified as national territory.

(A) I, II, III, and V

(B) II, III, IV, and V

(C) I, II, IV, and V

(D) I, II, III, and IV

(E) ALL of the above.

7. Select the best summary statement for the article as a whole.

(A) Using ancient methods based upon natural patterns and interactions, the Lacandon farmed the Mexican forest with remarkable success until they were placed on reservations.

(B) The Lacandon farmers caused damage to the forest that had been their home and then sold their forest land to ranchers.

(C) The Lacandon have been victimized over the centuries, but have, until recently, been able to maintain their ancient lifestyle.

(D) Simple, ancient methods of farming, such as those used by the Lacandon, embody a wisdom modern farmers have been unable to master.

(E) When natives of a region are forced to live in new conditions, it is not always possible for them to continue their traditional practices.

8. Which would be the primary purpose of allowing the *milpas* to lie fallow?

(A) Obtaining building material.

(B) Attracting wild animals needed for protein.

(C) Allowing the land to regenerate.

(D) Eliminating the weeds.

(E) Selling rubber to the loggers and cattle ranchers.

9. The Lacandon layering of crops in the *milpas* addresses which requirement of the various plants:

(A) soil

(B) nutrients

(C) isolation from other plants

(D) light

(E) water

10. The author's purpose in stating "Although most animals require the mature forest at critical times during their life cycles" (paragraph 4) is to:

(A) establish a contrast between certain animals that are common in the *milpas* and most forest animals.

(B) establish a cause-effect relationship.

(C) establish the fact that the *milpas* cannot be considered a substitute for the natural forest.

(D) embellish the information presented with interesting detail.

(E) elaborate upon a previously stated issue.

This practice passage is longer than a typical GMAT passage (which is approximately 500 words), and it has more questions than a typical GMAT passage.

Take a look at what you found out by *overviewing*:

Your overview of the passage has told you that (paragraph 1) the Maya did amazing things and the key to "it" was agriculture. (paragraph 2) The Lacandon Maya fled to Mexico and farmed there using ancient methods. They clear a plot by burning. (paragraph 3) They plant trees and crops, separating clumps of the same variety. (paragraph 4) The plot is cultivated for three to seven years. Certain animals are more common in a regenerating plot. (paragraph 5) Many peasant farmers migrated into Lacandon lands. The Lacandon are enticed to abandon their old ways.

Your overview of the questions themselves indicates that you are to gain information regarding:

1. the main idea of paragraph 1.

2. why the author mentions mahogany and cedar.

3. an inference (it would take too long to determine exactly about what).

4. the focus of the second paragraph.

5. the most significant factor affecting *milpas* productivity.

6. an inference (again, appearing to involve many aspects of the passage).

7. the main idea of the article as a whole.

8. the main purpose of allowing the *milpas* to lie fallow.

9. which plant requirement is accomplished by layering plants.

10. the author's purpose in making a statement about animals requiring mature forests.

Do not attempt to memorize what you overviewed. Remember, this exercise of overviewing is just to gain a general sense of direction rapidly.

Begin the Journey: One Day at a Time

The next step is to return to the passage for a careful reading. You will focus upon main ideas and related details. Each paragraph is like a day's journey on your trip. Your focus is to understand the structure and intention of this material. As you read you may mark or underline aspects of the passage that ring a bell as a result of your overview. Again, do not spend time deciding whether to underline something or not.

The goal of your trip is to arrive as soon as possible, alive and well.

Your search for main ideas will be aided if you:

1. can identify the *subject* of each paragraph. The subject tells *who* or *what* the author is talking about.

2. can identify the *topic* of each paragraph. The topic tells what *aspect* of the subject the author has decided to focus upon. Some readers can arrive at the topic immediately, making step 1 unnecessary. Regardless, when you think you know the topic, make sure that you do not need to further narrow your choice.

3. can state in a concise sentence what (overall) the author is attempting to convey about the topic.

     This statement is the *main idea* of the paragraph. A main idea is always a statement; it will never sound like a title. A good statement of main idea is supported by at least *most*, if not all, of the details. Keep in mind that the author *may* have written a main idea sentence for you. If you can spot the author's main idea sentence, you will not have to work so hard. Questions may refer to the main idea as the central focus, the central theme, or the central idea.

4. can see in the paragraph details that support your opinion of what the main idea is.

Read the first paragraph of the practice passage and state the subject of the paragraph. If you said, "the Maya," you will need to proceed to step 2 to state a more specific topic. You would ask yourself what *aspect* of the Maya the author was discussing. If you said "accomplishments of the Maya" as the *subject*, you would be unable to be more specific in step 2, and you would simply proceed to stating in a sentence that the author wants you to understand about the accomplishments of the Maya. The step of finding a TOPIC is merely a tool to make sure that you take your thinking to a level that is as specific as possible. If you are already THERE at that appropriately specific level, be happy and continue.

Your mental flowchart would look something like this (The arrows indicate that there must be a valid relationship between items connected by the arrows):

SUBJECT → TOPIC ⟷ MAIN IDEA ⟷ DETAILS

Here's an example:

children→ learning styles of children ⟷
(Subject)   (Topic)
children have several different learning styles
             (Main Idea)

Appropriate details would give specific examples of some of those styles, allowing you to see that your statement of main idea and topic were both correct.

If the passage discussed just *one* style, you would know your *main idea* was incorrect.

Using the logic of the flowchart can help you determine if your thinking "fits" the passage. Every level of generality (subject, topic, main idea, detail) contributes something to your understanding of other levels and provides you with checks and double checks. The double arrows flow in two directions to indicate that no reader processes print in a strict general-to-specific, or specific-to-general, pattern. Although each reader may have a preferred style, the double arrows show that readers switch gears, moving back and forth from the general to the specific as they search for meaning.

When reading for topics and main ideas, do not "study" the details. Just read them and notice what kinds of details appear in various locations of the passage. Let your reading be driven by the purpose of gaining a sense of the main idea, organization, and purpose of the paragraph. Use the details to see if they develop, support, or refute your educated guess of what each main idea is. Just as you don't shut your eyes while driving simply because your primary goal is to arrive at your destination, and you are not particularly interested in every small detail of the day's drive, you will not shut down your mind to detail. Detail will help you judge the appropriateness of your impressions of the nature and purpose of what you are reading. On the other hand, you will not attempt to commit every detail to memory.

Now answer question 1 of the practice passage and check your thinking (and flowchart) against the one provided in the answer explanation. Read the remainder of the passage carefully. Don't try to memorize. Remember, the passage will always be there for your reference. Then answer questions 4 and 7, checking your answers and reading the explanations. For additional practice, state the main ideas of paragraphs 3, 4, and 5.

Recall that the main idea is a sentence, not a title.

Your statements of main idea for paragraphs 3, 4, and 7 should be similar to these:

> Paragraph 3: Using the natural growth cycle of the area and effective arrangements of plants, the Lacandon pack the *milpas* with plants. (Notice that the main idea does not "rattle off" the details, but rather summarizes them.)

> Paragraph 4: When the yield of the *milpas* begins to drop, it is allowed to lie fallow, but remains useful to the Lacandon.

> Paragraph 5: Political events that began in the 1940s and modernization have threatened the old ways of the Lacandon.

Congratulations! You have now arrived at your destination. Now you must return home. Your reading has enabled you to complete each day's trip, arriving safely at your destination. As you return home, the remaining GMAT questions will send you to specific "tourist attractions" for specific purposes. Remember, your only job is to make the prescribed tours and answer questions correctly.

These are questions that will require you to *use* the information in the passage to conclude, evaluate, judge, predict, and determine the author's attitude and purpose and also tell how or why the author presented his case in a particular way. When you read for information that is *implied* in the passage, you are *making an inference or inferring*.

Use the information gained from your overview and initial reading to locate information rapidly. Questions that require you to read between and beyond the lines are difficult, require thought, and must be based entirely upon information the passage has provided. Unless you are absolutely positive of your choice, you should quickly refer to the passage to be certain that your information is correct.

Your "map" and "trip to your destination" should provide you with a fairly clear idea of where to look for various pieces of information as you check.

No questions will evaluate your background knowledge. All questions are passage-dependent. Your opinions and decisions must be based entirely upon what the author has told you. If you believe you are being asked for an opinion, remember that it is the *author's* opinion, not your own, that really matters.

Your answers must be based upon ALL the information in a passage. Unless the question directs you to a specific piece of information, decisions about the reading must be based upon *everything* the passage has said. You should not base a response on anything less than a single sentence. If you are referred to a specific sentence or specific lines in the passage and asked to determine the author's intended meaning, you should read information *around* that sentence or those lines, as well, so that you are considering the information in its context.

For example, assume that the text reads as follows: Some legislators lend overwhelming support to a flat-rate income tax, as do isolated elements of the general population. Many legislators and most citizens, finding themselves perplexed by the entire tax structure, simply don't know where to commit their support.

A question asks you to determine, according to the passage, what public opinion is regarding the flat tax. If you zip through the text, find the first reference to a flat tax located right after the words "overwhelming support," and decide that the public opinion is one of "overwhelming support," you will miss the question, as documented in the sentence following the reference to the flat tax.

As you visit tourist attractions, answering the author's questions, the following suggestions will help you notice the author's intended message:

Watch for transition words. Transition words are intended to guide you in following the author's thoughts and organization. They can be loosely grouped in several categories. A few examples of each type are included to give you the general idea.

More to Come, Same Type of Information As Before
> and, moreover, also, in addition, next, a final reason, similarly, furthermore

Change of Direction—Contrasting Information to Follow
> although, however, rather, but, nevertheless, conversely, yet

Sequence Signals
> next, now, first, after, later

Clarification to Follow
> for example, for instance, such as, similarly, as an illustration

Please Notice This
> major, vital, primary, central—any word that means *most* important

Reason-Result Relationship
> since, because, as a result, cause (-s, -ed, -ing), consequently, therefore (Watch for cause-effect relationships *without* transition words.)

Comparison Signals
> like, similarly, more, less, fewer

Don't Be So Sure
> apparently, maybe, almost, seems, could, might, probably, was reported/ alleged

Definition
> is, is called, can be referred to as, is known as

Notice the organization patterns used in paragraphs. There are commonly used patterns that authors rely heavily upon in organizing information. The author must decide, before beginning to write, what the point of each paragraph is, and how that point will be made in the paragraph. Commonly, authors generate paragraphs in which the main point is brought to the reader's attention by using an organizational pattern as a vehicle (illustration-example, definition, comparison-contrast, sequence, cause-effect, or description). You should be familiar with each type of paragraph, for spotting one as you read can make your task easier. However, you should also know that several patterns may appear in the same paragraph.

Spotting the paragraph type is a tool that may aid your cause, but it should not become a process that distracts you from considering what you are reading. The presence of various transition words in a paragraph may help you identify the paragraph pattern. Common patterns are described below:

Illustration-example: The author uses either one long illustration or several shorter examples to make the point in the paragraph. Typically, the order of the examples makes very little difference, and cumulatively they lead the reader to the main point. The first paragraph of the practice passage uses illustration-example to make the point that the Mayan accomplishments were noteworthy.

If the main point of a paragraph were that talented individuals may not do well in traditional educational settings, this point might be made by citing the educational experiences of Edison and Einstein, who were both considered unteachable by their early teachers.

Cause-effect: Cause-effect relationships may be presented with or without transition words. They may be stated or implied. Perceiving these relationships is of the utmost importance in higher-level comprehension. Consider the following paragraph:

Before the railroad arrived on the scene in the Great Plains, most citizens were farmers who met the needs of their families by growing their own food and who obtained what they needed within their geographical locality. With the railroad came improved ability to move goods from one location to another, making it unnecessary for each man to provide his own nourishment by farming. Citizens relocating could arrive without undergoing the rigors of stagecoach travel, and cities grew at railroad stops. Men left the farms to work in the cities . . . .

The arrival of the railroad *caused* some changes in American life that a careful reader should recognize while reading.

Definition: In a paragraph of definition the author goes to great length to explain a special or technical term to the reader. Consider the following (bare-bones) paragraph:

A typical tragic hero is one who falls from great height as a result of a "tragic flaw." The flaw, a character defect that may have previously lain dormant, manifests itself during the tragedy as a result of circumstances that are beyond the immediate control of the hero. Many writers of tragedy have interpreted the "fall" as one from a position of royalty or nobility. Oedipus, Macbeth, and Julius Caesar are characters who typify this view of tragedy.

Comparison-contrast: In a paragraph of comparison and contrast, the author's point is made by presenting likenesses, differences, or both. Consider the following paragraph:

Before World War II the typical American woman was expected to be in her home caring for her children, cooking, and attending to family affairs. Meal preparation was an elaborate affair that was expected to occupy considerable portions of the homemaker's day. As women entered the work-force during the war, replacing the men who had vacated a variety of jobs to join the military, the expectations of society changed. Recipes appeared that featured shortened preparation time, giving acknowledgment to the fact that many women had joined the workforce. The point is that the role of women (and their approach to cooking) changed.

One might argue that this is really a *cause-effect* paragraph since the war *caused* the change in the role of women. For our purposes, either view is acceptable, since we are using the pattern as a vehicle to follow the author's thought, not as an exercise in rhetoric.

Sequence of events: Incidents are presented in chronological, or time, order. The overall pattern of your practice passage was sequential since it began with the Spanish conquest and ended with the present time. Noting sequence is useful beyond simply listing events in time order. In noting the sequence, and then in asking yourself what this particular sequence really means, you will approach the underlying meaning.

Be aware of the author's craft: Questions of craftsmanship (for example, questions 2 and 10 of your practice passage) may ask you to tell *why* the author included certain information. Noting transition words and looking for organizational patterns will help you. The same patterns occur on a sentence level, on a paragraph level, and on a passage level.

Watch the author's use of language: While single-word adjectives and adverbs are most obviously helpful, verb usage gives us clues that are equally as important. While we all recognize the difference between an inquisitive child and a nosy child, we should also notice the difference between a person's walking into the room, sauntering into the room, or slithering into the room. The absence of words that carry with them certain tones of meaning is likely to mean that we are reading material of a technical or scientific nature in which the author has made a serious effort to avoid contaminating the material with any sort of emotional overlay.

Use the same skills you use in real life to "get the message" on all levels: Reading involves getting the message on a surface level as well as on deeper levels, understanding what is stated, what is implied, and what might be expected as a result. Reading involves reading "the lines," reading "between the lines," and reading "beyond the lines." Reflect on a time when an adult authority figure said, "No, you can't go to that movie [game, party; fill in the blank with your most vivid recollection]." Consider all the possible meanings of that single literal statement: 1. *You* can't go, but your sister can. 2. You can't go to that *movie*, but you can go to another type of activity. 3. You can go to *another* movie, but not *that* movie. 4. You can't leave the house for any purpose. In a situation like this, you probably knew *exactly* what the adult meant; it is unlikely that you had to ask questions to gain clarification. The same factors that gave you clear and certain enlightenment in that situation will give you the same enlighten-ment as a reader who moves smoothly from surface meaning to deep meaning.

Some of the factors that led you to understanding were: the general context of the comment, specific details that preceded and followed the comment, the tone of the comment, the volume of the comment, the body language that accompanied the comment. There was no need for you to consider these factors individually; it was simply that your experience enabled you to process them simultaneously and *understand*. You were probably also able to predict that this would not be a good time to ask for an increase in your allowance.

Practicing with materials that demand the skills you will use on the GMAT will provide that helpful experience in interpretation. It will also be beneficial to you to practice judging the tone, intensity, and body language, if you will, of reading material of varied content and difficulty.

ANSWERS AND EXPLANATIONS TO THE READING COMPREHENSION PRACTICE QUESTIONS

1. Explanation: This is a main-idea question. Your main-idea mental flowchart would be similar to this:

   Maya→ civilization of the Maya→ civilization of the Maya seemed impressive→ details such as calendar, buildings, frescoes, math, writing kept 14 million people alive. The correct choice (and the one that should be most similar to your thought progression) is D. You should reject A because it speaks only of the calendar, which is just one detail of many provided. In addition, choice A assumes an unjustified cause-effect relationship, suggesting that its emergence during the Dark Ages somehow made the Gregorian calendar less accurate than the Mayan calendar. Reject choice B, which emphasizes the number of Maya, another detail. Reject choice C, which emphasizes the concurrence of the Mayan civilization and the Dark Ages. Choice E, which does not specifically mention the Maya, but which refers to "older civilizations" and is too general to fit the paragraph.

2. The correct answer is C. This question asks you to understand the author's organizational scheme. The presence of mahogany or cedar (indigenous or native vegetation) indicates to the Lacandon that the land is too wet. Choice A should be rejected because the presence of mahogany or cedar trees does not prove that the Lacandon are successful. Choice B should be eliminated because mahogany and cedar trees ARE indigenous vegetation. Since the trees in question are not there as a result of the Lacandon's preservation efforts, choice D is not appropriate. A transition statement is one that serves as a bridge between two ideas; choice E should be eliminated because the trees are not mentioned as a vehicle to link ideas.

3. The correct answer is B. The passage states that the Lacandon watch indicator plants to determine when to plant certain of their crops. It can be inferred that the plants bloom when natural conditions are appropriate and that this is a better gauge of planting time than an arbitrary date. Choice A can be eliminated since the passage states that the Lacandon FLED, indicating that their move was a necessity, not a choice. Furthermore, the reader cannot assume that they fled in order to improve agriculture. Choice C is tempting since

the Lacandon do have certain types of agricultural knowledge that modern farmers do not have. It would be correct to say that the Lacandon are more successful in cultivating forest land than modern farmers are, but there is no basis to make a statement indicating that they are in general "more advanced." Choice D suggests a cause-effect relationship not intended in the passage. While it is true that the animals come to the regenerating *milpas*, it is not true that the Lacandon regenerate the *milpas* simply to attract animals. Choice E can be eliminated because the Lacandon are now using machetes rather than pulling weeds by hand.

4. The correct answer is D. This is a main-idea question. Your mental flowchart should have resembled this one: the *milpas*→ selecting and clearing the *milpas*→ selecting and clearing the *milpas* is an intricate process→ details of support (determining the type of soil, studying native plants that grow there to gain more information about what kind of land this is, clearing a fire wall, burning the area of the *milpas*). You would eliminate choice A because the differences between Lacandon and ancient Mayan methods are not discussed in the article. Choices B and D are details of the paragraph rather than its central idea. Neither issue is discussed at length or elaborated upon in the paragraph. Choice E is mentioned in the paragraph in passing, but is not an idea that is further developed.

5. The correct answer is A. This is an inference question, one that requires the reader to evaluate information provided in the passage. You would select choice A because the length of time the *milpas* may be used depends on weed control (paragraph 4, sentence 1). Inability to do daily weeding is mentioned in paragraph 5, sentence 5. Weed entrenchment caused by machete use is mentioned (paragraph 5, sentence 6). Both weed-related statements are among the "circumstances that make it difficult for them to continue their traditional way of life." The reader may infer that weed control is highly important, and since no other choices receive this degree of emphasis in the passage, the reader may infer that weed control is of primary importance. Choice B could be eliminated because indicator plants tell the Lacandon *when* to plant. Choice C should be eliminated since the number of years the *milpas* is *cultivated* is a better key to its productivity than the number of years it lies fallow. Choice D must be avoided because of lack of evidence. While the reader knows that crops are layered (paragraph 3), no information is implied regarding the relative importance of layering and crop placement. Choice E is not viable since a major point of the passage is that the Lacandon have used the ancient knowledge.

6. The correct answer is C. This inference question is made more difficult because of the number of inferences that must be considered in order to find the correct answer. The best approach is to consider each possible inference separately, accepting or rejecting it. Then make your answer choice. You would accept choice I. If certain plants, as paragraph 2 states, indicate that the land is too wet, then there must be other plants indicating by their pres-

ence or absence that the land is too dry or just right. II is a correct inference. A fallow *milpas* is planted with trees, and (according to paragraph 4) planted with some "useful species." Furthermore, animals that visit the fallow *milpas* are used by the Lacandon. Inference III cannot be accepted on the basis of the content of this passage. Although it is clear that the Lacandon did not benefit from the move, no information is provided to enable the reader to judge the government's action. Inference IV is correct. The Lacandon system is one that was practiced for hundreds of years. Although the planting arrangement is among the knowledge that has been handed down through the centuries, one cannot assume that a Lacandon farmer would necessarily know *why* crops should be placed as they are. Maybe the knowledge is just, "Don't plant the beans beside the corn." Inference V is correct because the peasants had to own the land in order to be able to sell it to the cattle ranchers. Correct inferences are I, II, IV, and V.

7. The correct answer is A. You can use the same procedure for arriving at the main point of a passage that you use to determine the main idea of a single paragraph. The difference is that the main points of component paragraphs now function as "details" of your passage's main idea. Your "map" would look something like this: Lacandon→ Lacandon farming→ Lacandon people successfully farmed the rain forest of Mexico until very recently→ supporting details (paragraph 1, accomplishments of Maya; paragraph 2, locating and clearing the *milpas*; paragraph 3, plant arrangement in the *milpas*; paragraph 4, the fallow *milpas*; paragraph 5, the decline of Lacandon agriculture). You would reject choice B because the Lacandon neither damaged the forest nor sold their land. Reject choice C because the passage does not focus on the Lacandon as "victims." Reject choices D and E for the same reason: they speak of generalities (ancient methods and "natives" of a region). Always select the choice that, while still summarizing, is as specific to the passage as possible.

8. The correct answer is C. Notice the word *primary* in the question. This is an inference question. Several choices seem possible, since paragraph 4 discusses building material, planting rubber trees, the attraction of animals to the *milpas*, and weeds. It might be tempting to select choice D, since this passage speaks so frequently of weeds and weed-related issues; however, consider that the *milpas* will lie fallow for from five to twenty years, a considerable time if weed removal is the only issue. Choices A and B are related to the fallow *milpas*, but are not the *purpose* of allowing the *milpas* to lie fallow; they are best seen as side benefits. Choice E is far-fetched. The key sentence supporting choice C is this: "When a plot is no longer suitable for intensive cultivation, it is planted with rubber, cacao, citrus, and other trees and left fallow for five to twenty years."

9. The correct answer is D. The passage states that "Each crop has unique soil, water, and light requirements as well as different responses to close associations with every other plant." The requirement most closely related to layering would be light; crops located beneath other crops would require less sunlight

than the plants above. Plants so "layered" would be in extreme proximity, making it probable that they would receive about the same amount of water, nutrients, and soil. Layered plants are not isolated.

10. The correct answer is A. The word *although* signals a contrast. No cause-effect relationship is intended. The author is not considering whether the

milpas is a substitute for the forest (choice C). Although authors do add information for the sake of interest, this choice would be appropriate only if no others worked. E is not an appropriate choice since the issue was not previously stated.

Now try your hand at the following review questions and check your answers carefully.

REVIEW QUESTIONS

Passage 1

A new revolution into the understanding of the roots of the English language is under way. While acknowledging Sanskrit as the form for grammatical forms and vocabulary, scholars are now finding the same ideas in the early Greek and Latin, leading to the conclusion that all three spring from the same source. The finding of this source has intrigued philologists for centuries. The evolution of paper has saved many documents; however, what about those centuries when there was no written form of communication, no paper upon which to salvage the rudiments of language, no way of preserving traditions, folkways, and mores? How do we reconstruct those eons of time?

The focus on language as a psychological phenomenon understood by a small group of scholars has begun to reveal that language is really the product of cultural evolution. When looking into the most aged forms of language, one finds a strange uniformity. A few linguists have even begun to prognosticate that the original language can be recon-

structed piece by piece into the language spoken at the dawn of human civilization.

Mankind has always sought to know about the peopling of the earth. Modern social scientists use the most modern of techniques to uncover hints into that foggy time. Because language is that form that separates man from beast, the curiosity into its evolvement has always been present. Uncovering the evolution of the language will, it is thought, lead to discoveries about how ancient peoples migrated into new lands, what they saw, what they ate, and how they came both to coexist and to collide with one another.

These findings have combined the use of anthropology, psychology, sociology, and linguistics. When combined, these disciplines have revealed that it is language that is the integral part of culture and that binds people together and signals their presence to other civilizations of both man and beast. Thus, as man has evolved, so has his language; and as he has become more intricate and involved, so has his vocabulary.

The conclusion is that new linguistic findings will neatly compare with the conclusions already drawn from a very different area of research. The human creature has produced a "family tree" whose branches closely mirror the branching of languages proposed by linguists and lead to the startling finding that both man and his language descend from a tiny population that lived more than 200,000 years ago.

1. The passage provides information to support which of the following generalizations?

    (A) Observations of the behavior of modern man reflect the culture of the original man.
    (B) Language is essential to the understanding, interpretation, and determination of the evolution of man.
    (C) Only anthropologists are capable of making the conclusions about language.
    (D) The interpretation of language demands the use of writing with paper and pen.
    (E) Seemingly, man's origin was in a number of sites yet to be discovered.

2. According to the author, which of the following is NOT true of investigating language beginnings?

    (A) Determining the survival of the fittest.
    (B) Locating the cradle of civilization.
    (C) Finding any artifacts possible.
    (D) Using the personality indicators.
    (E) Establishing migration patterns.

3. The passage suggests that in seeking the origin of language, many disciplines are involved because:

    (A) all of the determiners of man's beginnings are in language.
    (B) understanding motivation and habit can contribute to the discovery of language's beginning.
    (C) the entire man is involved in language, which is an important factor, but only ONE factor of man's existence.
    (D) treasures might be found, and determining worth is important.
    (E) the beginning of language has long been the concern of ONLY the linguist.

4. The author leads the reader to assume that with samples of writings:

    (A) the discovery of language would be more expeditious.
    (B) the alphabet would be explained.
    (C) the language could be determined to be Greek, Roman, or Sanskrit.
    (D) the original language would be readable by modern man.
    (E) the search for language beginnings would still be incomplete.

5. The idea of Sanskrit as the ONLY beginning language is:

    (A) indicated by this author.
    (B) enhanced by the findings of a group of scholars.
    (C) countermanded by findings concurrent with other languages.
    (D) definitively supported by the findings of scholars in disciplines other than linguistics.
    (E) can no longer be considered since it is not written.

6. The conclusion reached by this writer is that:

(A) language is so dissident that its origins will never be known.

(B) modern science is making discoveries of linguistic origins available.

(C) language is unnecessary to determine culture.

(D) the piecing together of man's beginnings may indicate that language is not an important part of our evolution.

(E) man's beginnings have been narrowed significantly to a place in time.

Passage 2

For every piano student who loves to practice, there are probably ten who think the road to Hell is paved with ivory. So, when a teacher declared the ability to make piano lessons fun, testers became curious.

The development of software for the computer for use in teaching piano is a unique concept indeed. While self-teaching courses for piano have been around for ages, this is the first self-teaching piano course that gives students feedback the way a real teacher would give and adapts its lessons for individual students.

For a generation caught up in the Nintendo craze and its attendant "games," such an approach to teaching piano is indeed appealing. Tailoring the piano program to work with the Nintendo system is also a positive approach to appealing to the reluctant piano student. Imagine, Mom and Dad are *urging* the would-be piano student to *use* the Nintendo. Where there have been woeful wailings about too much Nintendo,

imagine being *sent* to the Nintendo to play an amusing game.

The screen displays an electronic keyboard exactly like that of the piano. The student finds that it is touch-sensitive so that, like the piano, the harder the key is struck, the louder the notes sound. In addition, the electronic keyboard reproduces five other keyboard voices, a pipe organ, a vibraphone, and a harpsichord! What fun to switch from instrument to instrument!

There is also the availability of 122 other voices including flutes, drums, horns, and human choruses. The student is thus encouraged to master the lessons necessary in order to move to the instruments preferred, especially the drums.

The concept of the program is similar. The beginning lessons are like live instruction, except the explanations deal with monitor and keyboard. The early lessons are easily mastered, as the electronic keyboard displayed on the screen imitates the student's moves. When the note is played correctly, the student is prompted to move to the next note. As the program continues, the lesson plan is adjusted to provide more practice where needed.

When the student falters, an alarmed *"oops!"* flashes on the screen. The student is urged to try again. Like a real teacher, the Nintendo can sense the patterns of mistakes and suggest remedies. It can scold like a real teacher, too. If the student bangs on the keys in frustration, he is warned to "stop pounding."

The Nintendo version also tells the sloppy student: "We could write another piece using just the notes you missed!"

7. This passage provides information to support which of the following generalizations?

   (A) All children should learn to play the piano.

   (B) Playing the piano is a dull and uninteresting activity.

   (C) Using tools determined to be fun can promote learning.

   (D) Playing the piano by computer is impossible.

   (E) With a computer, all things are possible.

8. It can be inferred from the passage that computerized piano instruction provides all of the following EXCEPT:

   (A) positive feedback.

   (B) negative feedback.

   (C) individualized instruction.

   (D) human presence.

   (E) rewards for learning.

9. The inclusion of a number of voices is included in the lesson to do all of the following EXCEPT:

   (A) provide instruction in more instruments than the piano.

   (B) provide harmony.

   (C) encourage students to master their lessons.

   (D) increase incentives.

   (E) create interests in various instruments.

10. The teaching technique of the computer closely resembles that of the teacher in all of the following EXCEPT that it:

   (A) delivers lectures as a teaching technique.

   (B) critiques performance.

   (C) rewards good work.

   (D) adjusts to the student's ability level.

   (E) shows the image of a human while the message is relayed.

11. The author indicates that most young students prefer the voice of the:

   (A) teacher.

   (B) piano.

   (C) drum.

   (D) organ.

   (E) harpsichord.

12. Scolding a student for sloppy playing, the computer voice uses:

   (A) irony.

   (B) caution.

   (C) criticism.

   (D) sarcasm.

   (E) satire.

Passage 3

In teaching piano via the computer, some lessons are disguised as video games. Students learn notes, for example, by shooting ducks on a staff of music. They tap out proper rhythm to keep a cartoon of "Roboman" from falling off of a bridge. There is a parachute game that teaches chords.

After every group of lessons, the student is invited to "visit" the practice room, where there is a choice of practice pieces ranging from "Chopsticks" to "Greensleeves" to "Hound Dog." Students can elect to practice with one hand or with both hands, or to allow the computer to demonstrate.

There are more than one hundred practice pieces, more than twice as many as earlier versions of teaching piano by computer. The student can also record and play back student performances and track the progress over several selections. The teacher can use the record selection to track several students simultaneously.

The course takes from six to twelve months to complete, depending upon the amount of practice the student is willing to do. A music professor testing the program thought the time estimate to be rather optimistic. The reality is that the student will *not* come out of the program as an accomplished pianist. But the student can learn to read music, play chords, and perform rhythms with optional fingering.

The program is not without its flaws. There is the presence of a metronome in the computer program. In real-life instruction, a teacher uses the metronome sparingly and only with fairly advanced students. The computer program uses it regularly to monitor student progress. This can be quite intimidating, and the incessant ticking can confuse the student as well.

The computer often asks the impossible of the student. Notes struck only slightly late caused the computer to default and require the entire selection to be redone. The constant chiding for "pounding" became annoying when the student was playing softly.

And there is the big question: Does this type of teaching make practice and learning fun? The main issue seems to be that if a student does *not* like to play the piano, that student will not like the computer version either. The price is equal to twenty private lessons, and parents can get a good sense of the student's acumen for piano. If the student succeeds here, the tendency to continue with a human teacher will be enhanced. The student who dislikes it still has the inexpensive electronic keyboard with which to experiment.

13. The passage provides information to support which of the following generalizations?

   (A) Playing the piano is a difficult feat.
   (B) Learning music is not for everyone.
   (C) Finding out what one can do through the computer can be helpful.
   (D) The computer program is not a sure way to become an accomplished pianist.
   (E) Students are excited over the computer program.

14. The length of the course can be a factor that will influence the purchaser in all of the following EXCEPT:

   (A) there is no guarantee.
   (B) the possibility of completing the course in six to twelve months provides a framework for goal-setting.
   (C) the student has enough material to keep busy.
   (D) student progress is a determining factor.
   (E) the amount of practice is not specified.

15. The types of games provide:

   (A) entertainment while learning.
   (B) exposure to classical elements.
   (C) nonsubliminal instruction.
   (D) disguised learning.
   (E) nonviolent competition.

16. The inclusion of so many selections of music provides:

    (A) entertainment for the family.

    (B) something for everyone.

    (C) gradual increases of difficulty.

    (D) recognition of various eras of music.

    (E) holiday selections.

17. There are flaws in the system that include:

    (A) necessity of consistency.

    (B) continual practicing.

    (C) a pesky voice.

    (D) a metronome.

    (E) an on-screen report.

18. The conclusion one might make is that:

    (A) real pianos are not necessary anymore.

    (B) using the computer can enhance instruction.

    (C) the computer is not the best way to teach.

    (D) the computer is the best way to teach.

    (E) all great pianists learned on a computer.

ANSWERS TO REVIEW QUESTIONS

1. The correct answer is B. The point is carefully made that "Uncovering the evolution of the language will, it is thought, lead to discoveries about how ancient peoples migrated into new lands, what they saw, what they ate, and how they came both to coexist and to collide with one another."

2. The correct answer is A. Determining the "survival of the fittest" would not necessarily help in the discovery of languages' beginnings. In fact, determining those who do not survive might create more of a discovery.

3. The correct answer is B. While A is partly true, not *all* of the determiners are in language, but language evolved. But when psychologists and sociologists are able to determine habits and patterns, the beginnings of language become more clear.

4. The correct answer is A. The point is made that with the discovery of paper, culture can be more readily saved, leading to the assumption that without paper this could not happen.

5. The correct answer is C. The inclusion of the findings of psychologists and sociologists supports a correlation with Greek and Roman.

6. The correct answer is E. The discovery of man's beginnings 200,000 years ago seems to be the positive for determining time and place.

7. The correct answer is C. The Nintendo plays games and the student in question is accustomed to having time limited there. Using the Nintendo to teach piano is a welcomed activity by the student.

8. The correct answer is D. No human presence is needed.

9. The correct answer is B. There is no mention that the additional 122 voices provide harmony to the piano music. The implication is that each voice represents a separate instrument and is played separately, as is the piano voice.

10. The correct answer is E. There is no indicator of the image of a human delivering the lecture.

11. The correct answer is C. The article states: "The student is thus encouraged to master the lessons necessary in order to move to the instruments preferred, especially the drums."

12. The correct answer is D. The article states: "We could write another piece using just the notes you missed!"

13. The correct answer is D. The student will not be an accomplished pianist, may hate the practicing, but still enjoy the playing.

14. The correct answer is A. The lack of a guarantee can be detrimental to some purchasers of the program. However, the presence of no guarantee allows for the nonmusical student to experiment without pressure.

15. The correct answer is A. The student is allowed to do all the things that regular video games do, but with the requirement for performance via music rather than instinctual reaction.

16. The correct answer is C. The student chooses the selections according to individual preference.

17. The correct answer is D, the metronome. "In real-life instruction, a teacher uses the metronome sparingly and only with fairly advanced students."

18. The correct answer is B. The computer program takes one to twelve months and then the human instructor is needed.

$$\frac{15}{18} \quad 83\%$$

Unit 4

The Critical Reasoning problems on the GMAT may be characterized as arguments that you must analyze and evaluate. Each argument consists of three components: a *conclusion* and *facts* to support the conclusion as well as *assumptions* that relate facts to conclusion.

Consider the following sample argument:

United Artists' most recent film is based on a best-selling novel and stars Brad Heartthrob. Therefore, the film is expected to do well at the box office.

The first step in tackling a problem such as this is to identify the three components.

Fact 1: film based on popular novel

Fact 2: star is Brad H.

Conclusion: film should be successful

The assumptions are unstated (hereafter, *hidden assumptions* or HA's); they are additional pieces of information about each fact in the argument. For example:

HA for fact 1: Fans of book are expected to help sales of tickets.

HA for fact 2: Brad H.'s presence should contribute to the success of the film.

These HA's help you see how the facts lead to the conclusion given.

You can often, though not always, distinguish fact from conclusion by spotting "signal words" that introduce each component. Conclusions may be signaled by words like *as, therefore* (as in the example above), *so, thus,* and *in conclusion.* Detailed facts, which are more specific than conclusions, may be flagged by such words as *due to, because, a study shows,* and *in addition.*

Once you *identify* the components, you must answer questions that ask you to *evaluate* these components.

The GMAT offers three basic question types in the Critical Reasoning section, each focusing on one of the three components. They are, in descending order of frequency: the Additional Fact question, the Conclusion question, and the Hidden Assumption question. Following is a discussion of each type.

Additional Fact Questions

Additional Fact questions focus on the supporting details of the argument. You are presented with a complete argument and are asked to *either* weaken or strengthen the argument by considering five multiple-choice statements. These statements are new facts about the argument, which you must accept as true. Some Additional Fact questions ask for a weakening of an argument; others ask you to strengthen what you read.

For example, in the preceding argument regarding United Artists' new movie, an Additional Fact question might offer the following five choices:

(A) The film will play only in urban areas.
(B) The producers of the film have cast their next movie without Brad H.
(C) The film is not likely to win an Academy Award.
(D) The book upon which the film is based is a worldwide hit.
(E) Brad H.'s popularity ratings are at an all time low.

If the question asks you to weaken the argument, you will choose a statement that either weakens a given fact or disputes an HA and, in consequence, makes the conclusion illogical. Choice E best weakens this argument by disputing the HA that Brad H. will attract moviegoers. The conclusion no longer logically follows.

For a strengthening choice, you would choose a statement to bolster a given fact or HA to support the conclusion. The correct strengthening choice here would be D, for it elaborates on the fact about the book's popularity, thus supporting the conclusion.

Wrong choices, called distracters, usually follow a pattern. They may touch upon the argument only marginally (such as choices A, B, and C); they may accomplish the opposite task (strengthen when you want to weaken); or they may not be the best strengthening or weakening statement (e.g., choice A is not the best weakening statement when compared to E).

Conclusion Questions

At times, arguments will be missing the conclusion. A series of facts, along with unstated HA's, will lead to the final statement that you then must supply. Sound arguments are linear, in that you can usually predict in what general direction the facts are headed. You may also consider the conclusion an inference: you are inferring the conclusion from the specific statements and associated HA's.

Consider the following argument:

The newest book by England's favorite political satirist has received warm praise from critics. In addition, there is a strong market in the UK for political satire.

You are now asked to choose the statement that best completes this series of facts.

(A) Political satire transfers well to other countries.
(B) The author of this book is a member of Parliament.
(C) People read book reviews before making purchases.
(D) Such a book will be banned by the current Tory government.
(E) The book will do well in British bookstores.

Although a series of facts does not usually have just one possible conclusion, there is only one best conclusion in the given choices. The best answer here would be one that follows the path the facts are taking but goes one step beyond the facts by making a more general statement. The answer is E.

Distracters may read too much into the facts. In the preceding example, statement D is a choice that steps too far from the given facts; you cannot reach the conclusion from the facts alone. Another sort of distracter introduces more detail instead of making the leap to a conclusion; examples of this would be choices A, B, and C.

Hidden Assumption Questions

To tackle the Hidden Assumption question, you must directly face the hidden statements that underlie the argument. Each HA statement meets the following two criteria: it gives you extra information about the existing facts instead of supplying new facts, *and* it must be true for the argument to be valid.

For example:

The Republican candidate for governor of State X will get the education vote. More than $200,000 was donated to her campaign fund by the state teachers' union. The same union donated only half that amount to the Democratic candidate's campaign.

You would then be asked to choose the statement that best reveals an assumption underlying the preceding argument.

(A) The Republican candidate is a former teacher.

(B) The Democratic candidate will lose the election.

(C) A donation usually indicates approval of a candidate.

(D) Most teachers have joined the union.

(E) Unions endorse candidates in each election.

An excellent test of an HA is the "negation test": If you think a choice is an HA, negate it and see if it seriously affects the validity of the conclusion—the right answer should.

For example, suppose you are struggling between choices C and D. If choice D were falsified, you would now have the statement "Most teachers have not joined the union." Does that mean that the Republican candidate is now likely not to win the education vote? She may still.

Negation of choice C gives you, "Donations usually don't indicate approval of a candidate." This negative statement does the most direct harm to the conclusion that the Republican candidate will get teachers' votes; it makes the connection between the facts and conclusion illogical. Choice C is correct.

Distracters associated with this question type include choices such as D, which doesn't support the conclusion enough; as well as irrelevant statements such as A, B, and E; besides being marginal to the problem, these statements also introduce new facts, whereas choice C elaborates on the facts given.

Summary

The best possible suggestion for doing well on the Critical Reasoning section of the GMAT is to understand how the problems are constructed, what the test is asking you to do, and then to practice. Keep in mind the following steps when tackling this section of the exam:

1. Read each paragraph carefully.

2. Distinguish conclusion from fact and consider the HA's based on given facts.

3. Read the question carefully.

4. For Additional Fact questions, make sure of your task (strengthen or weaken) before proceeding. Choose the statement that directly addresses a given fact, HA, or conclusion.

5. For conclusion questions, think in a linear fashion: Where are the facts headed? Choose a statement that goes one logical step further from the given facts.

6. For HA questions, remember to choose a statement that supports the argument with more information about given issues. Try the "negation test."

7. Complete as many practice problems as you can. Note which question types you have the most difficulty with and which distracters trip you up most often. Being aware of your own strengths and weaknesses on this section should help you be more successful at it.

CRITICAL REASONING REVIEW QUESTIONS

Additional Fact Questions

1. The trend in the United States banking industry of several small community banks merging into fewer large, interstate banks has consumers worried about service. Many consumers worry that, as banks become larger and fewer in number, the competition in the banking industry will decrease, and consumers will lose services and will pay higher fees. As a result, many consumers are urging their legislators to enact legislation to limit the size of any individual banking company.

The fears of the consumers discussed in the preceding argument would most be allayed by which of the following facts?

(A) The federal government recently enacted legislation to increase the maximum amounts of deposits that will be insured.

(B) A limitation on mergers between interstate banks could be construed as a violation of the Commerce Clause of the United States Constitution.

(C) Larger banks are able to generate higher profits for their investors with lower levels of risk.

(D) As a bank increases in size, its overhead costs for operation will decrease, and it will be able to improve the services to its consumers.

(E) Large governmentally operated banks have functioned successfully in other countries for many years without any decrease in services to their consumers, and with service fees that are less than many private banks.

2. Of the graduating students from Governor Smith Academy, a private high school, 93 percent go on to college. From Eastern High, the public high school in the same city, only 74 percent go on to attend college. As a result, many parents with children about to enter high school believe that Governor Smith Academy gives students a better education than they can get at Eastern High School.

Which of the following statements, if true, would cast the most doubt on the conclusion about Governor Smith Academy?

(A) Until 1992, Governor Smith Academy was exclusively a girls' school, but Eastern High School has always been coeducational.

(B) Governor Smith Academy requires students to pass an admissions examination before entering, but Eastern High School admits all applicants who live in the city.

(C) Eastern High School has problems with severe student violence during school hours.

(D) Governor Smith Academy has a higher percentage of students attending Ivy League colleges than any other high school in the state.

(E) Eastern High School receives its funding from local property taxes, while Governor Smith Academy receives funding from tuition costs and from alumni donations.

3. *Television Advertisement:* "Leonardo da Vinci was a genius, and everyone recognizes his art as the greatest in the world. At Acme Art Supply Company, you can get modern, improved art supplies so you will be able to create works of art even better than Leonardo da Vinci's."

Which of the following statements, if true, most shows the flaws in the claims made in this advertisement?

(A) Leonardo da Vinci, at the time he was painting in the fifteenth century, was sponsored by patrons who provided him with the opportunity to use the best materials then available in the world.

(B) Most of the customers of Acme Art Supply Company are hobbyists who are not professionally trained and who do not realize the value of using professional-quality art supplies.

(C) The art supplies at Acme Art Supply Company are more expensive than similar supplies available at any other supply store in the area.

(D) An art professor from the local community college supplies all of his students with materials from the Acme Art Supply Company.

(E) Even when using supplies from Acme Art Supply Company, many amateur artists create projects that art critics call inferior and childish.

4. While some job loss is inevitable in a changing American economy, the current phase of corporate "downsizing" has reached the level of becoming an epidemic. Many employees are being fired simply to enhance profits for top management and company shareholders. Even so, some economists see improvement in the fact that the total number of new jobs being created is increasing at a steady rate.

Which of the following facts, if true, would show that the economists' view of improvement is incorrect?

(A)   The new jobs that are being created come as a result of governmental tax incentives to large corporations.

(B)   Corporate downsizing is not actually resulting in higher profits for shareholders as expected.

(C)   Many of the new jobs are low-paying entry-level positions that do not provide health-care or pension benefits.

(D)   A separate study of corporate shareholders reveals that many of them would be willing to forgo higher profits in order to increase hiring levels.

(E)   Other countries are experiencing similar increases in job creation.

5.   High doses of niacin in a person's diet have been shown to raise HDL levels, which doctors call the "good" cholesterol, and to lower levels of triglycerides and LDL, the so-called "bad" cholesterol. As a result of this study, some nutritionists are now recommending diets that are extremely high in niacin.

Which of the following facts, if true, would most question the recommendations of the nutritionists?

(A)   The original study was conducted on a sample of hospital patients who initially had dangerously high cholesterol levels.

(B)   High doses of niacin have been shown to reduce the clotting factors in blood, thereby reducing a person's ability to heal after receiving minor injuries.

(C)   When levels of triglycerides decrease, patients report higher levels of stamina and improved physical endurance.

(D)   The doctors reporting the results of the study had once been discredited for falsifying the results of their research.

(E)   Other studies have shown that the body eventually reaches a maximum plateau with regard to its LDL level.

Conclusion Questions

1.   A consumer watchdog group recently reported the results of a study surrounding the deregulation of the U.S. banking industry, which has allowed for more mergers between banks and has allowed banks more freedom in setting their interest rates for their customers. The report shows that customers now have access to higher savings interest rates and lower borrowing interest rates. At the same time, banks are reporting record profits.

From the results of this study, what can be concluded about the effect of deregulation of the American banking industry?

(A)   Deregulation has hurt the banking industry by limiting the number of options allowed to the customers of small local banks.

(B)   Deregulation has been a success because it has given the banks the ability to raise their interest rates and force their customers to pay the highest rates possible.

(C) As a result of the deregulation of the banking industry, investments in other industries will increase, resulting in a stronger economy nationwide.

(D) Deregulation has been a success because it allows both the banks and their customers to realize savings and profits at the same time.

(E) Because deregulation has lowered the interest rates that customers will have to pay, many banks will be driven out of business in the near future.

2. A report from the head of the city's school department reveals that the school department had a large surplus in its health insurance account at the end of 1994.

The same report showed that at the end of 1995 the school department suffered a deficit of $300,000 in the same account. Despite this decline, the school department reported no significant changes in costs over the two-year period studied.

What can be concluded from the results of this report?

(A) The school department's budget for health costs is excessively high.

(B) More teachers were provided with health insurance payments during 1995 than in 1994.

(C) The costs related to operating the school department's health insurance program must have increased dramatically from 1994 to 1995.

(D) The health insurance account received less funding in 1995 than it did in 1994.

(E) The health insurance budget will show an even greater deficit in 1996 than it did in 1995.

3. In a game of Monopoly, if a player owns a hotel on Boardwalk, he must own both Boardwalk and Park Place. If he owns a hotel in Marvin Gardens, he must own Marvin Gardens and either Boardwalk or Park Place. If he owns Park Place, he also owns Marvin Gardens.

If the player described above does not own Park Place, which of the following conclusions may be drawn?

(A) The player owns a hotel on Boardwalk.

(B) The player owns a hotel in Marvin Gardens but does not own a hotel on Boardwalk.

(C) The player owns Marvin Gardens and Boardwalk, but does not own a hotel on either property.

(D) The player does not own a hotel on Marvin Gardens.

(E) The player does not own a hotel on Boardwalk.

4. As the temperature of a solution of water and chemical X increases, the reactivity of chemical X also increases. As the temperature of a mixture of chemical X and chemical Y increases, the reactivity of chemical Y increases but the reactivity of chemical X remains constant. As the temperature of a solution of water and chemical Y increases, the reactivity of chemical Y remains constant.

From the above information, what conclusion may be drawn?

(A) A change in temperature has no effect on the reactivity of chemical Y.

(B) A change in temperature has no effect on the reactivity of chemical X.

(C) When combined, chemical X and chemical Y display different reaction levels than when studied separately.

(D) When combined with chemical X, chemical Y demonstrates the same reactive properties as it does when it is studied alone.

(E) A change in temperature produces a greater effect on chemical Y than it does on chemical X.

5. *Advertisement:* Seven out of ten municipal employees choose Green Arrow Underwriters as their health insurance provider.

From the information provided in this advertisement, what further conclusion may be drawn?

(A) Green Arrow Underwriters has the cheapest premium rates of any other insurance company available.

(B) All other health insurance providers, excluding Green Arrow Underwriters, provide services to less than 50 percent of the municipal employees.

(C) Municipal employees need less health insurance coverage than employees in other industries.

(D) Green Arrow Underwriters provides more valuable services and better customer assistance than any of its competitors.

(E) Except for Green Arrow Underwriters, the health insurance industry is suffering a decline in the rate of obtaining new customers.

Hidden Assumption Questions

1. In order to ensure a successful vote on the issue of abortion rights, the governor is pressuring the leaders of the state political party to replace several delegates to the national convention. The governor is insisting that certain individuals with a history of voting in favor of abortion rights be replaced with new delegates who have voted against abortion rights in the past.

The governor's actions demonstrate that he is making which of the following assumptions?

(A) Voting on abortion issues is an important part of the national political agenda.

(B) The current delegates will probably not share the governor's views on such issues as the national budget or federal spending limits.

(C) The proposed new delegates will continue to vote on abortion issues in the same way that they have voted in the past.

(D) The national delegation will not have an opportunity to vote on any issues other than abortion rights.

(E) Governors of other states will be making similar changes to their states' delegations, so that the issue of abortion rights will be guaranteed to be decided as this governor desires.

2. To travel on public transportation from City Hall to the convention center, the most direct route requires passengers to ride the Blue Bus line to Center Street, collect a token at Center Street station, then ride the subway to Middle Street. This weekend there will be a big political rally, so the city should hire extra token vendors for the Center Street station.

The conclusion for the preceding argument depends upon which of the following assumptions?

(A) The mayor will be working at City Hall this weekend and will need to use public transportation to go to the convention center.

(B) There is no way to get from City Hall to the convention center without going through the Center Street station.

(C) The political rally will draw thousands of people to the city from all parts of the state.

(D) Because of the political rally, traffic at the Center Street station will increase.

(E) The city's public transportation system does not allow passengers to buy tokens in advance.

3. The newspaper just reported that a man won this year's national baking contest for the first time in its history. The contest has used both male and female judges for many years. This must

have been the first year that the contest was open to male participants.

Which of the following is an assumption upon which the speaker's conclusion is based?

(A) The newspaper has never before reported the results of the national baking contest.

(B) Male judges are more likely to vote for a male contestant than a female contestant.

(C) Men have tried to enter the national baking contest for several years but have been denied.

(D) Men are generally superior to women and would be able to beat them in any kind of competition.

(E) Men are better bakers than women and could win this contest every year.

4. Today is Tuesday and yesterday was Monday. Therefore, tomorrow will be Wednesday.

This speaker's conclusion depends on which of the following assumptions?

(A) Wednesday is the day that precedes Thursday.

(B) Tuesday always follows Monday.

(C) If, in any given week, Tuesday follows Monday, then Wednesday will follow Tuesday.

(D) Every week consists of seven days arranged in a particular order.

(E) The speaker always schedules a certain meeting to occur on Wednesday.

5. In the animal world, when any species becomes overpopulated, naturalists observe that the animals begin fighting among themselves and become cannibalistic. Sociologists have been reporting for years that the human population of the world is growing at an uncontrollable rate, and the world's cities will be overpopulated in about ten years. As a result, human societies will begin experiencing a global breakdown and we can expect an international war within the next ten years.

Which of the following statements represents a hidden assumption upon which the preceding argument depends?

(A) Human social behaviors follow the same patterns as the behaviors of animals.

(B) Major cities do not always have adequate budgets to provide resources for all their residents.

(C) Naturalists and sociologists use the same research methods in studying their subjects and reporting results.

(D) The study that showed cannibalistic patterns in animals studied only carnivorous animals.

(E) The population of the world has doubled in the past five years, and its rate of growth will increase even faster in the future.

ANSWERS TO REVIEW QUESTIONS

Additional Fact Questions

1. (D) The consumers assume that bank mergers will result in higher fees and fewer services. Choice D contradicts this assumption and would be the best response for weakening the conclusion. Choice A is irrelevant, as nothing in the argument addresses insurance of deposits or federal involvement. Choice B is irrelevant because the argument is not concerned with whether or not such mergers are allowable but whether they are a good move for consumers. Choice C focuses on investors and not customers. Choice E is somewhat informative, but is not as directly addressed to this argument as choice D.

2. (B) This argument assumes that the percentage of students moving on to college reflects on the quality of the education at the two high schools. Choice B contradicts this assumption by suggesting that the students at Governor Smith Academy may have entered school with better academic abilities than the public school students. Choice A is incorrect because nothing in the argument suggests any difference between male and female students. Although student violence might reflect on students' abilities to learn, choice C is irrelevant to this particular argument without more information. Choice D addresses the end results of the students attending college, but too many other factors could be part of this result. Choice E is insufficient without more information in the argument that taxes or funding have anything to do with the quality of the education.

3. **(E)** This argument depends on the assumption that the quality of an artist's materials leads directly to the quality of the finished product and that no other factors are involved. Choice E shows that even with the best materials, some artists do not create excellent art. Choice A is incorrect in that it does not recognize the individual quality of the artist. Choice B does not address the quality of the finished product and so is insufficient. Choice C is irrelevant because nothing in the argument suggests that the cost of the materials is a factor. Choice D is insufficient without additional information about the finished works of art produced by the students involved.

4. **(C)** The economists assume that creation of any new jobs is a positive sign. Choice C questions this assumption by showing that the new jobs may be inadequate to support individuals or families, and thereby may not improve the general economy. Choice A provides irrelevant information, because the conclusion does not depend on the reason for the creation of the new jobs. Choices B and D are incorrect because the argument does not seem to be concerned with the motivation for downsizing. Choice E provides irrelevant information, because nothing in the argument suggests

that the economies in other countries are related to this issue.

5. **(B)** The nutritionists assume that people should take in high levels of niacin because high niacin shows a positive result in this one study. Choice B suggests that high doses of niacin may have a negative effect, despite the positive results of this study. Choice A might have an effect, but without further information linking the effect of this information on the result, the information provided is insufficient to weaken the argument. Choice C would strengthen, not weaken, the argument. Choice D illustrates an "ad homonym" attack by questioning the researchers and not the quality or results of the research. Choice E is irrelevant to the argument.

Conclusion Questions

1. **(D)** The information given in the argument shows that banks have benefited from deregulation by collecting higher profits, and customers have benefited by receiving better interest rates for both saving and borrowing. The best answer, then, is D, which reports both of these results. Choice B has the correct result, that deregulation has been a success, but it gives reasons that contradict the premises provided in the argument. Choices A, C, and E all go too far beyond the scope of the provided information and therefore do not make acceptable conclusions.

2. **(D)** The premises of this argument show that while costs remained constant for this two-year period, the final budget decreased. From this, a logical conclusion would be D, that the budget received less funding to start with in 1995 than in 1994.

   Choice A may or may not be true, but there is not enough information in the argument to make this decision. Choices B and C contradict the premise that costs remained constant. Choice E may be a reasonable inference for the future, but without additional information about the 1996 budget, it stretches too far beyond the information provided and is not as good a response as D.

3. **(E)** This is a direct "if-then" type argument. Choice A is incorrect because the first sentence of the argument required Park Place in order to own a hotel on Boardwalk. This same reasoning explains why choice E must be correct. [In fact, notice that A and E are direct opposites of one another—one of them must be true!] Choices B and C could both be true but cannot be concluded from the information given. Choice D is incorrect because the player could still own a hotel in Marvin Gardens by owning Boardwalk instead of Park Place.

4. **(C)** Choices A, B, and D are all incorrect because the premises show that both chemical X and chemical Y display changes in reactivity when combined. Choice C is the best answer because it reflects this change. Choice E is incorrect because nothing in the argument addresses the degree of the changes on either chemical.

5. **(B)** This is a very short statement, so there is not much that can be concluded. Choices A, C, D, and E all state conclusions that require information outside the scope of the information provided. Only choice B remains limited to the known material. If Green Arrow provides coverage to "seven out of ten"— i.e., 70 percent, the rest of the industry can only cover the remaining 30 percent. Therefore, choice B is a reasonable conclusion.

Hidden Assumption Questions

1. **(C)** The governor is choosing new delegates based upon their past voting records. This shows the assumption that they will continue to vote the same way, so choice C is the best answer. Choices A and D are incorrect because the importance of the issue is not made part of this argument; this argument is based upon the fact that the governor is making these decisions for whatever reason he chooses. Choice B is irrelevant to this particular argument because nothing in this argument mentions the budget issues. Choice E is incorrect because there is nothing in the argument to suggest that activities in other states have anything to do with this governor's actions.

2. **(D)** This argument concludes that additional token vendors are necessary as a result of the rally.

Choice D shows the best assumption, that the rally will increase use of the Center Street station, where token vendors will be required. Choice A is incorrect because there is no reason to believe that the mayor has anything to do with this particular rally. Choice B is incorrect because the argument merely says that the route discussed is the "best" route, not the "only" one. Choice C is probably the second-best choice, because it suggests that the traffic on public transportation will increase, but D is better by making this statement directly. Choice E is not directly related to the argument without making the connection directly to the Center Street station.

3. **(E)** The speaker considers that a man won in the first year that men were allowed to enter and assumes that men could win this contest anytime they enter. Choice E, therefore, is the best answer. Choice D is similar, but it goes too far beyond the argument. Choices A, B, and C do not address the results of this contest and are therefore irrelevant.

4. **(C)** This appears to be a simple argument because it presents a relatively common issue, the days of the week, but analysis may be complicated. Choices A, B, and D are all true statements, using the standard calendar, but they do not directly address this as a logical argument. Only choice C provides information that could be a hidden assumption for this argument, linking the information in the premise with the conclusion. Choice E is irrelevant because nothing in the argument suggests any connection to the speaker's meeting schedule.

5. **(A)** This argument begins with information about animal behavior and then makes a conclusion about human behavior. Thus, the best assumption is one that connects human behavior to the observed animal behavior. Choice B is incorrect because nothing in the argument considers cities' budgets. Choice C is close but is not as good an answer as A because it does not address the conclusion reached. Choice D might question the validity of the result of the animal study, but it does not make any connection to the human behavior. Choice E is incorrect because it makes no connection between the animal study and human behavior.

Unit 5

Although scored separately from the rest of the GMAT, the 1-hour Analytical Writing Assessment will be the first of the tests you will be taking. It consists of writing two 30-minute essays on two topics that you will not know ahead of time and for which you will not be given any choice. One of the topics will ask for an analysis of an issue, and the second will call for an analysis of an argument.

Why essays?

You may be wondering why a student of business management is required to demonstrate his or her writing skills. However, when you stop to consider what good management entails, it becomes clear that one of the most important qualities of a good manager is effective communication, which includes both written and verbal skills. Hence, this is the reason for the essay component of the GMAT.

Scoring

Each essay will be scored on a scale of 0 to 6 and an NR for a blank paper or a nonverbal response.

The general qualities that are taken into consideration for the essays are:

(A) thoughtful, perceptive analysis of the issue or a critique of the argument presented.

(B) development of ideas clearly, persuasively, or logically, using insightful reasons and/or relevant examples.

(C) coherent organization.

(D) language fluency.

(E) grammar, usage, and mechanics.

Based on the level of skill demonstrated in the above-mentioned areas, following is a summary score guide.

6 An outstanding essay
5 A strong essay
4 An adequate essay
3 A limited essay
2 A seriously flawed essay
1 A fundamentally deficient essay
0 An essay that is completely illegible or not written on the assigned topic

The essays are scored using the "holistic" method, which means the score will be based on the overall impression your essay makes rather than on attention to minor details. Each essay will be read by two readers, and if their scores fall within a point of each other's, which is usually the case, the two scores are averaged. If the scores differ by a wider spread, then the essay will be read by a third reader.

Since the holistic method is used, the readers must read with deliberate speed, averaging about 2 minutes per essay. Pet peeves like penmanship (unless it's illegible) and minor infractions of grammar and usage are supposed to be set aside in arriving at a score. Also, since you, the writer, have only 30 minutes to write each essay, cross-outs and edits are expected as all you have time for is one draft. However, be careful to make any changes you deem necessary as neatly and legibly as you can.

As mentioned earlier, the Analytical Writing Assessment requires that you write two 30-minute essays, one analyzing an issue stated in the topic, and the other critiquing an argument presented in the topic. The "issue" topic generally presents you with two positions on a subject, and you are expected to state and defend the position of your choice using reasons and persuasive examples. The "argument" topic presents you with one strong position on a subject, and you are expected to critique or find fault with the line of reasoning and the evidence employed to support it. Each essay should consist of 4 to 5 paragraphs.

However, before discussing the differences in how to approach the two types of essay, it might be worthwhile to focus on the common elements of a good essay.

What Is an Essay?

An essay is basically an attempt in writing to express a personal opinion on a subject as convincingly and persuasively as possible.

The fundamental *fives* of a good essay are:

1. Content
2. Cogency
3. Clarity
4. Coherency
5. Correctness

Let's discuss each one separately.

Content: People read an article to the end only if they find it interesting, surprising, or informative. However, in the context in which you are writing these essays, and the fact that the readers must read each essay to the end, use your common sense. Don't try too hard to be unique in your perspective or reasoning, but on the other hand, avoid clichés and well worn expressions. Try to avoid melodrama and under-

statement. In other words, take the subject seriously, respond honestly, and use examples from your own experience, the experience of people you know of personally or through your reading, and that will take care of ensuring both the individuality of your essay and the reader's interest.

Cogency: If you express your thoughts and point of view about the subject in the context of what you know and believe at the time of writing, you will have no difficulty in being convincing. Remember, no one expects you to be an expert on the subject of the topic since you will have no prior knowledge of what the topic will be. If you use a voice that is not yours, not only will the reader find it difficult to understand you, but the quality of your writing will suffer.

Clarity: Time is of the essence here, both for you and the readers. Avoid vague, general words and try to use concrete, specific examples and language to avoid wordiness.

Example:

Scenes depicting violence on many TV entertainment shows have a bad influence on viewers, particularly the young.

Better:

Scenes depicting violence on TV, such as the beating of a youth by a gang of teens in an episode of "In The Heat of the Night," encourage violence in young people, because they rarely show the result of violence, such as broken limbs or the bloodied face of the victim.

Coherency: Even though you explore several ideas about a subject in your essay, they should all be related or connected. Therefore, it is important that as you move from one idea to another, you make clear the connecting link between them. These connecting links can express opposition or contrast, addition or amplification, result or effect, relations in time or place, and time sequence to mention a few. This is where transitional words or phrases become very important, particularly when you move from exploring an idea in one paragraph to exploring another in the next paragraph. Some of the more frequently used transitions signal the following:

Opposition:

but, however, contrary to, although, nevertheless, in opposition to, on the other hand

Example:

Many people believe that marijuana is extremely harmful under any circumstance, and therefore should remain illegal. *However,* people with pain-wracked bodies cannot live without its soothing effect and believe it should be legalized.

Addition:

furthermore, in addition, moreover, further, also

Example:

Many teenage couples cannot handle financial pressure. *Furthermore,* they find it difficult to cope with the responsibility of raising a child.

Result:

consequently, thus, as a result, therefore

Example:

Ralph worked overtime all summer. *As a result*, he was able to pay his tuition fees for the fall.

Time:

sometimes, often, never, seldom, after, now, before, frequently, at the same time

Example:

Edward is determined to make a success of himself. He *often* tries to work on several different projects *at the same time.*

Place:

here, there, above, elsewhere, farther on, below

Example:

There are several dilapidated houses at the intersection of the roads. *Farther on* down Lake Road, however, several beautiful mansions dot the lakefront.

Time sequence:

first, second, last or lastly, then, before, next, finally

Example:

Pamela worked on her term paper into the early hours of the morning. *Finally*, at 7 a.m., she went to bed exhausted.

Correctness: If you have reached this stage in your formal education, chances are that you have more than a basic command of the English language. However, when you must write under the pressure of time, it is likely that you will make some mistakes in your essay. Sometimes, as you read over the essay, you will discover that you can express the same idea or information more succinctly. In other instances, you will find that you have inadvertently made an error in grammar or punctuation. As this may occur in both essays, this may be the appropriate time to point out some of the more common errors.

Sentence errors

Fragments:

The coolie tried to run away from the rampaging elephant. Although it was useless.

The coolie tried to run away from the rampaging elephant, although he knew it was useless.

Run-ons:

John and Mary wanted to leave, but their hostess asked them to stay, so they sat down again with the Johnsons to have another cup of coffee, and John even had another piece of the apple pie that Rita Johnson had made.

John and Mary wanted to leave, but their hostess asked them to stay. So they sat down again with the Johnsons to have another cup of coffee. John even had another piece of the apple pie that Rita Johnson had made.

Verb errors

The sergeant was ask to report to the colonel immediately.

The sergeant was ask*ed* to report to the colonel immediately.

Preposition errors

Parents often do not trust their children. As a result, they create avoidable problems.

(Who does the "they" refer to—the children or the parents?)

Watch out for those places where you have repeated a word or omitted a word in the rush to finish the essay on time.

Note: It is a good idea to skip a line between your written lines. This will give you room to edit, cross out, or add words legibly.

Process

There are four basic steps to writing an essay:

1. Read (about 2 minutes).

2. Plan (about 3 minutes).

3. Write (about 20 minutes).

4. Proofread and edit (about 5 minutes).

Step 1—*Reading the topic*

Read the topic to determine the issue to which you are asked to respond.

This may sound like unnecessary advice, but bear in mind that if you don't read the topic at least twice, you are in danger of misunderstanding what the issue is, or going off on a tangent. If that happens, you may wind up with a score of 0, no matter how well you write.

Step 2—*Planning the essay*

Unlike the essays or papers you write at home or in the library where there is no time limit and that you can write, revise, or even start over, this GMAT essay must be as near perfect as you can make it the first time you write it. The fact that you have a limited amount of time makes it imperative that you know ahead of time what your position is, what your main supporting points are, and what examples or information you will use to explain your points.

Step 3—*Writing the essay*

Once you have a basic plan, you are ready to begin.

Introduction: Many people find it difficult to begin at the beginning, partly from anxiety, and partly because the introduction or the first paragraph must be clear, strong, and effective. In fact, isn't it logical that you can introduce a subject better if you know what it is and how it is developed? Ask any author of a textbook, and you will discover that the introduction to the book was the last section written.

Body: It is a good idea to leave a few lines at the top of the first page for the introduction and begin by writing the second paragraph. We will discuss in the following section what the second and following paragraphs of the essay should cover for both kinds of analysis.

Conclusion: If the body paragraphs of your essay have done their jobs well, the concluding paragraph needs only to restate briefly your position and summarize the supporting ideas. If you have time, a sentence (or two) that suggests new areas of action or a solution can be included.

Step 4—*Proofreading and Editing*

Next to planning, this is the most crucial part of your essay. You must spend the last 4 to 5 minutes checking for errors that you made in your haste to finish on time. Some of these were discussed in the previous section under Correctness. Also, look out for words you may have omitted or repeated in haste, a punctuation mark that is either unclear or left out, letters in a word that have been transposed, and wordiness; then make the necessary corrections. Finally, only if you have time, change any words or phrases that you don't think express your idea clearly.

Writing the essays

I. *Analysis of an issue*: The analysis topic presents you with two positions on a subject. You are required to choose one position and explain the reasons for your choice.

Topic

There is a growing body of people who feel that affirmative action should be ended because it encourages reverse discrimination, exacerbates racial tensions, and throws doubt on the worth of any achievement by a member of a minority. However, there is also a large body of people who believe that the best way for white America to make reparations for slavery and other forms of discrimination against minorities is not only to continue, but to expand affirmative action programs.

Which position do you find more compelling? Explain your position using reasons and/or examples drawn from your personal experiences, observations, or readings.

Step 1. *Read* the topic to determine the issue and choose your position:

Position A—End affirmative action

Reasons

(A) reverse discrimination
(B) racial tensions
(C) devalues minority achievement

Position B—Continue and expand affirmative action

Reasons

(A) reparation for slavery
(B) other forms of discrimination

Notice that once you have read and analyzed the topic, you practically have an outline for your essay, particularly since the reasons to defend the position are also stated in the essay. All you have to plan beyond this is to think of examples to illustrate each of the supporting reasons. If you do not like all or some of the reasons presented, or if there are no reasons stated in the topic, spend a couple of minutes brainstorming for more and add them to the lists.

Let's see if we can come up with additional reasons:

Position A—End Affirmative Action

Reasons

(D) fails to challenge some recipients to do their best

(E) can actually inhibit sense of self-worth

Position B—Continue and expand affirmative action

Reasons

(C) helps to break down social segregation

(D) diminishes suspicions and prejudices between the groups through familiarity

Step 2. *Plan* Now you can create a brief outline for either position that will look somewhat like this:

Position A:

Paragraph 1—Introduction: End affirmative action

Paragraph 2—Reason A: encourages reverse discrimination

Paragraph 3—Reason B: throws doubt on the worth of a minority person's achievement

Paragraph 4—Reason C: does not build self-esteem in a recipient

Paragraph 5—Conclusion: restate your position and summarize the reasons once again

Position B:

The same format applies except that you state the opposing position in the introductory paragraph and present your reasons in paragraphs 2, 3, and 4. Again, the concluding paragraph will restate your position and summarize the reasons.

Step 3. *Now you're on your own. Write the essay!*

Step 4. *Proofread and edit (remember to save a few minutes for this step).*

Analysis of an Argument

The argument topic presents you with one strong, clear position on a controversial topic. What you are required to do is to find fault with the reasoning expressed in the argument and the evidence on which the argument is based. You are also expected to present alternative means by which the problem can be better remedied.

Topic:

The United States has one of the highest rates of murder in the world. Law enforcement agencies seem unable to cope with this problem. The only way to decrease the murder rate in the United States is to mandate the death penalty for murder.

How persuasive do you find this argument? Explain your point of view by analyzing the line of reasoning and the use of evidence in the argument. Discuss also what would make the argument more persuasive or would help you better evaluate its conclusion.

Step 1. *Read* the topic to identify the premises and the conclusion. Remember that your job here is to find fault or demonstrate the weakness in both the premise and the argument.

Premises:

A. The United States has one of the highest murder rates in the world.

B. Law enforcement agencies are unable to cope with the problem.

Conclusion: The only way to decrease the murder rate is to mandate the death penalty for murder.

Step 2. *Plan*

Paragraph 1—Introduction: Fault with the first premise—too general. How high is the rate? Is it increasing? Many countries' records are incomplete or nonexistent.

Paragraph 2—Fault with the second premise—Most countries do not have as efficient a record of tracking down murderers as the United States does, both because of technological sophistication and police training. This may partially explain the high statistics.

Paragraph 3—Fault with the conclusion: Very few murders are premeditated—most are committed in the heat of passion. (Cool, calculated murders are often committed for profit or by deranged minds; the first group of perpetrators considers the risk worth taking, and the second group is not even aware of the consequences.)

Paragraph 4—Fault with the conclusion: There are already several states where the death penalty is legal. None of them has demonstrated any appreciable decrease in murder when compared to states where it is not legal.

Paragraph 5—Conclusion: Thus, the death penalty is not a viable solution (restate why). Alternative—What might work better is to remove existing loopholes in the current penal system, such as parole from a life sentence. Life imprisonment should mean imprisonment for life.

Of course, you need to explain your points in greater depth than in the preceding outline. But the most important thing to remember is that in an argument, you must distinguish between the premise (or premises) and the conclusion and present evidence or reasoning to demonstrate the weaknesses in both. If you have time, you should indicate alternative solutions that you think may be better remedies.

Step 3. *Now write!*

Step 4. *Proofread and edit*
Good luck!

ADDITIONAL TOPICS FOR PRACTICE

Analysis of an Issue

1. The juvenile crime rate in the United States has been increasing steadily in the past few years and shows no signs of abating. Some people place the blame for this situation on lack of parental involvement and on personal responsibility on the part of juveniles. Others believe that the government's lack of commitment to successful youth-oriented programs such as Head Start, Job Corps, and drug treatment centers is where the blame lies.

2. Recently, President Clinton signed a $265-billion defense authorization bill, one of the provisions of which requires the Pentagon to discharge troops who have HIV, the virus that causes AIDS. Those who support this provision believe that the combat readiness of the military is jeopardized by the presence of troops with HIV. Those who plan to have the ouster provision repealed claim that people who live with HIV are able to lead productive lives, provide for their families, and contribute to the country's security and well-being.

3. A new kind of war against cancer is being waged among the pharmaceutical companies, the Food and Drug Administration, and many physicians on one side; and patients, their families, and their physicians on the other. The first contends that chemotherapy is the only scientifically proven treatment to combat cancer, and no alternative treatments should be included. In opposition, patients and their families, as well as their physicians, maintain that patients have a right to control their own lives, which includes the right to choose companion therapies.

4. Although the cold war era has ended, many people still believe that their causes are worth dying for. Some give their lives for their countries, others for their religions, and still others for their families or personal beliefs. Unless we can persuade these people that giving up their lives for their cause is useless, and even counterproductive, in the long run, the world will never be rid of war.

5. In recent years one of the ongoing controversies in our society and in the courts is the issue of prayer in public schools. People on both sides of the issue base their arguments on the Constitution of the United States that guarantees freedom of religious expression. Since prayer is the essential common element in all religions, time should be set aside for prayer in all American public schools.

Analysis of an Argument

1. Immigrants, both legal and illegal, have drained the nation's resources by stealing jobs from American citizens, overtaxing the public school system, and overburdening public assistance services such as health and housing. The only solution to this deteriorating situation is to declare a moratorium on immigration for a few years and to deport illegal immigrants immediately.

2. In developed and developing nations, hunger, poverty, disease, and illiteracy ravage the lives of countless men, women, and children every day. At the

same time, a large chunk of each nation's budget is devoted to increasing its arsenal of weapons and troops for use in real, imagined, or concocted hostility and war between tribes, ethnic groups, and neighboring nations. Unless this proclivity to war-making and warmongering is reversed, there will be nothing left worth fighting for since we will have destroyed humanity.

3. The landmark communications bill that President Clinton recently signed removes most prior restraints on companies in the communications industry in the spirit of free and open markets as a spur to competition. However, one of the provisions in the same bill places restrictions on the dissemination of pornographic material and other forms of indecent expression on the Internet. This is a blatant violation of one of the most dearly held freedoms of Americans, set forth in the First Amendment: the right of free speech and expression.

4. The cost of a college education is skyrocketting, as the availability of student loans and scholarships is shrinking. This situation is leading to many capable and deserving students being denied the right to a college education. These academically gifted students should be assisted by the federal government to attend the college of their choice.

5. The United States is a rich and colorful tapestry of ethnic groups—an intricate mosaic of cultures, religions, and social rituals. However, it is also a Tower of Babel of innumerable languages and dialects. If this country is to develop its unique identity through communication, understanding, and respect for its diversity, we must make English the official language of the nation.

Unit 6

Each GMAT test contains two multiple choice mathematical problem solving sections. You will be allotted 25 minutes for each section, and each section will contain 16 questions. The questions in this section are based on the mathematics that is usually covered in high school mathematics classes—arithmetic, algebra, and geometry.

There are two different types of arithmetic questions that will appear on the GMAT—one that asks you to perform a computation (add the fractions, multiply the decimals, manipulate the percents), and one that asks you to solve a word problem. Similarly, there will be algebraic computation problems (solve the equation, factor the expressions, manipulate the square roots), as well as word problems. As far as the geometry problems are concerned, you will only be asked to solve problems by working with geometric properties. You will not need to create proofs or state definitions.

In the following pages, you will find a thorough review of all of the mathematics covered on the GMAT. First, read the hints and strategies below, and remember them when you begin to practice problem solving.

HINTS AND STRATEGIES FOR MULTIPLE CHOICE MATH QUESTIONS

1. If you are not able to answer a question in one or two minutes, leave the question and move on to others. Each question, regardless of how easy or hard it is, is worth only one point. Wasting time on a very hard question may mean you won't have time to work on a number of easier ones.

2. Do not waste any time doing computations that are not necessary. Remember that one of the five answers must be the correct one. Estimate as much as you possibly can as you try to determine which of the five answers must be correct.

3. You will not be given any scrap paper on which to out work problems. You must do all of your writing in the margin of the test booklet. Be sure to write as small as you can to conserve space.

4. Do not worry if there are questions that you cannot answer. You can still get a good score even if you only answer slightly more than half of the questions correctly.

5. Be careful (especially when solving geometry problems) to give your answer in the same units of measure as the multiple choice answers.

6. All fractions that appear as the answers to questions will be expressed in reduced form. Therefore, if you solve a problem and obtain a fraction as the answer, this fraction must be reduced before you will find it among the multiple choice answers. Similarly, all square root answers must be expressed in reduced form. In geometrical problems involving π, look at the answer choices to determine if you are supposed to leave the answer in terms of π or use the approximate value $\dfrac{22}{7}$.

7. Of course, you are not permitted to use a calculator to perform your computations. This means that you should brush up on the rules for multiplying and dividing numbers with decimals, etc. However, the problems are, in general, designed to not include messy computations. If you ever find yourself thinking, "I wish I had a calculator to help me with this problem," carefully look at the problem once again. There is quite possibly an easier way to do it that you may have missed.

8. If the answer you obtain does not match one of the choices given, it might still be right. Try to write it in a different form, and then see if it matches. For example, the answer $x^2 + 3x$ can also be written as $x(x + 3)$.

9. Roughly speaking, the questions within each section of the GMAT are arranged in increasing order of difficulty. If, for example, you are working on a question in the first third of a particular math section, and there is an answer that seems obviously correct, it probably is correct. On the other hand, if you are working on a question on the last third of a section and there is an answer that seems immediately and obviously correct, it is advisable to mentally challenge the answer. Take another look at the problem to see if you can find anything wrong with the answer.

10. Make sure to answer the question that is being asked. People sometimes get a problem wrong because, after finding the value of x, they choose that value as the answer, when the problem was actually asking for the value, for example, of $x + 2$.

11. If you are stuck, try looking at the multiple choice answers. Since one of them has to be right, the answers may give you some idea of how to proceed.

In the following section, all of the mathematics that you need to know for the GMAT is reviewed. Once you have studied it—and understood it—you can then take the mathematics portion of the exams included in this book, with confidence.

ARITHMETIC

Whole Numbers

Definitions

The set of numbers {1, 2, 3, 4, . . .} is called the set of *counting numbers* and/or natural numbers, and/or sometimes the set *of positive integers.* (The notation { } means "set" or collection, and the three dots after the number 4 indicate that the list continues without end.) *Zero* is usually not considered one of the counting numbers. Together the counting numbers and zero make up the set of *whole numbers.*

Place Value

Whole numbers are expressed in a system of tens, called the *decimal* system. Ten *digits*—0, 1, 2, 3, 4, 5, 6, 7, 8, and 9—are used. Each digit differs not only in *face* value but also in *place* value, depending on where it stands in the number.

Example 1

237 means:

$(2 \cdot 100) + (3 \cdot 10) + (7 \cdot 1)$

The digit 2 has face value 2 but place value of 200.

Example 2

35,412 can be written as:

$(3 \cdot 10,000) + (5 \cdot 1,000) + (4 \cdot 100) + (1 \cdot 10) + (2 \cdot 1)$

The digit in the last place on the right is said to be in the units or ones place; the digit to the left of that in the tens place; the next digit to the left of that in the hundreds place; and so on.

Odd and Even Numbers

A whole number is *even* if it is divisible by 2; it is *odd* if it is not divisible by 2. Zero is thus an even number.

Example

2, 4, 6, 8, and 320 are even numbers; 3, 7, 9, 21, and 45 are odd numbers.

Prime Numbers

The positive integer p is said to be a prime number (or simply *a prime*) if $p = 1$ and the only positive divisors of p are itself and 1. The positive integer 1 is called a *unit.* The first ten primes are 2, 3, 5, 7, 11, 13, 17, 19, 23, and 29. All other positive integers that are neither 1 nor prime are *composite numbers.* Composite numbers can be *factored,* that is, expressed as products of their divisors or factors; for example, $56 = 7 \cdot 8 = 7 \cdot 4 \cdot 2$. In particular, composite numbers can be expressed as products of their *prime* factors in just one way (except for order).

To factor a composite number into its prime factors, proceed as follows. First try to divide the number by the prime number 2. If this is successful, continue to divide by 2 until an odd number is obtained. Then attempt to divide the last quotient by the prime number 3 and by 3 again, as many times as possible. Then move on to dividing by the prime number 5, and other successive primes until a prime quotient is obtained. Express the original number as a product of all its prime divisors.

Example

Find the prime factors of 210.

2)210
3)105
5) 35
    7

Therefore:

210 = 2 · 3 · 5 · 7 (written in any order) and 210 is an integer multiple of 2, of 3, of 5, and of 7.

Consecutive Whole Numbers

Numbers are consecutive if each number is the successor of the number that precedes it. In a consecutive series of whole numbers, an odd number is always followed by an even number, and an even number by an odd. If three consecutive whole numbers are given, either two of them are odd and one is even or two are even and one is odd.

Example 1

7, 8, 9, 10, and 11 are consecutive whole numbers.

Example 2

8, 10, 12, and 14 are consecutive even numbers.

Example 3

21, 23, 25, and 27 are consecutive odd numbers.

Example 4

21, 23, and 27 are *not* consecutive odd numbers because 25 is missing.

The Number Line

A useful method of representing numbers geometrically makes it easier to understand numbers. It is called the *number line.* Draw a horizontal line, considered to extend without end in both directions. Select some point on the line and label it with the number 0. This point is called the *origin.* Choose some convenient distance as a unit of length. Take the point on the number line that lies one unit to the right of the origin and label it with the number 1. The point on the number line that is one unit to the right of 1 is labeled 2, and so on. In this way, every whole number is associated with one point on the line, but it is not true that every point on the line represents a whole number.

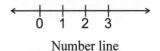

Number line

Ordering of Whole Numbers

On the number line the point representing 8 lies to the right of the point representing 5, and we say 8 > 5 (read "8 is greater than 5"). One can also say 5 < 8 ("5 is less than 8"). For any two whole numbers *a* and *b,* there are always three possibilities:

$$a < b, \qquad a = b, \qquad \text{or} \qquad a > b.$$

If *a = b,* the points representing the numbers *a* and *b* coincide on the number line.

Operations with Whole Numbers

The basic operations on whole numbers are addition (+), subtraction (−), multiplication (· or ×), and division (÷). These are all *binary* operations—that is, one works with two numbers at a time in order to get a unique answer. The operations of addition and multiplication on whole numbers are said to be *closed* because the answer in each case is also a whole number. The operations of subtraction and division on whole numbers are not closed because the unique answer is not necessarily a member of the set of whole numbers.

Examples

$3 + 4 = 7$ a whole number
$4 \cdot 3 = 12$ a whole number
$2 - 5 = -3$ not a whole number
$3 \div 8 = \dfrac{3}{8}$ not a whole number

Addition

If addition is a binary operation, how are three numbers—say, 3, 4, and 8—added? One way is to write:

$$(3 + 4) + 8 = 7 + 8 = 15$$

Another way is to write:

$$3 + (4 + 8) = 3 + 12 = 15$$

The parentheses merely group the numbers together. The fact that the same answer, 15, is obtained either way illustrates the *associative property* of addition:

$$(r + s) + t = r + (s + t)$$

The order in which whole numbers are added is immaterial—that is, $3 + 4 = 4 + 3$. This principle is called the *commutative property* of addition. Most people use this property without realizing it when they add a column of numbers from the top down and then check their results by beginning over again from the bottom. (Even though there may be a long column of numbers, only two numbers are added at a time.)

If 0 is added to any whole number, the whole number is unchanged. Zero is called the *identity element* for addition.

Subtraction

Subtraction is the inverse of addition. The order in which the numbers are written is important; there is no commutative property for subtraction.

$$4 - 3 \neq 3 - 4$$

The $\neq$ is read "not equal."

Multiplication

Multiplication is a commutative operation:

$$43 \cdot 73 = 73 \cdot 43$$

The result or answer in a multiplication problem is called the *product*.

If a number is multiplied by 1, the number is unchanged; the *identity element* for multiplication is 1.

Zero times any number is 0:

$$42 \cdot 0 = 0$$

Multiplication can be expressed with several different symbols:

$$9 \cdot 7 \cdot 3 = 9 \times 7 \times 3 = 9(7)(3)$$

Besides being commutative, multiplication is *associative:*

$$(9 \cdot 7) \cdot 3 = 63 \cdot 3 = 189$$

and

$$9 \cdot (7 \cdot 3) = 9 \cdot 21 = 189$$

A number can be quickly multiplied by 10 by adding a zero to the right of the number. Similarly, a number can be multiplied by 100 by adding two zeros to the right:

$$38 \cdot 10 = 380$$

and

$$100 \cdot 76 = 7,600$$

Division

Division is the inverse of multiplication. It is not commutative:

$$8 \div 4 \neq 4 \div 8$$

The parts of a division example are named as follows:

$$\text{divisor} \overline{)\, \text{dividend}}^{\text{quotient}}$$

If a number is divided by 1, the quotient is the original number.

Division by 0 is not defined (has no meaning). Zero divided by any number other than 0 is 0:

$$0 \div 56 = 0$$

Divisors and Multiples

The whole number b *divides* the whole number a if there exists a whole number k such that $a = bk$. The whole number a is then said to be an integer *multiple* of b, and b is called a *divisor* (or *factor*) of a.

Example 1

3 divides 15 because $15 = 3 \cdot 5$. Thus, 3 is a divisor of 15 (and so is 5), and 15 is an integer multiple of 3 (and of 5).

Example 2

3 does not divide 8 because $8 \neq 3k$ for a whole number k.

Example 3

Divisors of 28 are 1, 2, 4, 7, 14, and 28.

Example 4

Multiples of 3 are 3, 6, 9, 12, 15, . . .

Whole Number Problems

1. What is the prime factorization of 78?
2. What are the divisors of 56?
3. Which property is illustrated by the following statement?

   $$(3 + 5) + 8 = 3 + (5 + 8)$$

4. Which property is illustrated by the following statement?

   $$(5 \cdot 7) \cdot 3 = 7 \cdot (5 \cdot 3)$$

5. Find the first five multiples of 7.

Solutions:

1. $78 = 2 \cdot 39 = 2 \cdot 3 \cdot 13$
2. The divisors of 56 are 1, 2, 4, 7, 8, 14, 28, 56.
3. The associative property of addition
4. The commutative property of multiplication
5. 7, 14, 21, 28, 35

Fractions

Definitions

If a and b are whole numbers and $b \neq 0$, the symbol $\dfrac{a}{b}$ (or a/b) is called a fraction. The upper part, a, is called the *numerator,* and the lower part, b, is called the *denominator.* The denominator indicates into how many parts something is divided, and the numerator tells how many of these parts are taken. A fraction indicates division:

$$\frac{7}{8} = 8\overline{)7}$$

If the numerator of a fraction is 0, the value of the fraction is 0. If the denominator of a fraction is 0, the fraction is not defined (has no meaning):

$$\frac{0}{17} = 0$$

$$\frac{17}{0} \text{ not defined (has no meaning)}$$

If the denominator of a fraction is 1, the value of the fraction is the same as the numerator:

$$\frac{18}{1} = 18$$

If the numerator and denominator are the same number, the value of the fraction is 1:

$$\frac{7}{7} = 1$$

Equivalent Fractions

Fractions that represent the same number are said to be *equivalent*. If m is a counting number and $\frac{a}{b}$ is a fraction, then:

$$\frac{m \times a}{m \times b} = \frac{a}{b}$$

because $\frac{m}{m} = 1$ and $1 \times \frac{a}{b} = \frac{a}{b}$

Example

$$\frac{2}{3} = \frac{4}{6} = \frac{6}{9} = \frac{8}{12}$$

These fractions are all equivalent.

Inequality of Fractions

If two fractions are not equivalent, one is smaller than the other. The ideas of "less than" and "greater than" were previously defined and used for whole numbers.

For the fractions $\frac{a}{b}$ and $\frac{c}{b}$:

$$\frac{a}{b} < \frac{c}{b} \text{ if } a < c \text{ and if } b > 0$$

That is, if two fractions have the same denominator, the one with the smaller numerator has the smaller value.

If two fractions have different denominators, find a common denominator by multiplying one denominator by the other. Then use the common denominator to compare numerators.

Example

Which is smaller, $\frac{5}{8}$ or $\frac{4}{7}$?

$8 \cdot 7 = 56 = $ common denominator

$$\frac{5}{8} \times \frac{7}{7} = \frac{35}{56} \qquad \frac{4}{7} \times \frac{8}{8} = \frac{32}{56}$$

Since $32 < 35$,

$$\frac{32}{56} < \frac{35}{56} \text{ and } \frac{4}{7} < \frac{5}{8}$$

Reducing to Lowest Terms

The principle that

$$\frac{m \times a}{m \times b} = \frac{a}{b}$$

can be particularly useful in reducing fractions to lowest terms. Fractions are expressed in *lowest terms* when the numerator and denominator have no common factor except 1. To reduce a fraction to an equivalent fraction in lowest terms, express the numerator and denominator as products of their prime factors. Each time a prime appears in the numerator over the same prime in the denominator, $\frac{p}{p}$, substitute its equal value, 1.

Example

Reduce $\frac{30}{42}$ to an equivalent fraction in lowest terms:

$$\frac{30}{42} = \frac{2 \cdot 3 \cdot 5}{2 \cdot 3 \cdot 7} = 1 \cdot 1 \cdot \frac{5}{7} = \frac{5}{7}$$

In practice, this can be done even more quickly by dividing the numerator and the denominator by any number, prime or not, which will divide both evenly. Repeat this process until there is no prime factor remaining that is common to both the numerator and the denominator:

$$\frac{30}{42} = \frac{15}{21} = \frac{5}{7}$$

Proper Fractions, Improper Fractions, and Mixed Numbers

Definitions

A *proper fraction* is a fraction whose numerator is smaller than its denominator. Proper fractions always have a value less than 1:

$$\frac{3}{4} \qquad \frac{5}{8} \qquad \frac{121}{132} \qquad \frac{0}{1}$$

An *improper fraction* is a fraction with a numerator equal to or greater than the denominator. Improper fractions always have a value equal to or greater than 1:

$$\frac{3}{2} \qquad \frac{17}{17} \qquad \frac{9}{1} \qquad \frac{15}{14}$$

A *mixed number* is a number composed of a whole number and a proper fraction. It is always greater than 1 in value:

$$3\frac{7}{8} \qquad 5\frac{1}{4} \qquad 11\frac{3}{14}$$

The fraction $3\frac{7}{8}$ means $3 + \frac{7}{8}$ and is read "three and seven eighths."

To Change a Mixed Number into an Improper Fraction

Multiply the denominator by the whole number and add this product to the numerator. Use the sum so obtained as the new numerator, and keep the original denominator.

Example

Write $9\frac{4}{11}$ as an improper fraction:

$$9\frac{4}{11} = \frac{(11 \times 9) + 4}{11} = \frac{99 + 4}{11} = \frac{103}{11}$$

Note: In any calculation with mixed numbers, first change the mixed numbers to improper fractions.

To Change an Improper Fraction into a Mixed Number

Divide the numerator by the denominator. The result is the whole-number part of the mixed number. If there is a remainder in the division process because the division does not come out evenly, put the remainder over the denominator (divisor). This gives the fractional part of the mixed number:

$$\frac{20}{3} = 3\overline{)\begin{matrix} 6 \\ 20 \end{matrix}} \qquad = 6\frac{2}{3}$$
$$\frac{18}{2} \text{ remainder}$$

Multiplication

Proper and Improper Fractions

Multiply the two numerators and then multiply the two denominators. If the numerator obtained is larger than the denominator, divide the numerator of the resulting fraction by its denominator:

$$\frac{3}{8} \times \frac{15}{11} = \frac{45}{88} \qquad \frac{3}{8} \times \frac{22}{7} = \frac{66}{56} = 1\frac{10}{56}$$

Multiplication of fractions is commutative. Three or more fractions are multiplied in the same way; two numerators are done at a time and the result multiplied by the next numerator.

The product in the multiplication of fractions is usually expressed in lowest terms.

Canceling

In multiplying fractions, if any of the numerators and denominators have a common divisor (factor), divide each of them by this common factor and the value of the fraction remains the same. This process is called *canceling* or *cancellation*.

Example

$$\frac{27}{18} \times \frac{90}{300} =$$

$$\frac{27}{18} \times \frac{90}{300} = \frac{27}{18} \times \frac{9}{30} \qquad \text{Divide second}$$
$$\text{fraction by } \frac{10}{10}$$

$$= \frac{\overset{9}{\cancel{27}}}{\underset{2}{\cancel{18}}} \times \frac{\overset{1}{\cancel{9}}}{\underset{10}{\cancel{30}}} \qquad \begin{array}{l}\text{Cancel: 18 and 9 each}\\ \text{divisible by 9; 27 and 30}\\ \text{each divisible by 3}\end{array}$$

$$= \frac{9 \times 1}{2 \times 10} = \frac{9}{20} \qquad \begin{array}{l}\text{Multiply numerators;}\\ \text{multiply denominators}\end{array}$$

Another method:

$$\frac{\overset{3}{\cancel{27}}}{\underset{2}{\cancel{18}}} \times \frac{\overset{3}{\cancel{9}}}{\underset{10}{\cancel{30}}} = \frac{3 \times 3}{2 \times 10} = \frac{9}{20}$$

Cancel: 27 and 18 have common factor 9; 9 and 30 have common factor 3

Note: Canceling can take place only between a numerator and a denominator, in the same or a different fraction, never between two numerators or between two denominators.

Mixed Numbers

Mixed numbers should be changed to improper fractions before multiplying. Then multiply as described above.

Example

To multiply

$$\frac{4}{7} \times 3\frac{5}{8}$$

change $3\frac{5}{8}$ to an improper fraction:

$$3\frac{5}{8} = \frac{(8 \times 3) + 5}{8} = \frac{24 + 5}{8} = \frac{29}{8}$$

Multiply

$$\frac{\overset{1}{\cancel{4}}}{7} \times \frac{29}{\underset{2}{\cancel{8}}} = \frac{29}{14}$$

The answer can be left in this form or changed to a mixed number: $2\frac{1}{14}$

Fractions with Whole Numbers

Write the whole number as a fraction with a denominator of 1 and then multiply:

$$\frac{3}{4} \times 7 = \frac{3}{4} \times \frac{7}{1} = \frac{21}{4} = 5\frac{1}{4}$$

Note: When any fraction is multiplied by 1, its value remains unchanged. When any fraction is multiplied by 0, the product is 0.

Division

Reciprocals

Division of fractions involves reciprocals. One fraction is the *reciprocal* of another if the product of the fractions is 1.

Example 1

$\frac{3}{4}$ and $\frac{4}{3}$ are reciprocals since

$$\frac{\overset{1}{\cancel{3}}}{\underset{1}{\cancel{4}}} \times \frac{\overset{1}{\cancel{4}}}{\underset{1}{\cancel{3}}} = \frac{1 \times 1}{1 \times 1} = 1$$

Example 2

$\frac{1}{3}$ and 3 are reciprocals since

$$\frac{1}{\underset{1}{\cancel{3}}} \times \frac{\overset{1}{\cancel{3}}}{1} = 1$$

To find the reciprocal of a fraction, interchange the numerator and denominator—that is, invert the fraction, or turn it upside down.

Proper and Improper Fractions

Multiply the first fraction (dividend) by the reciprocal of the second fraction (divisor). Reduce by cancellation if possible. If you wish to, change the answer to a mixed number when possible:

Example

$$\frac{9}{2} \div \frac{4}{7} = \frac{9}{2} \times \frac{7}{4}$$ The reciprocal of $\frac{4}{7}$ is $\frac{7}{4}$

because $\frac{4}{7} \times \frac{7}{4} = 1$

$$= \frac{63}{8}$$

$$= 7\frac{7}{8}$$

Mixed Numbers and/or Whole Numbers

Both mixed numbers and whole numbers must first be changed to equivalent improper fractions. Then proceed as described above.

Note: If a fraction or a mixed number is divided by 1, its value is unchanged. Division of a fraction or a mixed number by 0 is not defined. If a fraction is divided by itself or an equivalent fraction, the quotient is 1:

$$\frac{19}{7} \div \frac{19}{7} = \frac{19}{7} \times \frac{7}{19}$$ Reciprocal of $\frac{19}{7}$ is $\frac{7}{19}$

$$= 1 \times 1 = 1$$

Addition

Fractions can be added only if their denominators are the same (called the *common denominator*). Add the numerators; the denominator remains the same. Reduce the sum to the lowest terms:

$$\frac{3}{8} + \frac{2}{8} + \frac{1}{8} = \frac{3 + 2 + 1}{8} = \frac{6}{8} = \frac{3}{4}$$

When the fractions have different denominators, you must find a common denominator. One way of doing this is to find the product of the different denominators.

Example

$$\frac{5}{6} + \frac{1}{4} = ?$$

A common denominator is $6 \cdot 4 = 24$.

$$\frac{5}{6} \times \frac{4}{4} = \frac{20}{24} \quad \text{and} \quad \frac{1}{4} \times \frac{6}{6} = \frac{6}{24}$$

$$\frac{5}{6} + \frac{1}{4} = \frac{20}{24} + \frac{6}{24}$$

$$= \frac{20 + 6}{24}$$

$$= \frac{26}{24}$$

$$= \frac{13}{12}$$

$$= 1\frac{1}{12}$$

Least Common Denominator

A denominator that is smaller than the product of the different denominators can often be found. If the denominator of each fraction will divide into such a number evenly and it is the *smallest* such number, it is called the *least* (or *lowest*) *common denominator*, abbreviated as LCD. Finding a least common denominator may make it unnecessary to reduce the answer and enables one to work with smaller numbers. There are two common methods.

First Method: By Inspection

$$\frac{5}{6} + \frac{1}{4} = ?$$

LCD = 12 because 12 is the smallest number into which 6 and 4 divide evenly. Therefore:

$$12 \div 6 = 2 \qquad \text{multiply } \frac{5}{6} \times \frac{2}{2} = \frac{10}{12}$$

$$12 \div 4 = 3 \qquad \text{multiply } \frac{1}{4} \times \frac{3}{3} = \frac{3}{12}$$

Then:

$$\frac{5}{6} + \frac{1}{4} = \frac{10}{12} + \frac{3}{12}$$

$$= \frac{13}{12}$$

$$= 1\frac{1}{12}$$

Second Method: By Factoring

This method can be used when the LCD is not recognized by inspection. Factor each denominator into its prime factors. The LCD is the product of the highest power of each separate factor, where *power* refers to the number of times a factor occurs.

Example

$$\frac{5}{6} + \frac{1}{4} = ?$$

Factoring denominators gives:

$$6 = 2 \cdot 3 \quad \text{and} \quad 4 = 2 \cdot 2$$
$$\text{LCD} = 2 \cdot 2 \cdot 3$$
$$\qquad = 12$$

Convert to LCD:

$$\frac{5}{6} \times \frac{2}{2} = \frac{10}{12} \qquad \frac{1}{4} \times \frac{3}{3} = \frac{3}{12}$$

$$\frac{5}{6} + \frac{1}{4} = \frac{10}{12} + \frac{3}{12}$$

$$= \frac{13}{12}$$

$$= 1\frac{1}{12}$$

The denominators 4 and 6 factor into $2 \cdot 2$ and $2 \cdot 3$, respectively. Although the factor 2 *appears* three times, its power is 2^2 from factoring 4. The factor 3 appears once, so its power is 3^1. Therefore, the LCD as a *product* of the *highest power of each separate factor* is $2 \times 2 \times 3$.

The factoring method of adding fractions can be extended to three or more fractions.

Example

$$\frac{1}{4} + \frac{3}{8} + \frac{1}{12} = ?$$

Factoring denominators gives:

$$4 = 2 \cdot 2 \qquad 8 = 2 \cdot 2 \cdot 2 \qquad 12 = 2 \cdot 2 \cdot 3$$
$$\text{LCD} = 2 \cdot 2 \cdot 2 \cdot 3$$
$$\qquad = 24$$

Convert to LCD:

$$\frac{1}{4} \times \frac{6}{6} = \frac{6}{24} \qquad \frac{3}{8} \times \frac{3}{3} = \frac{9}{24}$$

$$\frac{1}{12} \times \frac{2}{2} = \frac{2}{24}$$

$$\frac{1}{4} + \frac{3}{8} + \frac{1}{12} = \frac{6}{24} + \frac{9}{24} + \frac{2}{24}$$

$$= \frac{6 + 9 + 2}{24}$$

$$= \frac{17}{24}$$

Addition of Mixed Numbers

Change any mixed numbers to improper fractions. If the fractions have the same denominator, add the numerators. If the fractions have different denominators, find the LCD of all the denominators and then add numerators. Reduce the answer if possible. Write the answer as a mixed number if you wish.

Example

$$2\frac{2}{3} + 5\frac{1}{2} + 1\frac{2}{9} = ?$$

Factoring denominators gives:

$$3 = 3 \qquad 2 = 2 \qquad 9 = 3 \cdot 3$$

$$LCD = 2 \cdot 3 \cdot 3$$
$$= 18$$

Convert to LCD:

$$\frac{8}{3} \times \frac{6}{6} = \frac{48}{18} \qquad \frac{11}{2} \times \frac{9}{9} = \frac{99}{18}$$

$$\frac{11}{9} \times \frac{2}{2} = \frac{22}{18}$$

$$2\frac{2}{3} + 5\frac{1}{2} + 1\frac{2}{9} = \frac{8}{3} + \frac{11}{2} + \frac{11}{9}$$

$$= \frac{48}{18} + \frac{99}{18} + \frac{22}{18}$$

$$= \frac{48 + 99 + 22}{18}$$

$$= \frac{169}{18} = 9\frac{7}{18}$$

Subtraction

Fractions can be subtracted only if the denominators are the same. If the denominators are the same, find the difference between the numerators. The denominator remains unchanged.

Example

$$\frac{19}{3} - \frac{2}{3} = ?$$

$$= \frac{19 - 2}{3}$$

$$= \frac{17}{3}$$

$$= 5\frac{2}{3}$$

When fractions have different denominators, find equivalent fractions with a common denominator, and then subtract numerators.

Example

$$\frac{7}{8} - \frac{3}{4} = ?$$

Factoring denominators gives:

$$8 = 2 \cdot 2 \cdot 2 \qquad 4 = 2 \cdot 2$$

$$LCD = 2 \cdot 2 \cdot 2$$
$$= 8$$

Convert to LCD:

$$\frac{7}{8} = \frac{7}{8} \qquad \frac{3}{4} \times \frac{2}{2} = \frac{6}{8}$$

$$\frac{7}{8} - \frac{3}{4} = \frac{7}{8} - \frac{6}{8}$$

$$= \frac{7 - 6}{8}$$

$$= \frac{1}{8}$$

Mixed Numbers

To subtract mixed numbers, change each mixed number to an improper fraction. Find the LCD for the fractions. Write each fraction as an equivalent fraction whose denominator is the common denominator. Find the difference between the numerators.

Example

$$3\frac{3}{8} - 2\frac{5}{6} = ?$$

$$LCD = 24$$

$$3\frac{3}{8} - 2\frac{5}{6} = \frac{27}{8} - \frac{17}{6}$$

$$= \frac{81}{24} - \frac{68}{24}$$

$$= \frac{13}{24}$$

If zero is subtracted from a fraction, the result is the original fraction:

$$\frac{3}{4} - 0 = \frac{3}{4} - \frac{0}{4} = \frac{3}{4}$$

Fraction Problems

In the following problems, perform the indicated operations and reduce the answers to lowest terms.

1. $\dfrac{5}{12} \times \dfrac{4}{15}$

2. $\dfrac{1}{2} \div \dfrac{3}{8}$

3. $\dfrac{5}{12} + \dfrac{2}{3}$

4. $\dfrac{2}{3} - \dfrac{5}{11}$

5. $3\dfrac{1}{3} \times \dfrac{4}{5}$

6. $7\dfrac{4}{5} - 2\dfrac{1}{3}$

Solutions:

1. $\dfrac{5}{12} \times \dfrac{4}{15} = \dfrac{\cancel{5}^{1}}{\cancel{12}_{3}} \times \dfrac{\cancel{4}^{1}}{\cancel{15}_{3}} = \dfrac{1}{9}$

2. $\dfrac{1}{2} \div \dfrac{3}{8} = \dfrac{1}{2} \times \dfrac{8}{3} = \dfrac{1}{\cancel{2}_{1}} \times \dfrac{\cancel{8}^{4}}{3} = \dfrac{4}{3}$

3. $\dfrac{5}{12} + \dfrac{2}{3} = \dfrac{5}{12} + \dfrac{8}{12} = \dfrac{13}{12} = 1\dfrac{1}{12}$

4. $\dfrac{2}{3} - \dfrac{5}{11} = \dfrac{22}{33} - \dfrac{15}{33} = \dfrac{7}{33}$

5. $3\dfrac{1}{3} \times \dfrac{4}{5} = \dfrac{10}{3} \times \dfrac{4}{5} = \dfrac{\cancel{10}^{2}}{3} \times \dfrac{4}{\cancel{5}_{1}} = \dfrac{8}{3} = 2\dfrac{2}{3}$

6. $7\dfrac{4}{5} - 2\dfrac{1}{3} = \dfrac{39}{5} - \dfrac{7}{3} = \dfrac{117}{15} - \dfrac{35}{15} = \dfrac{82}{15} = 5\dfrac{7}{15}$

Decimals

Earlier, we stated that whole numbers are expressed in a system of tens, or the decimal system, using the digits from 0 to 9. This system can be extended to fractions by using a period called a *decimal point*. The digits after a decimal point form a *decimal fraction*. Decimal fractions are smaller than 1—for example, .3, .37, .372, and .105. The first position to the right of the decimal point is called the *tenths' place* since the digit in that position tells how many tenths there are. The second digit to the right of the decimal point is in the *hundredths' place*. The third digit to the right of the decimal point is in the *thousandths' place*, and so on.

Example 1

.3 is a decimal fraction that means

$$3 \times \dfrac{1}{10} = \dfrac{3}{10}$$

read "three-tenths."

Example 2

The decimal fraction of .37 means

$$3 \times \dfrac{1}{10} + 7 \times \dfrac{1}{100} = 3 \times \dfrac{10}{100} + 7 \times \dfrac{1}{100}$$

$$= \dfrac{30}{100} + \dfrac{7}{100} = \dfrac{37}{100}$$

read "thirty-seven hundredths."

Example 3

The decimal fraction .372 means

$$\frac{300}{1,000} + \frac{70}{1,000} + \frac{2}{1,000} = \frac{372}{1,000}$$

read "three hundred seventy-two thousandths."

Whole numbers have an understood (unwritten) decimal point to the right of the last digit (i.e., 4 = 4.0). Decimal fractions can be combined with whole numbers to make *decimals*—for example, 3.246, 10.85, and 4.7.

Note: Adding zeros to the right of a decimal after the last digit does not change the value of the decimal.

Rounding Off

Sometimes a decimal is expressed with more digits than desired. As the number of digits to the right of the decimal point increases, the number increases in accuracy, but a high degree of accuracy is not always needed. Then, the number can be "rounded off" to a certain decimal place.

To round off, identify the place to be rounded off. If the digit to the right of it is 0, 1, 2, 3, or 4, the round-off place digit remains the same. If the digit to the right is 5, 6, 7, 8, or 9, add 1 to the round-off place digit.

Example 1

Round off .6384 to the nearest thousandth. The digit in the thousandths' place is 8. The digit to the right in the ten-thousandths' place is 4, so the 8 stays the same. The answer is .638

Example 2

.6386 rounded to the nearest thousandth is .639, rounded to the nearest hundredth is .64, and rounded to the nearest tenth is .6.

After a decimal fraction has been rounded off to a particular decimal place, all the digits to the right of that place will be 0.

Note: Rounding off whole numbers can be done by a similar method. It is less common but is sometimes used to get approximate answers quickly.

Example

Round 32,756 to the nearest *hundred*. This means, to find the multiple of 100 that is nearest the given number. The number in the hundreds' place is 7. The number immediately to the right is 5, so 32,756 rounds to 32,800.

Decimals and Fractions

Changing a Decimal to a Fraction

Place the digits to the right of the decimal point over the value of the place in which the last digit appears and reduce if possible. The whole number remains the same.

Example

Change 2.14 to a fraction or mixed number. Observe that 4 is the last digit and is in the hundredths' place.

$$.14 = \frac{14}{100} = \frac{7}{50}$$

Therefore:

$$2.14 = 2\frac{7}{50}$$

Changing a Fraction to a Decimal

Divide the numerator of the fraction by the denominator. First put a decimal point followed by zeros to the right of the number in the numerator. Subtract and divide until there is no remainder. The decimal point in the quotient is aligned directly above the decimal point in the dividend.

Example

Change $\dfrac{3}{8}$ to a decimal.

Divide

$$\begin{array}{r} .375 \\ 8\overline{)3.000} \\ \underline{24} \\ 60 \\ \underline{56} \\ 40 \\ \underline{40} \end{array}$$

When the division does not terminate with a 0 remainder, two courses are possible.

First Method: Divide to three decimal places.

Example

Change $\dfrac{5}{6}$ to a decimal.

$$\begin{array}{r} .833 \\ 6\overline{)5.000} \\ \underline{48} \\ 20 \\ \underline{18} \\ 20 \\ \underline{18} \\ 2 \end{array}$$

The 3 in the quotient will be repeated indefinitely. It is called an *infinite decimal* and is written .833. . . .

Second Method: Divide until there are two decimal places in the quotient and then write the remainder over the divisor.

Example

Change $\dfrac{5}{6}$ to a decimal.

$$\begin{array}{r} .833 \\ 6\overline{)5.000} = .83\tfrac{1}{3} \\ \underline{48} \\ 20 \\ \underline{18} \\ 20 \end{array}$$

Addition

Addition of decimals is both commutative and associative. Decimals are simpler to add than fractions. Place the decimals in a column with the decimal points aligned under each other. Add in the usual way. The decimal point of the answer is also aligned under the other decimal points.

Example

$43 + 2.73 + .9 + 3.01 = ?$

$$\begin{array}{r} 43. \\ 2.73 \\ .9 \\ \underline{3.01} \\ 49.64 \end{array}$$

Subtraction

For subtraction, the decimal points must be aligned under each other. Add zeros to the right of the decimal point if desired. Subtract as with whole numbers.

Examples

21.567	21.567	39.00
−9.4	−9.48	−17.48
12.167	12.087	21.52

Multiplication

Multiplication of decimals is commutative and associative:

$$5.39 \times .04 = .04 \times 5.39$$
$$(.7 \times .02) \times .1 = .7 \cdot (.02 \times .1)$$

Multiply the decimals as if they were whole numbers. The total number of decimal places in the product is the sum of the number of places (to the right of the decimal point) in all of the numbers multiplied.

Example

$8.64 \times .003 = ?$

8.64	2	places to right of decimal point
× .003	+ 3	places to right of decimal point
.02592	5	places to right of decimal point

A zero had to be added to the left of the product before writing the decimal point to ensure that there would be five decimal places in the product.

Note: To multiply a decimal by 10, simply move the decimal point one place to the right; to multiply by 100, move the decimal point two places to the right.

Division

To divide one decimal (the dividend) by another (the divisor), move the decimal point in the divisor as many places as necessary to the right to make the divisor a whole number. Then move the decimal point in the dividend (expressed or understood) a corresponding number of places, adding zeros if necessary. Then divide as with whole numbers. The decimal point in the quotient is placed above the decimal point in the dividend after the decimal point has been moved.

Example

Divide 7.6 by .32.

$$.32\overline{)7.60} = 32\overline{)760.00}$$

with quotient 23.75:

$$
\begin{array}{r}
23.75 \\
32\overline{)760.00} \\
64 \\
\overline{120} \\
96 \\
\overline{240} \\
224 \\
\overline{160} \\
160 \\
\end{array}
$$

Note: "Divide 7.6 by .32" can be written as $\dfrac{7.6}{.32}$. If this fraction is multiplied by $\dfrac{100}{100}$, an equivalent fraction is obtained with a whole number in the denominator:

$$\frac{7.6}{.32} \times \frac{100}{100} = \frac{760}{32}$$

Moving the decimal point two places to the right in both the divisor and dividend is equivalent to multiplying each number by 100.

Special Cases

If the dividend has a decimal point and the divisor does not, divide as with whole numbers and place the decimal point of the quotient above the decimal point in the divisor.

If both dividend and divisor are whole numbers but the quotient is a decimal, place a decimal point after the last digit of the dividend and add zeros as necessary to get the required degree of accuracy. (*See* Changing a Fraction to a Decimal, page 144).

Note: To divide any number by 10, simply move its decimal point (understood to be after the last digit for a whole number) one place to the left; to divide by 100, move the decimal point two places to the left; and so on.

Percents

Percents, like fractions and decimals, are ways of expressing parts of whole numbers, as 93%, 50%, and 22.4%. Percents are expressions of hundredths—that is, of fractions whose denominator is 100. The symbol for percent is %.

Example

$$25\% = \text{twenty-five hundredths} = \frac{25}{100} = \frac{1}{4}$$

The word *percent* means *per hundred*. Its main use is in comparing fractions with equal denominators of 100.

Relationship with Fractions and Decimals

Changing Percent into Decimal

Divide the percent by 100 and drop the symbol for percent. Add zeros to the left when necessary:

$$30\% = .30 \qquad 1\% = .01$$

Remember that the short method of dividing by 100 is to move the decimal point two places to the left.

Changing Decimal into Percent

Multiply the decimal by 100 by moving the decimal point two places to the right, and add the symbol for percent:

$$.375 = 37.5\% \qquad .001 = .1\%$$

Decimal Problems

1. Change the following decimals into fractions, and reduce.
   a. 1.16
   b. 15.05

2. Change the following fractions into decimals.

   a. $\frac{3}{8}$

   b. $\frac{2}{3}$

In the following problems, perform the indicated operations.

3. 3.762 + 23.43

4. 1.368 − .559

5. 8.7 × .8

6. .045 ÷ .5

Solutions:

1. a. $1.16 = 1\frac{16}{100} = 1\frac{8}{50} = 1\frac{4}{25}$

   b. $15.05 = 15\frac{5}{100} = 15\frac{1}{20}$

2. a. $\frac{3}{8} = 8\overline{)3.000}$ $\quad.375$

$$\begin{array}{r} \underline{24} \\ 60 \\ \underline{-56} \\ 40 \end{array}$$

   b. $\frac{2}{3} = 3\overline{)2.00}$ $\quad.666\ldots$

$$\begin{array}{r} \underline{18} \\ 20 \\ \underline{-18} \\ 20 \end{array}$$

3. $\begin{array}{r} 3.762 \\ +23.43 \\ \hline 27.192 \end{array}$

4. $\begin{array}{r} 1.368 \\ -.559 \\ \hline .809 \end{array}$

5. $\begin{array}{r} 8.7 \\ \times\ .8 \\ \hline 6.96 \end{array}$

6. $.5\overline{)0.0.45}$ $\quad 0.09$

146

Changing Percent into Fraction

Drop the percent sign. Write the number as a numerator over a denominator of 100. If the numerator has a decimal point, move the decimal point to the right the necessary number of places to make the numerator a whole number. Add the same number of zeros to the right of the denominator as you moved places to the right in the numerator. Reduce where possible.

Examples

$$20\% = \frac{20}{100} = \frac{2}{10} = \frac{1}{5}$$

$$36.5\% = \frac{36.5}{100} = \frac{365}{1000} = \frac{73}{200}$$

Changing a Fraction into Percent

Use either of two methods.

First Method: Change the fraction into an equivalent fraction with a denominator of 100. Drop the denominator (equivalent to multiplying by 100) and add the % sign.

Example

Express $\frac{6}{20}$ as a percent.

$$\frac{6}{20} \times \frac{5}{5} = \frac{30}{100} = 30\%$$

Second Method: Divide the numerator by the denominator to get a decimal with two places (express the remainder as a fraction if necessary). Change the decimal to a percent.

Example

Express $\frac{6}{20}$ as a percent.

$$\frac{6}{20} = 20\overline{)6.00} = 30\%$$
$$\quad\;\; \frac{.30}{6.00}$$
$$\quad\;\; \underline{60}$$

Percent Problems

1. Change the following percents into decimals:
   a. 37.5%   b. 0.5%

2. Change the following decimals into percents:
   a. 0.625   b. 3.75

3. Change the following fractions into percents:
   a. $\frac{7}{8}$ b. $\frac{73}{200}$

4. Change the following percents into fractions:
   a. 87.5%   b. 0.02%

Solutions:

1. a. 37.5% = 0.375

   b. 00.5% = 0.005

2. a. 0.625 = 62.5%

   b. 3.75 = 375%

3. a. $\frac{7}{8} = 8\overline{)7.000} = 87.5\%$ (0.875)

   b. $\frac{73}{200} = 200\overline{)73.000} = 36.5\%$ (0.365)

4. a. $87.5\% = 0.875 = \frac{875}{1,000} = \frac{35}{40} = \frac{7}{8}$

   b. $0.02\% = 0.0002 = \frac{2}{10,000} = \frac{1}{5,000}$

Word Problems

When doing percent problems, it is usually easier to change the percent to a decimal or a fraction before computing. When we take a percent of a certain number, that number is called the *base*, the percent we take is called the *rate*, and the result is called the *percentage* or *part*. If we let B represent the base, R the rate, and P the part, the relationship between these quantities is expressed by the following formula:

$$P = R \cdot B$$

All percent problems can be done with the help of this formula.

Example 1

In a class of 24 students, 25% received an A. How many students received an A? The number of students (24) is the base, and 25% is the rate. Change the rate to a fraction for ease of handling and apply the formula.

$$25\% = \frac{25}{100} = \frac{1}{4}$$

$$P = R \times B$$

$$= \frac{1}{\cancel{4}} \times \frac{\cancel{24}^{6}}{1}$$

$$= 6 \text{ students}$$

To choose between changing the percent (rate) to a decimal or a fraction, simply decide which would be easier to work with. In Example 1, the fraction was easier to work with because cancellation was possible. In Example 2, the situation is the same except for a different rate. This time the decimal form is easier.

Example 2

In a class of 24 students, 29.17% received an A. How many students received an A?

Changing the rate to a fraction yields

$$\frac{29.17}{100} = \frac{2917}{10,000}$$

You can quickly see that the decimal is the better choice.

$$29.17\% = .2917$$

$$P = R \times B$$

$$= .2917 \times 24$$

$$= 7 \text{ students}$$

$$\begin{array}{r} .2917 \\ \times\ \ 24 \\ \hline 1.1668 \\ 5.834\ \ \\ \hline 7.0008 \end{array}$$

Example 3

What percent of a 40-hour week is a 16-hour schedule?

40 hours is the base and 16 hours is the part.

$$P = R \cdot B$$

$$16 = R \cdot 40$$

Divide each side of the equation by 40.

$$\frac{16}{40} = R$$

$$\frac{2}{5} = R$$

$$40\% = R$$

Example 4

A woman paid $15,000 as a down payment on a house. If this amount was 20% of the price, what did the house cost?

The part (or percentage) is $15,000, the rate is 20%, and we must find the base. Change the rate to a fraction.

$$20\% = \frac{1}{5}$$

$$P = R \times B$$

$$\$15,000 = \frac{1}{5} \times B$$

Multiply each side of the equation by 5.

$$\$75,000 = B = \text{cost of house}$$

Percent of Increase or Decrease

This kind of problem is not really new but follows immediately from the previous problems. First calculate the *amount* of increase or decrease. This amount is the P (percentage or part) from the formula $P = R \cdot B$. The base, B, is the original amount, regardless of whether there was a loss or gain.

Example

By what percent does Mary's salary increase if her present salary is $20,000 and she accepts a new job at a salary of $28,000?

Amount of increase is:

$$28,000 - \$20,000 = \$8000$$

$$P = R \cdot B$$

$$\$8000 = R \cdot \$20,000$$

Divide each side of the equation by $20,000. Then:

$$\frac{\overset{40}{\cancel{8,000}}}{\underset{100}{\cancel{20,000}}} = \frac{40}{100} = R = 40\% \text{ increase}$$

Discount and Interest

These special kinds of percent problems require no new methods of attack.

Discount: The amount of discount is the difference between the original price and the sale, or discount, price. The rate of discount is usually given as a fraction or as a percent. Use the formula of the percent problems $P = R \cdot B$, but now P stands for the part or discount, R is the rate, and B, the base, is the original price.

Example 1

A table listed at $160 is marked 20% off. What is the sale price?

$$P = R \cdot B$$
$$= .20 \cdot \$160 = \$32$$

This is the amount of discount or how much must be subtracted from the original price. Then:

$$\$160 - \$32 = \$128 \text{ sale price}$$

Example 2

A car priced at $9000 was sold for $7200. What was the rate of discount?

$$\text{Amount of discount} = \$9000 - \$7200$$
$$= \$1800$$

$$\text{discount} = \text{rate} \cdot \text{original price}$$

$$\$1800 = R \cdot \$9000$$

Divide each side of the equation by $9000:

$$\frac{\overset{20}{\cancel{1800}}}{\underset{100}{\cancel{9000}}} = \frac{20}{100} = R = 20\%$$

Successive Discounting: When an item is discounted more than once, it is called successive discounting.

Example 1

In one store, a dress tagged at $40 was discounted 15%. When it did not sell at the lower price, it was discounted an additional 10%. What was the final selling price?

$$\text{discount} = R \cdot \text{original price}$$
$$\text{First discount} = .15 \cdot \$40 = \$6$$
$$\$40 - \$6 = \$34 \text{ selling price after}$$
$$\text{first discount}$$

Second
$$\text{discount} = .10 \cdot \$34 = \$3.40$$
$$\$34 - \$3.40 = \$30.60 \text{ final selling price}$$

Example 2

In another store, an identical dress was also tagged at $40. When it did not sell, it was discounted 25% all at once. Is the final selling price lower or higher than in Example 1?

Discount = R · original price
= .25 · $40
= $10

$40 − $10 = $30 final selling price

This is a lower selling price than in Example 1, where two successive discounts were taken. Although the two discounts from Example 1 add up to the discount of Example 2, the final selling price is not the same.

Interest: Interest problems are similar to discount and percent problems. If money is left in the bank for a year and the interest is calculated at the end of the year, the usual formula $P = R \cdot B$ can be used, where P is the *interest,* R is the *rate,* and B is the *principal* (original amount of money borrowed or loaned).

Example 1

A certain bank pays interest on savings accounts at the rate of 4% per year. If a man has $6700 on deposit, find the interest earned after one year.

$$P = R \cdot B$$

interest = rate · principal

$$P = .04 \cdot \$6700 = \$268 \text{ interest}$$

Interest problems frequently involve more or less time than one year. Then the formula becomes:

interest = rate · principal · time

Example 2

If the money is left in the bank for three years at simple interest (the kind we are discussing), the interest is

$$3 \cdot \$268 = \$804$$

Example 3

Suppose $6700 is deposited in the bank at 4% interest for three months. How much interest is earned?

interest = rate · principal · time

Here the 4% rate is for one year. Since three months is $\frac{3}{12} = \frac{1}{4}$

interest = .04 · $6700 · $\frac{1}{4}$ = $67

Percent Word Problems

1. Janet received a rent increase of 15%. If her rent was $785 monthly before the increase, what is her new rent?

2. School bus fares rose from $25 per month to $30 per month. Find the percent of increase.

3. A dress originally priced at $90 is marked down 35%, then discounted a further 10%. What is the new reduced price?

4. Dave delivers flowers for a salary of $45 a day, plus a 12% commission on all sales. One day his sales amounted to $220. How much money did he earn that day?

5. A certain bank pays interest on money market accounts at a rate of 6% a year. If Brett deposits $7200, find the interest earned after one year.

Solutions:

1. Amount of increase = $785 × 15%
= $785 × .15 = $117.75
New rent = $902.75

2. Amount of increase = $30 − $25 = $5

Percent of increase = $\frac{5}{25} = \frac{1}{5}$ = 20%

3. Amount of first markdown = $90 × 35%
= $90 × .35 = $31.50

Reduced price =
$90 − $31.50 = $58.50

Amount of second markdown =
$58.50 × 10% = $58.50 × .1 = $5.85

Final price = $58.50 − $5.85 = $52.65

4. Commission =
$220 × 12% = $220 × .12 = $26.40

Money earned = $45 + $26.40 = $71.40

5. Interest =
$7200 × 6% = $7200 × .06 = $432

Signed Numbers

In describing subtraction of whole numbers, we said that the operation was not closed— that is, 4 − 6 will yield a number that is not a member of the set of counting numbers and zero. The set of *integers* was developed to give meaning to such expressions as 4 − 6. The set of integers is the set of all *signed* whole numbers and zero. It is the set {..., −4, −3, −2, −1, 0, 1, 2, 3, 4, ...}

The first three dots symbolize the fact that the negative integers go on indefinitely, just as the positive integers do. Integers preceded by a minus sign (called *negative integers*) appear to the left of 0 on a number line.

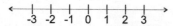

Decimals, fractions, and mixed numbers can also have negative signs. Together with positive fractions and decimals, they appear on the number line in this fashion:

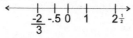

All numbers to the right of 0 are called *positive numbers*. They have the sign +, whether it is actually written or not. Business gains or losses, feet above or below sea level, and temperature above or below zero can all be expressed by means of signed numbers.

Addition

If the numbers to be added have the same sign, add the numbers (integers, fractions, decimals) as usual and use their common sign in the answer:

$$+9 + (+8) + (+2) = +19 \text{ or } 19$$
$$-4 + (-11) + (-7) + (-1) = -23$$

If the numbers to be added have different signs, add the positive numbers and then the negative numbers. Ignore the signs and subtract the smaller total from the larger total. If the larger total is positive, the answer will be positive; if the larger total is negative, the answer will be negative. The answer may be zero. Zero is neither positive nor negative and has no sign.

Example

$$+3 + (-5) + (-8) + (+2) = ?$$
$$+3 + (+2) = +5$$
$$-5 + (-8) = -13$$
$$13 - 5 = 8$$

Since the larger total (13) has a negative sign, the answer is −8.

Subtraction

The second number in a subtraction problem is called the *subtrahend*. In order to subtract, change the sign of the subtrahend and then continue as if you were *adding* signed numbers. If there is no sign in front of the subtrahend, it is assumed to be positive.

Examples

Subtract the subtrahend (bottom number) from the top number.

15	5	−35	−35	42
5	15	−42	42	35
10	−10	7	−77	7

Multiplication

If two and only two signed numbers are to be multiplied, multiply the numbers as you would if they were not signed. Then, if the two numbers have the *same sign,* the product is *positive.* If the two numbers have *different signs,* the product is *negative.* If more than two numbers are being multiplied, proceed two at a time in the same way as before, finding the signed product of the first two numbers, then multiplying that product by the next number, and so on. The product has a positive sign if all the factors are positive or there is an even number of negative factors. The product has a negative sign if there is an odd number of negative factors.

Example

$$-3 \cdot (+5) \cdot (-11) \cdot (-2) = -330$$

The answer is negative because there is an odd number (three) of negative factors.

The product of a signed number and zero is zero. The product of a signed number and 1 is the original number. The product of a signed number and -1 is the original number with its sign changed.

Examples

$$-5 \cdot 0 = 0$$
$$-5 \cdot 1 = -5$$
$$-5 \cdot (-1) = +5$$

Division

If the divisor and the dividend have the same sign, the answer is positive. Divide the numbers as you normally would. If the divisor and the dividend have different signs, the answer is negative. Divide the numbers as you normally would.

Examples

$$-3 \div (-2) = \frac{3}{2} = 1\frac{1}{2}$$
$$8 \div (-.2) = -40$$

If zero is divided by a signed number, the answer is zero. If a signed number is divided by zero, the answer does not exist. If a signed number is divided by 1, the number remains the same. If a signed number is divided by -1, the quotient is the original number with its sign changed.

Examples

$$0 \div (-2) = 0$$
$$-\frac{4}{3} \div 0 \qquad \text{not defined}$$
$$\frac{2}{3} \div 1 = \frac{2}{3}$$
$$4 \div -1 = -4$$

Signed Numbers Problems

Perform the indicated operations:

1. $+ 6 + (-5) + (+2) + (-8) =$
2. $- 5 - (-4) + (-2) - (+6) =$
3. $-3 \cdot (+5) \cdot (-7) \cdot (-2) =$
4. $9 \div (-.3) =$

Solutions:

1. $+6 + (-5) = +1$
   $+1 + (+2) = +3$
   $+3 + (-8) = -5$

2. $-5 -(-4) = -5 + 4 = -1$
   $-1 + (-2) = -3$
   $-3 - (+6) = -9$

3. $\quad -3 \cdot (+5) = -15$
   $-15 \cdot (-7) = +105$
   $+105 \cdot (-2) = -210$

4. $9 \div (-.3) = -30$

Powers, Exponents, and Roots

Exponents

The product $10 \cdot 10 \cdot 10$ can be written 10^3. We say 10 is raised to the *third power*. In general, $a \times a \times a \ldots a$ n times is written a^n. The *base a* is raised to the nth power, and n is called the *exponent*.

Examples

$3^2 = 3 \cdot 3$ read "3 squared"

$2^3 = 2 \cdot 2 \cdot 2$ read "2 cubed"

$5^4 = 5 \cdot 5 \cdot 5 \cdot 5$ read "5 to the fourth power"

If the exponent is 1, it is usually understood and not written; thus, $a^1 = a$. Since

$$a^2 = a \times a \quad \text{and} \quad a^3 = a \times a \times a$$

then

$$a^2 \times a^3 = (a \times a)(a \times a \times a) = a^5$$

There are three rules for exponents. In general, if k and m are any counting numbers or zero, and a is any number,

Rule 1: $a^k \times a^m = a^{k+m}$

Rule 2: $a^m \cdot b^m = (ab)^m$

Rule 3: $(a^k)^n = a^{kn}$

Examples

Rule 1: $2^2 \cdot 2^3 = 4 \times 8 = 32$
and $2^2 \times 2^3 = 2^5 = 32$

Rule 2: $3^2 \times 4^2 = 9 \times 16 = 144$
and $3^2 \times 4^2 = (3 \times 4)^2 = 12^2 = 144$

Rule 3: $(3^2)^3 = 9^3 = 729$
and $(3^2)^3 = 3^6 = 729$

Roots

The definition of roots is based on exponents. If $a^n = c$, where a is the base and n the exponent, a is called the nth *root* of c. This is written $a = \sqrt[n]{c}$. The symbol $\sqrt{}$ is called a *radical sign*. Since $5^4 = 625$, $\sqrt[4]{625} = 5$ and 5 is the fourth root of 625. The most frequently used roots are the second (called the square) root and the third (called the cube) root. The square root is written $\sqrt{}$ and the cube root is written $\sqrt[3]{}$.

Square Roots

If c is a positive number, there are two values, one negative and one positive, which when multiplied together will produce c.

Example

$+4 \cdot (+4) = 16 \quad \text{and} \quad -4 \cdot (-4) = 16$

The positive square root of a positive number c is called the *principal* square root of c (briefly, the *square root* of c) and is denoted by $\sqrt{c}$:

$$\sqrt{144} = 12$$

If $c = 0$, there is only one square root, 0. If c is a negative number, there is no real number that is the square root of c:

$$\sqrt{-4} \text{ is not a real number}$$

Cube Roots

Both positive and negative numbers have real cube roots. The cube root of 0 is 0. The cube root of a positive number is positive; that of a negative number is negative.

Examples

$2 \cdot 2 \cdot 2 = 8$

Therefore $\sqrt[3]{8} = 2$

$-3 \cdot (-3) \cdot (-3) = -27$

Therefore $\sqrt[3]{-27} = -3$

Each number has only one real cube root.

Example 1

Simplify $\sqrt{98}$

$\sqrt{98} = \sqrt{2 \times 49}$

$\qquad = \sqrt{2} \times \sqrt{49}$ where 49 is a square number

$\qquad = \sqrt{2} \times 7$

Therefore, $\sqrt{98} = 7\sqrt{2}$ and the process terminates because there is no whole number whose square is 2. $7\sqrt{2}$ is called a radical expression or simply a *radical*.

Example 2

Which is larger, $\left(\sqrt{96}\right)^2$ or $\sqrt{2^{14}}$?

$\left(\sqrt{96}\right)^2 = \sqrt{96} \times \sqrt{96} = \sqrt{96 \times 96}$
$= 96$

$\sqrt{2^{14}} = 2^7 = 128$ because $2^{14} = 2^7 \times 2^7$ by

Rule 1 or because $\sqrt{2^{14}} = (2^{14})^{1/2} = 2^7$
by Rule 3

Since $128 > 96$,

$\sqrt{2^{14}} > \left(\sqrt{96}\right)^2$

Example 3

Which is larger, $2\sqrt{75}$ or $6\sqrt{12}$?

These numbers can be compared if the same number appears under the radical sign. Then the greater number is the one with the larger number in front of the radical sign.

$\sqrt{75} = \sqrt{25 \times 3} = \sqrt{25} \times \sqrt{3} = 5\sqrt{3}$

Therefore:

$2\sqrt{75} = 2(5\sqrt{3}) = 10\sqrt{3}$

$\sqrt{12} = \sqrt{4 \times 3} = \sqrt{4} \times \sqrt{3} = 2\sqrt{3}$

Therefore:

$6\sqrt{12} = 6(2\sqrt{3}) = 12\sqrt{3}$

Since $12\sqrt{3} > 10\sqrt{3}$,

$6\sqrt{12} > 2\sqrt{75}$

Note: Numbers such as $\sqrt{2}$ and $\sqrt{3}$ are called *irrational* numbers to distinguish them from *rational* numbers, which include the integers and the fractions. Irrational numbers also have places on the number line. They may have positive or negative signs. The combination of rational and irrational numbers, all the numbers we have used so far, make up the *real* numbers. Arithmetic, algebra, and geometry deal with real numbers. The number π, the ratio of the circumference of a circle to its diameter, is also a real number; it is irrational, although it is approximated by 3.14159. . . . Instructions for taking the GMAT say that the numbers used are real numbers. This means that answers may be expressed as fractions, decimals, radicals, or integers, whatever is required.

Radicals can be added and subtracted only if they have the same number under the radical sign. Otherwise, they must be reduced to expressions having the same number under the radical sign.

Example

Add

$$2\sqrt{18} + 4\sqrt{8} - \sqrt{2}.$$

$$\sqrt{18} = \sqrt{9 \times 2} = \sqrt{9} \times \sqrt{2} = 3\sqrt{2}$$

therefore,

$$2\sqrt{18} = 2(3\sqrt{2}) = 6\sqrt{2}$$

and

$$\sqrt{8} = \sqrt{4 \times 2} = \sqrt{4} \times \sqrt{2} = 2\sqrt{2}$$

therefore,

$$4\sqrt{8} = 4(2\sqrt{2}) = 8\sqrt{2}$$

giving

$$2\sqrt{18} + 4\sqrt{8} - \sqrt{2}$$

$$= 6\sqrt{2} + 8\sqrt{2} - \sqrt{2} = 13\sqrt{2}$$

Radicals are multiplied using the rule that

$$\sqrt[k]{a \times b} = \sqrt[k]{a} \times \sqrt[k]{b}$$

Example

$$\sqrt{2}\left(\sqrt{2} - 5\sqrt{3}\right) = \sqrt{4} - 5\sqrt{6}$$
$$= 2 - 5\sqrt{6}$$

A quotient rule for radicals similar to the product rule is:

$$\sqrt[k]{\frac{a}{b}} = \frac{\sqrt[k]{a}}{\sqrt[k]{b}}$$

Example

$$\sqrt{\frac{9}{4}} = \frac{\sqrt{9}}{\sqrt{4}} = \frac{3}{2}$$

Exponents, Powers, and Roots Problems

1. Simplify $\sqrt{162}$.

2. Find the sum of $\sqrt{75}$ and $\sqrt{12}$.

3. Combine $\sqrt{80} + \sqrt{45} - \sqrt{20}$.

4. Simplify $\sqrt{5}(2\sqrt{2} - 3\sqrt{5})$.

5. Divide and simplify $\dfrac{15\sqrt{96}}{5\sqrt{2}}$.

6. Calculate $5^2 \times 2^3$.

Solutions:

1. $\sqrt{162} = \sqrt{2 \cdot 81} = \sqrt{2} \cdot \sqrt{81} = 9\sqrt{2}$

2. $\sqrt{75} + \sqrt{12} = 5\sqrt{3} + 2\sqrt{3} = 7\sqrt{3}$

3. $\sqrt{80} + \sqrt{45} - \sqrt{20}$

$\quad = 4\sqrt{5} + 3\sqrt{5} - 2\sqrt{5} = 5\sqrt{5}$

4. $\sqrt{5}\left(2\sqrt{2} - 3\sqrt{5}\right)$

$\quad = 2\sqrt{10} - 3\sqrt{25} = 2\sqrt{10} - 3(5)$

$\quad = 2\sqrt{10} - 15$

5. $\dfrac{15\sqrt{96}}{5\sqrt{2}} = \dfrac{15(4\sqrt{6})}{5\sqrt{2}} = \dfrac{60\sqrt{6}}{5\sqrt{2}} = 12\sqrt{3}$

6. $5^2 \times 2^3 = 25 \times 8 = 200$

ALGEBRA

Algebra is a generalization of arithmetic. It provides methods for solving problems that cannot be done by arithmetic alone or that can be done by arithmetic only after long computations. Algebra provides a shorthand way of reducing long verbal statements to brief formulas, expressions, or equations. After the verbal statements have been reduced, the resulting algebraic expressions can be simplified. Suppose that a room is 12 feet wide and 20 feet long. Its perimeter (measurement around the outside) can be expressed as:

$$12 + 20 + 12 + 20 \text{ or } 2(12 + 20)$$

If the width of the room remains 12 feet but the letter *l* is used to symbolize length, the perimeter is:

$$12 + l + 12 + l \text{ or } 2(12 + l)$$

Further, if *w* is used for width, the perimeter of *any* rectangular room can be written as $2(w + l)$. This same room has an area of 12 feet by 20 feet or $12 \cdot 20$. If *l* is substituted for 20, any room of width 12 has area equal to $12l$. If *w* is substituted for the number 12, the area of any rectangular room is given by *wl* or *lw*. Expressions such as *wl* and $2(w + l)$ are called *algebraic expressions*. An *equation* is a statement that two algebraic expressions are equal. A *formula* is a special type of equation.

Evaluating Formulas

If we are given an expression and numerical values to be assigned to each letter, the expression can be evaluated.

Example

Evaluate $2x + 3y - 7$ if $x = 2$ and $y = -4$.
Substitute given values
$2(2) + 3(-4) - 7 = ?$

Multiply numbers using rules for signed numbers
$4 + -12 - 7 = ?$

Collect numbers
$4 - 19 = -15$

We have already evaluated formulas in arithmetic when solving percent, discount, and interest problems.

Example

The formula for temperature conversion is:

$$F = \frac{9}{5} C + 32$$

where C stands for the temperature in degrees Celsius and F for degrees Fahrenheit. Find the Fahrenheit temperature that is equivalent to 20°C.

$$F = \frac{9}{5} (20°C) + 32 = 36 + 32 = 68°F$$

Algebraic Expressions

Formulation

A more difficult problem than evaluating an expression or formula is to translate from a verbal expression to an algebraic one:

Verbal	Algebraic
Thirteen more than *x*	$x + 13$
Six less than twice *x*	$2x - 6$
The square of the sum of *x* and 5	$(x + 5)^2$
The sum of the square of *x* and the square of 5	$x^2 + 5^2$
The distance traveled by a car going 50 miles an hour for *x* hours	$50x$
The average of 70, 80, 85, and *x*	$\dfrac{70 + 80 + 85 + x}{4}$

Simplification

After algebraic expressions have been formulated, they can usually be simplified by means of the laws of exponents and the common operations of addition, subtraction, multiplication, and division. These techniques will be described in the next section. Algebraic expressions and equations frequently contain parentheses, which are removed in the process of simplifying. If an expression contains more than one set of parentheses, remove the inner set first and then the outer set. Brackets, [ ], which are often used instead of parentheses, are treated the same way. Parentheses are used to indicate multiplication. Thus $3(x + y)$ means that 3 is to be multiplied by the sum of x and y. The *distributive law* is used to accomplish this:

$$a(b + c) = ab + ac$$

The expression in front of the parentheses is multiplied by each term inside. Rules for signed numbers apply.

Example

Simplify $3[4(2 - 8) - 5(4 + 2)]$.

This can be done in two ways.

Method 1: Combine the numbers inside the parentheses first:

$$3[4(2 - 8) - 5(4 + 2)] = 3[4(-6) - 5(6)]$$
$$= 3[-24 - 30]$$
$$= 3[-54] = -162$$

Method 2: Use the distributive law:

$$3[4(2 - 8) - 5(4 + 2)] = 3[8 - 32 - 20 - 10]$$
$$= 3[8 - 62]$$
$$= 3[-54] = -162$$

If there is a (+) before the parentheses, the signs of the terms inside the parentheses remain the same when the parentheses are removed. If there is a (−) before the parentheses, the sign of each term inside the parentheses changes when the parentheses are removed.

Once parentheses have been removed, the order of operations is multiplication and division, then addition and subtraction from left to right.

Example

$(-15 + 17) \cdot 3 - [(4 \cdot 9) \div 6] = ?$

Work inside the parentheses first:
$(2) \cdot 3 - [36 \div 6] = ?$

Then work inside the brackets:
$2 \cdot 3 - [6] = ?$

Multiply first, then subtract, proceeding from left to right:
$6 - 6 = 0$

The placement of parentheses and brackets is important. Using the same numbers as above with the parentheses and brackets placed in different positions can give many different answers.

Example

$-15 + [(17 \cdot 3) - (4 \cdot 9)] \div 6 = ?$

Work inside the parentheses first:
$-15 + [(51) - (36)] \div 6 = ?$

Then work inside the brackets:
$-15 + [15] \div 6 = ?$
Since there are no more parentheses or brackets, proceed from left to right, dividing before adding:

$$-15 + 2\frac{1}{2} = -12\frac{1}{2}$$

Operations

When letter symbols and numbers are combined with the operations of arithmetic ($+, -, \cdot, \div$) and with certain other mathematical operations, we have an *algebraic expression*. Algebraic expressions are made up of several parts connected by a plus or a minus sign; each part is called a *term*. Terms with the same letter part are called *like terms.* Since algebraic expressions represent numbers, they can be added, subtracted, multiplied, and divided.

When we defined the commutative law of addition in arithmetic by writing $a + b = b + a$, we meant that a and b could represent any number. The expression $a + b = b + a$ is an *identity* because it is true for all numbers. The expression $n + 5 = 14$ is not an identity because it is not true for all numbers; it becomes true only when the number 9 is substituted for n. Letters used to represent numbers are called *variables*. If a number stands alone (the 5 or 14 in $n + 5 = 14$), it is called a *constant* because its value is constant or unchanging. If a number appears in front of a variable, it is called a *coefficient*. Because the letter x is frequently used to represent a variable, or *unknown*, the times sign ×, which can be confused with it in handwriting, is rarely used to express multiplication in algebra. Other expressions used for multiplication are a dot, parentheses, or simply writing a number and letter together:

$$5 \cdot 4 \text{ or } 5(4) \text{ or } 5a$$

Of course, 54 still means fifty-four.

Addition and Subtraction

Only like terms can be combined. Add or subtract the coefficients of like terms, using the rules for signed numbers.

Example 1

Add $x + 2y - 2x + 3y$.

$$x - 2x + 2y + 3y = -x + 5y$$

Example 2

Perform the subtraction:

$$
\begin{array}{r}
-30a - 15b + 4c \\
-(-\ 5a +\ \ 3b -\ c + d)
\end{array}
$$

Change the sign of each term in the subtrahend and then add, using the rules for signed numbers:

$$
\begin{array}{r}
-30a - 15b + 4c \\
5a -\ 3b +\ c - d \\
\hline
-25a - 18b + 5c - d
\end{array}
$$

Multiplication

Multiplication is accomplished by using the *distributive property*. If the multiplier has only one term, then

$$a(b + c) = ab + bc$$

Example

$$9x(5m + 9q) = (9x)(5m) + (9x)(9q)$$
$$= 45mx + 81qx$$

When the multiplier contains more than one term and you are multiplying two expressions, multiply each term of the first expression by each term of the second and then add like terms. Follow the rules for signed numbers and exponents at all times.

Example

$$(3x + 8)(4x^2 + 2x + 1)$$
$$= 3x(4x^2 + 2x + 1) + 8(4x^2 + 2x + 1)$$
$$= 12x^3 + 6x^2 + 3x + 32x^2 + 16x + 8$$
$$= 12x^3 + 38x^2 + 19x + 8$$

If more than two expressions are to be multiplied, multiply the first two, then multiply the product by the third factor, and so on, until all factors have been used.

Algebraic expressions can be multiplied by themselves (squared) or raised to any power.

Example 1

$$(a + b)^2 = (a + b)(a + b)$$
$$= a(a + b) + b(a + b)$$
$$= a^2 + ab + ba + b^2$$
$$= a^2 + 2ab + b^2$$

since $ab = ba$ by the commutative law

Example 2

$$(a + b)(a - b) = a(a - b) + b(a - b)$$
$$= a^2 - ab + ba - b^2$$
$$= a^2 - b^2$$

Factoring

When two or more algebraic expressions are multiplied, each is called a factor, and the result is the *product*. The reverse process of finding the factors when given the product is called *factoring*. A product can often be factored in more than one way. Factoring is useful in multiplication, division, and solving equations.

One way to factor an expression is to remove any single-term factor that is common to each of the terms and write it outside the parentheses. It is the distributive law that permits this.

Example

$$3x^3 + 6x^2 + 9x = 3x(x^2 + 2x + 3)$$

The result can be checked by multiplication.

Expressions containing squares can sometimes be factored into expressions containing letters raised to the first power only, called *linear factors*. We have seen that

$$(a + b)(a - b) = a^2 - b^2$$

Therefore, if we have an expression in the form of a difference of two squares, it can be factored as:

$$a^2 - b^2 = (a + b)(a - b)$$

Example

Factor $4x^2 - 9$.

$$4x^2 - 9 = (2x)^2 - (3)^2 = (2x + 3)(2x - 3)$$

Again, the result can be checked by multiplication.

A third type of expression that can be factored is one containing three terms, such as $x^2 + 5x + 6$. Since

$$(x + a)(x + b) = x(x + b) + a(x + b)$$
$$= x^2 + xb + ax + ab$$
$$= x^2 + (a + b)x + ab$$

an expression in the form $x^2 + (a + b)x + ab$ can be factored into two factors of the form $(x + a)$ and $(x + b)$. We must find two numbers whose product is the constant in the given expression and whose sum is the coefficient of the term containing x.

Example 1

Find factors of $x^2 + 5x + 6$.

First find two numbers which, when multiplied, have +6 as a product. Possibilities are 2 and 3, −2 and −3, 1 and 6, −1 and −6. From these select the one pair whose sum is 5. The pair 2 and 3 is the only possible selection, and so:

$$x^2 + 5x + 6 = (x + 2)(x + 3) \quad \text{written in}$$
$$\text{either order}$$

Example 2

Factor $x^2 - 5x - 6$.

Possible factors of −6 are −1 and 6, 1 and −6, 2 and −3, −2 and 3. We must select the pair whose sum is −5. The only pair whose sum is −5 is + 1 and −6, and so

$$x^2 - 5x - 6 = (x + 1)(x - 6)$$

In factoring expressions of this type, notice that if the last sign is plus, both *a* and *b* have the same sign and it is the same as the sign of the middle term. If the last sign is minus, the numbers have opposite signs.

Many expressions cannot be factored.

Division

Write the division example as a fraction. If numerator and denominator each contain one term, divide the numbers using laws of signed numbers and use the laws of exponents to simplify the letter part of the problem.

Example

Method 1: Law of Exponents

$$\frac{36mx^2}{9m^2x} = 4m^1x^2m^{-2}x^{-1}$$

$$= 4m^{-1}x^1 = \frac{4x}{m}$$

Method 2: Cancellation

$$\frac{36mx^2}{9m^2x} = \frac{\overset{4}{\cancel{36}mxx}}{\cancel{9}mmx} = \frac{4x}{m}$$
$$\underset{1}{}$$

This is acceptable because

$$\frac{ac}{bc} = \frac{a}{b}\left(\frac{c}{c}\right) \text{ and } \frac{c}{c} = 1$$

so that $\dfrac{ac}{bc} = \dfrac{a}{b}$

If the divisor contains only one term and the dividend is a sum, divide each term in the dividend by the divisor and simplify as you did in Method 2.

Example

$$\frac{9x^3 + 3x^2 + 6x}{3x} = \frac{\overset{3x^2}{\cancel{9x^3}}}{\cancel{3x}} + \frac{\overset{x}{\cancel{3x^2}}}{\cancel{3x}} + \frac{\overset{2}{\cancel{6x}}}{\cancel{3x}}$$

$$= 3x^2 + x + 2$$

This method cannot be followed if there are two terms or more in the denominator since

$$\frac{a}{b+c} \neq \frac{a}{b} + \frac{a}{c}$$

In this case, write the example as a fraction. Factor the numerator and denominator if possible. Then use laws of exponents or cancel.

Example

Divide $x^3 - 9x$ by $x^3 + 6x^2 + 9x$.

Write as:

$$\frac{x^3 - 9x}{x^3 + 6x^2 + 9x}$$

Both numerator and denominator can be factored to give:

$$\frac{x(x^2 - 9)}{x(x^2 + 6x + 9)} = \frac{\cancel{x}(x+3)(x-3)}{\cancel{x}(x+3)(x+3)} = \frac{x-3}{x+3}$$

Algebra Problems

1. Simplify $4[2(3-7) - 4(2+6)]$
2. Subtract
   $(-25x + 4y - 12z) - (4x - 8y - 13z)$
3. Multiply $(5x + 2)(3x^2 - 2x + 1)$
4. Factor completely $2x^3 + 8x^2 - 90x$
5. Factor completely $32x^2 - 98$
6. Divide $\dfrac{x^2 + 2x - 8}{x^2 - x - 20}$

Solutions:

1. $4[2(3-7) - 4(2+6)] = 4[2(-4)-4(8)]$
   $= 4[-8 - 32] = 4(-40) = -160$
2. $(-25x + 4y - 12z) - (4x - 8y - 13z)$
   $= -25x + 4y - 12z - 4x + 8y + 13z$
   $= -29x + 12y + z$
3. $(5x + 2)(3x^2 - 2x + 1)$
   $= 5x(3x^2 - 2x + 1) + 2(3x^2 - 2x + 1)$
   $= 15x^3 - 10x^2 + 5x + 6x^2 - 4x + 2$
   $= 15x^3 - 4x^2 + x + 2$
4. $2x^3 + 8x^2 - 90x = 2x(x^2 + 4x - 45)$
   $= 2x(x + 9)(x - 5)$
5. $32x^2 - 98 = 2(16x^2 - 49)$
   $= 2(4x - 7)(4x + 7)$
6. $\dfrac{x^2 + 2x - 8}{x^2 - x - 20} = \dfrac{(x + 4)(x - 2)}{(x - 5)(x + 4)}$

   $= \dfrac{\overset{1}{\cancel{(x+4)}}(x - 2)}{(x - 5)\cancel{(x+4)}} = \dfrac{x - 2}{x - 5}$
   $$\underset{1}{}$$

Equations

Solving equations is one of the major objectives in algebra. If a variable x in an equation is replaced by a value or expression that makes the equation a true statement, the value or expression is called a *solution* of the equation. (Remember that an equation is a mathematical statement that one algebraic expression is equal to another.)

An equation may contain one or more variables. We begin with one variable. Certain rules apply to equations whether there are one or more variables. The following rules are applied to give equivalent equations that are simpler than the original:

Addition: If $s = t$, then $s + c = t + c$.
Subtraction: If $s + c = t + c$, then $s = t$.
Multiplication: If $s = t$, then $cs = ct$.
Division: If $cs = ct$ and $c \neq 0$, then $s = t$.

To solve for x in an equation in the form $ax = b$ with $a \neq 0$, divide each side of the equation by a:

$$\frac{ax}{a} = \frac{b}{a} \quad \text{yielding} \quad x = \frac{b}{a}$$

Then, $\frac{b}{a}$ is the solution to the equation.

Example 1

Solve $4x = 8$.

Write $\dfrac{4x}{4} = \dfrac{8}{4}$

$ x = 2$

Example 2

Solve $2x - (x - 4) = 5(x + 2)$ for x.

$2x - (x - 4) = 5(x + 2)$
$2x - x + 4 = 5x + 10$ Remove parentheses by distributive law.
$x + 4 = 5x + 10$ Combine like terms.
$x = 5x + 6$ Subtract 4 from each side.
$-4x = 6$ Subtract $5x$ from each side.
$x = \dfrac{6}{-4}$ Divide each side by -4.
$= -\dfrac{3}{2}$ Reduce fraction to lowest terms. Negative sign now applies to the entire fraction.

Check the solution for accuracy by substituting in the original equation:

$$2\left(-\frac{3}{2}\right) - \left(-\frac{3}{2} - 4\right) \stackrel{?}{=} 5\left(-\frac{3}{2} + 2\right)$$

$$-3 - \left(-\frac{11}{2}\right) \stackrel{?}{=} 5\left(\frac{1}{2}\right)$$

$$-3 + \frac{11}{2} \stackrel{?}{=} \frac{5}{2}$$

$$\frac{6}{2} + \frac{11}{2} \stackrel{?}{=} \frac{5}{2} \quad \text{check}$$

Equations Problems

Solve the following equations for x:

1. $3x - 5 = 3 + 2x$

2. $3(2x - 2) = 12$

3. $4(x - 2) = 2x + 10$

4. $7 - 4(2x - 1) = 3 + 4(4 - x)$

Solutions:

1. $3x - 5 = 3 + 2x$
   $\underline{-2x \qquad\quad -2x}$
   $\quad x - 5 = 3$
   $\quad \underline{+5 \; +5}$
   $\qquad x = 8$

2. $3(2x - 2) = 12$
   $\quad 6x - 6 = 12$
   $\qquad\quad 6x = 18$
   $\qquad\quad\; x = 3$

3. $4(x - 2) = 2x + 10$
   $\quad 4x - 8 = 2x + 10$
   $\qquad 4x = 2x + 18$
   $\qquad 2x = 18$
   $\qquad\; x = 9$

4. $7 - 4(2x - 1) = 3 + 4(4 - x)$
   $\quad 7 - 8x + 4 = 3 + 16 - 4x$
   $\qquad 11 - 8x = 19 - 4x$
   $\qquad\quad\; 11 = 19 + 4x$
   $\qquad\quad -8 = 4x$
   $\qquad\quad\; x = -2$

Word Problems Involving One Unknown

In many cases, if you read a word problem carefully, assign a letter to the quantity to be found, and understand the relationships between known and unknown quantities, you can formulate an equation in one unknown.

Number Problems and Age Problems

These two kinds of problems are similar to one another.

Example

One number is 3 times another, and their sum is 48. Find the two numbers.

Let x = second number. Then the first is $3x$. Since their sum is 48,

$3x + x = 48$
$\quad\; 4x = 48$
$\qquad x = 12$

Therefore, the first number is $3x = 36$.

$36 + 12 = 48$ check

Distance Problems

The basic concept is:

distance = rate · time

Example

In a mileage test, a man drives a truck at a fixed rate of speed for 1 hour. Then he increases the speed by 20 miles per hour and drives at that rate for 2 hours. He then reduces that speed by 5 miles per hour and drives at that rate for 3 hours. If the distance traveled was 295 miles, what are the rates of speed over each part of the test?

Let x be the first speed, $x + 20$ the second, and $x + (20 - 5) = x + 15$ the third. Because distance = rate · time, multiply these rates by the time and formulate the equation by separating the two equal expressions for distance by an equal sign:

$1x + 2(x + 20) + 3(x + 15) = 295$
$\quad x + 2x + 3x + 40 + 45 = 295$
$\qquad\qquad\qquad\qquad\; 6x = 210$
$\qquad\qquad\qquad\qquad\;\; x = 35$

The speeds are 35, 55, and 50 miles per hour.

Consecutive Number Problems

This type usually involves only one unknown. Two numbers are consecutive if one is the successor of the other. Three consecutive numbers are of the form x, $x + 1$, and $x + 2$. Since an even number is divisible by 2, consecutive even numbers are of the form $2x$, $2x + 2$, and $2x + 4$. An odd number is of the form $2x + 1$.

Example

Find three consecutive whole numbers whose sum is 75.

Let the first number be x, the second $x + 1$, and the third $x + 2$. Then:

$$x + (x + 1) + (x + 2) = 75$$
$$3x + 3 = 75$$
$$3x = 72$$
$$x = 24$$

The numbers whose sum is 75 are 24, 25, and 26. Many versions of this problem have no solution. For example, no three consecutive whole numbers have a sum of 74.

Work Problems

These problems concern the speed with which work can be accomplished and the time necessary to perform a task if the size of the workforce is changed.

Example

If Joe can type a chapter alone in 6 days and Ann can type the same chapter in 8 days, how long will it take them to type the chapter if they both work on it?

We let x = number of days required if they work together, and then put our information into tabular form:

	Joe	Ann	Together
Days to type chapter	6	8	x
Part typed in 1 day	$\dfrac{1}{6}$	$\dfrac{1}{8}$	$\dfrac{1}{x}$

Since the part done by Joe in 1 day plus the part done by Ann in 1 day equals the part done by both in 1 day, we have

$$\frac{1}{6} + \frac{1}{8} = \frac{1}{x}$$

Next we multiply each member by $48x$ to clear the fractions, giving:

$$8x + 6x = 48$$
$$14x = 48$$
$$x = 3\frac{3}{7} \text{ days}$$

Word Problems in One Unknown Problems

1. If 18 is subtracted from six times a certain number, the result is 96. Find the number.

2. A 63-foot rope is cut into two pieces. If one piece is twice as long as the other, how long is each piece?

3. Peter is now three times as old as Jillian. In six years, he will be twice as old as she will be then. How old is Peter now?

4. Lauren can clean the kitchen in 30 minutes. It takes Kathleen 20 minutes to complete the same job. How long would it take to clean the kitchen if they both worked together?

5. A train travels 120 miles at an average rate of 40 mph, and it returns along the same route at an average rate of 60 mph. What is the average rate of speed for the entire trip?

6. The sum of two consecutive odd integers is 68. Find the integers.

Solutions:

1. Let x = the number.

Then, $6x - 18 = 96$

$$6x = 114$$
$$x = 19$$

The number is 19.

2. Let x = the length of the short piece.

Then, $2x$ = the length of the longer piece.

And, $x + 2x = 63$

$$3x = 63$$
$$x = 21$$
$$2x = 42$$

The pieces are 21 feet and 42 feet.

3. Let J = Jillian's age now;

$3J$ = Peter's age now;

$J + 6$ = Jillian's age in 6 years;

$3J + 6$ = Peter's age in 6 years.

Then,

$$3J + 6 = 2(J + 6)$$
$$3J + 6 = 2J + 12$$
$$3J = 2J + 6$$
$$J = 6$$
$$3J = 18$$

Peter is currently 18 years old.

4. Let x = the number of minutes to do the job working together.

Lauren does $\dfrac{x}{30}$ of the job.

Kathleen does $\dfrac{x}{20}$ of the job.

$$\frac{x}{30} + \frac{x}{20} = 1 \text{ (Multiply by 60)}$$
$$2x + 3x = 60$$
$$5x = 60$$
$$x = 12$$

It would take 12 minutes to do the job together.

5. The train takes $120/40 = 3$ hours out, and

the train takes $120/60 = 2$ hours back.

The total trip takes 5 hours.

The total distance traveled is 240 miles.

Then,

rate = distance/time = $240/5 = 48$

The average rate is 48 mph.

6. Let x = the first odd integer.

Then, $x + 2$ = the second odd integer, and,

$$x + x + 2 = 68$$
$$2x + 2 = 68$$
$$2x = 66$$
$$x = 33$$
$$x + 2 = 35$$

The numbers are 33 and 35.

Literal Equations

An equation may have other letters in it besides the variable (or variables). Such an equation is called a *literal equation*. An illustration is $x + b = a$, with x the variable. The solution of such an equation will not be a specific number but will involve letter symbols. Literal equations are solved by exactly the same methods as those involving numbers, but we must know which of the letters in the equation is to be considered the variable. Then the other letters are treated as constants.

Example 1

Solve $ax - 2bc = d$ for x.

$$ax = d + 2bc$$
$$x = \frac{d + 2bc}{a} \text{ if } a \neq 0$$

Example 2

Solve $ay - by = a^2 - b^2$ for y.

$y(a - b) = a^2 - b^2$	Factor out common term.
$y(a - b) = (a + b)(a - b)$	Factor expression on right side.
$y = a + b$	Divide each side by $a - b$ if $a \neq b$.

Example 3

Solve for S in the equation

$$\frac{1}{R} = \frac{1}{S} + \frac{1}{T}$$

Multiply every term by RST, the LCD:

$$ST = RT + RS$$
$$ST - RS = RT$$
$$S(T - R) = RT$$
$$S = \frac{RT}{T - R} \qquad \text{If } T \neq R$$

Quadratic Equations

An equation containing the square of an unknown quantity is called a *quadratic* equation. One way of solving such an equation is by factoring. If the product of two expressions is zero, at least one of the expressions must be zero.

Example 1

Solve $y^2 + 2y = 0$.

$\qquad y(y + 2) = 0$ Remove common factor.

$\qquad y = 0$ or $y + 2 = 0$ Since product is 0, at least one of factors must be 0.

$\qquad y = 0$ or $y = -2$

Check by substituting both values in the original equation:

$$(0)^2 + 2(0) = 0$$
$$(-2)^2 + 2(-2) = 4 - 4 = 0$$

In this case there are two solutions.

Example 2

Solve $x^2 + 7x + 10 = 0$.

$x^2 + 7x + 10 = (x + 5)(x + 2) = 0$

$\qquad x + 5 = 0 \qquad$ or $x + 2 = 0$

$\qquad\qquad x = -5 \quad$ or $\qquad x = -2$

Check:

$$(-5)^2 + 7(-5) + 10 = 25 - 35 + 10 = 0$$
$$(-2)^2 + 7(-2) + 10 = 4 - 14 + 10 = 0$$

Not all quadratic equations can be factored using only integers, but solutions can usually be found by means of a formula. A quadratic equation may have two solutions, one solution, or occasionally no real solutions. If the quadratic equation is in the form $Ax^2 + Bx + C = 0$, x can be found from the following formula:

$$x = \frac{-B \pm \sqrt{B^2 - 4AC}}{2A}$$

Example

Solve $2y^2 + 5y + 2 = 0$ by formula.

Assume

$A = 2$, $B = 5$, and $C = 2$.

$$x = \frac{-5 \pm \sqrt{5^2 - 4(2)(2)}}{2(2)}$$

$$= \frac{-5 \pm \sqrt{25 - 16}}{4}$$

$$= \frac{-5 \pm \sqrt{9}}{4}$$

$$= \frac{-5 \pm 3}{4}$$

This yields two solutions:

$$x = \frac{-5 + 3}{4} = \frac{-2}{4} = \frac{-1}{2} \text{ and}$$

$$x = \frac{-5 - 3}{4} = \frac{-8}{4} = -2$$

So far, each quadratic we have solved has had two distinct answers, but an equation may have a single answer (repeated), as in

$$x^2 + 4x + 4 = 0$$
$$(x + 2)(x + 2) = 0$$
$$x + 2 = 0 \text{ and } x + 2 = 0$$
$$x = -2 \text{ and } x = -2$$

The only solution is -2.

It is also possible for a quadratic equation to have no real solution at all.

Example

If we attempt to solve $x^2 + x + 1 = 0$, by formula, we get:

$$x = \frac{-1 \pm \sqrt{1 - 4(1)(1)}}{2} = \frac{-1 \pm \sqrt{-3}}{2}$$

Since $\sqrt{-3}$ is not defined, this quadratic has no real answer.

Rewriting Equations

Certain equations written with a variable in the denominator can be rewritten as quadratics.

Example

Solve $-\dfrac{4}{x} + 5 = x$

$-4 + 5x = x^2$	Multiply both sides by $x \neq 0$.
$-x^2 + 5x - 4 = 0$	Collect terms on one side of equals and set sum equal to 0.
$x^2 - 5x + 4 = 0$	Multiply both sides by -1.
$(x - 4)(x - 1) = 0$	Factor
$x - 4 = 0$ or $x - 1 = 0$	
$x = 4$ or $x = 1$	

Check the result by substitution:

$-\dfrac{4}{4} + 5 \stackrel{?}{=} 4$ and $-\dfrac{4}{1} + 5 \stackrel{?}{=} 1$

$-1 + 5 = 4 \qquad -4 + 5 = 1$

Some equations containing a radical sign can also be converted into a quadratic equation. The solution of this type of problem depends on the principle that

If $A = B$ then $A^2 = B^2$

and If $A^2 = B^2$ then $A = B$ or $A = -B$

Example

Solve $y = \sqrt{3y + 4}$

$$y = \sqrt{3y + 4}$$
$$y^2 = 3y + 4$$
$$y^2 - 3y - 4 = 0$$
$$(y - 4)(y + 1) = 0$$
$$y = 4 \text{ or } y = -1$$

Check by substituting values into the original equation:

$4 \stackrel{?}{=} \sqrt{3(4) + 4}$ and $-1 \stackrel{?}{=} \sqrt{3(-1) + 4}$

$4 \stackrel{?}{=} \sqrt{16} \qquad\qquad -1 \stackrel{?}{=} \sqrt{1}$

$4 = 4 \qquad\qquad\qquad -1 \neq 1$

The single solution is $y = 4$: the false root $y = -1$ was introduced when the original equation was squared.

Equation Solving Problems

Solve the following equations for the variable indicated:

1. Solve for W: $P = 2L + 2W$

2. Solve for x: $ax + b = cx + d$

3. Solve for x: $8x^2 - 4x = 0$

4. Solve for x: $x^2 - 4x = 21$

5. Solve for y: $\sqrt{y + 1} - 3 = 7$

Solutions:

1. $P = 2L + 2W$

$2W = P - 2L$

$W = \dfrac{P - 2L}{2}$

2. $ax + b = cx + d$

$ax = cx + d - b$

$ax - cx = d - b$

$x(a - c) = d - b$

$x = \dfrac{d - b}{a - c}$

3. $8x^2 - 4x = 0$

$\quad 4x(x - 2) = 0$

$\quad\quad\quad x = 0, 2$

4. $\quad\quad x^2 - 4x = 21$

$\quad x^2 - 4x - 21 = 0$

$\quad (x - 7)(x + 3) = 0$

$\quad\quad\quad\quad\quad x = 7, -3$

5. $\sqrt{y + 1} - 3 = 7$

$\quad\quad \sqrt{y + 1} = 10$

$\quad (\sqrt{y + 1})^2 = 10^2$

$\quad\quad\quad y + 1 = 100$

$\quad\quad\quad\quad\quad y = 99$

Linear Inequalities

For each of the sets of numbers we have considered, we have established an ordering of the members of the set by defining what it means to say that one number is greater than the other. Every number we have considered can be represented by a point on a number line.

An *algebraic inequality* is a statement that one algebraic expression is greater than (or less than) another algebraic expression. If all the variables in the inequality are raised to the first power, the inequality is said to be a *linear inequality*. We solve the inequality by reducing it to a simpler inequality whose solution is apparent. The answer is not unique, as it is in an equation, since a great number of values may satisfy the inequality.

There are three rules for producing equivalent inequalities:

1. The same quantity can be added or subtracted from each side of an inequality.

2. Each side of an inequality can be multiplied or divided by the same *positive* quantity.

3. If each side of an inequality is multiplied or divided by the same *negative* quantity, the sign of the inequality must be reversed so that the new inequality is equivalent to the first.

Example 1

Solve $5x - 5 > -9 + 3x$.

$5x > -4 + 3x$ Add 5 to each side.

$2x > -4$ Subtract $3x$ from each side.

$x > -2$ Divide by $+2$.

Any number greater than -2 is a solution to this inequality.

Example 2

Solve $2x - 12 < 5x - 3$.

$2x < 5x + 9$ Add 12 to each side.

$-3x < 9$ Subtract $5x$ from each side.

$x > -3$ Divide each side by -3, changing sign of inequality.

Any number greater than -3—for example, $-2\frac{1}{2}$, 0, 1, or 4—is a solution to this inequality.

Linear Equations in Two Unknowns

Graphing Equations

The number line is useful in picturing the values of one variable. When two variables are involved, a coordinate system is effective. The Cartesian coordinate system is constructed by placing a vertical number line and a horizontal number line on a plane so that the lines intersect at their zero points. This meeting place is called the *origin*. The horizontal number line is called the x axis, and the vertical number line (with positive numbers above the x axis) is called the y axis. Points in the plane correspond to ordered pairs of real numbers.

Example

The points in this example are:

x	y
0	0
1	1
3	−1
−2	−2
−2	1

A first-degree equation in two variables is an equation that can be written in the form $ax + by = c$, where a, b, and c are constants. *First-degree* means that x and y appear to the first power. *Linear* refers to the graph of the solutions (x, y) of the equation, which is a straight line. We have already discussed linear equations of one variable.

Example

Graph the line $y = 2x − 4$.
First make a table and select small integral values of x. Find the value of each corresponding y and write it in the table:

x	y
0	−4
1	−2
2	0
3	2

If $x = 1$, for example, $y = 2(1) − 4 = −2$. Then plot the four points on a coordinate system. It is not necessary to have four points; two would do since two points determine a line, but plotting three or more points reduces the possibility of error.

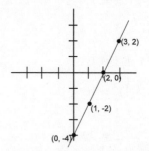

After the points have been plotted (placed on the graph), draw a line through the points and extend it in both directions. This line represents the equation $y = 2x − 4$.

Solving Simultaneous Linear Equations

Two linear equations can be solved together (simultaneously) to yield an answer (x, y) if it exists. On the coordinate system, this amounts to drawing the graphs of two lines and finding their point of intersection. If the lines are parallel and therefore never meet, no solution exists.

Simultaneous linear equations can be solved in the following manner without drawing graphs. From the first equation find the value of one variable in terms of the other; substitute this value in the second equation. The second equation is now a linear equation in one variable and can be solved. After the numerical value of the one variable has been found, substitute that value into the first equation to find the value of the second variable. Check the results by putting both values into the second equation.

Example 1

Solve the system

$2x + y = 3$
$4x - y = 0$

From the first equation, $y = 3 - 2x$. Substitute this value of y into the second equation to get

$4x - (3 - 2x) = 0$
$4x - 3 + 2x = 0$
$6x = 3$
$x = \dfrac{1}{2}$

Substitute $x = \dfrac{1}{2}$ in the first of the original equations:

$2\left(\dfrac{1}{2}\right) + y = 3$
$1 + y = 3$
$y = 2$

Check by substituting both x and y values into the second equation:

$4\left(\dfrac{1}{2}\right) + -2 = 0$
$2 - 2 = 0$

Example 2

A change-making machine contains $30 in dimes and quarters. There are 150 coins in the machine. Find the number of each type of coin.

Let x = number of dimes and y = number of quarters. Then:

$x + y = 150$

Since $.25y$ is the product of a quarter of a dollar and the number of quarters, and $.10x$ is the amount of money in dimes,

$.10x + .25y = 30$

Multiply the last equation by 100 to eliminate the decimal points:

$10x + 25y = 3,000$

From the first equation, $y = 150 - x$. Substitute this value in the equivalent form of the second equation.

$10x + 25(150 - x) = 3,000$
$-15x = -750$
$x = 50$

This is the number of dimes. Substitute this value in $x + y = 150$ to find the number of quarters, $y = 100$.

Check:

$.10(50) + .25(100) = 30$
$\$5 + \$25 = \$30$

Linear Inequalities and Equations Problems

1. Solve for x: $12x < 5(2x + 4)$

2. Solve for y: $6y + 2 < 8y + 14$

3. Find the common solution:
   $x - 3y = 3$
   $2x + 9y = 11$

4. A coin collection consisting of quarters and nickels has a value of $4.50. The total number of coins is 26. Find the number of quarters and the number of nickels in the collection.

5. Mr. Linnell bought 3 cans of corn and 5 cans of tomatoes for $3.75. The next week, he bought 4 cans of corn and 2 cans of tomatoes for $2.90. Find the cost of a can of corn.

Solutions:

1. $12x < 5(2x + 4)$
   $12x < 10x + 20$
   $2x < 20$
   $x < 10$

2. $6y + 2 < 8y + 14$
   $6y < 8y + 12$
   $-2y < 12$
   $y > -6$

3. $x - 3y = 3$

$2x + 9y = 11$

Multiply the first equation by 3.

$3(x - 3y) = 3(3)$

$2x + 9y = 11$

$3x - 9y = 9$

$\underline{2x + 9y = 11}$

$5x \quad\quad = 20$

$x = 4$

Now substitute this answer for x in the second equation.

$2(4) + 9y = 11$

$8 + 9y = 11$

$9y = 3$

$y = \dfrac{1}{3}$

4. Let Q = the number of quarters in the collection.

Let N = the number of nickels in the collection.

Then, $.25Q + .05N = 4.50$

$Q + N = 26$

Multiply the top equation by 100 to clear the decimals:

$25Q + 5N = 450$

$Q + N = 26$

Multiply the bottom equation by −5 and add:

$25Q + 5N = 450$

$\underline{-5Q - 5N = -130}$

$20Q \quad\quad = 320$

$Q = 16$

$N = 10$

There are 16 quarters and 10 nickels.

5. Let c = the cost of a can of corn, and t = the cost of a can of tomatoes.

Then,

$3c + 5t = 3.75$

$4c + 2t = 2.90$

Multiply the top equation by 2, the bottom one by −5, and add:

$6c + 10t = 7.50$

$\underline{-20c - 10t = -14.50}$

$-14c \quad\quad = -7.00$

$c = .50$

A can of corn costs 50¢.

Ratio and Proportion

Many problems in arithmetic and algebra can be solved using the concept of *ratio* to compare numbers. The ratio of a to b is the fraction $\dfrac{a}{b}$. If the two ratios $\dfrac{a}{b}$ and $\dfrac{c}{d}$ represent the same comparison, we write:

$$\frac{a}{b} = \frac{c}{d}$$

This equation (statement of equality) is called a *proportion*. A proportion states the equivalence of two different expressions for the same ratio.

Example 1

In a class of 39 students, 17 are men. Find the ratio of men to women.

39 students − 17 men = 22 women

Ratio of men to women is 17/22, also written 17:22.

Example 2

A fertilizer contains 3 parts nitrogen, 2 parts potash, and 2 parts phosphate by weight. How many pounds of fertilizer will contain 60 pounds of nitrogen?

The ratio of pounds of nitrogen to pounds of fertilizer is 3 to $3 + 2 + 2 = 3/7$. Let x be the number of pounds of mixture. Then:

$$\frac{3}{7} = \frac{60}{x}$$

Multiply both sides of the equation by $7x$ to get:

$3x = 420$

$x = 140$ pounds

Computing Averages

Mean

Several statistical measures are used frequently. One of them is the *average* or *arithmetic mean.* To find the average of N numbers, add the numbers and divide their sum by N.

Example 1

Seven students attained test scores of 62, 80, 60, 30, 50, 90, and 20. What was the average test score for the group?

$$62 + 80 + 60 + 30 + 50 + 90 + 20 = 392$$

Since there are 7 scores, the average score was

$$\frac{392}{7} = 56$$

Example 2

Joan allotted herself a budget of $50 a week, on the average, for expenses. One week she spent $35, the next $60, and the third $40. How much can she spend in the fourth week without exceeding her budget?

Let x be the amount spent in the fourth week. Then:

$$\frac{35 + 60 + 40 + x}{4} = 50$$

$$35 + 60 + 40 + x = 200$$
$$135 + x = 200$$
$$x = 65$$

She can spend $65 in the fourth week.

PLANE GEOMETRY

Plane geometry is the science of measurement. Certain assumptions are made about undefined quantities called points, lines, and planes, and then logical deductions about relationships between figures composed of lines, angles, and portions of planes are made based on these assumptions. The process of making the logical deduction is called a *proof*. In this summary we are not making any proofs but are giving the definitions frequently used in geometry and stating relationships that are the results of proofs.

Lines and Angles

Angles

A line in geometry is always a straight line. When two straight lines meet at a point, they form an *angle*. The lines are called *sides* or *rays* of the angle, and the point is called the *vertex*. The symbol for an angle is ∠. When no other angle shares the same vertex, the name of the angle is the name given to the vertex, as in angle *A:*

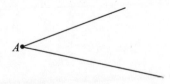

An angle may be named with three letters. Following, for example, *B* is a point on one side and *C* is a point on the other. In this case the name of the vertex must be the middle letter, and we have angle *BAC*.

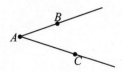

Occasionally an angle is named by a number or small letter placed in the angle.

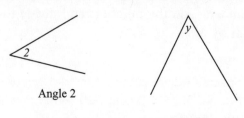

Angle 2

Angle *y*

Angles are usually measured in degrees. An angle of 30 degrees, written 30°, is an angle whose measure is 30 degrees. Degrees are divided into minutes; 60′ (read "minutes") = 1°. Minutes are further divided into seconds; 60″ (read "seconds") = 1′.

Vertical Angles

When two lines intersect, four angles are formed. The angles opposite each other are called *vertical angles* and are equal to each other.

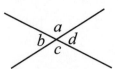

a and *c* are vertical angles.
∠*a* = ∠c
b and *d* are vertical angles.
∠*b* = ∠d

Straight Angle

A *straight angle* has its sides lying along a straight line. It is always equal to 180°.

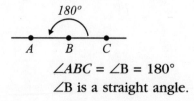

∠*ABC* = ∠B = 180°
∠B is a straight angle.

Adjacent Angles

Two angles are *adjacent* if they share the same vertex and a common side but no angle is inside another angle. ∠*ABC* and ∠*CBD* are adjacent angles. Even though they share a common vertex *B* and a common side *AB*, ∠*ABD* and ∠*ABC* are not adjacent angles because one angle is inside the other.

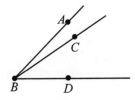

Supplementary Angles

If the sum of two angles is a straight angle (180°), the two angles are *supplementary* and each angle is the supplement of the other.

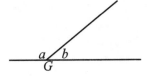

∠G is a straight angle = 180°.
∠*a* + ∠*b* = 180°
∠*a* and ∠*b* are supplementary angles.

Right Angles

If two supplementary angles are equal, they are both *right* angles. A *right* angle is one-half a straight angle. Its measure is 90°. A right angle is symbolized by ∟.

∠G is a straight angle.
∠*b* + ∠*a* = ∠G, and ∠*a* = ∠*b*. ∠*a* and ∠*b* are right angles.

Complementary Angles

Complementary angles are two angles whose sum is a right angle (90°).

∠Y is a right angle.
∠*a* + ∠*b* = ∠Y = 90°.
∠*a* and ∠*b* are complementary angles.

Acute Angles

Acute angles are angles whose measure is less than 90°. No two acute angles can be supplementary angles. Two acute angles can be complementary angles.

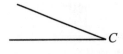

∠C is an acute angle.

Obtuse Angles

Obtuse angles are angles that are greater than 90° and less than 180°.

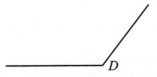

∠D is an obtuse angle.

Example 1

In the figure, what is the value of *x*?

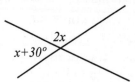

Since the two labeled angles are supplementary angles, their sum is 180°.

$$(x + 30°) + 2x = 180°$$
$$3x = 150°$$
$$x = 50°$$

173

Example 2

Find the value of x in the figure.

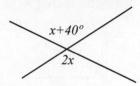

Since the two labeled angles are vertical angles, they are equal.

$$x + 40° = 2x$$
$$40° = x$$

Example 3

If angle Y is a right angle and angle b measures $30°15'$, what does angle a measure?

Since angle Y is a right angle, angles a and b are complementary angles and their sum is $90°$.

$$\angle a + \angle b = 90°$$
$$\angle a + 30°15' = 90°$$
$$\angle a = 59°45'$$

Lines

A *line* in geometry is always assumed to be a straight line. It extends infinitely far in both directions. It is determined if two of its points are known. It can be expressed in terms of the two points, which are written as capital letters. The following line is called *AB*.

Or, a line may be given one name with a small letter. The following line is called line *k*.

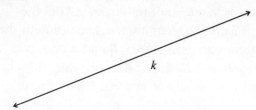

A *line segment* is a part of a line between two *endpoints*. It is named by its endpoints, for example, *A* and *B*.

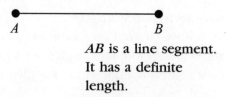

AB is a line segment. It has a definite length.

If point *P* is on the line and is the same distance from *A* as from *B*, then *P* is the *midpoint* of segment *AB*. When we say *AP = PB*, we mean that the two line segments have the same length.

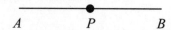

A part of a line with one endpoint is called a *ray*. *AC* is a ray of which *A* is an endpoint. The ray extends infinitely far in the direction away from the endpoint.

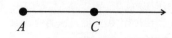

Parallel Lines

Two lines meet or intersect if there is one point that is on both lines. Two different lines may either intersect in one point or never meet, but they can never meet in more than one point.

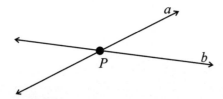

Two lines in the same plane that never meet no matter how far they are extended are said to be *parallel,* for which the symbol is ∥. In the following diagram $a \parallel b$.

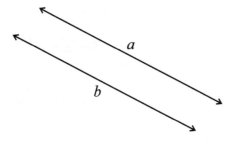

If two lines in the same plane are parallel to a third line, they are parallel to each other. Since $a \parallel b$ and $b \parallel c$, we know that $a \parallel c$.

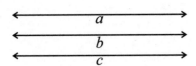

Two lines that meet each other at right angles are said to be *perpendicular,* for which the symbol is ⊥. Line a is perpendicular to line b.

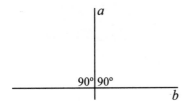

Two lines in the same plane that are perpendicular to the same line are parallel to each other.

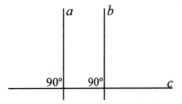

Line a ⊥ line c and line b ⊥ line c.
Therefore, $a \parallel b$.

A line intersecting two other lines is called a *transversal.* Line c is a transversal intersecting lines a and b.

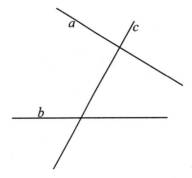

The transversal and the two given lines form eight angles. The four angles between the given lines are called *interior angles;* the four angles outside the given lines are called *exterior angles.* If two angles are on opposite sides of the transversal, they are called *alternate angles.*

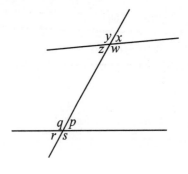

∠z, ∠w, ∠q, and ∠p are interior angles.
∠y, ∠x, ∠s, and ∠r are exterior angles.
∠z and ∠p are alternate interior angles; so
  are ∠w and ∠q.
∠y and ∠s are alternate exterior angles; so
  are ∠x and ∠r.

Pairs of *corresponding* angles are y and
∠q; ∠z and ∠r; ∠x and ∠p; and ∠w and ∠s.
Corresponding angles are sometimes called
exterior-interior angles.

When the two given lines cut by a
transversal are parallel lines:

1. the corresponding angles are equal
2. the alternate interior angles are equal
3. the alternate exterior angles are equal
4. interior angles on the same side of the
   transversal are supplementary

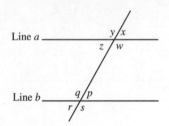

If line *a* is parallel to line *b:*

1. ∠y = ∠q, ∠z = ∠r, ∠x = ∠p, and
   ∠w = ∠s.
2. ∠z = ∠p and ∠w = ∠q.
3. ∠y = ∠s and ∠x = ∠r.
4. ∠z + ∠q = 180°, and ∠p + ∠w
   = 180°

Because vertical angles are equal, ∠p =
∠r, ∠q = ∠s, ∠y = ∠w, and ∠x = ∠z. If any
one of the four conditions for equality of
angles holds true, the lines are parallel; that
is, if two lines are cut by a transversal and
one pair of the corresponding angles is
equal, the lines are parallel. If a pair of
alternate interior angles or a pair of alternate
exterior angles is equal, the lines are
parallel. If interior angles on the same side

of the transversal are supplementary, the
lines are parallel.

Example

In the figure, two parallel lines are cut by
a transversal. Find the measure of angle *y*.

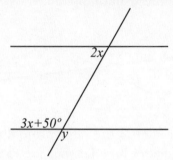

The two labeled angles are supplementary.
$2x + (3x+50°) = 180°$
$$5x = 130°$$
$$x = 26°$$

Since ∠y is vertical to the angle whose
measure is $3x + 50°$, it has the same
measure.

$y = 3x + 50° = 3(26°) + 50° = 128°$

Polygons

A *polygon* is a closed plane figure
composed of line segments joined together
at points called *vertices* (singular, *vertex*). A
polygon is usually named by giving its
vertices in order.

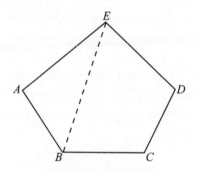

Polygon *ABCDE*

In the figure, points *A, B, C, D,* and *E* are the vertices, and the sides are *AB, BC, CD, DE,* and *EA. AB* and *BC* are *adjacent* sides, and *A* and *B* are adjacent vertices. A *diagonal* of a polygon is a line segment joining any two nonadjacent vertices. *EB* is a diagonal.

Polygons are named according to the number of sides or angles. A *triangle* is a polygon with three sides, a *quadrilateral* a polygon with four sides, a *pentagon* a polygon with five sides, and a *hexagon* a polygon with six sides. The number of sides is always equal to the number of angles.

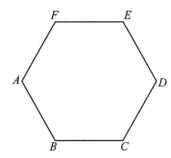

Hexagon

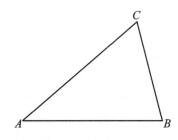

Triangle

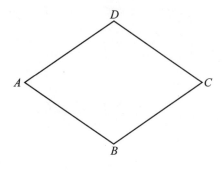

Quadrilateral

The *perimeter* of a polygon is the sum of the lengths of its sides. If the polygon is regular (all sides equal and all angles equal), the perimeter is the product of the length of *one* side and the number of sides.

Congruent and Similar Polygons

If two polygons have equal corresponding angles and equal corresponding sides, they are said to be *congruent.* Congruent polygons have the same size and shape. They are the same in all respects except possibly position. The symbol for congruence is ≅.

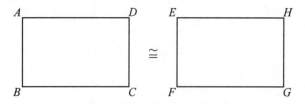

When two sides of congruent or different polygons are equal, we indicate the fact by drawing the same number of short lines through the equal sides.

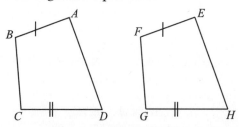

This indicates that *AB = EF* and *CD = GH.*

Two polygons with equal corresponding angles and corresponding sides in proportion are said to be *similar.* The symbol for similar is ∼.

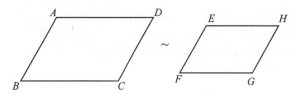

Similar figures have the same shape but not necessarily the same size.

A *regular polygon* is a polygon whose sides are equal and whose angles are equal.

Triangles

A *triangle* is a polygon of three sides. Triangles are classified by measuring their sides and angles. The sum of the angles of a plane triangle is always 180°. The symbol for a triangle is Δ. The sum of any two sides of a triangle is always greater than the third side.

Equilateral

Equilateral triangles have equal sides and equal angles. Each angle measures 60° because $\frac{1}{3}(180°) = 60°$.

$$AB = AC = BC$$
$$\angle A = \angle B = \angle C = 60°$$

Isosceles

Isosceles triangles have two equal sides. The angles opposite the equal sides are equal. The two equal angles are sometimes called the *base* angles and the third angle is called the *vertex* angle. Note that an equilateral triangle is isosceles.

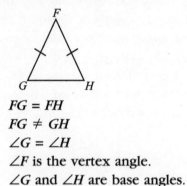

$$FG = FH$$
$$FG \neq GH$$
$$\angle G = \angle H$$
$\angle F$ is the vertex angle.
$\angle G$ and $\angle H$ are base angles.

Scalene

Scalene triangles have all three sides of different length and all angles of different measure. In scalene triangles, the shortest side is opposite the angle of smallest measure, and the longest side is opposite the angle of greatest measure.

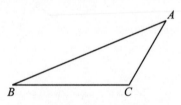

$$AB > BC > CA; \text{ therefore}$$
$$\angle C > \angle A > \angle B.$$

Right

Right triangles contain one right angle. Since the right angle is 90°, the other two angles are complementary. They may or may not be equal to each other. The side of a right triangle opposite the right angle is called the *hypotenuse*. The other two sides are called *legs*. The *Pythagorean theorem* states that the square of the length of the hypotenuse is equal to the sum of the squares of the lengths of the legs.

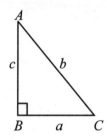

AC is the hypotenuse.
AB and BC are legs.
$\angle B = 90°$
$\angle A + \angle C = 90°$
$a^2 + c^2 = b^2$

Examples

If ABC is a right triangle with right angle at B, and if $AB = 6$ and $BC = 8$, what is the length of AC?

$$AB^2 + BC^2 = AC^2$$
$$6^2 + 8^2 = 36 + 64 = 100 = AC^2$$
$$AC = 10$$

If the measure of angle A is 30°, what is the measure of angle C ?

Since angles A and C are complementary:

$$30° + C = 90°$$
$$C = 60°$$

If the lengths of the three sides of a triangle are a, b, and c and the relation $a^2 + b^2 = c^2$ holds, the triangle is a right triangle and side c is the hypotenuse.

Example

Show that a triangle of sides 5, 12, and 13 is a right triangle.
The triangle will be a right triangle if $a^2 + b^2 = c^2$.

$$5^2 + 12^2 = 13^2$$
$$25 + 144 = 169$$

Therefore, the triangle is a right triangle and 13 is the length of the hypotenuse.

Area of a Triangle

An *altitude* (or height) of a triangle is a line segment dropped as a perpendicular from any vertex to the opposite side. The area of a triangle is the product of one-half the altitude and the base of the triangle. (The base is the side opposite the vertex from which the perpendicular was drawn.)

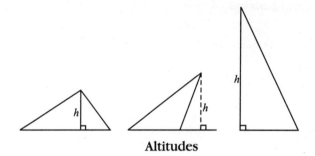

Altitudes

Example

Find the area A of the following isosceles triangle.

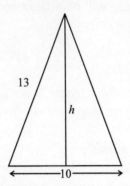

In an isosceles triangle the altitude from the vertex angle bisects the base (cuts it in half).

The first step is to find the altitude. By the Pythagorean theorem, $a^2 + b^2 = c^2$; $c = 13$, $a = h$, and $b = \frac{1}{2}(10) = 5$.

$$b^2 + 5^2 = 13^2$$
$$b^2 + 25 = 169$$
$$b^2 = 144$$
$$b = 12$$
$$A = \frac{1}{2} \cdot \text{base} \cdot \text{height}$$
$$= \frac{1}{2} \cdot 10 \cdot 12$$
$$= 60$$

Similarity

Two triangles are *similar* if all three pairs of corresponding angles are equal. The sum of the three angles of a triangle is 180°; therefore, if two angles of triangle I equal two corresponding angles of triangle II, the third angle of triangle I must be equal to the third angle of triangle II and the triangles are similar. The lengths of the sides of similar triangles are in proportion to each other. A line drawn parallel to one side of a triangle divides the triangle into two portions, one of which is a triangle. The new triangle is similar to the original triangle.

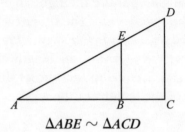

$$\triangle ABE \sim \triangle ACD$$

Example

In the following figure, if $AC = 28$ feet, $AB = 35$ feet, $BC = 21$ feet, and $EC = 12$ feet, find the length of DC if $DE \parallel AB$.

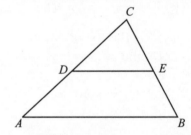

Because $DE \parallel AB$, $\triangle CDE \sim \triangle CAB$. Since the triangles are similar, their sides are in proportion:

$$\frac{DC}{AC} = \frac{EC}{BC}$$
$$\frac{DC}{28} = \frac{12}{21}$$
$$DC = \frac{12 \cdot 28}{21} = 16 \text{ feet}$$

Quadrilaterals

A *quadrilateral* is a polygon of four sides. The sum of the angles of a quadrilateral is 360°. If the opposite sides of a quadrilateral are parallel, the quadrilateral is a *parallelogram*. Opposite sides of a parallelogram are equal and so are opposite angles. Any two consecutive angles of a parallelogram are supplementary. A diagonal of a parallelogram divides the parallelogram into congruent triangles. The diagonals of a parallelogram bisect each other.

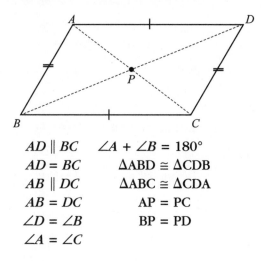

$AD \parallel BC$ $\angle A + \angle B = 180°$
$AD = BC$ $\triangle ABD \cong \triangle CDB$
$AB \parallel DC$ $\triangle ABC \cong \triangle CDA$
$AB = DC$ $AP = PC$
$\angle D = \angle B$ $BP = PD$
$\angle A = \angle C$

Definitions

A *rhombus* is a parallelogram with four equal sides. The diagonals of a rhombus are perpendicular to each other.

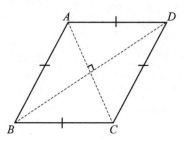

A *rectangle* is a parallelogram with four right angles. The diagonals of a rectangle are equal and can be found using the Pythagorean theorem if the sides of the rectangle are known.

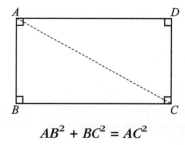

$$AB^2 + BC^2 = AC^2$$

A *square* is a rectangle with four equal sides.

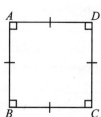

A *trapezoid* is a quadrilateral with only one pair of parallel sides, called *bases*. The nonparallel sides are called *legs*.

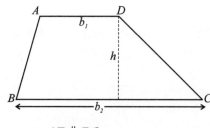

$AD \parallel BC$
AD and BC are bases.
AB and DC are legs.
h = altitude

181

Finding Areas

The area of any *parallelogram* is the product of the base and the height, where the height is the length of an altitude, a line segment drawn from a vertex perpendicular to the base.

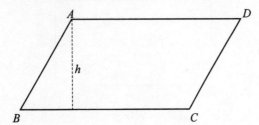

Since rectangles and squares are also parallelograms, their areas follow the same formula. For a *rectangle,* the altitude is one of the sides, and the formula is length times width. Since a *square* is a rectangle for which length and width are the same, the area of a square is the square of its side.

The area of a *trapezoid* is the height times the average of the two bases. The formula is:

$$A = h \, \frac{b_1 + b_2}{2}$$

The bases are the parallel sides, and the height is the length of an altitude to one of the bases.

Example 1

Find the area of a square whose diagonal is 12 feet. Let s = side of square. By the Pythagorean theorem:

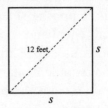

$$s^2 + s^2 = 12^2$$
$$2s^2 = 144$$
$$s^2 = 72$$
$$s = \sqrt{72}$$

Use only positive value because this is the side of a square.

Since $A = s^2$

$$A = 72 \text{ square feet}$$

Example 2

Find the altitude of a rectangle if its area is 320 and its base is 5 times its altitude. Let altitude = h. Then base = $5h$. Since $A = bh$,

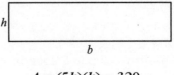

$$A = (5h)(h) = 320$$
$$5h^2 = 320$$
$$h^2 = 64$$
$$h = 8$$

If a quadrilateral is not a parallelogram or trapezoid but is irregularly shaped, its area can be found by dividing it into triangles, attempting to find the area of each, and adding the results.

Circles

Definitions

Circles are closed plane curves with all points on the curve equally distant from a fixed point called the *center*. The symbol ⊙ indicates a circle. A circle is usually named by its center. A line segment from the center to any point on the circle is called the *radius* (plural, radii). All radii of the same circle are equal.

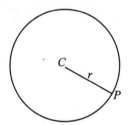

C = center
CP = radius = r

A *chord* is a line segment whose endpoints are on the circle. A *diameter* of a circle is a chord that passes through the center of the circle. A diameter, the longest distance between two points on the circle, is twice the length of the radius. A diameter perpendicular to a chord bisects that chord.

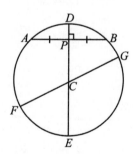

AB is a chord.
C is the center.
DCE is a diameter.
FCG is a diameter.
AB ⊥ DCE so AP = PB.

A *central angle* is an angle whose vertex is the center of a circle and whose sides are radii of the circle. An *inscribed angle* is an angle whose vertex is on the circle and whose sides are chords of the circle.

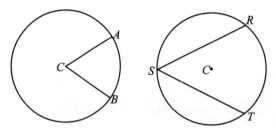

∠ACB is a central angle.
∠RST is an inscribed angle.

An *arc* is a portion of a circle. The symbol ⌒ is used to indicate an arc. Arcs are usually measured in degrees. Since the entire circle is 360°, a semicircle (half a circle) is an arc of 180°, and a quarter of a circle is an arc of 90°.

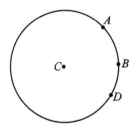

⌒
ABD is an arc.
⌒
AB is an arc.
⌒
BD is an arc.

A central angle is equal in measure to its intercepted arc.

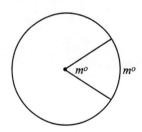

An inscribed angle is equal in measure to one-half its intercepted arc. An angle inscribed in a semicircle is a right angle because the semicircle has a measure of 180°, and the measure of the inscribed angle is one-half of that.

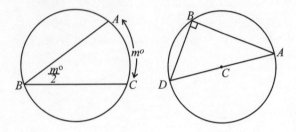

$$\overset{\frown}{DA} = 180°; \text{ therefore,}$$
$$\angle DBA = 90°.$$

Perimeter and Area

The perimeter of a circle is called the *circumference*. The length of the circumference is πd, where d is the diameter, or $2\pi r$, where r is the radius. The number π is irrational and can be approximated by 3.14159..., but in problems dealing with circles it is best to leave π in the answer. There is no fraction exactly equal to π.

Example

If the circumference of a circle is 8π feet, what is the radius?

Since $C = 2\pi r = 8\pi$, $r = 4$ feet.

The length of an arc of a circle can be found if the central angle and radius are known. Then, the length of arc is $\dfrac{n°}{360°}(2\pi r)$, where the central angle of the arc is $n°$. This is true because of the proportion:

$$\frac{\text{arc}}{\text{circumference}} = \frac{\text{central angle}}{360°}$$

Example

If a circle of radius 3 feet has a central angle of 60°, find the length of the arc intercepted by this central angle.

$$\text{Arc} = \frac{60°}{360°}(2\pi3) = \pi \text{ feet}$$

The area A of a circle is πr^2, where r is the radius. If the diameter is given instead of the radius,

$$A = \pi\left(\frac{d}{2}\right)^2 = \frac{\pi d^2}{4}.$$

Example 1

Find the area of a circular ring formed by two concentric circles of radii 6 and 8 inches, respectively. (Concentric circles are circles with the same center.)

The area of the ring will equal the area of the large circle minus the area of the small circle.

$$\begin{aligned}
\text{Area of ring} &= \pi8^2 - \pi6^2 \\
&= \pi(64 - 36) \\
&= 28\pi \text{ square inches}
\end{aligned}$$

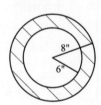

Example 2

A square is inscribed in a circle whose diameter is 10 inches. Find the difference between the area of the circle and that of the square.

If a square is inscribed in a circle, the diagonal of the square is the diameter of the circle. If the diagonal of the square is 10 inches, then, by the Pythagorean theorem,

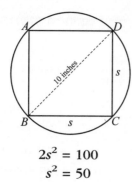

$$2s^2 = 100$$
$$s^2 = 50$$

The side of the square s is $\sqrt{50}$, and the area of the square is 50 square inches. If the diameter of the circle is 10, its radius is 5 and the area of the circle is $\pi 5^2 = 25\pi$ square inches. Then, the difference between the area of the circle and the area of the square is:

$25\pi - 50$ square inches
$= 25\,(\pi-2)$ square inches

Distance Formula

In the arithmetic section, we described the Cartesian coordinate system when explaining how to draw graphs representing linear equations. If two points are plotted in the Cartesian coordinate system, it is useful to know how to find the distance between them. If the two points have coordinates (a, b) and (p, q), the distance between them is:

$$d = \sqrt{(a-p)^2 + (b-q)^2}$$

This formula makes use of the Pythagorean theorem.

Example

Find the distance between the two points $(-3, 2)$ and $(1, -1)$.

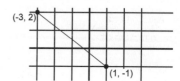

Let $(a, b) = (-3, 2)$ and $(p, q) = (1, -1)$.

Then:

$$d = \sqrt{(-3-1)^2 + [2 - (-1)]^2}$$
$$= \sqrt{(-4)^2 + (2+1)^2}$$
$$= \sqrt{(-4)^2 + 3^2}$$
$$= \sqrt{16 + 9} = \sqrt{25} = 5$$

Plane Geometry Problems

1. In triangle QRS, $\angle Q = \angle R$ and $\angle S = 64°$. Find the measures of $\angle Q$ and $\angle R$.
2. In parallelogram ABCD, $\angle A$ and $\angle C$ are opposite angles. If $\angle A = 12x°$ and $\angle C = (10x + 12)°$, find the measures of $\angle A$ and $\angle C$.

3. What is the area of a trapezoid whose height is 5 feet, and whose bases are 7 feet and 9 feet?

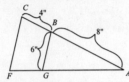

4. In the preceding figure, CF ∥ BG. Find the length of CF.

5. The hypotenuse of a right triangle is 25 feet. If one leg is 15 feet, find the length of the other leg.

6. Find the area of a circle whose diameter is 16 inches.

7. Find the distance between the points $(-1, -2)$ and $(5, 7)$.

Solutions:

1. $\angle Q + \angle R + \angle S = 180°$

$\angle Q + \angle R + 64° = 180°$

$\angle Q + \angle R = 116°$

Since $\angle Q = \angle R$, they must each have measures of 58°.

2. The opposite angles in a parallelogram are equal. Thus,

$12x = 10x + 12$

$2x = 12$

$x = 6$

Thus, $12x = 12(6) = 72$.

$\angle A$ and $\angle C$ both measure 72°.

3. $A = h\left(\dfrac{b_1 + b_2}{2}\right)$

$= 5\left(\dfrac{7 + 9}{2}\right) = 5\left(\dfrac{16}{2}\right) = 5(8) = 40$

The area of the trapezoid is 40.

4. Since CF ∥ BG, $\triangle ACF \sim \triangle ABG$.

Therefore, $\dfrac{6}{CF} = \dfrac{8}{12}$

$8\,CF = 72$

$CF = 9$ inches.

5. Using the Pythagorean theorem,

$a^2 + 15^2 = 25^2$

$a^2 + 225 = 625$

$a^2 = 400$

$a = \sqrt{400} = 20$

The length of the other leg is 20.

6. If $d = 16$, $r = 8$. $A = \pi r^2 = \pi(8)^2 = 64\pi$

The area of the triangle is 64π.

7. $d = \sqrt{(5 - (-1))^2 + (7 - (-2))^2}$

$= \sqrt{6^2 + 9^2} = \sqrt{36 + 81} = \sqrt{117}$

The distance between the points is equal to $\sqrt{117}$.

Unit 7

A data sufficiency question is a particular type of math problem in which, instead of actually answering the question, you are simply asked to determine whether or not you have been given sufficient information to answer the question.

Data sufficiency questions are the only problems on the GMAT for which you are not given five possible answers to the question being asked; instead, the five answer choices A through E represent a code to enable you to indicate whether the information you have been given is enough to answer the question.

Each data sufficiency question has the same format. First, you are asked a question for which there is not enough information to answer. Sample questions of this type are: "What is the value of x?," "Is Bob older than Paul?," etc. You are then given two additional statements, providing additional information about the question. Your job is to analyze these statements and decide if either or both of them gives you enough information to answer the question. Based upon what you decide, you then select one of the five answer choices.

You will have one 25-minute section of data sufficiency questions on the GMAT. You will be asked a total of 20 questions in this section.

The directions for the data sufficiency section of the GMAT read as follows:

Directions: Each of the data sufficiency problems below consists of a question and two statements, labeled (1) and (2), in which certain data are given. You

have to decide whether the data given in the statements are *sufficient* for answering the question. Using the data given in the statements *plus* your knowledge of mathematics and every-day facts (such as the number of days in July or the meaning of *counterclock-wise*), you are to fill in the oval.

A. If statement (1) ALONE is sufficient, but statement (2) alone is not sufficient to answer the question asked;

B. If statement (2) ALONE is sufficient, but statement (1) alone is not sufficient to answer the question asked;

C. If BOTH statements (1) and (2) TOGETHER are sufficient to answer the question asked, but NEITHER statement ALONE is sufficient;

D. If EACH statement ALONE is sufficient to answer the question asked;

E. If statements (1) and (2) TO-GETHER are NOT sufficient to answer the question asked, and additional data specific to the problem are needed.

Note: A figure in a data sufficiency problem will conform to the information given in the question, but will not necessarily conform to the additional information given in statements (1) and (2).

Example:

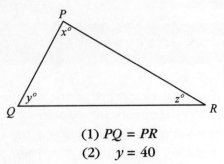

(1) $PQ = PR$
(2) $y = 40$

In $\triangle PQR$, what is the value of x?

Explanation:

According to statement (1), $PQ = PR$; therefore, $\triangle PQR$ is isosceles and $y = z$. Since $x + y + z = 180$, it follows that $x + 2y = 180$. Since statement (1) does not give a value for y, you cannot answer the question using statement (1) alone. According to statement (2), $y = 40$; therefore, $x + z = 140$. Since statement (2) does not give a value for z, you cannot answer the question using statement (2) alone. Using both statements together you can find y and z; therefore, you can find x, and the answer to the problem is C.

The proper mode of working these questions is as follows:

1. Read statement (1). If statement (1) includes sufficient information to enable you to answer the question, write the letter "S" (for *Sufficient*) next to the (1). If (1) does not contain enough information to enable you to answer the question, write the letter "I" (for *Insufficient*) next to the (1).

2. Read statement (2). It is **crucial** at this time to treat statement (2) by itself—that is, to ignore the information statement (1) contained. If statement (2) includes sufficient information to enable you to answer the question, write the letter "S" (for *Sufficient*) next to the (2). If (2) does not contain enough information to enable you to answer the question, write the letter "I" (for *Insufficient*) next to the (2).

At this point in time, your paper will look like one of the four following possibilities:

S (1)	I (1)	I (1)	S (1)
I (2)	S (2)	I (2)	S (2)

In case number one (the first statement, by itself, is sufficient and the second is not), the answer is A. In case number two (the first statement by itself is insufficient, but the second is sufficient), the answer is B. In the *fourth* case (both statements, by themselves, are sufficient), the answer is D.

In the third case (both statements, by themselves, are insufficient), you must go one step further. In this case, and in this case only, consider the two statements together. If, together, they enable you to answer the question, answer C. If, even with both statements together you cannot answer the question, the answer is E.

	I (1)		I (1)
S <		I <	
	I (2)		I (2)

Answer: C   Answer: E

Note that, since the answers A through E are the same on every GMAT, you can save a lot of time by memorizing their meanings in advance and skipping the instructions when you actually take the GMAT.

So that you will better understand the answer choices A through E, five examples follow. Note that the answers have been designed so that the first question has answer A, the second question has answer B, and so on.

1. Pumps A and B, working together, can remove all the water from a tank in 30 minutes. How long will it take pump A to remove all the water in the tank?

   (1) Pump B alone can remove the water in 75 minutes.

   (2) Pump A's pipe is smaller than pump B's pipe.

Analysis

A is the correct answer. (1) enables you to set up the equation as follows:

Pump B can remove $\frac{1}{75}$ in 1 minute.

Pump A can remove $\frac{1}{x}$ in 1 minute.

$$\frac{1}{75} + \frac{1}{x} = \frac{1}{30}$$

Pump A can remove the water in 50 minutes. (Of course, it is not necessary to solve the equation as long as you know that it can be solved.)

(2) is not relevant to the problem.

2. How far is it from point P to point Q?

   (1) Brian ran half the distance from P to Q in 12 minutes.

   (2) Janet ran in a straight line from P to Q in 20 minutes, at an average speed of 9 miles per hour.

Analysis

B is the correct answer. Without knowing Brian's speed, you cannot determine the distance that he ran. Therefore, (1) is insufficient. However, since Janet ran for 20 minutes at an average speed of 9 miles per hour, she ran a distance of 9 mph × $\frac{1}{3}$ hour = 3 miles. Therefore, (2) is sufficient.

3. In triangle ABC, does angle $C = 30°$?

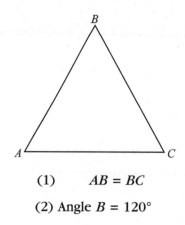

   (1) $AB = BC$

   (2) Angle $B = 120°$

Analysis

C is the correct answer. Both (1) and (2) are necessary. (1) tells you that the triangle is isosceles; therefore, angle $A =$ angle C. Because of information in (2), you know that angle A + angle $C = 60°$. (The sum of the angles in a triangle must equal 180°.) Therefore, angle $C = 30°$.

4. Pipe A and pipe B, working together, can fill a water tank in $1\frac{1}{3}$ hours. How long will it take for pipe A to fill the tank without pipe B?

   (1) Pipe B could fill the tank in 4 hours without pipe A.

   (2) Pipe A pumps in twice as much water as pipe B.

Analysis

D is the correct answer. According to (1), B could fill $\frac{1}{4}$ of the tank in one hour.

Pipe A would fill $\frac{1}{x}$ of the tank in one hour.

In $1\frac{1}{3}$ hours they would fill $\frac{4}{3}\left(\frac{1}{4}+\frac{1}{x}\right) = 1$.

(1) gives us an answer for the length of time needed for A to fill the tank alone.

(2) tells us that if A can pump in $\frac{1}{x}$ in one hour, B would pump in $\frac{1}{2x}$ in one hour. In $1\frac{1}{3}$hours, they would fill $\frac{4}{3}\left(\frac{1}{x}+\frac{1}{2x}\right) = 1$.

Each statement alone answers the question.

5. Is y greater than x?

(1) $5x = 3k$

(2) $k = y^2$

Analysis

E is the correct answer. (1) describes x and (2) describes y in terms of a common element, k, so that both (1) and (2) are needed. Combining (1) and (2), we obtain

$5x = 3y^2$, or $x = \frac{3}{5}y^2$. Then if, for example, y = 1, we have $x = \frac{3}{5}$, and y is bigger than x.

Or, if y = 2, we have $x = \frac{12}{5}$, and x is bigger than y. And, of course, it could be possible that $x = y = 0$. Since we cannot determine the relative size, the answer is E.

Hints for Answering Data Sufficiency Questions

1. The "**What is the value of . . .?**" Question. More than half of the data sufficiency questions on the GMAT ask if you can determine the *value* of a certain quantity. Remember that for this type of question, a statement (or combination of statements) is sufficient only if it enables you to determine a single unique numerical value. Statements that determine two values or a range of values are always insufficient.

Example 1

What is the value of x?

(1) $4x = 12$

(2) $6x < 24$

Solution

Statement (1) is sufficient since it tells us that x is 3. Statement (2) is insufficient since it tells us that x is any number less than 4.

The answer is A.

Example 2

What is the value of x?

(1) $x = 2y$

(2) $x^2 = 16$

Solution

Since x varies as y varies, x can be any number. Therefore, statement (1) is insufficient. Statement (2) is also insufficient since it tells us that x is either 4 or -4. Even together, we cannot determine the value of x.

The answer is E.

Example 3

What is the value of x?

(1) $x + y = 6$

(2) $x - y = 4$

Solution

Statement (1) is insufficient since without knowing the value of y it is impossible to determine a numerical value for x. Statement (2) is insufficient for the same reason. However, when you take (1) and (2) together, you obtain a system of simultaneous equations that can be solved for x.

The answer is C.

Typically, when each statement either gives you or contains the information to write an equation with two unknowns, the answer will be C, as above. However, look out for examples like those below.

Example 4

What is the value of x?

(1) $x + y = 6$

(2) $3x + 3y = 18$

Solution

Statement (1) is insufficient, since without knowing the value of y it is impossible to determine a numerical value for x. Statement (2) is insufficient for the same reason. When you take (1) and (2) together, you still cannot determine x, since (1) and (2), in fact, contain different forms of the same equation.

The answer is E.

Example 5

What is the value of $3x - 5y$?

(1) $x + y = 6$

(2) $6x - 10y = 18$

Solution

Statement (1) is insufficient, since without knowing the value of y it is impossible to determine a numerical value for x. Statement (2), however, is sufficient, because if you divide both sides of the equation by 2, you obtain $3x - 5y = 9$.

The answer is B.

2. The "**Is . . .?**" Question. The other type of data sufficiency question on the GMAT asks if a certain quantity has a certain value ("Is $x = 17$?"), or if a certain geometric figure has a certain shape ("Is quadrilateral ABCD a parallelogram?"). Remember that in questions of this type, "Is . . .?" means "Does it absolutely have to be?" rather than, "Could it possibly be?"

The best way to approach these questions is to read one of the statements, then reread the question. If your answer to the question is, "Yes, it has to be," then the statement is sufficient. If, on the other hand, your answer is "Maybe it is, or maybe it isn't," then the statement is insufficient.

Example 6

Is $x = 0$?

(1) The sum of x and 4 is 4

(2) The product of x and 0 is 0

Solution

Statement (1) tells us that $x + 4 = 4$. The only solution to this equation is $x = 0$, so statement (1) is sufficient. Statement (2) tells us that $x \cdot 0 = 0$. In this case, x could be 0, but it also might not be.

The answer is A.

Example 7

Is triangle PQR a right triangle?

(1) The measure of angle P is 35°

(2) The measure of angle Q is 55°

Solution

Neither statement (1) by itself nor statement (2) by itself, is sufficient since the knowledge of one of the angles of a triangle is not enough to tell us what the other angles are. If, however, we take the two statements together, we can determine if the triangle is a right triangle, since if we know two angles, we can determine the third.

3. Guessing on Data Sufficiency Questions. Often, when solving a data sufficiency question, you will find yourself in the situation of being unsure of whether one of the two given statements is sufficient or insufficient. Note that in any problem where you know the status of one of the statements, but do not know the status of the other, you are, in fact, able to make an extremely educated guess, which will greatly improve your chances of coming up with the correct answer.

In the situation described below, you are able to eliminate all but two of the possible answers.

Situation 1

If you are certain that statement (1) is sufficient, but are unsure about statement (2), then the only possible answers are A or D.

> S (1)
>
> ? (2)
>
> Guess A or D

Situation 2

If you are certain that statement (2) is sufficient, but are unsure about statement (1), then the only possible answers are B or D.

> ? (1)
>
> S (2)
>
> Guess B or D

Situation 3

If you are certain that each statement alone is insufficient, but are unsure about both statements together, then the only possible answers are C or E.

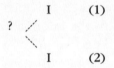

> Guess C or E

In the situations described below, you are able to eliminate only two of the possible answers, but it is generally still to your benefit to guess.

Situation 4

If you are certain that statement (1) is insufficient, but are unsure about statement (2), then the only possible answers are B, C, or E.

> I (1)
>
> ? (2)
>
> Guess B, C, or E.

Situation 5

If you are certain that statement (2) is insufficient, but are unsure about statement (1), then the only possible answers are A, C, or E.

> ? (1)
>
> I (2)
>
> Guess A, C, or E

4. Don't do more than necessary. Remember that your job is only to determine whether you actually have enough information to find the answer. Do not waste your time trying to find the answer; stop once you have determined whether it is possible to find one or not.

5. Be careful to isolate statements initially. Remember that both statements must be considered alone before you consider them together. When analyzing statement (1), be sure not to read statement (2). Similarly, when analyzing statement (2), be sure to forget the information in statement (1). Consider the statements together only after you have determined that they are both insufficient.

Following are several more solved examples to help you understand data sufficiency questions. Then, there is a practice test for you to try.

Additional Solved Problems

1. What is the value of x?

   (1) $x + y = 7$
   (2) $3x + 3y = 21$

Analysis

E is the correct answer. Both (1) and (2) are the same. [Multiply both sides of (1) by 3, and you will get (2)]. In general, when you have two unknowns, you need two equations to solve for the unknowns. Since we really only have one unique equation, the answer is E.

2. A cylindrical tank holds 10,000 gallons. What is its height?

   (1) A gallon of liquid equals 13 cubic feet.

   (2) The diameter of the tank is 10 feet.

Analysis

C is the correct answer. (1) will help you obtain the cubic volume of the tank in cubic feet but will not give you the dimensions. By giving you one dimension in (2), the necessary dimension (height) can be found. (In a cylinder, $V = \pi r^2 h$.)

3. An author is guaranteed minimum royalties of $1,856. How many copies of the book must be sold before additional royalties are earned?

   (1) The author is to receive 5 percent of the net price received by the publisher.

   (2) The list price of the book is $10.95.

Analysis

E is the correct answer. In order to determine how many copies of the book must be sold to reach the guaranteed minimum, you have to know the royalty rate and the net price received by the publisher.

(1) gives you the royalty rate, but (2) does not tell you what the publisher receives for the book. He certainly does not receive the list price, which is the price in the bookstore.

4. A train traveled for 5 hours and went from A to B. What is the distance between A and B?

    (1) The train had to go through some hilly country and traveled at an average speed of only 50 miles an hour in that terrain.

    (2) The train covered 150 miles through hilly country.

Analysis

    E is the correct answer. (1) and (2) together inform you that the train traveled through hilly country for 3 hours. However, neither statement gives you any information about the speed used in the remaining time. No solution is possible with this data.

Data Sufficiency Practice Questions

Directions: Each of the data sufficiency problems below consists of a question and two statements, labeled (1) and (2), in which certain data are given. You have to decide whether the data given in the statements are *sufficient* for answering the question. Using the data given in the statements *plus* your knowledge of mathematics and everyday facts (such as the number of days in July or the meaning of *counterclockwise*), you are to fill in oval:

A. If statement (1) ALONE is sufficient, but statement (2) alone is not sufficient to answer the question asked;

B. If statement (2) ALONE is sufficient, but statement (1) alone is not sufficient to answer the question asked;

C. If BOTH statements (1) and (2) TOGETHER are sufficient to answer the question asked, but NEITHER statement ALONE is sufficient;

D. If EACH statement ALONE is sufficient to answer the question asked;

E. If statements (1) and (2) TOGETHER are NOT sufficient to answer the question asked, and additional data specific to the problem are needed.

Note: A figure in a data sufficiency problem will conform to the information given in the question, but will not necessarily conform to the additional information given in statements (1) and (2).

Example

In $\triangle PQR$, what is the value of x?

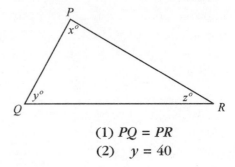

    (1) $PQ = PR$
    (2) $y = 40$

Explanation

    According to statement (1), $PQ = PR$; therefore, $\triangle PQR$ is isosceles and $y = z$. Since $x + y + z = 180$, it follows that $x + 2y = 180$. Since statement (1) does not give a value for y, you cannot answer the question using statement (1) alone. According to statement (2), $y = 40$; therefore, $x + z = 140$. Since statement (2) does not give a value for z, you cannot answer the question using statement (2) alone. Using both statements together you can find y and z; therefore, you can find x, and the answer to the problem is C.

1. The number of eligible voters is 200,000. How many eligible voters voted?

   (1) 57 percent of the eligible men voted.
   (2) 91,200 men voted.

2. Together, Joyce and Ellen weigh 300 pounds. How much does Ellen weight?

   (1) Joyce weighs $1\frac{1}{2}$ times as much as Ellen.
   (2) Ellen is 5 feet 3 inches tall.

3. How much did it cost the Linnell Corporation for liability insurance in 1994?

   (1) The company spent a total of $29,000 for liability insurance in 1993, 1994, and 1995.
   (2) The company paid $7,000 for liability insurance in 1995.

4. Does line AC = 5?

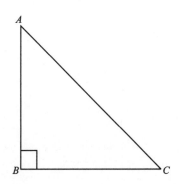

   (1) $(AB)^2 + (BC)^2 = 25$
   (2) $AB + BC = 7$

5. How many male business school graduates from a particular school will not work for state agencies?

   (1) 60 out of the 300 business school graduates from the school were women.
   (2) 30 percent of the male graduates will work for state agencies.

6. What are the dimensions of a box of 60 cubic feet of material?

   (1) The length of the box is 6 feet.
   (2) The depth of the box is $\frac{1}{3}$ of the length.

7. Is x larger than 4?

   (1) x is larger than 0.
   (2) $x^2 - 25 = 0$.

8. Did the MN Corporation have higher profits in 1993 or 1994?

   (1) In 1995 the profits were two times that of 1994.
   (2) In 1993 the profits were twice the average of the profits for 1993, 1994, and 1995.

9. Is AD perpendicular to BC? AD and BC are intersecting straight lines.

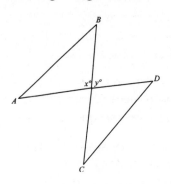

   (1) $x° = y°$
   (2) $AB = CD$

10. How long will it take to empty a water tank if both faucet A and faucet B are used?

   (1) The tank will empty in 36 minutes if only faucet A is used.
   (2) The tank will empty in 45 minutes if only faucet B is used.

11. How much does each book on the bookshelf weigh?

   (1) The books and the bookshelf weigh 43 pounds.
   (2) The books are uniform in size.

12. K is an integer. Is K divisible by 14?

   (1) K is divisible by 7.
   (2) K is divisible by 2.

13. Is triangle ABC congruent to triangle DEF if AB = BC and DE = EF?

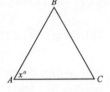 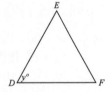

   (1) Angle x° = y°
   (2) AB = DE

14. Is ABCD a parallelogram?

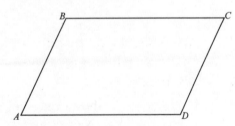

   (1) Angle B = 100°
   (2) AB = CD

15. Is n > p?

   (1) $\dfrac{m}{n} = n + p$
   (2) n > m

16. Do doctors make more than lawyers and accountants?

   (1) An accountant's average salary is 20 percent higher than that of a lawyer.
   (2) An accountant's average salary is 10 percent higher than that of a doctor.

17. Circle O is inscribed in parallelogram ABCD, whose base is 12 inches. Find the area of the shaded portion.

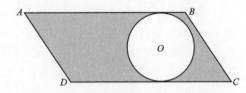

   (1) The radius of the circle is 4 inches.
   (2) DC is twice as long as AD.

18. How many students registered for the Accounting I lecture?

   (1) There are 80 girls registered for the lecture.
   (2) 60 percent of the students in the lectures are boys.

19. Is x always less than y?

   (1) $x < 3$
   (2) $y > 3$

20. Ava, Doris, and Linda earn salaries totaling $120,000. What is Linda's salary?

   (1) Doris's salary is 125 percent of Ava's salary.
   (2) Linda's salary is 120 percent of Doris's salary.

21. An architect is planning a small rectangular entryway. The length of the hallway is to be $\frac{3}{4}$ of the width. What will the dimensions be?

   (1)   The area is to be 108 square feet.

   (2)   The ceiling will be $9\frac{1}{2}$ feet high.

22. How long would it take 12 men, each working at the same rate, to dig a trench?

   (1)   Sewer pipes will be placed in the trench.

   (2)   It would take 9 of the men $1\frac{1}{2}$ hours to dig a trench of the required size.

23. If it takes A and B 6 hours to paint a room, how long will it take A to do the room alone?

   (1)   B can paint the room alone in 15 hours.

   (2)   Both painters use latex paint and rollers.

24. What is the diameter of circle O?

   (1)   The area of circle O = the circumference of the circle.

   (2)   The circle has four central angles of 90° each.

25. One hundred eighty students are taking either accounting or law or both. How many attend each class?

   (1)   50 students are taking only law.

   (2)   130 students are taking accounting.

26. If n and k are even integers, is $\frac{n}{3} + \frac{k}{2}$ an integer?

   (1)   n is a multiple of 3.

   (2)   k is a multiple of 4.

27. The projected school tax rate is set at $11.25 per $1,000. What is X's house assessed for?

   (1)   Mr. X will pay $202.50 in school taxes under the proposed new budget.

   (2)   He paid $217.85 last year.

28. The area of circle A is 36% less than the radius of circle B. What is the radius of circle A?

   (1)   The perimeter of circle B = 20π.

   (2)   The diameter of circle B = 20 inches.

29. Is $x > y$?

   (1) $\frac{x+y}{2} > 0$

   (2) $y^2 - x^2$

30. What is the approximate distance between New York City and Montauk Point, Long Island?

   (1)   Road map A shows that the distance from New York City to Hicksville is approximately 15 inches when 1 inch = 1.3 miles.

   (2)   Road map B shows that the distance from Hicksville to Montauk Point is approximately 36 inches when 1 inch = 2.6 miles.

31. One hundred students are taking both law and accounting. How many students are taking only accounting?

   (1)   180 students are taking either law or accounting.

   (2)   50 students are taking law but not accounting.

32. If AB = BC, how large is inscribed angle ABC?

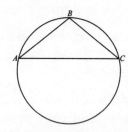

   (1)   A = 40°

   (2)   AC is not a diameter.

33. Find the area of △ABD if BC = 8 inches.

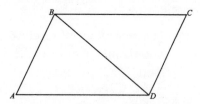

   (1)   A line dropped perpendicular to BC from AD = 5 inches.

   (2)   ABCD is a parallelogram.

34. What is the length of the edge of a cube?

   (1)   The number of square inches in its total surface area is equal to 30 times the length of the edge.

   (2)   25 times the length of the edge is equal to the number of cubic inches in the cube.

35. What is the value of y?

   (1) $x + 2y = 7$

   (2) $3x - y = 9$

36. Is x a positive number?

   (1) $ax^2 = 16a$

   (2) $x - a > 0$

37. What part of the distance from New York to Paris does the Concorde travel in $1\frac{1}{4}$ hours?

   (1)   The Concorde travels at 750 miles per hour.

   (2)   The Concorde travels from New York to Paris in $3\frac{1}{2}$ hours.

38. Does angle x = angle y?

   (1)   AB is not parallel to CD.

   (2) $x = 70°$

39. Is it cheaper to drive to Boston from New York City than it is to fly the 250-mile distance?

   (1)   Round-trip airfare is $276 on shuttle flights.

   (2)   The average price per gallon of regular gas is $106\frac{9}{10}$¢.

40. A man walked around the outside of a field. How far did he walk?

   (1)   The field has an area of 900 square feet.

   (2)   The length of the field is $1\frac{1}{2}$ times it width.

ANSWERS

1. (E) is the correct answer. Both (1) and (2) give us information about the men who voted. You have no information about the number or the percentage of eligible women who might have voted.

2. (A) is the correct answer. (1) gives you a relationship between Ellen's and Joyce's weight so that an algebraic solution can be found.

3. (E) is the correct answer. Even taking (1) and (2) together, we cannot determine any specific information about 1994. Without this information the question cannot be answered.

4. (A) is the correct answer. The Pythagorean theorem tells us that $AC^2 = 25$; therefore, $AC = 5$, as per information in (1). (2) alone will not help us find AC. The sides can be 6 inches and 1 inch, as well as 2 inches and 5 inches. Therefore, (2) does not help you.

5. (C) is the correct answer. You need both (1) and (2) to determine how many male graduates of the 300 will work for state agencies. Once you know that, you have enough information to determine how many will not.

6. (C) is the correct answer. (1) and (2) give us two of the dimensions of the box. The volume of the box = 60 cubic feet = length × width × depth (or height). $60 = 6 \times w \times 2$.

7. (C) is the correct answer. (1) tells you that x is a positive number, but it gives you no information about its size. (2) becomes $x^2 = 25$. This does not answer the question by itself since x could be either +5 or −5. However, taking (1) and (2) together, we see that x must be 5.

8. (B) is the correct answer. (1) is insufficient since it does not relate profits to 1994 and 1993. Let x = average profit. As per (2), profits for 1993 were $2x$, and the combined profits for 1994 and 1995 had to equal x. Therefore, 1993 was larger than 1994.

9. (A) is the correct answer. (1) in effect tells you that angle x and angle y are 90° each, or right angles ($x° + y° = 180°$). Therefore, line AD is perpendicular to BC. (2) is of no use.

10. (C) is the correct answer. Faucet A will drain $\frac{1}{36}$ of the tank in one minute. Faucet B will drain $\frac{1}{45}$ of the tank each minute. Therefore, faucets A and B will drain $\frac{1}{36} + \frac{1}{45}$ per minute, or $\frac{5}{180} + \frac{4}{180} = \frac{9}{180} = \frac{1}{20}$ of the tank will drain in one minute. The entire tank will drain in 20 minutes. Both (1) and (2) are necessary.

11. (E) is the correct answer. Neither statement (1) nor (2) nor both together are sufficient. You must have information on the weight of the bookshelf and the number of books.

12. (C) is the correct answer. In order for K to be divisible by 14, it would have to be divisible by both 7 and 2; therefore, both statements together are sufficient, but each statement alone is not.

13. (C) is the correct answer. There are two isosceles triangles here. (1) indicates that the triangles are similar, since angle $x°$ = angle $y°$, but it does not tell us anything about congruence. (2) indicates that two sides of each triangle are equal to themselves and to each other. (1) gives us the information that the similar angles are equal. Therefore, the triangles are congruent.

14. (E) is the correct answer. Neither statement (1) nor (2) nor both together give you the information necessary. (1) provides you with no relationship about the other angles. (2) gives you no information, other than size, about the lines AB and CD.

15. (E) is the correct answer. Since there is no restriction placed on n, except that it is larger than m, n can be a negative or a positive number. A quick check can be made:

Let $n = -1$; $m = -3$.

Then (1) becomes

$$\frac{m}{n} = n + p$$

$$\frac{m}{n} - n = p$$

$$\frac{-3}{-1} - (-1) = p$$

$+3 + 1$ or $4 = p$

Therefore, p is larger than n in this case. However, if $n = 4$ and $m = 2$, p would equal $-\frac{3}{2}$.

16. (C) is the correct answer. This can be determined by using (1) and (2), which together give a comparison for all three professions.

17. (A) is the correct answer. In order to find the area of the shaded portion, it is necessary to find the area of the parallelogram and subtract the area of the circle. (1) gives us the information to derive the area of the circle, which is πr^2, or 16π square inches. Since the circle is inscribed in the parallelogram, twice its radius is equal to the altitude of the figure. The area of the parallelogram is base × height, or 12 inches × 8 inches, or 96 square inches. (2) is of no use.

18. (C) is the correct answer. (2) tells us that 40 percent of the students in the lecture are girls. If 40 percent of the total group equals 80, then $.4x = 80$, and $x = 200$ for a total. Both (1) and (2) are needed.

19. (C) is the correct answer. (1) tells us only that x is less than 3. (2) gives us the information about y (greater than 3) that makes it possible to answer the question.

20. (C) is the correct answer. Neither (1) nor (2) alone gives you enough of a relationship to answer the question. Both (1) and (2) are needed. If Ava's salary $= x$, then Doris's salary, as per statement (1), $= 1.25x$. Then Linda's salary, as per (2), equals $1.20 (1.25x)$. The three salaries, then, are $x + 1.25x + 1.2 (1.25x) = \$120,000$.

21. (A) is the correct answer. With the information in (1), the question can be answered because an algebraic relationship is established. The

width $= x$; the length is $\left(\dfrac{3}{4}\right)x$. $x \times \left(\dfrac{3}{4}\right)x = 108$ square feet. The height of the ceiling is irrelevant.

22. (B) is the correct answer. (1) gives you no mathematical relationship, but (2) does. Each of the 9 men completed $\dfrac{1}{9}$ of the job in $1\dfrac{1}{2}$ hours. Therefore, in 1 hour each would complete

$\dfrac{1}{9} \div \dfrac{3}{2}$ or $\dfrac{1}{9} \times \dfrac{2}{3}$ or $\dfrac{2}{27}$ of the job. Twelve men would complete $\dfrac{24}{27} \times$ Time $= 1$ job.

$T = \dfrac{27}{24}$ or $\dfrac{9}{8}$ or $1\dfrac{1}{8}$ hours. (Solution is not necessary.)

23. (A) is the correct answer. If B can paint a room in 15 hours, he paints $\dfrac{1}{15}$ in 1 hour; therefore, in 6 hours he paints $\dfrac{6}{15}$. A paints $\dfrac{1}{x}$ of the room in 1 hour, or $\dfrac{6}{x}$ in 6 hours.

$$\dfrac{6}{15} + \dfrac{6}{x} = 1 \text{ job}$$

$$\dfrac{2}{5} + \dfrac{6}{x} = 1$$

$$2x + 30 = 5x$$

$$30 = 3x$$

$$10 \text{ hours} = x$$

Only (1) helps us answer the question. Once again, note that it is not necessary to work the solution out in full.

24. (A) is the correct answer. According to (1), the area, $\pi r^2 =$ the circumference, $2\pi r$. Therefore, $r = 2$ and the diameter is 4 inches. Any size circle would have four central angles of 90° each. Therefore, (2) does not help you.

25. (E) is the correct answer. Since neither (1) nor (2) tells us how many students are taking both accounting and law, we cannot determine how many students are taking the law class.

26. (A) is the correct answer. If n is an even whole number, it would equal 2p, where p is an odd or even integer.

(1) means that n = 3 × 2q, or 6q, where q is an integer, so that $\frac{n}{3}$ is always an integer. Since k is an even number, $\frac{k}{2}$ is an integer, so that (1) gives us the answer. (2) adds nothing that we need to know.

27. (A) is the correct answer. (1) tells you what Mr. X will pay in taxes. Dividing $202.50 by .01125, the tax rate, will give you the assessed value of Mr. X's house. Information in (2) is irrelevant.

28. (D) is the correct answer. (1) means that the perimeter of the circle B is $2\pi r = 20\pi$. Therefore, the radius is 10. The area of the circle would be πr^2, or 100π. Therefore, the area of circle A would be 64 percent of 100π and the radius would be 8. (2) tells you that the radius of circle B = 10 inches, and the calculation would be the same as for (1).

29. (E) is the correct answer. The average shown in (1), $\frac{x+y}{2}$, would have to fall between x and y, but x could be a negative number and y a positive number; the average could still be greater than 0. In (2), if $x = 5$ and $y = 7$, the relationship would be 49 − 25 > 0. Conversely, if $x = 5$ and $y = -7$, the relationship would still be 49 − 25 > 0.

30. (E) is the correct answer. Neither statement nor both together can help you. There is nothing in the given facts to indicate that Hicksville is on the direct line that leads from New York City to Montauk Point. It could be farther north or south.

31. (C) is the correct answer. (1) tells you that the entire population that exists equals 180 students. "Either . . . or" includes people taking both subjects or one (accounting) or the other (law). With (2), the entire population taking law is determined by the 100 students taking both law and accounting, plus the 50 students who are taking only law, which totals 150. Total population minus the students taking law (180 − 150) = 30, the number of students who are only taking accounting.

32. (A) is the correct answer. If AB = BC, line AB = line BC and angle A = angle C. Since (1) gives us a value for angle A and angle C, then inscribed angle ABC = 100°. All (2) tells us is that angle B is not a right angle.

33. (C) is the correct answer. Since ABCD is a parallelogram, according to (2), $\triangle ABD = \triangle BDC$. The area of $\triangle BDC = \frac{1}{2} \times 5$ inches (the height) $\times 8$ inches (base). Both statements are needed.

34. (D) is the correct answer. There are 6 surfaces to a cube, and each surface has an area of x^2. The area of the 6 sides together = $6x^2 = 30x$. Therefore, $x = 5$. (2) the volume of the cube is x^3. With (2) the relationship becomes $x^3 = 25x$ or $x^2 = 25$ with $x = 5$.

35. (C) is the correct answer. Neither equation by itself enables you to find y, but, using both equations together y can be determined.

36. (E) is the correct answer. According to (1), $x^2 = 16$ or ± 4. If $x = -4$ and a is a negative number smaller than -4, then (2) would be true, but we have no information about a, so the question cannot be answered.

37. (B) is the correct answer. The question does not ask how many miles, but what part of the distance; thus, (1) is of no help, since it gives you no information about the total distance. (2) gives you a time relationship, so that $1\frac{1}{4}$ hours divided by $3\frac{1}{2}$ hours will tell you what part of the entire distance has been traveled.

38. (A) is the correct answer. Since AB is not parallel to CD as stated in (1), angle x cannot = angle y. (2) adds nothing to the problem.

39. (E) is the correct answer. (1) gives you the cost of the air flight. (2) does not give you enough information to determine the amount of gallons of gas needed, nor does it give you the cost per mile to run the car.

40. (C) is the correct answer. In order to know how far the man walks, you must know the perimeter of the field. (1) is not sufficient because the area is composed of length × width, and many different combinations can equal 900 square feet. (2) gives you a relationship that specifically expresses the length in terms of the width. Taking (1) and (2) together, you can write a single equation in one unknown, and solve it for the length. Therefore, the question can be answered by using both statements together. Neither statement alone helps.

Practice Test 1

Directions: For each question in this section, select the best of the answer choices given.

1. Students who consistently receive low scores on standardized tests have also demonstrated lower-than-average levels of self-esteem. As a result, educators believe that lowering the requirements for success on standardized tests will increase the students' levels of self-esteem.

   Which of the following, if true, shows a flaw in the reasoning of the educators in the above situation?

   (A) A person's level of self-esteem is usually established by the time he or she begins attending school and does not change.

   (B) The scales for standardized tests are based on nationwide sample tests and not on any local factors.

   (C) Changing the grading scale for standardized tests will have no effect on students' ability to succeed in college or graduate school.

   (D) Self-esteem is a very fragile part of a person's psyche and is highly susceptible to changes caused by outside factors.

   (E) Because standardized test scores are based on very large testing populations, any change in the grading scale would have to be very drastic in order to have any impact on an individual test-taker.

2. Light bulbs that emit lower-intensity light save energy by requiring less electricity. Therefore, if homeowners use only low-intensity light bulbs, their electric bills will decrease.

   Which of the following represents a necessary assumption for the preceding argument?

   (A) Homeowners are always concerned with lowering their utility bills.

   (B) By lowering electricity use, homeowners can help decrease pollution levels in their communities.

   (C) Low-intensity light bulbs are less expensive than more standard light bulbs.

   (D) The low-intensity light bulbs are as effective in providing light as standard light bulbs.

   (E) Low-intensity light bulbs have been shown to create less stress on eyes, and people using low-intensity light bulbs have fewer medical problems.

3. Most boat engines run well on gasoline with octane levels of 87 or higher, whether it is conventional gas or the new cleaner-burning reformulated gas (RFG). RFG contains added oxygen, which makes the gas burn more thoroughly and cleaner. Therefore, it is expected that all boat owners will begin using RFG in the near future.

Which of the following details, if true, would most weaken the conclusion about the predicted use of RFG?

(A) Because RFG is much less expensive to produce than conventional gasoline, retail sellers are expected to receive higher profits than with conventional gasoline.

(B) Conventional gasoline creates environmental problems when it is spilled into fragile ecological systems.

(C) RFG will be available to the general public only in small amounts.

(D) Because RFG burns more efficiently than conventional gasoline, boat owners will need to use less RFG than they would conventional gasoline.

(E) Federal regulations regarding RFG production will make the cost of production higher than the cost of producing equal amounts of conventional gasoline.

4. Municipal records indicate that City X's level of recycling efficiency dropped from 33 percent two years ago to 29 percent last year. One official explained that the decrease does not accurately suggest that the amount of recycling activity has decreased because the total level of trash increased dramatically from two years ago to last year.

The city official's conclusion depends upon which of the following factors?

(A) As time passes, the recycling plant loses its ability to maintain a consistently high level of efficiency.

(B) The increase in the total level of trash consisted primarily of nonrecyclable materials.

(C) City X does not place a high level of importance on the level of its recycling efficiency.

(D) The population of City X has increased dramatically over the past two years, resulting in an increase in the total level of trash collected.

(E) Recycling efforts require separating the collected trash into separate categories of recyclable materials and nonrecyclable materials.

5. A survey of 250 local residents by an environmental organization reported that 84 percent of the residents supported a new bill that would expand the current law requiring deposits at the time of sale of cans and bottles. Based on the results of its survey, the organization then strongly urged the state legislature to enact such a measure because the citizens of the state strongly support it.

Which of the following statements, if true, would most weaken the environmental organization's argument to the legislature?

(A) The citizens who were polled have a history of reacting more favorably to legislation on environmental topics than citizens in other areas of the state.

(B) Expanding the current law would not require any significant increase in funding from the state budget.

(C) Because of high levels of recycling currently in use throughout the state, the increased deposit requirements would not significantly increase the level of recycling.

(D) The population of the town that was surveyed is only 1 percent of the entire population of the state.

(E) The terms of office of state legislators are limited by the state constitution, so the legislators are less concerned with satisfying the desires of their constituents.

Questions 6 and 7 come from the following selection.

In the domain of genetics, natural reproduction will be forbidden. A stable population will be necessary, and it will consist of the highest human types. Artificial insemination will be employed. This, according to Nobelist J. H. Muller, will "permit the introduction into a carrier uterus of an ovum fertilized in vitro, ovum and sperm . . . having been taken from persons representing the masculine ideal and the feminine ideal, respectively. The reproductive cells in question will preferably be those of persons dead long enough that a true perspective of their lives and works, free of all personal prejudice, can be seen. Such cells will be taken from cell banks and will represent the most precious genetic heritage of humanity. . . . The method will have to be applied universally. If the people of a single country were to apply this intelligently and intensively . . . they would quickly attain a practically invincible level of superiority. . . ." Here is a future Huxley never dreamed of.

6. The author's preference is based most upon which of the following assumptions?

(A) Journeys into space will solve many of society's needs.

(B) Research in genetic engineering will lead to a better human product.

(C) Governments are the best judges of their people's needs.

(D) The everyday experiences of daily life enrich existence.

(E) People can be trained to do any kind of work.

7. Which of the following represents the author's effort to state an effective view?

   (A) Only accomplishments possible on the basis of present knowledge are listed.

   (B) The need of federal support to initiate scientific research is stressed.

   (C) The author extols the contributions of Nobel Prize winners.

   (D) What will have been accomplished by A.D. 2000 is exaggerated.

   (E) The author expresses hope for the future in a population created in vitro.

8. Perhaps instead of marveling or being shocked, we ought to reflect a little. A question no one ever asks when confronted with the scientific wonders of the future concerns the interim period. Consider, for example, the problems of automation, which will become acute in a very short time. How are the prodigious economic problems, for example, of unemployment, to be solved? In Muller's more distant Utopia, how shall we get humanity to refrain from begetting children naturally? How shall we force them to submit to constant and rigorous hygienic controls? How shall man be persuaded to accept a radical transformation of his traditional modes of nutrition? How and where shall we relocate a billion and a half persons who today make their livings from agriculture and who, in the promised ultra-rapid conversion of the next forty years, will become completely useless as cultivators of the soil? How shall we handle the control and occupation of outer space in order to provide a *modus vivendi*? How shall national boundaries be made to disappear? There are many other "hows," but they are left conveniently unformulated.

Which of the following best represents the author's concerns?

   (A) The process by which a scientific and humane Utopia will be achieved.

   (B) Feeding a growing population.

   (C) The problems involved in eliminating illiteracy.

   (D) The question of how increasing numbers of elderly people can be supported.

   (E) The opposition of chauvinistic politicians to a world state.

9. **Bill**: Our state government should allow the operation of gambling casinos, because they create jobs and generate taxes. As a result, the economy will improve.

Dave: No, you're wrong. If the government allows gambling casinos, people with low incomes will become addicted to gambling as a way to try to make more money. In fact, they will lose more money than they earn, and the economy will be depressed.

The argument between Bill and Dave is created by which of the following?

(A) They disagree on the applicable definition of the term "economy."
(B) They assume mutually exclusive fact scenarios.
(C) Bill is focusing on a global effect of allowing casinos, while Dave is focusing on a more local effect.
(D) Gambling has been proven to be a highly addictive activity that most people cannot break away from without years of counseling.
(E) Bill more accurately understands the effects that tax laws will have on the allowance of gambling casinos.

10. Only a year after rejecting the President's proposed health-care bill, Congress passed a health-care bill of its own. Most political commentators at the time suggested that this demonstrated a complete lack of respect by the Republican Congress for the Democratic president.

Which of the following facts, if true, would most weaken the commentators' conclusion?

(A) The office of president has been continuously held by the Democratic party for the past twenty-four years.
(B) This president has vetoed more legislation in the past year than any other president this century.
(C) The current Congress has passed more legislation directly proposed by the President than any other Congress in history.

(D) Census polls of the nation have shown that more voters are registered as Democrats than Republicans.
(E) Because no legislation for term limits for members of Congress has yet been enacted, the members of Congress are more concerned with the desires of their constituents than with the proposals of the president.

11. Professional athletes today are more concerned with making high salaries than athletes in the past. Because athletes are willing to play wherever they can earn the most money, local fan loyalties have been decreasing and ticket sales to local sporting events have declined.

Which of the following presents the best evidence to contradict the preceding argument?

(A) A professional figure skater who turns down a multimillion-dollar contract to endorse a product because she doesn't believe in the integrity of the advertising.
(B) A professional tennis player who agrees to play without compensation in a tournament to benefit cancer research.
(C) A professional football player who turns down more lucrative offers from several teams around the country in order to stay in his hometown.
(D) A professional hockey player from Canada who decides to play in New York because he will receive more public exposure.
(E) A professional baseball player who negotiates with the management of his team for the highest salary in the league.

208

12. We are forced to conclude that our scientists are incapable of any but the emptiest of platitudes when they stray from their specialties. . . . Their pomposities, in fact, do not rise to the level of the average. They are vague generalities inherited from the nineteenth century, and the fact that they represent the furthest limits of thought of our scientific worthies must be symptomatic of arrested development or mental block.

Which of the following statements, if true, would least specifically establish the best of all possible worlds for human beings?

(A) Scientists and technologists are engaged in probing the mysteries of birth.

(B) Conditions for a one-world society would be established.

(C) Scientists and technologists would engage in planning for the adequate nourishment of all people on earth.

(D) How the universe came into existence would be determined.

(E) Computers would be refined to do complex jobs beyond the capacity of the human brain.

13. Particularly disquieting is the gap between the enormous power they wield and their critical ability, which must be estimated as null. To wield power well entails a certain faculty of criticism, judgment, and option. It is impossible to have confidence in men who apparently lack these faculties. Yet it is apparently our fate to be facing a "golden age" in the power of sorcerers who are totally blind to the meaning of the human adventure.

Which of the following statements, if true, would most accurately reflect the major function of the scientist?

(A) Scientists must engage in efforts to prolong human life.

(B) Changes in people's eating habits must be enforced.

(C) The mystery of how the universe was created must be explained.

(D) The problems that improve the quality of everyday life must be solved.

(E) Science and religion must be reconciled.

Questions 14 and 15 come from the following selection.

To be beneficent when we can is a duty; and besides this, there are many minds so sympathetically constituted that, without any other motive of vanity or self-interest, they find a pleasure in spreading joy around them, and can take delight in the satisfaction of others so far as it is their own work.

14. Which of the following, if true, would most strengthen the author's definition of sense of duty?

(A) An outgrowth of patriotism is a sense of duty.

(B) The production of one's heredity and environment is embodied in a sense of duty.

(C) A sense of duty is forced upon one by an authority.

(D) A sense of duty is the true source of beneficence.

(E) A sense of duty is acquired through education.

15. Which of the following can be concluded from the preceding information?

(A) The author's belief arises from inclination.

(B) The author's belief can be compared to the sublime in literature.

(C) The author's belief is unrelated to any emotional feeling.

(D) The author's belief has its source in all that's good in human beings.

(E) The author's belief is inculcated in school and church.

16. All employees of a particular company must enroll in the company's insurance program. Some but not all of the employees' spouses have enrolled in the same program. No one who is not enrolled in the company insurance program may enter the assembly-line work space.

Based on the preceding information, which of the following conclusions must be true?

  I.   Some employees' spouses are also employees of the company.

 II.   No employees' spouses are also employees of the company.

III.   No employee's spouse may enter the assembly-line work space.

(A) I only

(B) II only

(C) I and II only

(D) I, II, and III

(E) None of the above

SECTION 2   TIME—25 MINUTES   16 QUESTIONS

Directions: In this section solve each problem, using any available space on the page for scratchwork. Then indicate the best of the answer choices given.

Numbers: All numbers used are real numbers.

Figures: Figures that accompany problems in the text are intended to provide information useful in solving the problems. They are drawn as accurately as possible EXCEPT when it is stated in a specific problem that its figure is not drawn to scale. All figures lie in a plane unless otherwise indicated.

1. Five women had the following amounts of money in their wallets: $12.50, $11.83, $10.40, $0.74, and $0.00. What was the average amount of money carried by these women?

   (A) $7.09
   (B) $7.62
   (C) $9.88
   (D) $35.47
   (E) $7.83

2. Each inch on a map corresponds to a distance of 110 miles. What distance corresponds to 5.5 inches on the map?

   (A) 20 miles
   (B) 550 miles
   (C) 605 miles
   (D) 660 miles
   (E) 1,100 miles

3. 84.2 is 42.1% of:

   (A) 42.1
   (B) 50
   (C) 84.2
   (D) 100
   (E) 200

4. Mr. Tower and Mr. Scalisi leave two towns and travel toward one another in their cars. Mr. Tower averages 40 mph, and Mr. Scalisi averages 50 mph. If the two towns are 270 miles apart, how many miles does Mr. Tower travel before they meet?

   (A) 80
   (B) 90
   (C) 110
   (D) 120
   (E) 150

5. Three congruent squares are arranged in a row. If the perimeter of *ABCD* is 80, the area of *ABCD* is:

   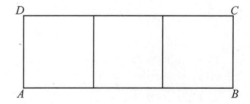

   (A) 64
   (B) 100
   (C) 193
   (D) 300
   (E) 260

6. On a certain day at school, 72 students were absent. This represents 9% of the enrollment. How many students were enrolled?

   (A) 720
   (B) 800
   (C) 6,552
   (D) 80
   (E) 600

7. If the length of a square is doubled, then:

   (A) the perimeter and area are both doubled
   (B) the perimeter and area are each multiplied by 4
   (C) the area is multiplied by 4 and the perimeter is doubled
   (D) the perimeter is multiplied by 4 and the area is doubled
   (E) none of the above

8. Calculate the volume of a spherical storage tank if the diameter is 2.4 feet long using the formula

   $$\text{volume} = \left(\frac{4}{3}\right)\pi r^3 \qquad \left(\pi = \frac{22}{7}\right).$$

   (A) 3.6 cu ft
   (B) 7.2 cu ft
   (C) 3.4 cu ft
   (D) 8.3 cu ft
   (E) 9.7 cu ft

9. Express the fraction $\dfrac{N^2 + N - 6}{2N + 6}$ in lowest terms.

   (A) $\dfrac{N-1}{N}$
   (B) $\dfrac{N-2}{2}$
   (C) $\dfrac{N+2}{N}$
   (D) $\dfrac{N}{2}$
   (E) $\dfrac{N}{2} + N + 6$

10. It takes Ms. Smith Y hours to complete typing a manuscript. After 2 hours, she was called away. What fractional part of the assignment was left to be completed?

    (A) $\dfrac{2-Y}{Y}$
    (B) $\dfrac{Y}{2}$
    (C) $Y - 2$
    (D) $\dfrac{Y-2}{2}$
    (E) $\dfrac{Y-2}{Y}$

11. Which of the following is the smallest?

    (A) (0.11)(0.11)
    (B) 0.00112
    (C) 0.001(1.2)
    (D) 0.00121
    (E) 0.001101

12. The length of a side of a square is represented by $x + 2$, and the length of a side of an equilateral triangle by $2x$. If the square and the equilateral triangle have equal perimeters, find x.

(A) 24
(B) 16
(C) 12
(D) 8
(E) 4

13. If $\dfrac{px - r}{x - 1} = s$, then $x =$

(A) $\dfrac{s - p}{r - s}$

(B) $\dfrac{p}{r}$

(C) $\dfrac{p - s}{p - r - 1}$

(D) $\dfrac{r - s}{p - s}$

(E) $\dfrac{1 - p}{s - r}$

14. What is the area of square $ABCD$?

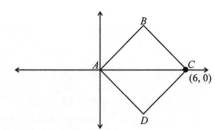

(A) $3\sqrt{2}$
(B) $6\sqrt{2}$
(C) 12
(D) $12\sqrt{2}$
(E) 18

15. EBD and FBC are right angles. If the degree measurement of EBF and FBD is in the ratio $5:4$, what is the degree measurement of EBA?

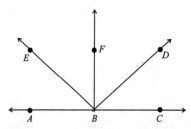

(A) 40°
(B) 50°
(C) 55°
(D) 60°
(E) 45°

16. The measures of angles of a triangle are in the ratio $1:3:5$. Find the number of degrees in the measure of the smallest angle of a triangle.

(A) 20°
(B) 60°
(C) 100°
(D) 180°
(E) 40°

SECTION **3** TIME—25 MINUTES 20 QUESTIONS

Figures

A figure in a data sufficiency problem will conform to the information given in the question, but will not necessarily conform to the additional information given in statements (1) and (2).

Note

In questions that ask for the value of a quantity, the data given in the statements are sufficient only when it is possible to determine exactly one numerical value for the quantity.

Example

In $\triangle PQR$, what is the value of x?

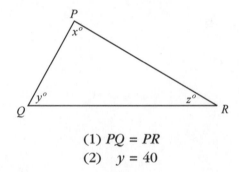

    (1) $PQ = PR$
    (2) $y = 40$

Explanation

According to statement (1), $PQ = PR$; therefore, $\triangle PQR$ is isosceles and $y = z$. Since $x + y + z = 180$, it follows that $x + 2y = 180$. Since statement (1) does not give a value for y, you cannot answer the question using statement (1) alone. According to statement (2), $y = 40$; therefore, $x + z = 140$. Since statement (2) does not give a value for z, you cannot answer the question using statement (2) alone. Using both statements together, since $x + 2y = 180$ and the value of y is given, you can find the value of x. Therefore, the answer is C.

1. A gardener is hired for five days. Each day he works 1 hour more than the preceding day. How many hours did he work the first day?

   (1) He is paid $4 an hour.
   (2) His total wages equal $140.

2. Are two triangles congruent?

   (1) Both triangles are isosceles triangles.
   (2) Both triangles have the same perimeter.

3. The figure ABCD is inscribed in the circle. What is the length of AB?

   (1) ABCD is a square.
   (2) The radius of the circle is 9 inches.

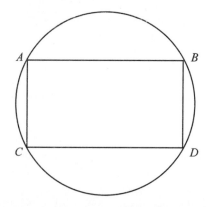

4. Ms. Newman made $25,000 in 1993. What is her average yearly income for the years 1993 through 1995?

   (1) Her total combined income for 1994 and 1995 was $63,000.
   (2) Ms. Newman had a 20 percent wage increase in 1994 and a 10 percent wage increase in 1995.

5. An SST plane is circling over Kennedy Airport. At what maximum speed per hour may it circle?

   (1) An SST flies at speeds of 750 miles an hour once it breaks the sonic barrier.
   (2) Planes circling Kennedy are limited to a speed of $\frac{1}{9}$ mile per second.

6. The Popular Corporation has 5,000 employees. What is the average yearly wage of its executives?

   (1) The total yearly payroll for the company is $50,000,000.
   (2) The company has 1,500 executives.

7. Is ABCD a parallelogram?

   (1) x and $y = 120°$
   (2) AB//CD

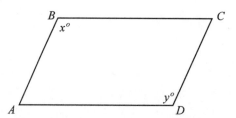

8. What was Mr. Pump's income tax for 1993?

   (1) The total income tax paid for 1992, 1993, and 1994 amounted to $70,000.
   (2) He paid 30 percent more in 1994 than he paid in 1992.

9. Mr. Kelly and Mr. Thomas are both salespeople for the same car dealership. Which of the two received the greater amount of commission money last year?

    (1) Mr. Thomas received a commission equal to 12 percent of his sales.

    (2) Mr. Kelly received a commission equal to 10 percent of his sales.

10. Is y an integer?

    (1) $7y$ is an integer.

    (2) $y + 7$ is an integer.

11. What is the value of $6x - y$?

    (1) $12x - 2y = 14$

    (2) $x + 2y = 12$

12. Is x greater than zero?

    (1) $x^3 + 27 = 0$

    (2) $x^4 - 81 = 0$

13. A piece of picture-frame molding is 4 feet long. When it is cut, what is the longer dimension of the picture it will frame?

    (1) One side of the picture is 9 inches long.

    (2) One side of the picture is $\dfrac{3}{5}$ that of the other side.

14. Matt and Jay, standing near each other in the sun, cast shadows of 15 feet and 12 feet, respectively. How tall is Jay?

    (1) Matt is standing 3 feet away from Jay.

    (2) Matt is 6 feet tall.

15. Mr. Smith wishes to lay a rectangular patio with an area of 240 square feet. What is the length of the patio?

    (1) The width of the patio will be 8 feet less than the length.

    (2) The width of the patio will be $\dfrac{3}{5}$ the length.

16. What is the profit on 20 boxes of bath soap?

    (1) Each box contains 12 cakes of soap, with a total weight of 2 lbs. 8 oz.

    (2) The cost of manufacturing and packaging 1,000 boxes of soap is $1,249.

17. Are angles x and y equal?

    (1) AB and CD are straight lines.

    (2) Angle $x = 80°$.

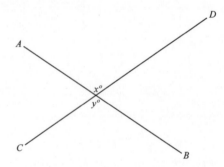

18. Do sides $AC + CD$ = lines $AE + EI + IF$ $+ FJ + JG + GH + HD$?

    (1) $ABCD$ is a parallelogram.

    (2)   Angles x, y, and z = angle C.

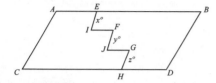

19. What is the value of $x^6 - y^6$?

    (1) $x^3 - y^3 = 0$

    (2) $x^3 + y^3 = 60$

20. Is x a positive number if m is an integer?

    (1) $m^2 = x$

    (2) $x \neq 0$

SECTION 4	TIME—25 MINUTES	22 QUESTIONS

Directions: In each of the following sentences, some part of the sentence or the entire sentence is underlined. Beneath each sentence you will find five ways of phrasing the underlined part. The first of these repeats the original; the other four are different. If you think the original is better than any of the alternatives, choose answer A; otherwise choose one of the others. Select the best version and fill in the corresponding oval on your answer sheet.

This is a test of correctness and effectiveness of expression. In choosing answers, follow the requirements of standard written English; that is, pay attention to grammar, choice of words, and sentence construction. Choose the answer that expresses most effectively what is presented in the original sentence; this answer should be clear and exact, without awkwardness, ambiguity, or redundancy.

1. He was suspended not only for his excessive absence but <u>because he was not meeting</u> the school's standards of achievement.

    (A) because he was not meeting
    (B) for his inability to meet
    (C) since he was not meeting
    (D) because he wasn't meeting
    (E) because of he wasn't meeting

2. <u>If he knew he was</u> awarded the prize, he would not have laughed at the judges.

    (A) If he knew he was
    (B) If he knows he was
    (C) If he had known he was
    (D) If he knew he were
    (E) If he had known he were

3. Her insulting habit of correcting everyone she meets, accompanied by her loud voice, her inability to listen to anyone, and her nervous giggles, <u>prevent her from doing well as an</u> administrator.

    (A) prevent her from doing well as
    (B) prevent her doing well as
    (C) prevent her doing good as
    (D) prevents her from doing good as
    (E) prevents her from doing well as

4. Mouth agape, Mark looked <u>more like a credible child than</u> the sophisticated attorney he actually was.

    (A) more like a credible child than
    (B) more as a credible child than
    (C) more as a credulous child then
    (D) more like a credulous child than
    (E) more like a credible child then

5. Having inherited great wealth, <u>her desire to continue her study of archae-ology</u> would not be thwarted by lack of funds.

   (A) her desire to continue her study of archaeology
   (B) her study of archaeology
   (C) she was able to continue her study of archaeology; she
   (D) the opportunity to continue her study of archaeology
   (E) studying archaeology

6. <u>Judge Shaffer had integrity and never hesitated</u> to render an unpopular decision.

   (A) Judge Shaffer had integrity and never hesitated
   (B) Judge Shaffer had integrity, and never hesitated
   (C) Judge Shaffer had integrity and he never hesitated
   (D) Judge Shaffer had integrity. And never hesitated
   (E) Judge Shaffer had integrity; and he never hesitated

7. Because <u>I was late. My mother was</u> angry.

   (A) I was late. My mother
   (B) I was late, my mother
   (C) I was late; my mother
   (D) I was late and my mother
   (E) I was late my mother

8. I shall give the writing prize to <u>who-ever in my opinion</u> deserves it.

   (A) whoever in my opinion
   (B) whomever in my opinion
   (C) whoever; in my opinion
   (D) whomever, in my opinion
   (E) whichever in my opinion

9. <u>To complete law school,</u> commitment is an important asset.

   (A) To complete law school,
   (B) To complete law school
   (C) If you want to complete law school,
   (D) When completing law school,
   (E) Upon completion of law school,

10. Some athletes compete to the point of complete <u>fatigue; this</u> may result in physical damage.

    (A) fatigue; this
    (B) fatigue; it
    (C) fatigue, this practice
    (D) fatigue; this practice
    (E) fatigue, this

11. The professor told the class <u>he would either expect</u> a term paper or an oral report.

    (A) he would either expect
    (B) , he would either expect
    (C) he either would expect
    (D) that he would either expect
    (E) he would expect either

12. He said, "Remember our <u>slogan, 'Do or die!'"</u>

    (A) slogan, 'Do or die!'"
    (B) slogan; 'Do or die!'"
    (C) slogan, "Do or die!""
    (D) slogan, 'do or die!'"
    (E) slogan, "do or die!""

13. Riding a bicycle <u>is like when you're riding</u> a motorcycle.

    (A) like when you're riding
    (B) like when your riding
    (C) similar to riding
    (D) like a ride on
    (E) similar to you're riding

14. The producer and director <u>will tell you about his work</u>.

   (A) will tell you about his work.
   (B) will tell you about their work.
   (C) will tell to you about his work.
   (D) will tell, you about his work.
   (E) will tell you, about his work.

15. <u>Henry Jame's novels are easier to read than James Joyce's</u>.

   (A) Henry Jame's novels are easier to read than James Joyce's.
   (B) Henry James's novels are easier to read than James Joyce's.
   (C) Henry James' novels are easier to read than James Joyces'.
   (D) Henry James's novels are easier to read than James Joyces's.
   (E) Henry Jamess' novels are easier to read than James Joyce.

16. Judith is <u>as pretty, if not prettier, than</u> Sheila.

   (A) as pretty, if not prettier, than
   (B) as pretty than Sheila
   (C) , if not prettier, as pretty than
   (D) as pretty as, if not prettier than
   (E) if as pretty, then not prettier than

17. Everyone is responsible <u>for their unique vision of the world</u>.

   (A) for their unique vision of the world.
   (B) for his unique vision of the world.
   (C) for their particular vision of the world.
   (D) for the way he views the world.
   (E) for the way they view the world.

18. His talent <u>is no greater than any other student</u> in playing the violin.

   (A) is no greater than any other student
   (B) is not greater than anyone else
   (C) is no greater than any other student's
   (D) is as great as any other
   (E) is as great as any other student

19. A writer's theme—<u>his message and purpose for writing—is as important as</u> examining his style.

   (A) A writer's theme—his message and purpose for writing—is
   (B) A writer's theme—his message and purpose for writing—are
   (C) The study of a writer's theme—his message and purpose for writing—are
   (D) Studying a writer's theme—his message and purpose for writing—are
   (E) Studying a writer's theme—his message and purpose for writing—is

20. <u>Continually late and guilty of disruptive behavior, the professor had the student expelled from class</u>.

   (A) Continually late and guilty of disruptive behavior, the professor had the student expelled from class.
   (B) Continually late and disruptive, the professor has the student expelled from his class.
   (C) Continually late and guilty of disruptive behavior, the student was expelled from the professor's class.
   (D) Although he was continually late and guilty of disruptive behavior, the professor dropped the student from class.
   (E) Since he was continually late and guilty of disruptive behavior, the professor had the student expelled from his class.

21. Claire is a strange one; the reason why is that she is not aware of the fact that she views the world in a peculiar way.

- (A) Claire is a strange one; the reason why is that she is not aware of the fact that she views the world in a peculiar way.
- (B) Claire is strange because she views the world peculiarly.
- (C) Claire is a strange one because she views the world in a peculiar way.
- (D) Claire is a strange one because she views the world in a way that is peculiar.
- (E) Claire is a strange one because she views the world in a peculiar fashion.

22. Jack excels at socializing with his customers, although Bob is the better salesman and who makes more money.

- (A) is the better salesman and who makes more money.
- (B) is the best salesman who makes more money.
- (C) is the best salesman and makes more money.
- (D) is the better salesman and makes more money.
- (E) is the better salesman who makes the most money.

| SECTION **5** | TIME—25 MINUTES | **16 QUESTIONS** |

Directions: In this section solve each problem, using any available space on the page for scratchwork. Then indicate the best of the answer choices given.

Numbers

All numbers used are real numbers.

Figures

Figures that accompany problems in the text are intended to provide information useful in solving the problems. They are drawn as accurately as possible EXCEPT when it is stated in a specific problem that its figure is not drawn to scale. All figures lie in a plane unless otherwise indicated.

1. If $A > B$ and C is a positive number, which of the following relationships is not true?

   (A) $AC > BC$
   (B) $C - A > C - B$
   (C) $A + C > B + C$
   (D) $A - C > B - C$
   (E) $A \div C > B \div C$

2. Determine the area between the curve and the x and y axes.

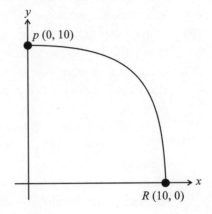

   (A) 100π
   (B) 25π
   (C) 20π
   (D) 400π
   (E) 250π

3. A dealer sold 200 pairs of ski poles. Some were sold at $6 per pair, and the remainder was sold at $11 per pair. The total receipts from this sale were $1600. How many pairs of poles did he sell at $6 each?

   (A) 120
   (B) 150
   (C) 60
   (D) 80
   (E) 140

4. If $ab = 5$ and $(a - b)^2 = 19$, what is the value of $a^2 + b^2$?

   (A) 14
   (B) 19
   (C) 24
   (D) 25
   (E) 29

5. After a discount of 20%, a pair of shoes sells for $84. What was the price of the shoes before the discount?

(A) $95
(B) $100.80
(C) $104
(D) $105
(E) $110

6. The area of a triangle is 40. If its height is 2 units more than its base, what is the length of its base?

(A) 4
(B) 6
(C) 8
(D) 10
(E) 12

7. What percent of the entire figure is shaded?

(A) $\frac{1}{4}$%
(B) 40%
(C) 25%
(D) 50%
(E) 60%

8. One wheel rotates once every 3 minutes, and another wheel rotates once every 7 minutes. If both wheels begin to rotate at the same time, after how many minutes will they both begin a rotation together?

(A) 3
(B) 7
(C) 14
(D) 10
(E) 21

9. From a workforce of 500,000 employed last year, 8 percent of the total employees had to be fired. How many were dismissed at that time?

(A) 100,000
(B) 200,000
(C) 30,000
(D) 40,000
(E) 8,000

10. What is the probability that a random selection of a ball drawn from a box containing two red balls, three white balls, and four blue balls will be white?

(A) $\frac{2}{9}$

(B) $\frac{4}{9}$

(C) $\frac{7}{9}$

(D) $\frac{2}{7}$

(E) $\frac{1}{3}$

11. (*RB* is parallel to *TD*.)

If $BAC = (a + 30)°$, then: *ACD* expressed in terms of *a* is:

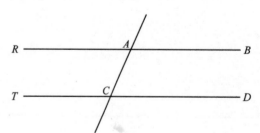

(A) $a + 30$
(B) $a + 120$
(C) $150 - a$
(D) $60 - a$
(E) $60 + a$

12. Jennifer is now 3 years older than Peter. If, in 12 years, the sum of their ages will be 61, how old is Jennifer now?

(A) 15
(B) 17
(C) 19
(D) 20
(E) 21

13. $\left(4 + \dfrac{1}{5}\right)^2 - 16 =$

(A) $\dfrac{1}{25}$

(B) $\dfrac{1}{5}$

(C) $\dfrac{24}{25}$

(D) $\dfrac{26}{25}$

(E) $\dfrac{41}{25}$

14. In the diagram, $QR = QS$ and R, S, and P are on a straight line. It is always true that:

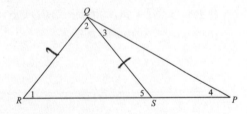

(A) $\angle 1 > \angle 2$
(B) $\angle 1 > \angle 4$
(C) $\angle 3 > \angle 4$
(D) $\angle 4 > \angle 2$
(E) $\angle 1 = \angle 4$

15. Multiply $(4 + \sqrt{5})(4 - \sqrt{5})$.

(A) 11
(B) $10 - \sqrt{5}$
(C) $11 - 8\sqrt{5}$
(D) $16 - 2\sqrt{5}$
(E) $8 - \sqrt{5}$

16. A piece of wood 34 inches in length is sawed into two pieces, one 6 inches longer than the other. What is the ratio of the length of the smaller piece to the length of the longer piece?

(A) 2:17
(B) 1:6
(C) 3:7
(D) 4:7
(E) 7:10

SECTION 6   TIME—30 MINUTES   21 QUESTIONS

Directions: Each passage in this group is followed by questions based on its content. After reading a passage, choose the best answer to each question and fill in the corresponding oval on the answer sheet. Answer all questions following a passage on the basis of what is *stated* or *implied* in that passage.

Reading 1

Line The trenchant observations embedded in Aristotle's *Poetics* as we know it may actually have originated in Aristotle's lecture notes, or even those of one of his
5 students. Regardless of the origin, Cooper refers to *Poetics*, written prior to 323 B.C., as "one of the most illuminating and influential books ever produced by the sober human mind."
10   Although it cannot be disputed that translations of Aristotle's work were available elsewhere, no evidence exists indicating that European scholars had access to it between the fifth and ninth
15 centuries. Aristotle was known in Syria, and a Nestorian monk of the ninth century translated the *Poetics* into Syriac from a complete Greek manuscript now lost. The work was translated from the Syriac in
20 Arabic in the year 935; from this translation Avorres of Córdoba, a Moslem philosopher, produced an abridged translation in the twelfth century intended to "determine how much of Aristotle's book *On Poetry* is
25 concerned with universal rules common to all nations or to most; for most of what is found in this book consists either of rules proper to their poetry and their usage, or they are found in Arabian poetry, or they
30 are found in other languages." Avorres substituted Arabic examples for the Greek, possessed no conception of literature as an imitation of life, and failed to comprehend

much of the sense of the treatise. It was,
35 however, Avorres' translation, translated into Latin by Hermannus Alemanus in the thirteenth century, published in Venice in 1481 and reprinted in 1515, that was the first vehicle enabling Renaissance scholars
40 to consider the content of *Poetics*. This version of *Poetics* circulated freely, leaving no indication that it influenced critical literature. The existence of translations into Latin (1498), into Greek by Erasmus in
45 1532, and into Italian by Segini in 1594 has been documented.
     When the Italian Renaissance scholars were able to consider the work of Aristotle, the result was skewed not only by the
50 number and quality of translations, but also by the nature of the Italian Renaissance itself, questions of the intended meaning of key words and phrases, and the pervasive influence of Horace and the ancient
55 Platonic tradition in the Renaissance.
     The Italians' particular zeal for form established the foundation for the dissemi-nation of Aristotelian "rules," which evolved from imperfectly grasped principles
60 of the *Poetics* and included the additions of unity of place, interpretation of "nobility" to mean outward nobility, the Horatian five acts, and an arbitrary exclusion of a fourth person in dialogue. In Giraldi Cinthio's
65 work, Aristotle's requirement that the poet, in contrast to the historian, relate what *could* happen is interpreted as a require-ment that the poetry represent things as they *should* occur. Other scholars freely
70 augmented Aristotle's work, completing his statements by adding much of the collec-tion of medieval precepts and a healthy dose of Christian thought.
     Aristotle is generally interpreted to
75 have required that the tragic hero be "noble." Italian scholars took this to mean that the tragic hero be highly renowned and prosperous, and the rank of the *dramatis personae* became such a signifi-
80 cant consideration in the Renaissance that it

was felt to be the distinguishing factor between comedy and tragedy. Other aspects of drama—plot, scenery, number of characters, and verse—were molded by this interpretation.

1. The central idea of this passage is that:

   (A) Aristotle's *Poetics*, after experiencing a circuitous rebirth, influenced the Italian Renaissance.

   (B) Aristotle's *Poetics* was not properly understood by those who later studied it.

   (C) literary criticism of the Renaissance had its own particular flavor.

   (D) ehen Italian scholars encountered *Poetics*, several factors influenced their consideration of this work.

   (E) Documents of one era are often misunderstood by those from another era

2. It can be inferred that Aristotle's view of literature included the concept that:

   (A) literature should be written for the consideration of "noble" readers.

   (B) drama should have five acts.

   (C) literature should reflect the concerns of reality.

   (D) Greek language is preferable to Arabic for artistic purposes.

   (E) literature should follow the conventions of history.

3. Select from the following statements that which best states the function of paragraph 3.

   (A) It clarifies the idea of the first paragraph by indicating that *Poetics* did eventually become known during the Italian Renaissance.

   (B) It states the author's opinion of the perceptions of Renaissance scholars who studied *Poetics*.

   (C) It is a paragraph of transition.

   (D) It is a paragraph of restatement of ideas previously stated or implied.

   (E) It establishes the author's negative stance toward Horace.

4. Select the choice that contains all correct completions of the question stem. Giraldi Cinthio:

   I. was a scholar who considered *Poetics* during the Italian Renaissance.

   II. believed that Aristotle saw moralistic value in literature.

   III. was Arabic.

   IV. misinterpreted Aristotle's intention.

   V. felt that Aristotle required literature to be realistic.

   (A) I, II, and III

   (B) I, III, and IV

   (C) II, III, IV, and V

   (D) I, II, III, and IV

   (E) I, II, and IV

5. Which of the following had the LEAST influence upon Renaissance interpretation of Aristotle?

(A) Renaissance regard for "form"
(B) The quality and number of translations
(C) Renaissance views of literature
(D) Difficulties in determining what Aristotle meant to say
(E) Hermannus Alemanus's version of Aristotle

6. According to the passage one way tragedy was defined was:

(A) in consideration of the social status of the characters.
(B) by counting the number of acts in the drama.
(C) in agreement with Horace.
(D) by *dramatis personae*.
(E) to consider social implications of the drama.

7. Which of the following statements about the Italian Renaissance is neither stated nor implied in the passage?

(A) An interest in Classical Greece was evidenced during the Italian Renaissance.
(B) The work of Italian Renaissance scholars lacked clarity and direction.
(C) During the Italian Renaissance, scholars who turned to Aristotle interpreted his works in terms of their own perspectives.
(D) During the Renaissance, one aim of literature was to instruct or inculcate moral values.
(E) Later scholarship has identified some errors of Italian Renaissance scholars who studied Aristotle.

Reading 2

Line Not long ago the region between the extreme northern section of California and southern British Columbia was considered an unlikely setting for an earthquake of
5   great magnitude; however, such earthquakes have occurred in the past and will in all probability occur in the future.

To determine the chronology of earthquakes in the Pacific Northwest area
10   of Cascadia, researchers have sought traces of past earthquakes in the geologic record. Excavation of coastal salt marshes indicated that distinct layers below the present marshes (spaced at successive depths of
15   about a meter) contain peat formed from remains of vegetation identical to flora currently extant in the intertidal zone. Many of the buried peat layers are covered by sand washed in by huge tsunamis that
20   rushed into the subsided coast. Theoretical modeling, as well as preserved geologic effects on the shoreline, indicates that these attained heights of 10 meters on the open coast.
25   After the tsunami dissipated, mud filled the subsided region, and marsh vegetation returned. Repeated sequences of peat, sand, and mud make the geologic point, but do not provide sufficient
30   evidence to date the events with certainty. However, coastal fir trees have been found that were drowned by the ocean after the land abruptly subsided. Examining growth rings and measuring radiocarbon in these
35   trees, researchers have estimated that they died in the last great earthquake to hit the area about 300 years ago.

The existence of the last great quake and of similar events that apparently struck
40   at irregular intervals of about 500 years is suggested by unusual deposits found on the ocean floor at quite a distance from land. When scientists studied these sea-floor sediments, they found fine-grained mud
45   alternating with sandier layers. Mud, accumulating from continuous precipitation of sediment from the ocean above, is common. High-energy earthquakes might have initiated huge submarine landslides

50 that carried coastal sediments out into the deep ocean floor.

The sediments themselves do not ordinarily provide precise chronology. A particular sample, however, contains 55 volcanic ash from the cataclysmic eruption 7,700 years ago of the former Mt. Mazama, whose legacy is Crater Lake, in Oregon. Assuming a steady precipitation of mud onto the sea floor, the calendar in the 60 seabed coincides with that of the coastal peat deposits and places the most recent event at 300 years ago with the twelve previous landslides separated by 300- to 900-year periods.

65 Reports of a disaster are preserved in the oral history of the natives of British Columbia. According to native tradition records, an earthquake devastated Pachena Bay on the west coast of Vancouver Island 70 one winter night, obliterating the village at the head of the bay. A similar account, to which no precise date can be attributed, has been found in the unwritten lore of northernmost California.

75 Japanese written records indicate that a 2 meter-high tsunami washed onto the coast of Honshu nearly 300 years ago. That the earthquake that generated the tsunami occurred along the American coast on 80 January 26, 1700, at about 9 p.m. was determined by adjusting for time zone changes and for the time required for the wave to reach Japan.

8. The occurrence of identical flora in the intertidal zone and in layers of peat probably indicates that:

(A) the sea his risen over the eons.
(B) a former salt marsh sank and was inundated by ocean water.
(C) the flora in question thrive in an ocean environment as well as on land.
(D) the flora grows only in an environment of sand.
(E) theoretical modeling can be inaccurate.

9. Which of the following statements is most directly supported by the text?

(A) It is difficult to date peat accurately.
(B) All peat contains marine plant life.
(C) Peat is located only on ocean floors.
(D) Peat bogs cause instability that gives rise to earthquakes.
(E) Where sand covers peat, an unstable suspension occurs.

10. The most appropriate title for the article would be:

(A) Cascadia's Story
(B) Secrets of the Geologic Record
(C) In Search of Cascadia's Quake History
(D) Scientists Find Answers in Cascadia
(E) Giant Earthquakes of the Pacific Northwest

11. Which evidence is LEAST conclusive as proof that earthquakes have occurred in Cascadia?

(A) Existence of identical layers of peat beneath present peat marshes.
(B) Geologic evidence on the shoreline.
(C) Repeated sequences of peat, sand, and mud.
(D) Fine-grained mud alternating with sandier layers.
(E) Documentation of the date of the Honshu tsunami.

12. The author mentions the "drowned" coastal fir trees in paragraph 3:

(A) to document the devastation of earthquakes.

(B) as a contrast to data obtained in peat.

(C) to explain the presence of radio carbon.

(D) as evidence used to date the last quake.

(E) for comparison with the Honshu quake.

13. Which of the following kinds of evidence were used by the authors in reaching the conclusion that large earthquakes do occur in Cascadia?

    I. native stories
  II. sedimentary deposits
 III. Japanese writing
 IV. geologic effects on the shoreline

(A) I and III

(B) II, III, and IV

(C) I, III, and IV

(D) I, II, and III

(E) All of the above

14. The author provides information related to the Honshu tsunami primarily to:

(A) compare the geologic past of Honshu with that of the Pacific northwest.

(B) prove that even early written records contain references to earthquakes.

(C) present evidence that coincides historically with previously presented evidence.

(D) add validity to the unwritten native stories of the Pacific northwest.

(E) provide the reader with a diversion from the previous more technical discussions.

Reading 3

Line Because adult Karimojong take their formal name from a favorite steer in their herd, I purchased an animal from my missionary friend Bob. In my new identity as Apalon-
5 goronyang—Father of the Roan Ox with the Tan Face—I seemed more accepted. My adoptive brother took my name-ox into his own herd, taught me how to care for it, how to decorate it with collar and bell,
10 how (with salt) to make it come when I called. When it first came to me he was happy, because that was proper between a man and the ox of his identity. I had not mastered the language yet, so friends
15 composed simple lyrics about it for m, and insisted I take my turn singing its praises at dances, as a man should for the ox that is his identity. And they taught me my battle cry, which contained my ox-name, so I
20 could assert who I truly was when I needed my courage and charged my enemies.

    The Karimojong call such an animal "a beloved ox"; mine became so for me. Then disease struck my brother's herd,
25 killing cattle, among them my name-ox. I sat dejected when I heard the news, uncharitably certain that my brother would have been more watchful with his own animal. When neighbors came to sympa-
30 thize, I thought only that they discerned this and were trying to rid me of unfair suspicion. But I was mistaken.

    Day after day, men stopped in to see me. Some had walked 30 or 40 miles to do
35 so. Their faces were concerned, their voices low, and always their remarks followed the same pattern: "We are sad about your ox. We are very sad. It is a bad thing. The land is bad now. Did you hear
40 that at such a place they have had sickness? Did you hear that so-and-so has lost his cattle? And so-and-so, he has lost many cows. They say there is very little milk for his people now. And your ox. It is a bad
45 time this. That is a bad business. Every- where now things seem bad." Gradually I came to see that in this they did me great kindness, for it is not unknown for a man to commit suicide at such a loss. They

50 came to protect me, to emphasize that I
was not uniquely the victim of misfortune.
    In their kindness they revealed much
of themselves. People feel such grief where
they regard their animals as in some sense
55 companions, tied to their own being—not
merely as objects to be possessed and
disposed of. Their commitment to herding
springs from this sense of being-in-cattle.
This merging of identities makes bearable
60 an otherwise intolerable round of labor in
harsh circumstances that begins long before
dawn and ends long after dark—that leaves
even the night hours to be spent stretched
on a cowhide at a little fire by the corral,
65 one ear open for sounds of unrest and
danger. Bringing the herd back full after a
long day's grazing, yourself empty-bellied
and apprehensive of things that prey at
night, you sing softly to the cattle of the
70 hours you have shared, and so feel easier in
your mind.

15. The author's adoptive brother was:

(A) careless in caring for the author's ox.
(B) a missionary.
(C) a mentor to the author.
(D) suspicious.
(E) the cattle master of the Karimojong.

16. The Karimojong perceive the death of a "beloved ox" as:

(A) a personal tragedy.
(B) a loss of income.
(C) a suspicious occurrence.
(D) an inevitable event.
(E) a sign from the gods.

17. The remarks of the men in paragraph 3 are intended to:

(A) establish the belief that life is difficult.
(B) fill some lonely hours and pass the time.
(C) inform the author of a widespread cattle disease.
(D) punish the author.
(E) relieve the author of guilt and isolation.

18. A Karimojong views his name-ox as

  I. a possession with which he may do as he wishes.
 II. a part of himself.
III. of great value, but secondary to himself.
 IV. so important that its welfare is of primary importance.

(A) All of the above
(B) I and II
(C) II and IV
(D) I, II, and III
(E) I, II, and IV

19. What adjective best describes the author's attitude toward the Karimojong?

(A) Empathetic
(B) Altruistic
(C) Apprehensive
(D) Ecstatic
(E) Anguished

20. It can be inferred that:

(A) the author will probably lead the Karimojong toward modernization.

(B) the Karimojong did not accept the author.

(C) kindness is lacking among the Karimojong.

(D) abandoning herding would improve the economic status of the Karimojong.

(E) among the Karimojong a man's ox-identity is a part of his spiritual nature.

21. Select the best statement of the topic of this selection:

(A) spiritual ties between a man and his name-ox.

(B) relationships between a Karimojong and his name-ox.

(C) life in a Karimojong village.

(D) observations and experiences of an adopted Karimojong.

(E) superstitions of a herding society.

QUICK-SCORE ANSWERS

ANSWERS FOR PRACTICE TEST 1

Section 1 Critical Reasoning	Section 2 Problem Solving	Section 3 Data Sufficiency	Section 4 Sentence Corrections	Section 5 Problem Solving	Section 6 Reading Comprehension
1. A	1. A	1. C	1. B	1. B	1. A
2. D	2. C	2. E	2. C	2. B	2. C
3. C	3. E	3. C	3. E	3. A	3. C
4. B	4. D	4. D	4. D	4. E	4. E
5. A	5. D	5. B	5. C	5. D	5. E
6. A	6. B	6. E	6. A	6. C	6. A
7. D	7. C	7. C	7. B	7. C	7. B
8. A	8. B	8. E	8. A	8. E	8. B
9. C	9. B	9. E	9. C	9. D	9. A
10. C	10. E	10. B	10. D	10. E	10. C
11. C	11. E	11. A	11. E	11. C	11. D
12. D	12. E	12. A	12. A	12. D	12. D
13. D	13. D	13. D	13. C	13. E	13. E
14. D	14. E	14. B	14. A	14. B	14. C
15. A	15. A	15. D	15. B	15. A	15. C
16. E	16. A	16. E	16. D	16. E	16. A
		17. A	17. B		17. E
		18. C	18. C		18. C
		19. A	19. E		19. A
		20. C	20. C		20. E
			21. B		21. D
			22. D		

EXPLANATORY ANSWERS FOR PRACTICE TEST 1

Critical Reasoning

1. The correct answer is A. The argument depends on an assumption that altering the tests so that students will receive higher scores will have a positive effect on the students' self-esteem levels. Choice A, if true, contradicts this by showing that self-esteem is already set and cannot be changed by something like test scores. Choices B and E address the methods of scoring the tests and of altering the grading scales, but they do not mention the effect that the scores may have on students. Choice C is irrelevant because the argument says nothing about a student's ability to succeed in college. Choice D, if true, would strengthen and not weaken this argument.

2. The correct answer is D. This argument assumes that homeowners can receive as much useful light using the same amount of low-intensity bulbs as they can with standard bulbs. If, on the other hand, the bulbs were half as bright and required homeowners to use twice as many bulbs, then electric costs may not actually decrease. Choice D repeats this necessary assumption. Choice A seems an obvious truth, but it addresses a homeowner's motivation rather than the actual effect of using the low-intensity bulbs. Choices B and E address other effects of using the special bulbs but say nothing about electric bills. Choice C addresses lowering the cost of purchasing bulbs but not using them.

3. The correct answer is C. This argument assumes that, because the RFG is better, all boat owners will want to use it and will be able to use it. Choice C contradicts this assumption by showing that all boat owners may not have access to RFG and so may not be able to use it, whether or not they want to. Choices A and E focus on the costs of producing RFG and the effects on retail sellers, but not on boat owners. Although it is possible to assume that these effects on the retail sellers might translate to the boat owners, this additional assumption makes these answers not as directly relevant as C. Choices B and D, to the extent that they are relevant to the argument, would strengthen and not weaken the argument by making RFG more desirable than conventional gasoline.

4. The correct answer is B. The city official assumes that the town is recycling at the same rate as before despite the increase in total trash. Choice B supports this by accepting that the added trash would not be recyclable anyway, despite the town's efforts. Choice A would contradict the conclusion by showing that the recycling plant actually becomes less efficient. Choice C is irrelevant by focusing on the town's motivation rather than its actual recycling efforts. Choice D is a close answer, but is not as good as B because it does not explain the drop in efficiency. Choice E is irrelevant unless the work required in recycling has changed over the time period considered.

5. The correct answer is A. The lobbying group assumes that a survey of 250 local residents is indicative of statewide public opinion. Choice A contradicts this assumption by showing that the surveyed citizens do not generally vote the same as the rest of the state. Choice B is irrelevant because budget concerns have nothing to do with the argument. Choice C is a possible answer, but not as good as A because it does not address the flaw in the conclusion based on the survey. Choice D is close to A, but without the added information about the voting history, choice D is not enough. Choice E is completely irrelevant because it addresses the legislators' possible motivations for voting on such a bill, but not the reasons for the public support of the legislation.

6. The correct answer is A. While the choice of genetic engineering and the retraining of people are viable options, the utilization of government and enriching life would not be viable for the author who prefers venturing into new eras.

7. The correct answer is D. The author realizes that some of his presentation is exaggerated for the nearness of A.D. 2000, but prefers that to miring the scientific community in the present or even in the *in vitro* concept.

8. The correct answer is A. The author is approaching all of the future in the sense of scientific development; therefore, the contemporary problems of hunger, illiteracy, the elderly, and chauvinism would be addressed as social problems and not be in the realm of scientific development.

9. The correct answer is C. Bill is looking at improvements to the statewide economy that will come from allowing casinos, while Dave is focusing on problems that can occur to individuals. Thus, C is the selection that closest reflects this contradiction. There is no support in the argument for choices A, B and E. Choice D may be true, but the argument does not show that Bill disagrees with this statement.

10. The correct answer is C. The argument assumes that Congress voted against the president's proposal only because of political party differences. Choice C contradicts this by showing evidence that Congress does, in fact, support many proposals from this president. Choices A and D provide facts that do not address the dynamics of enacting legislation between the Congress and the president. Choice B addresses the issue of legislation, but it focuses on the president's overriding Congress's proposals, and not the other way around. Choice E shows more a lack of respect for constituents than for the president.

11. The correct answer is C. The argument assumes that athletes do not care as much for the cities and towns where they play as they do for high salaries. Choice C directly contradicts this by showing someone who turns down high salary offers to stay in a particular town. Choices A and B contradict the argument in the sense that they show athletes who stress certain principles over high income, but they do not address the issue of loyalty to a certain location. Choice D, to the extent it is relevant, would strengthen the argument rather than weaken it because it shows someone willing to move. Choice E is not relevant because it does not directly address the issue of loyalty to a location.

12. The correct answer is D. When establishing (building) a world for the future
or even the present, the how of
creation of this universe would not be a
factor. Instead, those charged with that
responsibility would look forward, NOT
backward.

13. The correct answer is D. As a scientist,
one is charged with solving problems in
order to make things better, not with
the past, nor even the present.

14. The correct answer is D. One's sense of
duty springs from a desire to "spread
joy." Therefore, such a sense is not
learned, but is innate, and is, therefore,
true beneficence. It is not forced upon
us (choice C), nor is it acquired
(choice E).

15. The correct answer is A. The concept of
morality is not incorporated into
personal emotion or reason. Morality is
duty.

16. The correct answer is E. The best
approach to a question that presents
three Roman numeral selections is to
treat each one as a separate true-false
question. In this case, each of the three
selections is false. The first selection
could be true based on the information
that some spouses have enrolled in the
program, but it is possible that spouses
might be enrolled without being
employees. Thus, selection I is not a
conclusion that must be true. Selection
II is false for the same reason. The third
selection is one that must be false,
because the argument states that some
spouses are enrolled and would
therefore be allowed to enter the
workspace. Therefore, the correct
answer is E, none of the above.

Problem Solving

1. (A) To add decimals, the decimal
points should be positioned
directly under one another.

$$
\begin{array}{r}
12.50 \\
11.83 \\
10.40 \\
0.74 \\
\underline{0.00} \\
\$35.47
\end{array}
$$

To find the average, divide the sum
of all items by the number of
items.

$$\frac{\$35.47}{5} = \$7.09$$

2. (C) Set up a proportion:

$$\frac{1 \text{ inch}}{110 \text{ miles}} = \frac{5.5 \text{ inches}}{x \text{ miles}} \quad \begin{array}{l}\text{cross-} \\ \text{multiply}\end{array}$$

$$x = (5.5)(110) = 605 \text{ miles}$$

3. (E) The easiest way to do this problem
is to set up a proportion.

$$\frac{\text{part}}{\text{whole}} = \frac{\text{percent}}{100}$$

$$\frac{84.2}{x} = \frac{42.1}{100} \quad \text{cross-multiply}$$

$$8{,}420 = 42.1x \quad \text{divide by 42.1}$$

$$x = 200$$

4. (D)

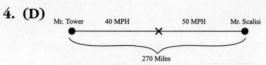

Let T = the number of hours they travel before meeting. Then,

$$40T + 50T = 270$$
$$90T = 270$$
$$T = 3 \text{ hours}$$

In 3 hours, Mr. Tower can go 40(3) = 120 miles.

5. (D) The perimeter of the rectangle is equal in length to 8 sides of the squares. Since the perimeter is 80, each side of each square must be 10.

$$\text{area of rectangle} = (\text{length}) \cdot (\text{width})$$
$$\text{length}(DC) = 30$$
$$\text{width}(AD) = 10$$
$$A = (30)(10)$$
$$A = 300$$

6. (B) Let N = the number of students enrolled. Then,

9% of N = 72, or

.09 · N = 72 divide by .09

$$N = \frac{72}{.09} = 800$$

7. (C) Doubled means to be multiplied by 2.

 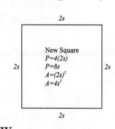

Original	New
$P = 4s$	$8s \rightarrow$ multiply by 2
$A = s^2$	$4s^2 \rightarrow$ multiply by 4

8. (B) Substitute in the formula. Use a radius of 1.2.

$$V = \frac{4}{3}\left(\frac{22}{7}\right)(1.2)(1.2)(1.2)$$
$$= 7.2 \text{ cu ft}$$

9. (B) $N^2 + N - 6$ can be factored into:
$(N + 3)(N - 2)$

$2N + 6$ can be factored into:
$2(N + 3)$

$$\frac{(N + 3)(N - 2)}{2(N + 3)}$$

$\dfrac{N - 2}{2}$ cross out common factor $(N + 3)$ in numerator and denominator

10. (E) Find the ratio

$$\frac{\text{time required to finish the job}}{\text{time to do whole job}} = \frac{\text{part of task}}{\text{not done}}$$

$$\frac{Y - 2}{Y} = \text{part of task not done}$$

11. (E)

$$(0.11)(0.11) = 0.0121$$
$$0.00112 = 0.00112$$
$$0.001(1.2) = 0.0012$$
$$0.00121 = 0.00121$$
$$0.001101 = 0.001101$$

The easiest way to determine the smallest number is to add zeros to the end of the five numbers until they all have the same number of digits. Then, ignore the decimal points and look for the smallest number.

The numbers become:
0.012100
0.001120
0.001200
0.001210
0.001101 → This is the smallest.

12. (E) The perimeter of a square $= 4s$. The perimeter of an equilateral triangle $= 3s$.

$$P = 4s \qquad P = 3s$$
$$= 4(x + 2) \qquad = 3(2x)$$
$$= 4x + 8 \qquad = 6x$$

$$4x + 8 = 6x$$
$$8 = 2x$$
$$4 = x$$

13. (D) $\dfrac{px - r}{x - 1} = s$

Cross-multiply: $\qquad px - r = s(x - 1)$
$$px - r = sx - s$$

Collect like terms: $\qquad px - sx = r - s$

Factor out x: $\qquad x(p - s) = r - s$

Divide by $p - s$: $\qquad \dfrac{x(p - s)}{p - s} = \dfrac{r - s}{p - s}$

$$x = \dfrac{r - s}{p - s}$$

14. (E)

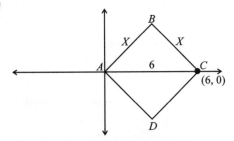

Since $ABCD$ is a square, triangle ABC is a right triangle. The hypotenuse, AC, is equal to 6. Let $AB = BC = x$.

$$x^2 + x^2 = 6^2$$
$$2x^2 = 36$$
$$x^2 = 18$$
$$x = \sqrt{18} = 3\sqrt{2}$$

The area of the square is $(3\sqrt{2})^2$ $= (9)(2) = 18$.

15. (A)

$$EBF + FBD = EBD = 90°$$
$$5x + 4x = 90°$$
$$9x = 90°$$
$$x = 10°$$

Therefore, $\quad EBF = 50°$

Then, $\quad EBA + EBF = 90°$
$$EBA + 50° = 90°$$
$$EBA = 40°$$

16. (A) Let:

$x =$ number of degrees in smallest angle

$3x =$ number of degrees in second angle

$5x =$ number of degrees in third angle

$$1x + 3x + 5x = 180$$
$$9x = 180$$
$$x = 20 \text{ (smallest angle)}$$

Data Sufficiency

1. (C) is the correct answer. (1) gives you no relationship between the hours worked and the amount collected. When you combine (1) and (2), however, the algebraic equation becomes $\$4(x+x+1+x+2+x+3+x+4)$ $= \$140$, where $x =$ the number of hours worked the first day. Both statements must be used.

2. (E) is the correct answer. Each isosceles triangle has one side equal to another, but (1) does not tell you if the equal sides of one triangle equal the sides in the other, nor does it give you any information about the size of the angles. (2) merely tells you that the sums of the sides of each triangle are equal but gives you no information about the size of any individual side. No relationship can be inferred about the lengths of the sides.

3. (C) is the correct answer. Draw the radii of the center to the vertices *A, B, C,* and *D.* According to (1) the four triangles that are formed are congruent to each other. The angle at *O* for each triangle is 90° (360° in a circle ÷ 4 = 90°).

Therefore, with the information given in statement (2), *AB* is the hypotenuse of a right triangle *ABD*, in which the other two sides are each 9 inches. Therefore, $(AB)^2 = 9^2 + 9^2$.

4. (D) is the correct answer. (1) provides you with the information to find the total income for years 1993-1995 so that an average can be found; $\dfrac{(\$63,000 + \$25,000)}{3}$. (2) gives you the information to find the income for 1994 and 1995. The income for those years added to the 1993 income gives you the figures for all three years.

Either (1) or (2) is sufficient.

5. (B) is the correct answer. (1) is not relevant, since a circling plane is not breaking the sonic barrier. (2) alone gives you the information needed because simple arithmetic will translate the speed per second to speed per hour.

6. (E) is the correct answer. Neither (1) or (2) alone nor both together give you sufficient data to answer the question. There is no way to determine the amount of the payroll that is exclusively for executives or even exclusively for nonexecutive personnel.

7. (C) is the correct answer. (1) tells you nothing about the other angles in the diagram. (2), however, expands our information. Angle *B* is supplementary to angle *C.* If two parallel lines are intersected by a transversal, then the interior angles on the same side are supplementary to each other. Angle *C* = 60°. Angle *A* = 60° as well, since angles of a quadrilateral add up to 360°. If opposite angles are equal in a quadrilateral, the figure is a parallelogram.

8. (E) is the correct answer. If you knew the amount of tax paid in 1992 and 1994, you could deduce the income tax paid in 1993, so (1) is not sufficient. (2) gives you a relationship between tax paid in 1992 and 1994, but you must know the amount paid in either 1992 or 1994 to use the relationship.

9. (E) is the correct answer. Since we do not know the amount of the sales of either salesperson, we do not know how much they received in commission.

10. (B) is the correct answer. (1) leaves open the possibility that y could be a fraction like $\frac{1}{7}$. However, if $y + 7$ in an integer, y must be an integer as well.

11. (A) is the correct answer. Taking the equation in (1) and dividing it by 2 gives us $6x - y = 7$. No useful information can be obtained from (2).

12. (A) is the correct answer. (1) resolves itself into $x^3 = -27$. Therefore, $x = -3$. In (2), $x^4 = 81$ and x can be either -3 or $+3$. (1) provides the answer.

13. (D) is the correct answer. (1) alone gives you sufficient information to find the longer dimension of the picture. Twice 9 inches = 18 inches, which leaves 30 inches for the other sides, or 15 inches as the longer dimension.

According to (2), let the longer side = x. Then $2x + 2\left(\frac{3}{5}\right)x = 48$ inches. $x = 15$ inches, as indicated in (1). Either statement alone can answer the question.

14. (B) is the correct answer. The distance that both are standing apart tells you nothing about the relationship between their heights.

Statement (2) gives us a proportion that can be used. Let x = Jay's height. Then $x : 6 = 12 : 15$ or $15x = 72$. Jay's height can thus be found.

15. (D) is the correct answer. (1) will give you the length of the patio algebraically. Let x = length; $x - 8$ = width. Then $x(x - 8) = 240$ or $x^2 - 8x = 240$ or $x^2 - 8x - 240 = 0$. The equation when factored becomes:

$(x + 12)(x - 20) = 240$
$x = -12$ (has no relevance)

$x = 20$ feet
Length = 20
Width = 12

(2) alone gives you enough information to solve the problem algebraically as well.

16. (E) is the correct answer. In order to determine profit, you must be given information or be able to obtain information about cost and selling price. (2) makes it possible to determine cost, but selling price is not determinable.

17. (A) is the correct answer. (1) is sufficient. When straight lines intersect, the vertical angles are equal to each other. (2) alone will not provide sufficient information to answer the question.

18. **(C)** is the correct answer. Both (1) and (2) are necessary. Three imaginary parallelograms result because $x° = y° = z° = C$.

    $EI + FJ + GH = AC$
    $AE + IF + JG + HD = CD$

    EI has to be parallel to *AC*, *FJ* has to be parallel to *AC*, and so on.

    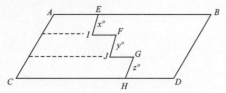

19. **(A)** is the correct answer. Note that $x^6 - y^6 = (x^3 - y^3)(x^3 + y^3)$. If $x^3 - y^3 = 0$, then $x^6 - y^6 = 0$, regardless of the value of $x^3 + y^3$.

20. **(C)** is the correct answer. According to (1), x will be a positive number whether m is a positive or negative number, but if $m = 0$, x would equal 0. (2) only indicates that x is not equal to zero. Both statements are necessary.

Sentence Corrections

1. The correct answer is B. The use of the phrase *for his excessive absence* requires parallel use of a phrase, *for his inability to meet*. The original sentence contains a clause, *because he was not meeting*. C is also a clause and is therefore incorrect. D is the same as the original except for the contraction *wasn't*. E is completely incorrect.

2. The correct answer is C. The use of the present perfect in the main clause requires a reference to a more previous time by use of the past perfect. In B the present tense is incorrect. In D and E the use of the subjunctive *were* is incorrect.

3. The correct answer is E. The subject of the sentence is *habit*, which is singular. The verb must also be singular. In this case *prevents* is correct. D is incorrect because of the use of an adjective, *good*, instead of an adverb, *well*.

4. The correct answer is D. The word *credible* means "believable," which is illogical in this sentence. *Credulous* makes sense because it means "gullible." C is incorrect because *as* is a conjunction and cannot be used in this sentence. *Then* is also incorrect because it is an adverb, and the conjunction *than* is needed.

5. The correct answer is C. The given sentence contains a dangling participle, *Having inherited great wealth*. This participle modifies *she*, and *she* must be the subject of the sentence.

6. The correct answer is A. The given sentence is correct because a compound predicate does not use a comma before *and*. C is incorrect because a comma must appear before *and* in a compound sentence. D is an example of a sentence fragment. The semicolon in E is used incorrectly.

7. The correct answer is B. *Because I was late* is a dependent or subordinate clause. It is separated from the independent or main clause, *my mother was angry*, by a comma.

8. The correct answer is A. *Whoever* is the subject of the verb *deserves* and must be in the nominative case. *Whomever* is in the objective case. C is incorrect because the semicolon is misused. In E, *whichever* is incorrect because it is not used to refer to people, and we can assume only people would win a writing prize.

9. The correct answer is C because it is the only choice that provides a subject for the verb *complete*.

10. The correct answer is D. This choice provides a noun, *practice*, as subject of the verb, *may result. This* (or *it* in choice B) by itself has no antecedent and cannot serve as a subject. Also, the two independent clauses must be separated by a semicolon.

11. The correct answer is E. In this sentence the correlatives *either . . . or* refer to the nouns *paper* and *report*; therefore, *either* is misplaced in the original and in the other choices.

12. The correct answer is A. is correct and provides a model for the correct form of a quote within a quote. Notice this special use of commas, capitals, and quotation marks.

13. The correct answer is C. The use of *like when* is incorrect. D does not use parallel structure. E uses *you're* (you are) incorrectly.

14. The correct answer is A. B uses *their* incorrectly. This subject is singular. If it were plural, it would be written as *The producer and* the *director*. C adds *to* incorrectly. D and E include a comma incorrectly.

15. The correct answer is B. The apostrophe is used correctly for both authors' names. In A, *Henry Jame's* is incorrect. In C, *James Joyces'* is incorrect. In D, *James Joyces's* is incorrect. In E, *James Joyce* is incorrect, and so is *Henry Jamess'*.

16. The correct answer is D. The use of *than* with *as pretty* in A, B, and C is incorrect. E changes the meaning of the sentence.

17. The correct answer is B. *Everyone* must agree with the pronoun *his*; since *everyone* is singular, *their* is incorrect. D and E repeat *view* and are redundant.

18. The correct answer is C. This question tests illogical comparisons. "Talent" is being compared with "student," which are not like items. The only choice that corrects this error is C—"any other student's" implies that we are comparing talents.

19. The correct answer is E. This question tests the subject-verb agreement and illogical comparisons. *His message and purpose for writing* does not make the subject plural, so B, C, and D are incorrect. *Theme* is not conceptually comparable to *examining*. In order to make the sentence parallel, *studying* is comparable to *examining*.

20. This question tests misplaced modifiers. C is the correct answer. *Continually late and guilty of disruptive behavior* describes the behavior of the student, not the professor. C is the only choice in which this is true.

21. The correct answer is B. This question tests wordiness. The word *one* is not necessary. *The reason why* is a wordy phrase that means because. *In a peculiar way* can more precisely and economically be expressed by the adverb *peculiarly*. All the choices are wordy except B.

22. The correct answer is D. This question tests sentence fragments as well as the comparative and superlative degrees. A is grammatically incorrect—it is not a complete thought. The word *best* in B and C is the superlative rather than the comparative form and changes the meaning. The word *most* is the superlative form and changes the meaning in E. The correct choice is therefore D.

Problem Solving

1. **(B)** If unequals are subtracted from equals, the differences are unequal in opposite order.

   Consider the equation $C = C$. Subtract A from the lefthand side of this equation, and subtract B from the righthand side. Since $A > B$, we obtain $C - A < C - B$. Thus, statement B is false.

   If $A > B$ and C is positive:

   (A) $\quad AC > BC \quad$ True

   (C) $A + C > B + C \quad$ True

   (D) $A - C > B - C \quad$ True

   (E) $A \div C > B \div C \quad$ True

2. **(B)** The region shown is $\frac{1}{4}$ of an entire circle with radius 10. The area of the curve is, therefore, $\frac{1}{4}$ that of the entire circle.

$$A = \pi r^2$$

$$A \text{ of } \frac{1}{4} \text{ circle} = \frac{1}{4}(\pi)(10)^2$$

$$A = \frac{1}{4}(\pi)(100)$$

$$= 25\pi$$

3. **(A)** Let:

   x = number of poles at $6 per pair

   y = number of poles at $11 per pair

   (1) $x + y = 200$

   (2) $6x + 11y = 1600$ "number of poles, x, times price per pole, $6, plus number of poles, y, times price per pole, $11 = total receipt"

   Substitute from equation (1) (that $x = 200 - y$) into equation (2):

$$6(200 - y) + 11y = 1,600$$
$$1,200 - 6y + 11y = 1,600$$
$$1,200 + 5y = 1,600$$
$$5y = 400$$
$$y = 80 \text{ pairs of skis sold at } \$11$$
$$x = 200 - y = 120$$

   pairs of skis sold at $6

4. **(E)** $(a - b)^2 = (a - b)(a - b)$
   $= a^2 - 2ab + b^2 = 19$

   Since $ab = 5$, then $2ab = 10$
   $a^2 + b^2 = (a^2 - 2ab + b^2) + 2ab$
   $= 19 + 10 = 29$

5. (D) Let P = the price of the shoes before the discount. Then:

$$P - 20\%(P) = 84 \text{ or}$$
$$(80\%)P = 84 \text{ so}$$
$$.8P = 84 \text{ and}$$

$$P = \frac{84}{.8} = \$105$$

6. (C) Area = $\frac{1}{2}$bh. We are given that h = 2 + b. Thus:

$$40 = \frac{1}{2}b(2 + b) \text{ Multiply and}$$
$$\text{distribute.}$$
$$80 = 2b + b^2$$
$$b^2 + 2b - 80 = 0$$
$$(b + 10)(b - 8) = 0$$

b = 8, or −10 Since b is a length, b $\neq$ −10

Hence, only (C) can be true.

7. (C) The total number of triangles is 16; the total number of shaded triangles is 4.

Ratio of

$$\frac{\text{shaded triangles}}{\text{total number of triangles}} = \frac{4}{16} = \frac{1}{4} = 25\%$$

8. (E) Find multiples of 3: 3, 6, 9, 12, 15, 18, 21, 24, etc. Find multiples of 7: 7, 14, 21, 28, etc. Since the least-common multiple is 21, they will start a rotation together after 21 minutes.

9. (D) *Of* means to multiply. 8% = .08

$$\begin{array}{r} 500,000 \\ \times \quad .08 \\ \hline 40,000.00 \end{array} = 40,000 \text{ dismissed}$$

10. (E) There are a total of 9 balls, and since there are 3 white balls, this represents 3 chances out of 9 of selecting 1 white ball; $\frac{3}{9} = \frac{1}{3}$

11. (C) *BAC* and *ACD* are supplementary angles; hence, *mBAC* + *mACD* = 180.

Substitute a + 30 + *mACD* = 180
$$mACD = 180 - (a + 30)$$
$$= 180 - a - 30$$
$$= 150 - a$$

12. (D) Let $\quad$ J = Jennifer's age now

Then $\quad$ J − 3 = Peter's age now

and $\quad$ J + 12 = Jennifer's age in 12 years

$$J - 3 + 12 = J + 9$$
$$= \text{Peter's age in 12 years}$$

Then,
$$(J + 12) + (J + 9) = 61$$
$$2J + 21 = 61$$
$$2J = 40$$
$$J = 20$$

13. (E) $\left(4 + \frac{1}{5}\right)^2 - 16$

$$= 16 + \frac{4}{5} + \frac{4}{5} + \frac{1}{25} - 16$$

$$= \frac{4}{5} + \frac{4}{5} + \frac{1}{25} = \frac{20}{25} + \frac{20}{25} + \frac{1}{25} = \frac{41}{25}$$

243

14. (B) In the diagram, $\angle 1 = \angle 5$ because $\triangle RQS$ is isosceles since $QR = QS$. Angle 5 is an exterior angle of triangle QSP and is equal to the sum of $\angle 3$ and $\angle 4$. Hence, $\angle 5 >$ either $\angle 3$ or $\angle 4$, $\angle 5 > \angle 4$. Substitute: $\angle 1 > \angle 4$

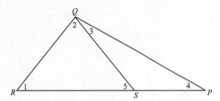

15. (A) Multiply $(4 + \sqrt{5})(4 - \sqrt{5})$ in the following manner:

(1) Multiply first terms: $(4)(4) = 16$

(2) Add inner and outer products:

$$(4 + \sqrt{5}) \quad (4 - \sqrt{5}) \rightarrow$$

$$(-4\sqrt{5})$$

$$(+4\sqrt{5})$$

$$(-4\sqrt{5}) + (4\sqrt{5}) = 0$$

(3) Multiply last terms:

$$(+\sqrt{5})(-\sqrt{5}) = -\sqrt{25} = -5$$

(4) Combine results: $16 - 5 = 11$

16. (E) Let s = length of the shorter piece Then $s + 6$ = length of the longer piece

$$s + (s + 6) = 34$$
$$2s + 6 = 34$$
$$2s = 28$$
$$s = 14, \text{ and } s + 6 = 20$$

Thus, the ratio is

$$\frac{\text{smaller}}{\text{larger}} = \frac{14}{20} = \frac{7}{10} = 7 : 10$$

Reading Comprehension

1. The correct answer is A. This answer choice blankets both the historical background of the passage of *Poetics* from oblivion into the Italian Renaissance and the influence it had upon the Italian Renaissance. The passage itself expands upon these two ideas. Choice B ignores the historical passage of *Poetics* into Italy and passes a value judgment upon scholars who considered it. Choice C is too general since this passage discusses literary criticism of only one work, *Poetics*. Choice D is a good summary of the second half of the passage, but not an accurate summary of the whole passage. Choice E is not specific enough, since it does not identify the eras or the documents to which it refers.

2. The correct answer is C. When paragraph 2 states that Avorres had no conception of literature as an imitation of life, the implication is that Aristotle *did* have such a conception. Furthermore, paragraph 4 mentions Aristotle's requirement that the poet relate what *could* happen. There is, then, no doubt that Aristotle intended literature to be a reflection of life. Choice B is incorrect since the passage states that Italian scholars added the requirement of the Horatian five acts. Choice D is inappropriate since Aristotle was Greek, wrote in Greek, and had no idea that his work would ever be translated into Arabic. Choice E suggests that Aristotle felt that literature should reflect what *has* happened, a suggestion neither stated nor implied in the passage.

3. The correct answer is C. Paragraph 3 is a vehicle designed to enable the author to go on to discuss the skewed consideration of *Poetics* during the Italian Renaissance. The paragraph establishes that the work of Aristotle did eventually come to the Italian Renaissance (bringing to a close the narrative of paragraph 2) and prepares the way for paragraph 4. Choice A, then, is incorrect since it presents only one aspect of the purpose. Choices B and E are incorrect in that they assume the purpose of the paragraph to be one of passing along an opinion. Choice D is incorrect because the comments that describe the skewed results have not been previously discussed in the passage and, therefore, cannot be considered a restatement.

4. The correct answer is E. Questions of this kind are best handled by deciding which completion statements are applicable, then finding the answer choice containing them. Completion I is applicable since paragraph 3 indicates that there will be a discussion of Italian Renaissance scholars' interpretations of Aristotle, and Giraldi Cinthio is mentioned in paragraph 4 as a specific example. Completion II is applicable. Giraldi Cinthio *interpreted* (believed) Aristotle as requiring that poetry represent things as they should occur (moralistic). Completion III is incorrect: Giraldi Cinthio is presented as an Italian living during the Renaissance. Completion IV is correct since the passage states that Aristotle's requirement (stated in the sentence) is interpreted as . . . (something different from Aristotle's requirement). Giraldi Cinthio's interpretation is, then, not correct. Completion V is not applicable because Giraldi Cinthio felt that Aristotle wanted poetry to represent what *should* happen, or what would be best, not what would be probable or realistic.

5. The correct answer is E. The passage states in paragraph 2 that there was no evidence that this version influenced the Renaissance in Italy. Paragraph 3 lists factors that *did* influence interpretation, including translations (choice A), the nature of the Renaissance itself (choice C, also implied by the discussion of Giraldi Cinthio), and questions of intended meaning (choice D). The first sentence of paragraph 4 mentions the Renaissance regard for form.

6. The correct answer is A. The final paragraph states that rank of the *dramatis personae* was felt to be the distinguishing factor between tragedy and comedy. References to the "Horatian five acts" (choices B and C) are unrelated to any discussion of defining tragedy. Choice D, although it contains the exact wording of a phrase in the passage, is too vague to be considered. Choice E is, likewise, not stated or implied in the passage.

7. The correct answer is B. While no evidence suggests that Renaissance scholars were aimlessly drifting with no direction, all other answer choices are directly supported. Choice A is indicated by the number of translations of Aristotle's *Poetics* that appeared in the late 1400s and early 1500s, as well as by the fact that literary critics had an interest in studying Aristotle. Choice C is indicated by the particular interpretations (for example, of "nobility") and by the Italians' love of "form," which inspired them to make "rules" of Aristotle's work. Choice D can be verified by considering Giraldi Cinthio's interpretation of Aristotle. Choice E is obviously an implication of the passage as a whole.

8. The correct answer is B. Since peat layers below the current salt marshes contain the same kinds of plants, and since those peat layers were covered by sand washed in by huge waves, it can be assumed that a previous marsh sank and was covered by ocean water and sand. Choice A is an unlikely choice since the passage makes no reference to the rise or fall of ocean levels. Choice C is incorrect since the "identical flora" are not growing in the ocean. Although the plants obviously grow in sandy environments, this passage does not discuss or imply other locations; choice D is beyond the data of this passage. Choice E uses a technical term from the passage (theoretical modeling) pulled from a sentence discussing wave height, not flora.

9. The correct answer is A. The passage (in paragraph 3) states that sequences of peat, sand, and mud do not provide evidence to date the events with certainty. The passage tells the reader that peat contains plant life (flora), but not that all peat contains marine plant life; choice B is not correct. Choice C can be eliminated because the passage does not indicate that *any* peat is on ocean floors. The cause-effect relationship stated in choice D is nearly a converse of the correct relationship: earthquakes can give rise to peat bogs. Choice E is not acceptable because the reader has no basis upon which to make a decision regarding unstable suspensions.

10. The correct answer is C. This title is the most specific available that blankets the content of the passage as a whole. Choice A is more vague (what story?), as are choices B (what secrets?) and D (what answers?). Choice E is too broad; this passage does not discuss the earthquakes themselves, but focuses upon evidence indicating that they did occur.

11. The correct answer is D. The passage states in paragraph 4 that huge earth-quakes *might* have caused landslides. All other choices are presented as definite cause-effect situations.

12. The correct answer is D. Growth rings and radiocarbon dating establish that the trees died 300 years ago when a large earthquake produced an ocean wave that drowned their roots, killing the trees. The age of dead trees does not document the seriousness of an earthquake, so choice A can be eliminated. Peat layers do not provide sufficient evidence to date the layers with accuracy; peat data does not contrast with tree data; choice B is incorrect. Choice C is incorrect, since drowned trees do not explain the presence of radiocarbon, which occurs in all living things. As for choice E, there was no Honshu quake, only a Honshu tsunami.

13. The correct answer is E. All choices are correct. Native stories from different locations told of quakes. Sedimentary deposits on the ocean floor enabled researchers to date such a quake. Japanese writing also enabled a date to be established. Geologic evidence on shorelines is cited in paragraph 2.

14. The correct answer is C. The author has presented information that enables the conclusion that: 1) earthquakes have occurred in this region; and 2) the last one occurred about 300 years ago. The documentation of the date of the Honshu tsunami coincides with the period of time the drowned pine trees have been dead and with the date indicated by the ocean floor layer that contained volcanic ash. Choice A is incorrect because it gives no purpose for the comparison. Choice B is not specific in regard to time or location. Choice D is the second-best choice, but choice C is better because it relates to the passage as a whole. Choice E suggests that the author included loosely related material, which is not correct.

15. The correct answer is C. The adoptive brother taught the author what he needed to know about his ox and showed happiness when the ox came when the author called it. The brother functioned as an encouraging role model for the author. Choice B applies to Bob who is not the author's adoptive brother. Choice D is incorrect since the passage states that it was the author who was suspicious of the brother's care of the ox. Nothing in the passage states or suggests choice E.

16. The correct answer is A. Loss of a beloved ox is perceived as such a serious loss that others might walk 30 or 40 miles to offer condolence, and the owner of the ox might commit suicide. No evidence supports choices B and E. The suspicion of choice C does not accompany the death of every ox, but describes only how the author felt when his ox died. Since the passage neither states nor suggests that *every* man will *always* lose his ox, this passage does not emphasize the inevitability of death (choice D).

17. The correct answer is E. The men came as friends, intending to console the author. The references to others who have lost cattle are intended to let the author know he was not alone, that he was not suspected of having caused his ox's death. Choice A is second-best; however, the surrounding context relates specifically to the death of the ox. Choice B also ignores the larger context of the remarks. Since there is no reason to assume that all cattle in the region died of *one* disease, choice C should be eliminated. Choice D is unsupported.

18. The correct answer is C. Option I must be eliminated since the passage states that animals are regarded *not* merely as objects. Option II is true, since the passage mentions the animals as "tied to their own being" and refers to a "merging of identities." Option III must be eliminated, since, though the herder may be "empty-bellied" and apprehensive, he has still seen that the herd are taken care of. Option IV, then, is correct, since the welfare of the herd is first in importance.

19. The correct answer is A. The author is empathetic; he has an intimate understanding of the Karimojong and their beliefs. Choice B is not correct since the word *altruistic* suggests putting the needs of another before your own, and there is no evidence to suggest that the author has denied himself in that manner. The author feels no fear or uneasiness regarding the Karimojong, so choice C must be eliminated. Neither is the author overjoyed, as choice D would suggest. He is not anguished. Notice that the question is very specific, asking only for the author's attitude toward the Karimojong themselves.

20. The correct answer is E. Because the owner sings about his name-ox at dances and uses a battle cry containing the ox-name to assert his true identity, choice E can be correctly inferred. Choice B can be eliminated, since there is no information indicating that the author would want to change or modernize the Karimojong, whom he clearly respects as they are. The Karimojong adopt the author, guide him, allow him to join their activities as an equal; hence, choice C is not substantiated in the text. Choice D is incorrect. While the passage informs the reader of the hardships of herding for the Karimojong, there is no information to support the idea that abandoning herding would bring an improved economy.

21. The correct answer is D. Since this selection is a first-person narrative, it shows us Karimojong life as filtered through the sensibilities of the author. Choice D emphasizes the role of the narrator in the account. Choice A suggests that the passage is a discussion of spirituality. Choice B ignores human-to-human relationships. Choice B is too general to fit the content; there are many aspects of village life that the reader does not learn. Certainly, choice E does not give the focus of the passage.

Practice Test 2

Directions: In this section solve each problem, using any available space on the page for scratchwork. Then indicate the best of the answer choices given.

Numbers

All numbers used are real numbers.

Figures

Figures that accompany problems in the text are intended to provide information useful in solving the problems. They are drawn as accurately as possible EXCEPT when it is stated in a specific problem that its figure is not drawn to scale. All figures lie in a plane unless otherwise indicated.

1. If $\frac{4}{5}$ of a number is 12, what is $\frac{5}{6}$ of the number?

   (A) $\frac{4}{5}$

   (B)   9

   (C)   12.5

   (D)   15

   (E)   18

2. Express as a trinomial:
   $(3a + 5)(2a - 3)$

   (A) $5a^2 - 15$

   (B) $6a^2 + 15$

   (C) $6a^2 - 4a - 15$

   (D) $6a^2 + a - 15$

   (E) $6a^2 - a + 15$

3. Which expression represents the number of cents, c, that a customer received in change from a \$1 bill after buying n articles each costing 5 cents?

   (A) $c = 1 - 5n$

   (B) $c = 100 - 5n$

   (C) $c = 95n$

   (D) $c = 100 - \dfrac{n}{5}$

   (E) $c = 1 - \dfrac{n}{5}$

4. If $4x - 3 = 17$, then $x =$

   (A) -5

   (B) 5

   (C) $-3\dfrac{1}{2}$

   (D) $32\dfrac{1}{2}$

   (E)   None of the above

5. In triangle ABC, $AB = AC$ and the measure of angle A is twice the measure of angle B. Find the number of degrees in the measure of the exterior angle at C.

   (A) $145°$

   (B) $135°$

   (C) $125°$

   (D) $95°$

   (E) $45°$

Use this line graph for questions 6 and 7.

249

6. During what 2-hour period was the temperature constant?

(A) 2 a.m.—4 a.m.
(B) 8 a.m.—10 a.m.
(C) Noon—2 p.m.
(D) 4 p.m.—6 p.m.
(E) 6 p.m.—8 p.m.

7. At what two times of the day was the temperature 76°?

(A) 10 a.m. and 10 p.m.
(B) 8 a.m. and 8 p.m.
(C) 10 a.m. and 9 p.m.
(D) 10 a.m. and 12 p.m.
(E) Noon and 10 p.m.

8. How far does a rolling wheel with a 4-inch radius travel in 8 revolutions?

(A) 8π ft
(B) $5\frac{1}{3}\pi$ ft
(C) 12π ft
(D) 4π ft
(E) $10\frac{1}{3}\pi$ ft

9. Find the value of $\dfrac{8}{3-x}$ if $x = -1$.

(A) $\dfrac{8}{5}$
(B) $\dfrac{1}{4}$
(C) 4
(D) 2
(E) $\dfrac{1}{2}$

10. If $\dfrac{x}{3} + \dfrac{x}{4} = 7$, then $\dfrac{x}{6} = ?$

(A) 2
(B) 4
(C) 6
(D) 10
(E) 12

11. Line AB is parallel to CD. Line EG bisects $\angle BEF$. How many degrees are there in angle GFD?

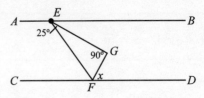

(A) 65
(B) 105
(C) 45
(D) 90
(E) 25

12. The recipe for a cake called for $\dfrac{2}{3}$ cup of sugar. How many cakes did Jane bake for a baked-goods sale if she used 4 cups of sugar?

(A) 2
(B) 3
(C) 4
(D) 5
(E) 6

13. In a class election, 190 votes were cast for three candidates. Jack received 6 votes more than twice as many as Sam received, while Arthur received 8 votes less than three times as many as Sam. How many votes did Jack receive?

(A) 32
(B) 88
(C) 70
(D) 80
(E) 90

14. A formula for finding the volume of a cylinder is V= $\pi r^2 h$, where r is the radius of the base and h is the altitude of the cylinder. Find the volume of a cylinder in which the radius of the base is 7 and the altitude is 10.

(Use $\pi = \dfrac{22}{7}$.)

(A) 220
(B) 170
(C) 154
(D) 2,200
(E) 1,540

15. *ROS* is a diameter of circle *O*. Radius *OT* and chords *RT* and *TS* are drawn. If *TRO* = 50°, find the measure of 1.

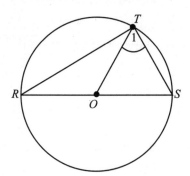

(A) 40°
(B) 50°
(C) 60°
(D) 80°
(E) 90°

16. A new copy machine can run off 1,500 workbooks in 8 hours, while it takes an older copy machine 12 hours to do the same job. What is the total number of hours that it would take both copy machines working at the same time, but independently, to run off the 1,500 workbooks?

(A) 4.4
(B) 4.6
(C) 4.8
(D) 5
(E) 10

SECTION 2   TIME—25 MINUTES   22 QUESTIONS

Directions: In each of the following sentences, some part of the sentence or the entire sentence is underlined. Beneath each sentence you will find five ways of phrasing the underlined part. The first of these repeats the original; the other four are different. If you think the original is better than any of the alternatives, choose answer A; otherwise choose one of the others. Select the best version and fill in the corresponding oval on your answer sheet.

This is a test of correctness and effectiveness of expression. In choosing answers, follow the requirements of standard written English; that is, pay attention to grammar, choice of words, and sentence construction. Choose the answer that expresses most effectively what is presented in the original sentence; this answer should be clear and exact, without awkwardness, ambiguity, or redundancy.

1. He had a professorship at the university, thus providing him with an income.

   (A) He had a professorship at the university, thus providing him with an income.
   (B) His professorship was at the university, thus providing him with an income.
   (C) His professorship at the university provided him with an income.
   (D) Provided with an income, his professorship was at the university.
   (E) Providing him with an income, he had a professorship.

2. He had hoped to have received his raise in next week's check.

   (A) He had hoped to have received his raise in next week's check.
   (B) He hopes to receive his raise in next week's check.
   (C) He had been hoping to be receiving his raise in next week's check.
   (D) He has hoped to have received his raise in next week's check.
   (E) He was hoping to have received his raise in next week's check.

3. They said that if they had had more time, they would have gone.

   (A) if they had had more time, they would have gone.
   (B) if they had had more time, they will go.
   (C) if they had more time, they would be going.
   (D) if they were to have more time, they would have gone.
   (E) if they were to have more time, they will go.

4. The world-famous flier, Charles Lindbergh, honored throughout the world.

   (A) The world-famous flier, Charles Lindbergh, honored throughout the world.
   (B) Charles Lindbergh, the world-famous flier, being honored throughout the world.
   (C) The world-famous flier, Charles Lindbergh, was honored throughout the world.
   (D) Being Charles Lindbergh, the world-famous flier, honored throughout the world.
   (E) The world-famous flier, honored throughout the world, Charles Lindbergh.

5. After becoming president, his hometown became prosperous.

   (A) After becoming president, his hometown
   (B) Becoming prosperous after he became president his hometown
   (C) After becoming president his hometown
   (D) His hometown, becoming president
   (E) After he became president, his home town

6. Did you ever visited at San Juan?

   (A) Did you ever visited San Juan?
   (B) Was you ever visiting in San Juan?
   (C) Have you ever visit San Juan?
   (D) Have you ever visited San Juan?
   (E) Has San Juan ever was visited by you?

7. His becoming upset, that was quite unnecessary.

   (A) His becoming upset, that was quite unnecessary.
   (B) That his becoming upset was quite unnecessary.
   (C) It was not necessary, his becoming quite upset.
   (D) Him becoming upset was quite unnecessary.
   (E) His becoming upset was quite unnecessary.

8. She said it was a long time since she read such a good book.

   (A) She said it was a long time
   (B) She said it is a long time
   (C) She says it was a long time
   (D) It was a long time she said
   (E) She said it had been a long time

9. The current reader is neither careful or demanding in his choices.

   (A) is neither careful or demanding
   (B) is neither careful nor demanding
   (C) is either careful nor demanding
   (D) is neither careful nor demands
   (E) are neither careful nor demanding

10. His books are entertaining, perceptive, and worthwhile.

   (A) are entertaining, perceptive, and worthwhile.
   (B) are entertaining, perceptive, and they have value.
   (C) are both entertaining, perceptive, and worthwhile.
   (D) entertain, are perceptive, and worthwhile.
   (E) is entertaining, perceptive and worthwhile.

11. He had often asked for a date, but I am unwilling to go out with him.

    (A) but I am unwilling to go out with him.
    (B) but I unwillingly go out with him.
    (C) but I was unwilling to go out with him.
    (D) unwilling to go out with him.
    (E) but I am not willing to go out with him.

12. This pile of books are among my favorites.

    (A) This pile of books are among my favorites.
    (B) These pile of books are among my favorites.
    (C) This pile of books contain my favorites.
    (D) This pile of books contains my favorites.
    (E) My favorites is among this pile of books.

13. When among them, it is obvious I am at peace.

    (A) When among them, it is obvious I am at peace.
    (B) When among them, I am obviously at peace.
    (C) Peace is obviously among them.
    (D) Among them peace is obviously for me.
    (E) Among them, peace is obvious for me.

14. Because they were angry, they could not act logically.

    (A) Because they were angry, they could not act logically.
    (B) They acted illogically because they were angry.
    (C) It was logical because they were angry.
    (D) They acted angrily, because they were illogical.
    (E) Logically, because they were angry, they could not act logically.

15. Did you now or were you ever a member of that group?

    (A) Did you now or were you ever
    (B) Are you ever, or were you
    (C) Were you ever, or are you now
    (D) Were you now, or are you
    (E) Were you ever, or did you ever be

16. Clearly, they had lost there way.

    (A) Clearly, they had lost there way.
    (B) They had lost their way clearly.
    (C) They had lost their clear way clearly.
    (D) They had clearly lost their way.
    (E) Clearly, they lost there way.

254

17. It is interesting to compare the teachings of Jesus and Mohammed. Jesus preaches love, whereas Mohammed's teachings were more militant.

   (A) Jesus preaches love, whereas Mohammed's teachings were more militant.

   • (B) Jesus preached love; whereas Mohammed's teachings are more militant.

   (C) Jesus preached love but Mohammed's teachings are more militant.

   (D) Jesus preaches love but Mohammed's teachings were more militant.

   (E) Jesus preaches love; whereas Mohammed's teachings are more militant.

18. The teacher agrees to give the make-up exam to whomever wants it.

   (A) to whomever wants it.
   (B) to whoever wants it.
   (C) to whomever wants to take the exam.
   (D) to whoever wants to take the exam.
   (E) to whoever would wish to take the exam.

19. The doors opened, the crowd surged in, pandemonium erupted.

   (A) The doors opened, the crowd surged in, pandemonium erupted.
   (B) The doors opened as the crowd surged in, pandemonium erupted.
   (C) Pandemonium erupted as the doors opened, the crowd surged in.
   (D) The doors opened, the crowd surged in as pandemonium erupted.
   (E) As the doors opened, the crowd surged in. Pandemonium erupted.

20. The student did not recognize the literary allusion, which adversely affected his test score.

   (A) allusion, which adversely affected his test score.
   • (B) illusion, which adversely effected his test score.
   (C) allusion, which adversely effected his test score.
   • (D) illusion, which adversely affected his test score.
   (E) allusion, a fact which adversely effected his test score.

21. The celebrity was arrogant, with a hot temper and has a pampered way about him.

   (A) with a hot temper and has a pampered way about him.
   (B) with a hot temper and has a pampered way.
   (C) with a hot temper and a pampered way.
   (D) hot-tempered, and pampered.
   (E) and has a hot temper as well as a pampered way.

22. To study the unities, to follow Aristotle's precepts, and venerating climactic dramatic structure were all crucial to neoclassicists.

   (A) to follow Aristotle's precepts, and venerating.
   (B) and to follow Aristotle's precepts, venerating.
   (C) as well as following Aristotle's precepts and to venerate.
   (D) as well as to follow Aristotle's precepts and venerating.
   (E) to follow Aristotle's precepts, and to venerate.

SECTION 3   TIME—25 MINUTES   20 QUESTIONS

Directions: Each of the data sufficiency problems below consists of a question and two statements, labeled (1) and (2), in which certain data are given. You have to decide whether the data given in the statements are *sufficient* for answering the question. Using the data given in the statements *plus* your knowledge of mathematics and everyday facts (such as the number of days in July or the meaning of *counterclockwise*), you are to fill in oval:

A. If statement (1) ALONE is sufficient, but statement (2) alone is not sufficient to answer the question asked;

B. If statement (2) ALONE is sufficient, but statement (1) alone is not sufficient to answer the question asked;

C. If BOTH statements (1) and (2) TOGETHER are sufficient to answer the question asked, but NEITHER statement ALONE is sufficient;

D. If EACH statement ALONE is sufficient to answer the question asked;

E. If statements (1) and (2) TOGETHER are NOT sufficient to answer the question asked, and additional data specific to the problem are needed.

Numbers

All numbers used are real numbers.

Figures

A figure in a data sufficiency problem will conform to the information given in the question, but will not necessarily conform to the additional information given in statements (1) and (2).

Note

In questions that ask for the value of a quantity, the data given in the statements are sufficient only when it is possible to determine exactly one numerical value for the quantity.

Example

In $\triangle PQR$, what is the value of x?

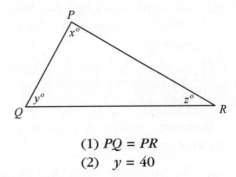

(1) $PQ = PR$
(2) $y = 40$

Explanation

According to statement (1), $PQ = PR$; therefore, $\triangle PQR$ is isosceles and $y = z$. Since $x + y + z = 180$, it follows that $x + 2y = 180$. Since statement (1) does not give a value for y, you cannot answer the question using statement (1) alone. According to statement (2), $y = 40$; therefore, $x + z = 140$. Since statement (2) does not give a value for z, you cannot answer the question using statement (2) alone. Using both statements together, since $x + 2y = 180$ and the value of y is given, you can find the value of x. Therefore, the answer is C.

1. Is N a positive number?

    (1) $5N + 5 > 0$
    (2) $5N + 7 < 27$

2. What are the coordinates of one particular corner of a square whose sides are 3 units long?

   (1)   The corner opposite the desired corner has coordinates (2, 1).
   (2)   The area of the square is 9 units.

3. How much does a car dealer make on the sale of a new car that lists for $8,900?

   (1)   The dealer gets a 25 percent discount from the manufacturer.
   (2)   The dealer accepted the purchaser's car for a trade-in value of $1,900.

4. One hundred ten car owners were surveyed. Each had either a stereo system or CB radio or both. How many cars are equipped with both stereo systems and CB radios?

   (1)   80 had stereo equipment in their cars.
   (2)   100 had CB radios

5. Is ΔABE congruent to ΔCED?

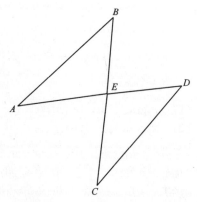

   (1)   AD and BC are straight lines that intersect at E.
   (2)   AB ∥CD; BE = EC

6. Does Area A have a better health-care system than Area B?

   (1)   Area A has an infant mortality rate of 22 per 1,000.
   (2)   Area B has an infant mortality rate of 45 per 1,000.

7. What is the perimeter of triangle ABC?

   (1)   AB = 7
   (2)   Triangle ABC is isosceles.

8. Upon the completion of a weight reduction program, Don weighed 187 pounds. What percent of his former weight did Don lose?

   (1)   Don lost 33 pounds through the weight reduction program.
   (2)   Don weighed 220 pounds prior to starting the weight reduction program.

9. One hundred ten car owners were surveyed. How many cars are equipped with both stereo and CB radios?

   (1)   80 had stereo equipment in their cars.
   (2)   100 had CB radios.

10. What is the number of degrees in angle x?

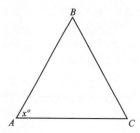

   (1)   AB = BC.
   (2) $\frac{1}{5}$ of the supplement of angle x = the complement of angle x.

11. Do food chains make a greater profit on the sale of generic products than on the sale of brand names?

    (1) Generic products are sold at considerably lower prices than brand items.

    (2) Generic products usually cost less than brand items.

12. Charles doubled the amount of the sales tax shown on his restaurant tab to determine the tip. His total cost was $14.88. What is the cost of his meal before the tax and tip were added?

    (1) The sales tax rate is 8 percent.

    (2) The sales tax on his bill amounted to $.96.

13. What is the value of p?

    (1) $p^2 - 7p = -12$

    (2) p is positive.

14. Find the fifth consecutive odd number.

    (1) The sum of the first number and the third number is 26.

    (2) The product of the first and second number is 143.

15. What is the value of $3x^2 + 4x^4 - x^6$?

    (1) $3x^2 + 4x^4 - x^6 + 380 = 2$

    (2) x is equal to either 3 or −3.

16. Does the area of sector $OAB = \frac{1}{4}$ of the area of the circle if O is the center?

    (1) Angle $O = 90°$.

    (2) The radius of the circle is 10 feet.

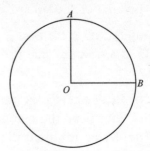

17. What is the value of $\frac{1}{a} + \frac{1}{b}$?

    (1) $7ab = a + b$

    (2) $a = 6b$

18. What is the measure of angle y?

    (1) Straight lines AB and CD are parallel.

    (2) Angle $x = 120°$.

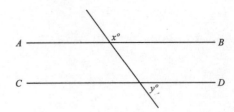

19. Is $x \cdot y$ positive?

    (1) x and y are negative.

    (2) x is larger than y.

20. A man's summer suit sells for $150. After a month, the suit, if unsold, is offered for sale at a discount of 40 percent. Will the seller make a profit on the sale of the suit?

    (1) The mark-up taken on the cost of the suit is 50 percent.

    (2) The seller's average gross profit is 23 percent.

SECTION 4　　　　TIME—25 MINUTES　　　　16 QUESTIONS

Directions: For each question in this section, select the best of the answer choices given.

1. All cars from Manufacturer X are made with driver's-side airbags. Of those cars with driver's-side airbags, 50 percent also have passenger's-side airbags. All of the cars with passenger airbags also have impact-reducing roll bars and shatterproof glass.

    If a car from Manufacturer X has shatterproof glass, which of the following can be concluded about that car?

    I. That car has an impact-reducing roll bar.
    II. That car has a driver's-side airbag.
    III. That car has a passenger's-side airbag.

    (A) I only
    (B) II only
    (C) I and III only
    (D) II and III only
    (E) I, II, and III

2. A new public welfare law requires that teenage parents who have not yet graduated from high school and who wish to receive welfare must remain in high school or enroll in a high school equivalency program at least 30 hours a week. Opponents of this law argue that it is unfair because it will require the parents to place their children in day-care programs, and the welfare income is insufficient to pay for the day care.

Which of the following facts, if true, would most support the law against this attack?

(A) Without at least a high school education, teenage parents will never be able to obtain jobs that will enable them to support their children.

(B) Teenage parents are not old enough to vote, so their interests should not be a factor in deciding whether to pass the new welfare law.

(C) The welfare law will contain a provision that high schools will provide in-house day-care facilities at no charge to their students.

(D) Requiring teenage parents to attend school for only 30 hours a week still allows them plenty of time for working.

(E) The opponents of the welfare law are also people who were teenage parents and they are only looking for handouts from the government.

3. I maintain that in the case of sympathetic beneficence, such an action of this kind, however proper, however amiable it may be, has nevertheless no true moral worth, but is on a level with other inclination to honor, which, if it is happily directed to that which is in fact of public utility and accordant with duty, and consequently honorable, deserves praise and encouragement, but esteemed.

Which of the following can be concluded from the preceding information?

(A) Moral duty arises from inclination.
(B) Moral duty is inculcated in school and church.
(C) Moral duty is unrelated to any emotional feeling.
(D) Moral duty has its source in all that's good in human beings.
(E) Moral duty can be compared to the sublime in literature.

Questions 4 and 5 come from the following selection.

Unquestionably, it is just in this that the moral worth of the character is brought out that is incomparably the highest of all, namely, that he is beneficent, not from inclination but from duty.

4. Which of the following least represents the word *inclination* in context?

(A) a predisposition
(B) a bias in favor of a positive action
(C) willingness
(D) a way of thinking and acting
(E) strong determination

5. Which of the following, if true, shows least the structure and content of this selection, a flaw in the reasoning of the educators in the above situation?

(A) The central theme is obvious.
(B) The idea of philanthropist covers many manifestations a conception of different kinds of duty.
(C) The spiritual elements are inherent in the concept of morality.
(D) The author's thesis has been presented leading to this climax.
(E) A well-structured argument for absolute morality has been offered.

6. A media watchdog group says the government should regulate advertising on computer bulletin boards that are used by children. This advertising, the group claims, exploits children by using entertaining computer programs that are nothing more than video games using the advertisers' products.

Which of the following statements should most alleviate the group's concerns?

(A) The computer advertising is available only to people with appropriate computer hardware.
(B) Studies have shown that children are not any more susceptible to advertising than are adults.
(C) Regulations of advertising on computer bulletin boards would be very difficult to monitor or enforce.
(D) Studies of children who are exposed to the advertising on computer bulletin boards have shown that the advertising is not actually an effective marketing tool, as the children do not retain the information to which they are exposed.
(E) Children are exposed to much more advertising on television and radio than on computer bulletin boards.

7. Stock prices for any given company usually rise when information about a pending merger involving that company becomes public. XYZ Corp. just made a public announcement that it will be merging with ABC Corp.

If the stock prices for XYZ Corp. decline after the announcement, what conclusion can be inferred?

(A) The price of stocks in XYZ Corp. is too high for average investors.

(B) ABC Corp. has only a limited number of stocks available for sale.

(C) The merger between XYZ and ABC creates a major conglomerate with a monopoly on the market, whose stocks are no longer desirable.

(D) The merger between XYZ and ABC can only be accomplished after long periods of negotiations between executives from each company.

(E) The announcement of the merger between XYZ and ABC became public on the same day that the government announced a decrease in prime lending rates.

8. John Doe, a well-known business leader, has a history of taking control over companies that later have to file for bankruptcy. Investors in a company that has just named John Doe its president are calling for his resignation before their company is also forced into bankruptcy.

Which of the following, if true, most contradicts the conclusion reached by the investors?

(A) The president of a business has little control over factors that determine whether it will file for bankruptcy.

(B) A company's filing bankruptcy does not always mean that its investors will lose money.

(C) The other businesses previously controlled by John Doe did not sell the same kinds of materials that the current company sells.

(D) Federal bankruptcy laws require a vote of a full board of directors in order for a company to file for bankruptcy.

(E) If this company files for bankruptcy, John Doe is likely to receive a large severance package.

Questions 9, 10, and 11 come from the following selection.

Further still, if nature has but little sympathy in the heart of this or that man; if he, supposed to be an upright man, is by temperament cold and indifferent to the sufferings of others, perhaps because in respect of his own he is provided with the special gift of patience and fortitude, and supposes or even requires, that others should have the same—and such a man would certainly not be the meanest product of nature—but if nature had not specially framed him for a philanthropist, would he not still find himself a source from whence to give himself a far higher worth than that of a good-natured temperament could be.

9. Which of the following least represents an assumption for the attitudes and characteristics of a philanthropist?

(A) Frozen by personal tragedy.
(B) Lacking the inclination to beneficence.
(C) Unsympathetic to the needs of others.
(D) Moved by repentance.
(E) Eager to make a fortune.

10. Which of the following statements, if true, would most seriously weaken the concept of "good" in a moral sense?

(A) Intelligence
(B) Goodwill
(C) Honor
(D) Power
(E) Perseverance

11. Which of the following, if true, would least describe the source of doing an act "in accord" with duty and doing an act "because of" duty?

(A) When the moral law is obeyed in defiance of all other inclinations.
(B) When there is an absolute and unmoving law of duty.
(C) When an action improves or corrects any situation that is destructive of nature or humanity.
(D) When the action is motivated entirely by the will to do good.
(E) When an individual acts out of duty alone.

12. A philosopher makes the following statements: "I think, therefore I am. If I am not, then I think not. If I think, then life means nothing."

If, applying the preceding argument, life does not mean nothing, then what more can the philosopher conclude?

(A) I am.
(B) I think.
(C) I do not think.
(D) I think and I am.
(E) I think not and I am.

Questions 13-16 come from this selection.

Assume that the mind of a philanthropist is clouded by sorrow of his own, extinguishing all sympathy with the lot of others, and that while he still has the power to benefit others in distress, he is not touched by their trouble because he is absorbed with his own; and now suppose that he tears himself out of this dead insensibility, and performs the action without any inclination to it, but simply from duty, then first has his action its genuine moral worth.

13. Which of the following, if true, would most strengthen the author's view of the best way to approach the question of goodness?

(A) From a principle based on experience.
(B) With wisdom culled from reading biographies.
(C) An abstract principle that is universal.
(D) A belief that nature has the answer.
(E) A mystic revelation.

14. Which of the following can be concluded about the preceding information?

    (A) The writing is involuted and intricate.
    (B) The author writes in a style that is poetic and graceful.
    (C) The author's style is angry and satiric.
    (D) The selection is forceful and direct.
    (E) The author's style is polished and graphic.

15. The author's conclusion of subject choice is based most upon which of the following assumptions?

    (A) Honor is the essential.
    (B) The subject is philanthropy.
    (C) Impulses toward charity provide the subject.
    (D) Ethics is the focus.
    (E) The subject is sympathy.

16. Which of the following best supports the speaker's point?

    (A) An uncompromising code of moral standards.
    (B) Acts of charity motivated by humanity.
    (C) Institutions dedicated to the needs of the poor.
    (D) "Goodness" for its own sake
    (E) The joys and satisfactions of philanthropy.

SECTION 5   TIME—25 MINUTES   16 QUESTIONS

Directions: In this section solve each problem, using any available space on the page for scratchwork. Then indicate the best of the answer choices given.

Numbers

All numbers used are real numbers.

Figures

Figures that accompany problems in the text are intended to provide information useful in solving the problems. They are drawn as accurately as possible EXCEPT when it is stated in a specific problem that its figure is not drawn to scale. All figures lie in a plane unless otherwise indicated.

1. If each interior angle of a regular polygon contains 150°, how many sides does the polygon have?

   (A) 12
   (B) 19
   (C) 3
   (D) 6
   (E) 8

2. Ben and David each receive a 6% annual raise. If Ben's raise is equal to $2400, and David's raise is equal to $2520, how much more is David's annual salary than Ben's after the raise?

   (A) $120
   (B) $1860
   (C) $2100
   (D) $2120
   (E) $2200

3. The number of points at a given distance from a given line, and also equally distant from two points on the given line is:

   (A) 1
   (B) 2
   (C) 3
   (D) 10
   (E) 6

4. In triangle *ABC*, line *DE* is parallel to *AC*. Find the length of *DE*.

   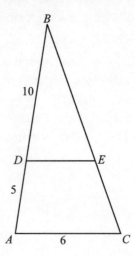

   (A) 10
   (B) 5
   (C) 15
   (D) 6
   (E) 4

5. If 40% of 50% of 100 is equal to 20M, then what is the value of M?

   (A) 0.01
   (B) 0.1
   (C) 1
   (D) −10
   (E) 100

6. If $\dfrac{(A-B)^2}{A^2-B^2} = 25$ then $\dfrac{A+B}{A-B} =$?

(A) $\dfrac{1}{25}$

(B) $\dfrac{1}{5}$

(C) 1

(D) 5

(E) 25

7. If $12 - 4W = Z$, then $8 - 4W =$?

(A) $Z + 4$

(B) $Z - 4$

(C) $2Z$

(D) $\left(\dfrac{3}{2}\right)Z$

(E) $\left(\dfrac{2}{3}\right)Z$

8. How long is chord AB of circle O?

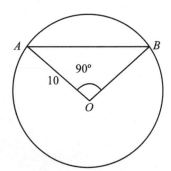

(A) $2\sqrt{10}$

(B) $10\sqrt{2}$

(C) 100

(D) 10

(E) $2\sqrt{50}$

9. It is possible to construct a triangle whose sides are:

(A) 7, 7, 16

(B) 5, 7, 12

(C) 4, 8, 13

(D) 5, 6, 10

(E) 5, 5, 10

10. In triangle ABC, altitude CD divides angle C into two parts, X and Y.,

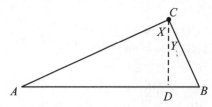

Which of the following must be true?

(A) $\angle X + \angle Y = \angle A + \angle B$

(B) $\angle X - \angle Y = \angle A - \angle B$

(C) $\angle X + \angle A = \angle Y + \angle B$

(D) $\angle X + \angle B = \angle Y + \angle A$

(E) $\angle X - \angle A = \angle Y + \angle B$

11. If the fractions $\dfrac{x+y}{3}$ and $\dfrac{x-y}{4}$ are added, the result is:

(A) $\dfrac{7x+y}{12}$

(B) $\dfrac{2x}{7}$

(C) $\dfrac{7x-y}{12}$

(D) $\dfrac{5x+4y}{12}$

(E) $\dfrac{x^2+y^2}{7}$

12. When $\dfrac{x^2-9}{x}$ is divided by $\dfrac{x-3}{5x}$, the quotient is:

(A) $\dfrac{(x-3)^2(x+3)}{5x^2}$

(B) $5x(x+3)$

(C) $5(x+3)$

(D) $5(x-3)$

(E) $\dfrac{5x}{x-3}$

13. The solution set of the inequality
$3x - 4 > 8$ is:

    (A) $x > 4$
    (B) $x < 4$
    (C) $x > -4$
    (D) $x = 4$
    (E) $x = -4$

14. Suppose there are seven roads between
Troy and Utica. In how many different
ways can Mr. Smythe travel from Troy
to Utica and return by a different route?

    (A) 36
    (B) 49
    (C) 35
    (D) 42
    (E) 54

15. A refrigerator that is originally priced at
M dollars is marked down to N dollars.
What is the percent of markdown?

    (A) $\left(\dfrac{M-N}{N}\right)100$

    (B) $\left(\dfrac{M-N}{M}\right)100$

    (C) $\left(\dfrac{N-M}{N}\right)100$

    (D) $\left(\dfrac{N-M}{M}\right)100$

    (E) $(M-N)100$

16. What is the area of the following
parallelogram?

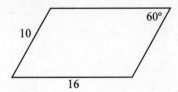

    (A) 20
    (B) 40
    (C) 60
    (D) 80
    (E) $80\sqrt{3}$

Directions: Each passage in this group is followed by questions based on its content. After reading a passage, choose the best answer to each question and blacken the corresponding space on the answer sheet. Answer all questions following a passage on the basis of what is *stated* or *implied* in that passage.

Passage 1

Line   Rebel uprising kills seventy! Plane crash leaves no survivors! Rock star dies of overdose!

5   Evening newscasts and metropolitan newspapers scream the bad news, the sensational, and the action.

     Audiences of today focus upon the sensational action, the violence, the loss, the terror. Individually, our lives are
10   redirected, our worlds reshaped, and our images warped. While wary of the danger of change, we human beings surrender daily to exploitation of values, opportunities, and sensitivity. The evolution has
15   brought us to the point that we believe little of what is presented to us as good and valuable; instead, we opt for suspicion and disbelief, demanding proof and something for nothing.

20   Therein lies the danger lurking for the writer seeking to break into the market of today. Journalists sell sensationalism— information as action. The journalist who loses sight of the simple truth and opts
25   *only* for the sensation loses the audience over the long run. Only those seeking a short-term thrill are intrigued enough to follow the journalistic thinking.

     How, then, do we capture the
30   audience of today and hold it, when the competition for attention is so hectic? The answer is writing to convey action, and the way to accomplish this is a simple one— action verbs.

35   The writer whose product suspends time for the reader or viewer is the successful writer whose work is sought and reread. Why?

     Time often will melt away in the face
40   of the reality of life's little responsibilities for the reader. Instead of puzzling over a punchier, more active, and more accurate verb, some journalists often limp through passive voice and useless tense to squeeze
45   the life out of an action-filled world and fill their writing with missed opportunities to appeal to the reader who seeks that moment of suspended time.

     Recently, a reporter wrote about
50   observing the buildings in a community ravished by rebel uprising as "thousands of bullet holes were in the hotel." A very sterile observation. Suppose he had written, "The hotel was pocked with bullet holes."
55   The visual image conjured up by the latter is far superior to the former.

     Here is the reader . . . comfortable in the easy chair before the fire with the dog as his feet. The verb *pocked* speaks to him.
60   Of course the verb *riddled* would also evoke an image. But *were* is the *be* verb that is bland vanilla as opposed to the Rocky Road of *pocked* or *riddled*. The reader moves on to the sports page without
65   feeling for the community.

     The journalist missed the opportunity to convey the reality.

1. This passage provides information to support which of the following?

    (A) Journalists of today find excitement that they convey to their readers.

    (B) The need for accurate reporting is obvious in the lack of human-interest stories.

    (C) In order to appeal to the public, one must write only about sensational topics.

    (D) Readers are often too concerned with themselves to care about others.

    (E) Writing that is bland escapes the reader's imagination.

2. One can infer that journalists write for an audience that is:

    (A) preoccupied with private interests.

    (B) uninterested in the world's problems.

    (C) illiterate and unable to understand extensive vocabulary.

    (D) focused on the sensational and able to sense the macabre.

    (E) ready to empathize with the subject of the article and react accordingly.

3. The journalist eager to succeed and capture the reader's attention will:

    (A) exploit the short attention span and sensationalize.

    (B) report only the familiar incidents in order to achieve the transfer of understanding.

    (C) attempt to spice the writing with contrived incidents that will fit the current situation.

    (D) utilize events and actions to transport the reader to the incident at hand.

    (E) appeal to emotions and evoke sympathy.

4. The passage suggests that readers are NOT affected by any of the following EXCEPT:

    (A) dull writing.

    (B) international incidents.

    (C) active writing.

    (D) local current events.

    (E) timely reporting.

5. One might conclude that readers prefer writing that will:

    (A) suspend reality.

    (B) refer to happy memories.

    (C) evoke sentiment.

    (D) capture the truth of the event.

    (E) fail to exploit them.

6. According to the author, which of the following might be true of journalists?

    (A) Most journalists are eager to report the truth.

    (B) Journalists only want to exploit the readers.

    (C) Language is the tool of journalists.

    (D) The more lurid the event, the greater the journalists' interests.

    (E) Journalists seek the easy way out.

7. According to this selection, journalists seize opportunities to communicate with readers by all of the following EXCEPT:

(A) colorful language.

(B) imaginative dialogue.

(C) bland or vanilla writing.

(D) action verbs.

(E) intriguing style.

Passage 2

Line Early in a writing career, one must understand that sloppy and distracted writing has no claim on a reader's attention. Some newsroom drones become nervous if the
5 writing is too active. The theory is that bright and lively writing is shameless and offends their sense of journalism that is ponderous and unbiased. The theory is that dealing in news means weighing down
10 articles with heavy words.

To achieve this somewhat questionable goal, the first impulse is to throw cover over the bare nouns and verbs, take the strong writing and active verbs down,
15 and shackle what might have been lively stories with jargon and erudite utterings.

The result is the same. The reader is lost. Terminally stuffy writing with its lofty vocabulary is no better than that which is
20 glutted and ponderous. The result is the remains of what once was lively writing.

Consider the following example:

"Additional strategies might include the placement of former camps of razor
25 wire, chain-link fencing, and riprap. . . ."

This line followed a discussion about the city worries about the homeless encamped in parks. The homeless were worried about being moved into camps
30 surrounded by fences. But in this line we see none of the concern nor realization of what *surrounding* or *ringing* might really mean. The verb is dead.

Another example is:
35 ". . . but no one from the building authority ever did an investigation."

Why not simply write: "Furthermore, no one investigated!" Get rid of the dead *be* verbs.
40 Fortunately, some writers demand more than passive voice and ponderous nouns. They snatch the extra instant they need to root around for a better verb. They stumble through the out-of-the-way places
45 in the language, uncovering rich verbs in unexplored crannies. Their writing is lively, provocative, and descriptive. It is filled with action. Consider this phrase:

"A warm but wild late spring storm
50 rumbled through New England on Monday. . . ."

This writer seized the opportunity to fill his reader's mind with the traditional thoughts of spring—*warm*—while at the
55 same time preparing that reader for the opposite—*wild*—when describing the storm. Additionally, the use of the verb *rumbled* evokes a further image of the storm moving slowly but with devastation
60 through a part of the country known to most Americans.

Another illustration of active writing is found in this passage:

"With three outs left in the regular
65 game, the Atlanta Braves—leading in the series four to three and with the score tied—mobilized themselves in the dugout to plot the strategy that would send their heaviest hitters to the plate in an effort to
70 claim the World Series title."

This writing seeks to envelop the reader in the suspense of the moment. Note the succinct handling of the building of the situation. The use of the verb
75 *mobilized* conjures the image of the team working as one unit to win the game. The adjective *heaviest* calls attention to the fact that there were those capable of carrying out the Herculean task at hand. And the last
80 phrase indicates the importance of this *one* game and this *one* inning.

8. The passage provides information to support which of the following generalizations?

(A) Writing for the public demands an extensive vocabulary.

(B) The public wants to read only what it can understand.

(C) Journalists can overdo the sensational vocabulary and allow the writing to become unwieldy.

(D) Writing that captures the reader and creates a visual image is preferred.

(E) Newsrooms are places to destroy creativity.

9. One might infer that working in a newsroom is:

(A) harrowing.
(B) distressing.
(C) easy.
(D) mundane.
(E) demanding.

10. In the first two examples, the writer is attempting to demonstrate the:

(A) underuse of action.
(B) reality of incidents.
(C) use of the creative.
(D) the destruction of vocabulary.
(E) the appeal to the lurid.

11. In the second two examples, the writer is attempting to demonstrate the:

(A) extensive vocabulary.
(B) suspension of reality.
(C) accuracy in reporting.
(D) use of imagination.
(E) depiction of heroes.

12. The conclusion one might draw from this writing is that:

(A) journalists have a big job.
(B) writing for a living is easy.
(C) word arrangement can determine readability.
(D) a good thesaurus is necessary.
(E) newspapers are unnecessary.

13. When one desires to become a writer, the best tool is:

(A) a selection of pens and paper.
(B) a good word processor.
(C) the knowledge of the language.
(D) identification with the reader.
(E) a creative instinct.

Passage 3

Line By the mid-1960s, not only was a great deal of good work being done on Southern literature, but the work was being accepted as legitimate scholarship by the profession
5 of literary critics. No longer was one an exotic if writing about literature in the South. The academic study of Southern literature had become a celebration of regional patriotism and local color.
10 　　During the next two decades, there evolved an expertise in critiquing the Southern writer that involved being able to see beyond the simplicity of language and the scope of the area into the deep and
15 passionate emotions that are typical in the South. That means that the leading writers on the scene led the profession into the great days of the Southern Renascence, or Renaissance, which lasted for about ten
20 years. These writers were in their fifties, sixties, or seventies and there seemed to be no one of significance coming along to take their places. What had once set the South and its literature apart from the rest of the
25 country, both for the good and the not so good, was now on the verge of extinction. Literary imagination was fast losing vitality. The novel appeared to be a dead art form,

and a new form, the nonfiction novel, was
30 being groomed to take its place.

      This has not become the case,
however. In fact, during the past decade,
there occurred a veritable explosion of
important and interesting young writers—
35 Southern novelists—ranging in age from 40
to 30 and even to 20. Their books were
read and reviewed not only everywhere in
America, but abroad as well. And, to the
surprise of all, the so-called nonfiction
40 novel, not the novel, was about to die.

      Not enough time has passed to
estimate how long this "Renaissance of the
Renaissance" will last; however, with the
important writing coming out of the South
45 in the 1990s, the reasoning is that the
promise is as real today as it was back in
those early years.

      Younger scholars have begun to
realize the importance of Southern litera-
50 ture and are selecting parts of it for their
theses, dissertations, essays, and even
books. New writers continue to emerge.
One of the virtues of Southern literary
study during the past forty years has been
55 its involvement in contemporary writing
and contemporary writers, and its merging
of criticism with historical scholarship. The
writing while anchored in reality is free of
never-never land. There is a recognition and
60 a need to explore both the continuity and
the change. Tradition is not dead; it is alive
and well in Southern literature.

14. The passage provides information to
support which of the following
generalizations?

(A) Southern writing is simple writing.

(B) Critics have not always recognized
Southern writing.

(C) Writing from other countries is
superior to Southern writing.

(D) Southern writers come from
simple roots.

(E) The genre of Southern writing is
still very new.

15. Which of the following best summa-
rizes the main point of the passage?

(A) Recent studies indicate a turning
away from writing done in the
South.

(B) The existence of the novel is
important to writing that is real.

(C) Southern writing is alive, well,
and growing in importance on a
global scale.

(D) The writing by Southerners is all
by older authors.

(E) Southern writing and Northern
writing are different.

16. When writing of the importance of
Southern writing, the word, *renascence*
or *renaissance* is used to mean:

(A) a renewing or rebirth.

(B) a separate identity and genre.

(C) similar to a great period in English
literature.

(D) a construction similar to that
following the Civil War.

(E) typical Southern language.

17. The passage suggests that those
devoted to the literature of the South
have evolved with the period and now
constitute:

(A) a majority of the writing population.

(B) only those born in the South.

(C) novelists only.

(D) a preponderance of fiction
writers.

(E) writers of all ages working in all
genres.

18. It can be inferred from this passage that Southern literature is destined to:

(A) evolve with the times and remain a part of the literary scene.

(B) increase in importance with the recognition of more and more critics and scholarship.

(C) decrease in popularity because of its limited form.

(D) suffer because of the demise of the nonfiction novel.

(E) experience a demise at the hand of modern scholars.

19. According to the author, which is true of the increase of Southern literature?

(A) A career in writing can be dangerous if correct decisions are not made.

(B) Authors writing in and about the South have not always been recognized for their labors and their distinction.

(C) The themes of racial prejudice are prevalent in Southern literature.

(D) Those writing about Southern literature are usually considered to be different.

(E) Bitter criticism of Southern writing made readers shy away from it.

20. The virtues of Southern literary study include all of the following EXCEPT:

(A) contemporary writing involvement.

(B) a merging of critical analysis and historical scholarship.

(C) use of modern writers.

(D) heavy use of family values.

(E) use of reality.

ANSWERS FOR PRACTICE TEST 2

Section 1 Problem Solving	Section 2 Sentence Correction	Section 3 Data Sufficiency	Section 4 Critical Reasoning	Section 5 Problem Solving	Section 6 Reading Comprehension
1. C	1. C	1. E	1. B	1. A	1. E
2. D	2. B	2. E	2. C	2. D	2. D
3. B	3. A	3. E	3. C	3. B	3. B
4. B	4. C	4. C	4. E	4. E	4. C
5. B	5. E	5. C	5. C	5. C	5. A
6. D	6. D	6. E	6. D	6. A	6. C
7. C	7. E	7. E	7. C	7. B	7. C
8. B	8. E	8. D	8. A	8. B	8. D
9. D	9. B	9. E	9. D	9. D	9. E
10. A	10. A	10. B	10. B	10. C	10. A
11. A	11. C	11. E	11. C	11. A	11. B
12. E	12. D	12. D	12. C	12. C	12. C
13. C	13. B	13. E	13. C	13. A	13. D
14. E	14. A	14. D	14. A	14. D	14. B
15. A	15. C	15. D	15. D	15. B	15. C
16. C	16. D	16. A	16. A	16. E	16. A
	17. E	17. A			17. E
	18. B	18. C			18. A
	19. E	19. A			19. B
	20. A	20. A			20. D
	21. D				
	22. E				

EXPLANATORY ANSWERS FOR PRACTICE TEST 2

Problem Solving

1. (C) Let x = the number.

Then $\frac{4}{5}x = 12$

$x = 12 \times \frac{5}{4} = 15$

and $\frac{5}{6} \times 15 = \frac{5}{\cancel{6}} \times \cancel{15}^{5} = \frac{25}{2} = 12.5$

2. (D) $(3a + 5)(2a - 3)$
first term = $(3a)(2a) = 6a^2$

Add inner and outer products:
$(3a)(-3) + (5)(2a) = -9a + 10a$
$\qquad\qquad\qquad\quad = 1a = a$

last term: $(5)(-3) = -15$
Now add: $6a^2 + a - 15$.

3. (B) 1 dollar = 100 cents

n = number of articles; each cost
5 cents; then
total cost = $5n$ cents
change from 100 cents − $5n$ cents:
$c = 100 - 5n$

4. (B) To solve equations use inverse operations. First, add 3 to both sides.

$$4x - 3 = 17$$
$$\underline{ + 3 = +3}$$
$$4x = 20$$

Then, divide both sides by 4.

$$\frac{4x}{4} = \frac{20}{4}$$
$$x = 5$$

5. (B) Draw $\angle ABC$ such that $AB = AC$.
$\angle B = \angle C$ since base angles of

isosceles Δ are equal

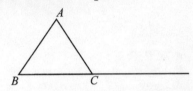

Let x = number of degrees in $\angle B$
$2x$ = number of degrees in $\angle A$

$\angle A + \angle B + \angle C = 180$
$2x + x + x = 180$
$4x = 180$
$x = 45$
$\angle C = 45$

The exterior angle at C is supplementary to $\angle C$. Hence,
$\angle C$ + exterior angle = 180
45 + exterior angle = 180
Exterior angle = 135

6. (D) The graph is horizontal between 4 p.m. and 6 p.m.

7. (C) Draw a horizontal line across from 76°. At the points of intersection with the curve, draw vertical lines down to the time axis. The two lines intersect the time axis at 10 a.m. and 9 p.m.

8. (B)
$$C = 2\pi r$$
$$= 2\pi(4)$$
$$= 8\pi \text{ inches in one}$$
revolution
$(8)(8\pi) = 64\pi$ inches

64π inches $\rightarrow 5\frac{1}{3}\pi$ ft

9. (D) Replace the value of x in the ratio:

$$\frac{8}{3-x} = \frac{8}{3-(-1)} = \frac{8}{3+1} = \frac{8}{4} = 2$$

10. (A) $\dfrac{x}{3} + \dfrac{x}{4} = 7$

$$\frac{\cancel{12} \cdot x}{\cancel{3}} + \frac{x \cdot \cancel{12}}{\cancel{4}} = 7 \cdot 12 \text{ Multiply by}$$
$$ \text{LCD} = 12$$

$$4x + 3x = 84$$

$$x = \frac{84}{7} = 12$$

Thus, $\dfrac{x}{6} = \dfrac{12}{6} = 2$

11. (A) Since acute angles of right $\triangle$ are complementary, $\angle GFE = 90 - 25 = 65$. If $\angle FEG = 25$, $\angle FEB = 2(25) = 50$ because $\angle BEF$ was bisected. $\angle EFC = \angle FEB$ because the measure of alternate interior angles is equal. Since the measure of a straight angle equals 180 degrees,

$$\angle EFC + \angle GFE + \angle GFD = 180$$
Substitute: $50 + 65 + x = 180$
$$115 + x = 180$$
$$x = 65$$

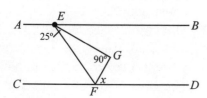

12. (E) Since 1 cake uses $\dfrac{2}{3}$ cup of sugar, let x = number of cakes for which you would need 4 cups of sugar. In the proportion:

$$\frac{1}{x} = \frac{\frac{2}{3}}{4}$$

$$(4)(1) = \frac{2}{3}x$$

$$4\left(\frac{3}{2}\right) = \left(\frac{3}{2}\right)\frac{2}{3}x \quad \text{cross-multiply;}$$
$$ \text{solve for } x$$

$$6 = x$$

13. (C) Let x = number of votes Sam received.

$2x + 6$ = number of votes Jack received

$3x - 8$ = number of votes Arthur received

$$x + 2x + 6 + 3x - 8 = 190$$

Collect like terms and solve for x.
$$6x - 2 = 190$$
$$6x = 192$$
$$x = 32 \text{ votes (Sam)}$$
$$2x + 6 = 70 \text{ votes (Jack)}$$
$$3x - 8 = 88 \text{ votes (Arthur)}$$

14. (E) Find $V = \pi r^2 h$ by substituting $r = 7$, $h = 10$, $\pi = \dfrac{22}{7}$.

$$V = \frac{22}{7}(7)^2(10)$$

$$= \frac{22}{7}(49)(10)$$

$$= (22)(7)(10)$$

$$= 1,540$$

15. (A) Diameter ROS divides circle O into two semicircles. Hence, $\angle RTS$ is a right angle because an angle inscribed in a semicircle is a right angle. Also, $OT = OR$, since they are equal radii in the same circle. Since $\triangle RTO$ is an isosceles triangle, $\angle TRO = \angle RTO$.

$$\angle RTS = \angle RTO + \angle 1$$

Substitute:

$$90° = 50° + \angle 1$$
$$40° = \angle 1$$

16. (C) Let x = the number of hours required to do the job with both machines working together. Every hour, the new machine does $\dfrac{1}{8}$ of the job, so in x hours the new machine will do $\dfrac{x}{8}$ of the job.

Every hour, the old machine does $\dfrac{1}{12}$ of the job, so in x hours the old machine will do $\dfrac{x}{12}$ of the job.

Thus, $\dfrac{x}{8} + \dfrac{x}{12} = 1$ (= 1 whole job done)

$$\frac{\overset{3}{\cancel{24}} \cdot x}{\underset{1}{\cancel{8}}} + \frac{x \cdot \overset{2}{\cancel{24}}}{\underset{1}{\cancel{12}}} = 1 \cdot 24 \quad \text{Multiply by LCD = 24}$$

$$3x + 2x = 24$$
$$5x = 24$$
$$x = \frac{24}{5} = 4.8 \text{ hours}$$

Sentence Corrections

1. The correct answer is C. It is the *professorship* that provided him with an income. The use of the word *thus* makes the entire sentence unclear.
2. The correct answer is B. After the initial verb—*hopes*—the infinitive form is called for.
3. The correct answer is A. No change is called for since the entire sequence is in the past.
4. The correct answer is C. This is the only choice that is a complete sentence.
5. The correct answer is E. This removes the dangling participle.
6. The correct answer is D. The expression is *"Have you ever visited . . .?"*
7. The correct answer is E. The participial phrase—*becoming upset*—is the subject. The use of the pronoun *that* is incorrect and confusing.
8. The correct answer is E. There are two actions in the past, one preceding the other.
9. The correct answer is B. The correlative *neither* is followed by *nor*.
10. The correct answer is A. This is correct—a good example of parallel construction.
11. The correct answer is C. Two past tenses are called for—one, the past perfect; the other, the simple past.
12. The correct answer is D. The subject is the singular noun *pile*; hence, the singular verb.
13. The correct answer is B. This is a misplaced modifier. The clause should modify *I*.
14. The correct answer is A. The introductory clause is correctly indicated as modifying *they*.

15. The correct answer is C. This, while it changes the order, is the correct sequence of tenses.

16. The correct answer is D. It is the spelling of the word *their* that is at issue here. In addition, the adverb *clearly* must be next to the verb *had lost*.

17. The correct answer is E. This question tests arbitrary tense shifts. There is no reason to mix present and past tense here. The only choice that is consistent with regard to tense is E.

18. The correct answer is B. *Whoever* is the subject of the clause; therefore, it must be in the nominative case. *Whomever* is in the accusative case and is incorrect. D and E are redundant, since the word *exam* is repeated. There is no reason to use the conditional *would* in E.

19. The correct answer is E. A, B, C, and D are all examples of run-on sentences. E is the only choice that ends an independent clause with a period rather than a comma or no punctuation at all.

20. The correct answer is A. This question tests proper word choice. *Allusions* is the correct choice, as is *affect* since affect is a verb. *Effect* is a noun. *Illusion* is not the intended meaning. E adds a wordy phrase—*a fact which*—in addition to using *effect* as a verb.

21. The correct answer is D. This question tests faulty parallelism. Since arrogant is an adjective describing the celebrity, the other two descriptions of the celebrity should be parallel in structure and should be adjectives. D is the only choice that makes that correction.

22. The correct answer is E. This question tests faulty parallelism. *To study* is an infinitive. To make the structure parallel, the other verbs should follow suit. The only choice in which all three verbs are in the infinitive form is choice E.

Data Sufficiency

1. **(E)** is the correct answer. Statement (1) can be simplified to tell us that N>−1. This, however, does not necessarily tell us that N is positive, since N could still be a number like −1/2. (2) can be simplified to tell us N<4, which also does not tell us if N is positive or negative. Together, we know that −1<N<4, which is also insufficient.

2. **(E)** is the correct answer. Statement (1) gives you the coordinates of one corner. But there are four squares that can be formed starting at points (2, 1), so that there will be four possible answers. Statement (2) contains information that is already known.

3. **(E)** is the correct answer. Statement (1) does not tell you whether the discount is based on the cost or the sale price of the car. Therefore, it is impossible to determine the cost of the car. Statement (2) does not tell you whether any further discount has been given on the price of the car. Neither statement (1) nor (2) alone nor both together give you enough information.

4. (C) is the correct answer. Both (1) and (2) are necessary. People who have stereo + people who have CB = 180. Since only 110 were surveyed, 180 − 110 = 70 who must have both. Those 70 people were counted in the group who had CB's and also counted in the group who had stereos. A Venn diagram helps.

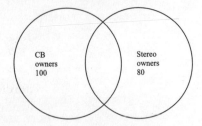

Since both circles have to represent 110 persons, there has to be an overlap of 70 people.

5. (C) is the correct answer. *AD* and *BC* are two intersecting lines, so that the vertical angles are equal, according to (1). Angle *AEB* = angle *CED*. Since *AB ∥ DC,* according to (2), angle *B* = angle *C.* If parallel lines are intersected by a transversal, alternate interior angles are equal. Since *BE = EC,* the triangles are congruent by the "angle-side-angle" theorem.

6. (E) is the correct answer. Statements (1) and (2) give you statistics that show that Area A has a lower infant mortality rate than Area B, but they give you no information about the health-care system on which to base a conclusion.

7. (E) is the correct answer. The fact that the triangle is isosceles tells us that two sides are equal, and that the third side is possibly different. Since we are given only the length of one side, we cannot answer the question.

8. (D) is the answer. Both (1) and (2) enable us to determine Don's weight before and after the program, so we can compute his percent of weight loss.

9. (E) is the correct answer. Neither (1) nor (2) helps. There could have been some car owners among the 110 who had neither stereo nor CB. The universe of the 110 car owners has four components— those with no radio equipment, those with stereo only, those with CB only, and those with both. We have information about only two groups and cannot answer the question.

10. (B) is the correct answer. Statement (1) does not give us enough information to determine angle size. Statement (2) gives us an algebraic equation: $\frac{1}{5}(180° − x°) = 90° − x°$

11. (E) is the correct answer. Neither (1) nor (2) gives a relationship between the rate of profit on unbranded products and that of branded products. Therefore, the answer to the question cannot be determined.

12. (D) is the correct answer. If the sales tax is 8 percent, then the tax plus the tip (16 percent) is 24 percent of the original cost, $1.24x = $14.88. Statement (2) also gives you enough information. Total cost, $14.88 − $.96 sales tax and − $1.92 for the tip equals the cost of the meal.

13. (E) is the correct answer. (1) tells us that $p^2 - 7p = -12$, or $p^2 - 7p + 12 = 0$. Factoring, $(p-4)(p-3) = 0$, so $p = 3$ or 4.

Since (1) does not give us a unique value for p, it is insufficient. (2) does not add anything to our knowledge of p.

14. (D) is the correct answer. Let x = first number, $x + 2$ = second number, $x + 4$ = third number, and so on.

Per statement (1),
$$x + x + 4 = 26$$
$$2x = 22$$
$$x = 11$$

The fifth number is 19.
Per statement (2),
$$(x)(x + 2) = 143$$
$$x^2 + 2x - 143 = 0$$
$$(x - 11)(x + 13) = 0$$
$$x = 11$$
$$x = -13 \text{ (not usable)}$$

The fifth number is 19.

15. (D) is the correct answer. (1) can be rewritten to tell us $3x^2 + 4x^4 - x^6 = -378$.

Knowing that $x = 3$ or -3 also enables us to answer the question since $3x^2 + 4x^4 - x^6$ has the same value for $x = 3$ or -3.

16. (A) is the correct answer. Since there are 360° in a circle and angle $O = 90°$, the area of the sector OAB would be $\frac{1}{4}$ of the total area of the circle.

(2) will not answer the question alone, nor is it of any use.

17. (A) is the correct answer. The sum of $\frac{1}{a}$ and $\frac{1}{b}$ is $\frac{a+b}{ab}$. (1) tells us that
$$\frac{a+b}{ab} = 7.$$

(2) does not supply any useful information.

18. (C) is the correct answer. Neither (1) nor (2) alone will help, but (1) and (2) provide you with the necessary information.

Since the lines are parallel, the angle supplementary to angle y = angle x, or 120°. Therefore, angle y is 60° (calculation is not even necessary).

19. (A) is the correct answer. (1) supplies you with the answer. The relative size of x and y is not important.

20. (A) is the correct answer. (1) enables us to determine the cost of the suit. The problem gives us enough information to determine the reduced sales price. Therefore, the question can be answered.

(2) simply gives us an overall gross profit percentage, which applies after markups and markdowns to *all* merchandise sold and tells us nothing about the cost of the specific suit.

Critical Reasoning

1. The correct answer is B. With the information provided, the only selection that must be true is II. Because every car made by Manufacturer X has a driver's-side airbag, it is clear that II must be true, no matter what other improvements it may have. Being told only that a car has shatterproof glass is not enough, with the information provided, to conclude anything else. If a car has a passenger's-side airbag, it is true that it must have a roll bar and shatterproof glass, but this statement does not work in reverse. It is possible that the car in question may have shatterproof glass and only a driver's-side airbag. Also, the statement that cars with passenger airbags will have both shatterproof glass and roll bars does not necessarily mean that shatterproof glass and roll bars must always be together.

2. The correct answer is C. The attack on the legislation assumes that the teenage parents will have to use their welfare money to pay for day care. Choice C directly contradicts this attack and supports the law. Choice A may be correct, but it goes beyond the scope of the argument and provides information that is irrelevant to the issue of welfare and day care. Choice B is completely irrelevant to the issue of whether or not the law is effective. Choice D is a possible answer, but it does not support the law as directly as C by not addressing the day-care issue. Choice E attacks the motives of the people attacking the bill but does not attack their argument.

3. The correct answer is C. Remember, the author is discussing *moral duty*, which is entirely unrelated to the "goodness" attributed to man and extolled in literature. There is *no* emotional feeling in *moral duty*. All answers except C deal with the acquired "goodness."

4. The correct answer is E. The word *inclination* indicates that which is innate, not learned. All answers except E deal with the innate.

5. The correct answer is C. The key word is *spiritual*. The selection deals with that which is observable, not that which is emotional.

6. The correct answer is D. This argument assumes that children using the computer bulletin boards are being "exploited." Choice D contradicts this assumption by showing that, even if the children are exposed to the advertising, they are not being exploited because the advertising has no practical effect. Choice A may or may not be true but it is irrelevant, because it does not address the problem that may affect people who do have the proper computer hardware. Choice B similarly avoids the issue, since showing that children and adults are equally susceptible does not present any cure for the problem. Choice C presents a problem with the proposed regulation but does not directly address the issue. Choice E may be true but ignores the specific issue of the advertising that does appear on the computer.

7. The correct answer is C. Based on the statements provided, one would expect the stock prices of XYZ to rise after the announcement. If the price decreases, then something about this particular merger must be causing a change in the opinion of investors. Choice C is the selection that repeats this conclusion. Choice A addresses only "average" investors, but nothing in the argument limits it to "average" investors. Choice B is irrelevant, or at best would contradict the argument by suggesting that the price should increase because of lower supply. Choice D is incorrect because nothing in the argument suggests any reliance on the negotiations involved in creating the merger. Choice E is incorrect because there is nothing in the argument suggesting that prime lending rates have any effect on stock prices.

8. The correct answer is A. The investors in this argument assume that John Doe is the cause of the bankruptcies of the other companies. Choice A, if true, directly contradicts this assumption. Choices B, C, and D focus on irrelevant information that does not directly affect the connection between John Doe and the bankruptcy filing. Choice E, if true, would support the conclusion reached by the investors rather than contradict it.

9. The correct answer is D. The word *philanthropist* denotes doing that which is good without hope of reward, and all of the answers except D indicate the absence of the desire to do good for its own good.

10. The correct answer is B. All answers except B evoke the connotation of that which one does from an acquired emotional thrust. Honor symbolizes that in which one believes and to which one is dedicated totally regardless of the outcomes.

11. The correct answer is C. The key phrase is *in accord* versus *because of*. Note that the first indicates obeying the rules in order to be obedient, while *because of* indicates the motivation of the rules. Only choice C calls for that motivation.

12. The correct answer is C. The conclusion of this argument can be reached by considering only the last sentence. The added information says that life does *not* mean nothing, thereby contradicting the conclusion of the last sentence of the argument. By contradicting the conclusion of an if-then sentence, one can conclude the opposite of the premise of the sentence, i.e., that "I do not think." Recognizing this, the only correct answers could be C or E. E is incorrect because the argument states that if the speaker does not think, then ". . . I am not." Therefore, the only correct answer is C.

13. The correct answer is C. The key word here is *goodness*. That which is good is a concept developed from that which is abstract (unknown in simple definition) and without human experience. Only C qualifies.

14. The correct answer is A. The author writes from the vantage point of deeply held moral convictions. Such concrete evaluations are neither poetic nor polished. In addition, there is no anger or force indicated here. The answer can only be A, and the reading of the passage clearly indicates that one must follow carefully the writer's thinking.

15. The correct answer is D. Consider the definitions of each of the choices: honor is that which is deeply entrenched and obeyed regardless; philanthropy is doing good without hope of reward; impulses implies no follow-through; and sympathy is not deeply rooted feeling for another. None of these is present; only the ethics of morality.

16. The correct answer is A. As in the previous question, the emotions toward sentimentality can all be disregarded in this selection, which eliminates all choices except A. The only standard that is uncompromising is morality.

Problem Solving

1. (A) The exterior angle of a regular polygon is the supplement of each interior angle, or the exterior angle = 180 − 150 = 30. The formula for an exterior angle is:

$$\frac{360}{N} = \text{exterior angle } (N = \text{number of sides})$$

$$\frac{360}{N} = 30 \text{ cross-multiply}$$

$$360 = 30N$$

$$12 = N \text{ (number of sides)}$$

2. (D) Let B = Ben's salary before the raise.

Let D = David's salary before the raise.

Then,

$$.06B = 2400 \qquad .06D = 2520$$

$$B = \frac{2400}{.06} = 40,000$$

$$D = \frac{2520}{.06} = 42,000$$

After the raise,

Ben's salary = 40,000 + 2,400
= $42,400

David's salary = 42,000 + 2,520
= $44,520

So: $44,520 − $42,400 = $2120

3. (B) Draw a line with two points, A and B, on it. The set of points equally distant from A and B is a line perpendicular to line AB. Choose points G and H to be the appropriate distance from AB. Then note that $GA = AB = HA = HB$. Thus, there are two points that are a given distance from line AB and equally distant from points A and B.

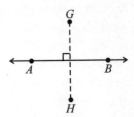

4. (E) If *DE* is parallel to *AC*, similar triangles *ABC* and *DBE* are formed. Corresponding sides of similar triangles are in proportion. Hence:

$$\frac{DE}{AC} = \frac{DB}{AB}$$

Substitute and cross-multiply:

$$\frac{x}{6} = \frac{10}{15}$$
$$15x = (6)(10)$$
$$x = 4$$

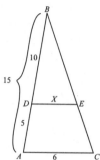

5. (C) We have: $.4 \times .5 \times 100 = 20M$, or
$$.2 \times 100 = 20M$$
$$20 = 20M$$
$$1 = M$$

6. (A) $\dfrac{(A-B)^2}{A^2 - B^2}$

$$= \frac{\overset{1}{\cancel{(A-B)}}(A-B)}{\underset{1}{\cancel{(A-B)}}(A+B)} = \frac{(A-B)}{(A+B)} = 25$$

If $\dfrac{A-B}{A+B} = 25$, then $\dfrac{A+B}{A-B} = \dfrac{1}{25}$

7. (B) Since $12 - 4W = Z$, we have
$$12 - 4W - 4 = Z - 4, \text{ or}$$
$$8 - 4W = Z - 4.$$

8. (B) $OA = OB$ because the radii in the same circle are equal. The triangle *AOB* is a 45-45-90 right triangle. In such a triangle,
$$\text{hypotenuse} = \sqrt{2} \cdot \text{leg.}$$
Thus, hypotenuse $= 10\sqrt{2}$

9. (D) In any triangle, the sum of any two sides must be greater than the third side. Only in example D is this true: $5 + 6 > 10$.

10. (C) Altitude *CD* is drawn, forming right angles: $\angle CDA = \angle CDB = 90°$. Hence, $\angle X + \angle A + \angle CDA = 180°$. Also, $\angle Y + \angle B + \angle CDB = 180°$. Substitute $\angle X + \angle A = \angle Y + \angle B$.

11. (A) Combine $\dfrac{x+y}{3}$ and $\dfrac{x-y}{4}$ into a single fraction. The least-common denominator is 12. Change each fraction into an equivalent fraction.

$$\frac{x+y}{3} = \frac{4x+4y}{12}$$

$$\frac{x-y}{4} = \frac{3x-3y}{12}$$

Combine like terms in the numerator:

$$\frac{4x + 4y + 3x - 3y}{12} = \frac{7x+y}{12}$$

12. (C) Invert the divisor so that the fractions can be multiplied.

$$\frac{x^2 - 9}{x} \cdot \frac{5x}{x - 3}$$

Factor $x^2 - 9 = (x - 3)(x + 3)$

Then, we have

$$\frac{(x - 3)(x + 3)}{x} \cdot \frac{5x}{x - 3}$$

Cancel out any common factors:

$$\frac{\overset{1}{\cancel{(x - 3)}}(x + 3)}{\underset{1}{\cancel{x}}} \cdot \frac{5\overset{1}{\cancel{x}}}{\underset{1}{\cancel{x - 3}}}$$

Multiply: $5(x + 3)$

13. (A) Solve the inequality:

$$3x - 4 > 8$$
$$3x > 8 + 4$$
$$3x > 12$$
$$x > 4$$

14. (D) Mr. Smythe can go in any of seven ways, but once a road is chosen there are only six roads to return by.

$$6 \cdot 7 = 42$$

15. (B) The amount of the markdown is $M - N$. To find the percent of the markdown:

$$\frac{\text{Markdown}}{\text{Original Price}} = \frac{\% \text{ Markdown}}{100}$$

$$\frac{M - N}{M} = \frac{\%}{100} \quad \text{Cross-multiply}$$

$$\left(\frac{M - N}{M}\right)100 = \% \text{ of Markdown}$$

16. (E) Since opposite angles in a parallelogram are congruent, the angle in the lower left must be 60°.

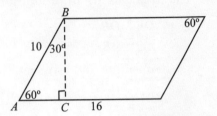

Points A, B, and C form a 30-60-90 triangle, as shown. We know that the side opposite the right angle is 10. Then the side opposite the 60° angle is $\frac{10}{2}\sqrt{3} = 5\sqrt{3}$.

$$A = bh = 16(5\sqrt{3}) = 80\sqrt{3}$$

Reading Comprehension

1. The correct answer is E. The concern is that readers cannot conceive of the meaning of the incident without writing that makes them feel what is happening. That can be done only with action verbs.

2. The correct answer is D. The audience is not attuned to the stories that are without "action" and therefore disengaging. The journalist must make the stories come alive and evoke pictures.

3. The correct answer is A. The journalist reports on the sensational rather than the ordinary. The use of action verbs allows this to work on the reader's imagination.

4. The correct answer is C. No matter how important or vital the incident reported, without active and lively writing it is unimportant. By the same token, any meaningless event can be important to the reader if the writing is alive.

5. The correct answer is A. Readers want the present to "melt away" and allow them to experience the incident at hand.

6. The correct answer is C. The journalist electing to use *riddled* rather than a *be* verb tends to capture the imagination of the reader.

7. The correct answer is C. The other choices are ways that a journalist *will* choose in order to intrigue the readers, while C is the one way that a writer would *never* use in order to intrigue the reader. *Bland* and *vanilla* are the words used to describe the writing that the reader passes over for the sports page.

8. The correct answer is D. In the examples presented, the reader is urged to *see* and to *feel* the tension of what is happening.

9. The correct answer is E. The selections indicate the tendencies of the newsroom to take away the creative and replace with the erudite or to destroy the writer's purpose.

10. The correct answer is A. The selection shows carefully that the overuse of words does not create the desired picture.

11. The correct answer is B. In order to capture a reader's attention, the writer must allow time to melt away and let the reader feel and see what is there.

12. The correct answer is C. The simple word arrangement in the second example made the selection more real.

13. The correct answer is D. When the writer can identify with the reader, then the news becomes real and memorable. One must use that realization when writing.

14. The correct answer is B. The careful point is made that Southern literature had to rise above the criticism and the conjecture and even then was viewed as becoming unimportant.

15. The correct answer is C. The point is made that the writings are read "not only everywhere in America but abroad as well."

16. The correct answer is A. The careful explanation of renaissance as rebirth is made to show that there is a coming of age or a new attention.

17. The correct answer is E. The point is made that the writers now include those down to the twenties and writing in theses, dissertations, etc.

18. The correct answer is A. The reader is led to believe that more and more scholarship is devoted to Southern literature, which will lead to its longevity.

19. The correct answer is B. The author leads the reader to understand that until the 1960s there was little if any attention given to Southern literature.

20. The correct answer is D. Southern literature does *not* focus on family values at all, but upon reality and the use of the contemporary.

Paying for School—Financing Your Graduate Education

Support for graduate study can take many forms, depending upon the field of study and program you pursue. For example, some 60 percent of doctoral students receive support in the form of either grants/fellowships or assistantships, whereas most students in master's programs rely on loans to pay for their graduate study. In addition, doctoral candidates are more likely to receive grants/fellowships and assistantships than master's degree students, and students in the sciences are more likely to receive aid than those in the arts and humanities.

For those of you who have applied for financial aid as an undergraduate, there are some differences for graduate students you'll notice right away. For one, aid to undergraduates is based primarily on need (although the number of colleges that now offer undergraduate merit-based aid is increasing), but graduate aid is often based on academic merit. Second, as a graduate student, you are automatically declared "independent" for federal financial aid purposes, meaning your parents' income and asset information is not required in assessing your need for federal aid. Third, at some graduate schools, the awarding of aid may be administered by the academic departments or the graduate school itself, not the financial aid office. That means that at some schools, you may be involved with as many as three offices: a central financial aid office, the graduate school, *and* your academic department.

Be Prepared

Being prepared for graduate school means you have to put together a financial plan. So, before you enter graduate school, you should have answers to these questions:

- What should I be doing now to prepare for the cost of my graduate education?

- What can I do to minimize my costs once I arrive on campus?

- What financial aid programs are available at each of the schools to which I am applying?

- What financial aid programs are available outside the university, at the federal, state, or private level?

- What financing options do I have if I cannot pay the full cost from my own resources and those of my family?

- What should I know about the loans I am being offered?

- What impact will these loans have on me when I complete my program?

You'll find your answers in three guiding principles: think ahead, live within your means, and keep your head above water.

Think Ahead

The first step to putting together your financial plan comes from thinking about the future: the loss of your income while you're attending school, your projected income after you graduate, the annual rate of inflation, additional expenses you will incur as a student and after you graduate, and any loss of income you may experience later on from unintentional periods of unemployment, pregnancy, or disability. The cornerstone of thinking ahead is following a step-by-step process.

1. *Set your goals.* Decide what and where you want to study, whether you will go full- or part-time, whether you'll work while attending, and what an appropriate level of debt would be. Consider whether you would attend full-time if you had enough financial aid or whether keeping your full-time job is an important priority in your life. Keep in mind that many employers have tuition reimbursement plans for full-time employees.

2. *Take inventory.* Collect your financial information and add up your assets—bank accounts, stocks, bonds, real estate, business and personal property. Then subtract your liabilities—money owed on your assets including credit card debt and car loans—to yield your net worth.

3. *Calculate your need.* Compare your net worth with the costs at the schools you are considering to get a rough estimate of how much of your assets you can use for your schooling.

4. *Create an action plan.* Determine how much you'll earn while in school, how much you think you will receive in grants and scholarships, and how much you plan to borrow. Don't forget to consider inflation and possible life changes that could affect your overall financial plan.

5. *Review your plan regularly.* Measure the progress of your plan every year and make adjustments for such things as increases in salary or other changes in your goals or circumstances.

Live Within Your Means

The second step in being prepared is knowing how much you spend now so you can determine how much you'll spend when you're in school. Use the standard cost of attendance budget published by your school as a guide, but don't be surprised if your estimated budget is higher than the one the school provides, especially if you've been out of school for a while. Once you've figured out your budget, see if you can pare down your current costs and financial obligations so the lean years of graduate school don't come as too large a shock.

Keep Your Head Above Water

Finally, the third step is managing the debt you'll accrue as a graduate student. Debt is manageable only when considered in terms of five things:

1. Your future income

2. The amount of time it takes to repay the loan

3. The interest rate you are being charged

4. Your personal lifestyle and expenses after graduation

5. Unexpected circumstances that change your income or your ability to repay what you owe

To make sure your educational debt is manageable, you should borrow an amount that requires payments of no more than 8 percent of your starting salary.

The approximate monthly installments for repaying borrowed principal at 5, 8–10, 12, and 14 percent are indicated below.

Estimated Loan Repayment Schedule
Monthly Payments for Every $1,000 Borrowed

Rate	5 years	10 years	15 years	20 years	25 years
5%	$18.87	$10.61	$ 7.91	$ 6.60	$ 5.85
8%	20.28	12.13	9.56	8.36	7.72
9%	20.76	12.67	10.14	9.00	8.39
10%	21.74	13.77	10.75	9.65	9.09
12%	22.24	14.35	12.00	11.01	10.53
14%	23.27	15.53	13.32	12.44	12.04

You can use this table to estimate your monthly payments on a loan for any of the five repayment periods (5, 10, 15, 20, and 25 years). The amounts listed are the monthly payments for a $1,000 loan for each of the interest rates. To estimate your monthly payment, choose the closest interest rate and multiply the amount of the payment listed by the total amount of your loan and then divide by 1,000. For example, for a total loan of $15,000 at 9 percent to be paid back over 10 years, multiply $12.67 times 15,000 (190,050), divided by 1,000. This yields $190.05 per month.

If you're wondering just how much of a loan payment you can afford monthly without running into payment problems, consult the following chart.

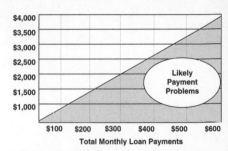

How Much Can You Afford to Repay?

Monthly Income (after taxes)

$4,000 / $3,500 / $3,000 / $2,500 / $2,000 / $1,500 / $1,000

Likely Payment Problems

$100 $200 $300 $400 $500 $600

Total Monthly Loan Payments

This graph shows the monthly cash-flow outlook based on your total monthly loan payments in comparison with your monthly income earned after taxes. Ideally, to eliminate likely payment problems, your monthly loan payment should be less than 15% of your monthly income.

Of course, the best way to manage your debt is to borrow less. While cutting your personal budget may be one option, there are a few others you may want to consider:

- *Ask Your Family for Help:* Although the federal government considers you "independent," your parents and family may still be willing and able to help pay for your graduate education. If your family is not open to just giving you money, they may be open to making a low-interest (or deferred-interest) loan. Family loans usually have more attractive interest rates and repayment terms than commercial loans. They may also have tax consequences, so you may want to check with a tax adviser.

- *Push to Graduate Early:* It's possible to reduce your total indebtedness by completing your program ahead of schedule. You can take more courses either per semester or during the summer. Keep in mind, though, that these options reduce the time you have available to work.

- *Work More, Attend Less:* Another alternative is to enroll part-time, leaving more time to work. Remember, though, to qualify for aid, you must be enrolled at least half-time, which is usually considered six credits per term. And if you're enrolled less than half-time, you'll have to start repaying your loans once the grace period has expired.

ROLL YOUR LOANS INTO ONE

There's a good chance that as a graduate student you will have two or more loans included in your aid package, plus any money you borrowed as an undergraduate. That means when you start repaying, you could be making loan payments to several different lenders. Not only can the recordkeeping be a nightmare, but with each loan having a minimum payment, your total monthly payments may be more than you can handle. If you owe more than $7,500 in federal loans, you can combine your loans into one consolidated loan at either a flat 9 percent interest rate

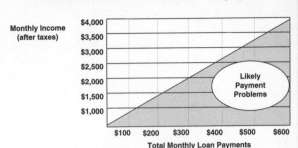

or a weighted average of the rates on the loans consolidated. Your repayment can also be extended to up to thirty years, depending on the total amount you borrow, which will make your monthly payments lower (of course, you'll also be paying more total interest). With a consolidated loan, some lenders offer graduated or income-sensitive repayment options. Consult with your lender about the types of consolidation provisions offered.

CREDIT: DON'T LET YOUR PAST HAUNT YOU

Many schools will check your credit history before they process any private educational loans for you. To make sure your credit rating is accurate, you may want to request a copy of your credit report before you start graduate school. You can get a copy of your report by sending a signed, written request to one of the three national credit reporting agencies at the address listed below. Include your full name, social security number, current address, any previous addresses for the past five years, date of birth, and daytime phone number. Call the agency before you request your report so you know whether there is a fee for this report. Note that you are entitled to a free copy of your credit report if you have been denied credit within the last sixty days. In addition, TRW currently provides complimentary credit reports once every twelve months.

Credit criteria used to review and approve student loans can include the following:

- Absence of negative credit

CREDIT REPORTING AGENCIES

TRW Consumer Assistance Center
P.O. Box 2350
Chatsworth, California 91313-2350
800-682-7654

Equifax
P.O. Box 105873
Atlanta, Georgia 30348
800-685-1111

CSC Credit Services
Consumer Assistance Center
P.O. Box 674402
Houston, Texas 77267-5979
800-759-5979

Trans Union Data Corporation
P.O. Box 390
760 Sproul Road
Springfield, Pennsylvania 19064-0390
610-690-4909

- No bankruptcies, foreclosures, repossessions, charge-offs, or open judgments

- No prior educational loan defaults, unless paid in full or making satisfactory repayments

- Absence of excessive past due accounts; that is, no 30-, 60-, or 90-day delinquencies on consumer loans or revolving charge accounts within the past two years

TYPES OF AID AVAILABLE

There are three types of aid: money given to you (grants, scholarships, and fellowships), money you earn through work, and loans.

Grants, Scholarships, and Fellowships

Most grants, scholarships, and fellowships are outright awards that require no service in return. Often they provide the cost of tuition and fees plus a stipend to cover living expenses. Some are based exclusively on financial need, some exclusively on academic merit, and some on a combination of need and merit. As a rule, grants are awarded to those with financial need, although they may require the recipient to have expertise in a certain field. Fellowships and scholarships often connote selectivity based on ability—financial need is usually not a factor.

Federal Support

Several federal agencies fund fellowship and trainee programs for graduate and professional students. The amounts and types of assistance offered vary considerably by field of study. The following are programs available for those studying engineering and applied sciences:

National Science Foundation. Graduate Research Program Fellowships include tuition and fees plus a $14,000 stipend and a $1,000 total allowance for three years of graduate study in engineering, mathematics, the natural sciences, the social sciences, and the history and philosophy of science. The application deadline is in early November. For more information, write to the National Science Foundation at Oak Ridge Associated Universities, P.O. Box 3010, Oak Ridge, Tennessee 37831-3010 or call 423-241-4300.

National Institutes of Health (NIH). NIH sponsors many different fellowship opportunities. For example, it offers training grants administered through schools' research departments. Training grants provide tuition plus a twelve-month stipend of $10,008. For more information, call 301-435-0714.

Veterans' Benefits. Veterans may use their educational benefits for training at the graduate and professional levels. Contact your regional office of the Veterans Administration for more details.

State Support

Many states offer grants for graduate study, with California, Michigan, New York, North Carolina,

Texas, and Virginia offering the largest programs. Due to fiscal constraints, however, some states have had to reduce or eliminate their financial aid programs for graduate study. To qualify for a particular state's aid you must be a resident of that state. Residency is established in most states after you have lived there for at least twelve consecutive months prior to enrolling in school. Many states provide funds for in-state students only; that is, funds are not transferable out of state. Contact your state scholarship office to determine what aid it offers.

Institutional Aid

Educational institutions using their own funds provide between $2 and $3 billion in graduate assistance in the form of fellowships, tuition waivers, and assistantships. Consult each school's catalog for information about aid programs.

Corporate Aid

Many corporations provide graduate student support as part of the employee benefits package. Most employees who receive aid study at the master's level or take courses without enrolling in a particular degree program.

Aid from Foundations

Most foundations provide support in areas of interest to them. The Foundation Center of New York City publishes several reference books on foundation support for graduate study. It also has a computerized databank called Grant Guides that, for a fee, will produce a listing of grant possibilities in a variety of fields. For more information call 212-620-4230.

Financial Aid for Minorities and Women

Patricia Roberts Harris Fellowships. This federal award provides support for minorities and women. Awards are made to schools, and the schools decide who receives these funds. Grants provide tuition and a stipend of $14,000 for up to four years. Consult the graduate school for more information. Funds for this program may be cut in the next federal budget.

Bureau of Indian Affairs. The Bureau of Indian Affairs (BIA) offers aid to students who are at least one quarter American Indian or native Alaskan and from a federally recognized tribe. Contact your tribal education officer, BIA area office, or call the Bureau of Indian Affairs at 202-208-3711.

The Ford Foundation Doctoral Fellowship for Minorities. Provides three-year doctoral fellowships and one-year dissertation fellowships. Predoctoral fellowships include an annual stipend of $11,500 to the fellow and an annual institutional grant of $6,000 to the fellowship institution in lieu of tuition and fees. Dissertation fellows receive a stipend of $18,000 for a twelve-month period.

Applications are due in early November. For more information contact the Fellowship Office, National Research Council at 202-334-2872.

National Consortium for Graduate Degrees in Engineering and Science (GEM). GEM was founded in 1976 to help minority men and women pursue graduate study in engineering and science by helping them obtain practical experience through summer internships at consortium work sites and finance graduate study toward a master's or Ph.D. degree. GEM administers the following programs:

Ph.D. Fellowship Program. The Ph.D. Science Fellowship and the Engineering Fellowship programs provide opportunities for minority students to obtain a Ph.D. in the natural sciences or in engineering through a program of paid summer research internships and financial support. Open to U.S. citizens who belong to one of the ethnic groups underrepresented in the natural sciences and engineering, GEM fellowships are awarded for a twelve-month period. Fellowships are tenable at universities participating in the GEM science or engineering Ph.D. programs. Awards include tuition, fees, and a $12,000 stipend. After the first year of study fellows are supported completely by their respective universities and support may include teaching or research assistantships. Forty fellowships are awarded annually in each program. The application deadline is December. Contact: GEM, Box 537, Notre Dame, Indiana 46556 or call 219-287-1097.

National Physical Sciences Consortium. Graduate fellowships are available in astronomy, chemistry, computer science, geology, materials science, mathematics, and physics for women and Black, Hispanic, and Native American students. These fellowships are available only at member universities. Awards may vary by year in school; the application deadline is November 1. Fellows receive tuition plus a stipend between $10,000 and $15,000. Contact National Physical Sciences Consortium, c/o New Mexico State University, O'Loughlin House, P.O. Box 30001, Department 3NPS, Las Cruces, New Mexico 88033-0001 or call 505-646-6037.

In addition, below are some books available that describe financial aid opportunities for women and minorities.

The Directory of Financial Aids for Women, fifth edition, by Gail Ann Schlachter (Reference Service Press, 1991), lists sources of support and identifies foundations and other organizations interested in helping women secure funding for graduate study.

The Association for Women in Science publishes *Grants-at-a-Glance,* a booklet highlighting fellowships for women in science. It can be ordered by calling 202-326-8940.

Books such as the *Directory of Special Programs for Minority Group Members,* fifth edition (Garrett Park, Md: Garrett Park Press, 1990), describe financial aid opportunities for minority students. If you register with the *Minority Graduate Student Locator Service* sponsored by the Educational Testing Service, you will be contacted by schools interested in increasing their minority student enrollment. Such schools may have funds designated for minority students.

Disabled students are eligible to receive aid from a number of organizations. *Financial Aid for the Disabled and Their Families, 1992-94* (Reference Service Press) lists aid opportunities for disabled students. The Vocational Rehabilitation Services in your home state can also provide information.

Researching Grants and Fellowships

The books listed below are good sources of information on grant and fellowship support for graduate education and should be consulted before you resort to borrowing. Keep in mind that grant support varies dramatically from field to field.

Annual Register of Grant Support: A Directory of Funding Sources, Wilmette, Ill.: National Register Publishing Co. This is a comprehensive guide to grants and awards from government agencies, foundations, and business and professional organizations.

Corporate Foundation Profiles, eighth edition. New York: Foundation Center, 1994. This is an in-depth, analytical profile of 250 of the largest company-sponsored foundations in the United States. Brief descriptions of all 700 company-sponsored foundations are also included. There is an index of subjects, types of support, and geographical locations.

The Foundation Directory, sixteenth edition. Edited by Stan Olsen. New York: Foundation Center, 1994. This directory, with a supplement, gives detailed information on U.S. foundations with brief descriptions of the purpose and activities of each.

The Grants Register 1995-97, fourteenth edition. Edited by Lisa Williams. New York: St. Martin's, 1995. This lists grant agencies alphabetically and gives information on awards available to graduate students, young professionals, and scholars for study and research.

Peterson's Grants for Graduate and Postdoctoral Study, fourth edition. Princeton: Peterson's Guides, 1994. Nearly 700 grants and fellowships are described. Originally compiled by the Office of Research Affairs at the Graduate School of the University of Massachusetts at Amherst, this guide is updated periodically by Peterson's.

Graduate schools sometimes publish listings of support sources in their catalogs, and some provide separate publications, such as the *Graduate Guide to Grants,* compiled by the Harvard Graduate School of Arts and Sciences. For more information, call 617-495-1814.

World Wide Web: A New Source of Funding Information

If you have not explored the financial resources on the World Wide Web (the Web, for short), your research is not complete. Now available on the Web is a wealth of information ranging from loan and entrance applications to minority grants and scholarships.

Web Mailing Lists

There is a mailing list or newsgroup, called GRANTS-L, for announcements of grants and fellowships of interest to graduate students. To subscribe, send mail to listserv@listproc.gsu.edu with ''subscribe GRANTS-L YOUR NAME'' in the body of the message.

University-Specific Information on the Web

Universities are now in the process of creating Web financial aid directories. Florida, Virginia Tech, Massachusetts, Emory, and Georgetown are just a few. Applications of admission can now be downloaded from the Web to start the graduate process. After that, detailed information can be obtained on financial aid processes, forms, and deadlines. University-specific grant and scholarship information can also be found, and more may be learned about financing by using the Web than by an actual visit. Questions can be asked on line.

Scholarships on the Web

Dictionary-size books listing scholarships will be obsolete in the future. When searching for scholarship opportunities, one can search the Web. First, many benefactors and other scholarship donors are creating pages on the Web listing pertinent information with regard to their specific scholarship. You can reach this information through a variety of methods. For example, you can find a directory listing minority scholarships, quickly look at the information on line, decide if it applies to you, and then move on. New scholarship pages are being added to the Web daily.

The Web also lists many services that will look for scholarships for you. *FastWeb* is one of these services. Some of these services cost money and advertise more scholarships per dollar than any other service. While some of these might be helpful, surfing the Web and using the traditional library resources on available scholarships (now often listed on the Web as stated above) are often just as productive and free. Some services such as *FastWeb,* which is an acronym for Financial aid search through the Web, may be free through your university. Check with your financial aid office to see if these services are available to you.

Bank and Loan Information on the Web

Banks and loan servicing centers are creating pages on the Web, making it easier to access loan information. Having the information on screen in front of you instantaneously is more convenient than being put on hold on the phone. Any loan information such as interest rate variations, descriptions of loans, loan consolidation programs, and repayment charts can all be found on the Web.

The Right Advice. The Right Tools. The Right Choice.

Logic & Reading Review for the GRE*, GMAT*, LSAT*, MCAT*
Hone skills required for top-notch performance with extensive preparation in logic games, analysis, and reading comprehension.
ISBN 0-7689-0229-0, $16.95 pb/$24.95 CAN, July 1999

Graduate Schools in the U.S. 1999
This overview of programs is the first tool a student needs to make the education decision of a lifetime. Includes CD with practice GRE and financial aid information.
ISBN 0-7689-0207-X, with CD, $24.95 pb/$36.95 CAN/£17.99 UK, January 1999

U.S. and Canadian Medical Schools 1999
Profiles of 400 accredited M.D. and combined medical degree programs in the U.S., Canada, and Puerto Rico. Plus—a full-length MCAT and financial aid options.
ISBN 0-7689-0150-2, $24.95 pb/$34.95 CAN/£17.99 UK, 1998

The Insider's Guide to Medical Schools
Profiles all 148 accredited medical colleges in the U.S., giving a student's view of each school, advice on med school, and articles on managing medical studies.
ISBN 0-7689-0203-7, $21.95 pb/$36.95 CAN/£17.99 UK, June 1999

Law Schools
The essential guide to legal education–everything prospective law students really need to know. Comprehensive coverage of all 181 nationally accredited U.S. law schools and a practice LSAT on CD.
ISBN 0-7689-0011-5, with CD, $24.95 pb/$34.95 CAN, 1998

MBA Programs 1999
A grad school essential! Details over 900 business schools offering full-time, part-time, joint-degree, dual-degree, international, and executive MBA programs.
ISBN 0-7689-0046-8, $26.95 pb/$37.95 CAN/£17.99 UK.

GRE* Success 2000
The only comprehensive test prep for both the written and computerized GRE format.
ISBN 0-7689-0240-1, with CD, $16.95 pb/$23.95 CAN/£14.99 UK, July 1999

LSAT* Success 2000
Inside advice on handling the essay and test questions from a designer of the LSAT.
ISBN 0-7689-0224-X, with CD, $16.95 pb/$23.95 CAN/£14.99 UK, July 1999

Gold Standard MCAT*
Delivers intensive coverage of science and math concepts and features practice exams.
ISBN 0-7689-0192-8, $44.95 pb/£37.99 UK, January 1999

GMAT* Success 2000
Results-oriented tips, strategies, and review for all content areas of the GMAT.
ISBN 0-7689-0233-9, with CD, $16.95/$23.95 CAN/£14.99 UK, July 1999

Financing Graduate School
Expert advice on securing assistantships, fellowships, loans, and internships.
ISBN 1-56079-638-3, $16.95 pb/$23.95 CAN/£12.99 UK, 1996

Grants for Graduate & Postdoctoral Study
Identify 1,900 grants, scholarships, and fellowships in this key guide.
ISBN 0-7689-0019-0, $32.95 pb/$45.95 CAN, 1998

How to Write a Winning Personal Statement for Graduate and Professional School
Exclusive tips from admissions officers at the nation's top graduate schools.
ISBN 1-56079-855-6 $12.95 pb/$17.50 CAN/9.99 UK, 1997

At fine bookstores near you.

To order direct, call 1-800-338-3282
Or fax your order to 609-243-9150

To order on line, access our Web site at
http://bookstore.petersons.com

P PETERSON'S
Princeton, New Jersey
www.petersons.com
Keyword on AOL: Petersons

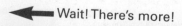

← Wait! There's more!